The Year's Best Sports Writing 2024

Edited and with an
introduction by
Jane McManus

TRIUMPH
B O O K S

Library of Congress Cataloging-in-Publication Data available upon request

This book is available in quantity at special discounts for your group or organization. For further information, contact:
    Triumph Books LLC
    814 North Franklin Street
    Chicago, Illinois 60610
    (312) 337-0747
    www.triumphbooks.com

Printed in U.S.A.

ISBN: 978-1-63727-652-5

Design by Sue Knopf
Page production by Patricia Frey

Contents

Introduction

There's no formal set of instructions when it comes to weaving a good tale. But you know it when you see it. It's in the way the material room you're sitting in starts to disappear, a desk or subway car becoming faded in the background until there you are on a tennis court hearing the *thwack* of a well-hit ball, watching Martina Navratilova and Chris Evert start a friendship that will pull them through the decades until they are fretted like the strings on the face of a racket.

Maybe, for just the next 10 minutes as you read Sally Jenkins' excellent column for *The Washington Post*, you feel part of that friendship yourself.

The best sports writing transports you. Jenkins is a deft teacher in her piece; reanimating Evert's steely temperament under her fetching young exterior, channeling the storm and danger of Navratilova's defection. Two athletes and a storyteller, lifetimes in the smeared ink of a daily newspaper.

Jenkins introduced her headliners:

> They are 26 and 24 years old, respectively, honed to fine edges. It's as if they were purposely constructed to test each other—and to whip up intense reactions from their audiences, the adorable blond American middle-class heroine with the frictionless grace against the flurrying Eastern European with sculpted muscles who played like a sword fighter.

For readers who became acquainted with these players as legends, it's easy to miss the context of their early years. We tend to do that, hummingbirds in our own lives. To remember what it was like to truly be some other time, to be able to conjure that, is a magic trick.

Over these pages you will have that experience, of slowing down and wading into someone else's moment. The storytellers here are deft, and some of the histories detailed in these pages are obscure enough to be a revelation. These tales are all woven around sports, but you don't have to care for sports to find yourself transfixed. League stats are irrelevant. Each of these tales transcends in its own way.

You could read these pieces on a screen, and many did as they were initially published, but there is solidity on a printed page even now. To read a book is an act of leisure that seems quaint given the pace required of us. That's why they come with us on vacations still. To unplug and read is a luxury. This book is an indulgence.

It has been a difficult year for sports media. As these stories were being written and edited, ground was giving way. Although the last decade has shrunk the pool of reporters and writers who are paid to report these kinds of stories, each week seemed to bring a new layoff. *The New York Times* even folded its sports section after buying The Athletic. Many of those unionized reporters opted for roles elsewhere at *The Times* rather than write or edit for the non-union Athletic. *Sports Illustrated* culled all but a small trove of writers. More layoffs at *The Washington Post*, Yahoo, *The Los Angeles Times*, and many others. Beyond the industry giants, more veteran writers announced they were again looking for work.

All that institutional knowledge.

As someone who has worked in higher education and taught sports writing and communication, it is a difficult moment. The need for fearless reporting has never been higher, but the infrastructure to support it is crumbling. Entry-level jobs can still be found, but those mid-career jobs have turned from professional class to freelance. The perspective that Jenkins brings to Evert and

Navratilova takes years to develop. That expertise, that mastery, it is invaluable.

Instead, there were major news outlets looking at ways to substitute artificial intelligence for reporters when it came to game coverage. You will not find Jenkins' level of prose in most high school sports sections writing game stories, but it is the training ground. The observation starts there, the tentative approach to opposing coaches to introduce yourself before the game, the hours in the stands to see it completed, chatting with parents and fans to learn more about the athletes in the numbered jerseys. Those are the games where there isn't a PR staff handing out halftime stats or pre-game emails with context.

But too many of today's media conglomerates often don't see the investment, just the cash to be skimmed from venerable institutions on the way down.

There are exceptions. Many of the stories here come from *The Washington Post*, The Athletic, and ESPN. Those three outlets have resources and editing. And quality editing can't be discounted. So many talented young writers need the guidance and development that comes from an in-house mentor. As for the masters of the craft, they are professionals and deserve to be compensated. Most freelancers would struggle to find international arms dealer Victor Bout, who was swapped in the prisoner trade that freed the WNBA's Brittney Griner. But ESPN's T.J. Quinn found him, and that incredible piece is on our honorable mentions list.

Longform is the format where structure is so important, and holes in reporting can undermine a well-written piece.

But I don't imagine readers of this volume need to be convinced of its value. You are here, and you are reading. So a word about what you can expect as you progress through these pages.

Each curator of this volume brings their own affinities. Mine come from three decades covering every sport imaginable for a local newspaper, and then football and women's sports for ESPN before becoming a columnist at the *New York Daily News*, Deadspin, and The Independent of London. Like so many of us,

I got into sports writing because I played sports. I got my first full-time job as the 1999 Women's World Cup cheers still echoed from the Rose Bowl, and soon came to recognize the paucity of coverage around women's sports. I can't ignore that my own experience has affected the choices in these pages.

Professor Cheryl Cooky at Purdue University and USC professor Michael Messner have been researching the issue of women's sports coverage since 1989. Their look at the amount of time highlight shows have dedicated to women's sports has yielded an oft-repeated statistic, that women's sports get just 4 to 5 percent of coverage.

Since they started tracking these numbers, other academics have looked at printed media, Olympics coverage, and other areas. The Olympics broadcasts are notable for their parity in the last decade, as Alabama professor Andrew Billings has researched, but written forms of traditional media have generally confirmed Cooky and Messner's number.

For many years of my career, the athletes who played in those women's leagues were some of the best stories never written.

In the year this writing is drawn from, women's sports made a huge leap in visibility. The NCAA women's college basketball championship—with stars Caitlin Clark and Angel Reese—drew 9.9 million viewers. In Nebraska, a volleyball court was installed in the middle of a football palace called Memorial Stadium and 92,003 fans came to watch the four-team tournament. The National Women's Soccer League expanded and signed a blockbuster media deal. Brittney Griner returned to the court after being released from an unjust imprisonment in Russia. Ratings, attendance, and investment everywhere—up, up, and up.

And so is the storytelling.

These have become some of the best-known players on the sports landscape, and it makes sense that the best writers would be assigned to pen profiles and cover their events. The Associated Press Sports Editors, the professional organization that runs the high-profile sports writing contest each year, introduced the Billie

Jean King Award for Excellence in Women's Sports Coverage, which will go to the writer with the strongest coverage of women's sports each year. It was designed to reward and incentivize this coverage, and King worked with *USA TODAY* columnist Nancy Armour, APSE president Naila Jean Meyers, and me to make it happen.

My eye was drawn to some incredible storytelling around these athletes, and Jenkins' lyric of a piece is just the starting point for this journey. Women's tennis had a two-decade head start over most other women's leagues, which is why Evert and Navratilova seem like old friends. But there are few other women's sports that have been covered so thoroughly for so long.

So let's get to know some of the athletes who may join Evert and Navratilova in the pantheon.

Iowa guard Caitlin Clark gets the MVP treatment from *The Washington Post*'s Ben Tolliver. Midway through her junior year, her impact was clear and Tolliver takes us on the road with her. Since this story, Clark has sold out games across the country, dozens more pieces have been written, and a documentary on her senior season was made by Omaha Productions, former NFL quarterback Peyton Manning's venture, and ESPN.

Tolliver tries to find the source of the budding star's motivation.

"If I wanted to hang out with the boys, I had to hold my own," Clark said during an interview at Carver-Hawkeye Arena. "They didn't take it easy on me. Every family function, it seemed like I would go inside crying. They wouldn't pass me the ball. In the Easter egg hunt, I wouldn't get enough eggs. It was just one thing after the next. I got picked on, but I loved it. That's what made me who I am."

Her college career has been at the very moment NCAA women's basketball has become as big a story as the men's in many ways. That's for a few reasons, but one is the ability for college athletes to endorse products. Steve Politi of NJ.com explores this phenomenon through LSU gymnast Livvy Dunne, who has capitalized on changes in Name, Image, and Likeness rules in college sports to build a million-dollar business. Rather than a flat look at a pretty athlete, Politi gets into influencer culture and the online threats that have marred Dunne's college experience.

The Washington Post's Candace Buckner writes an astute column about Spanish soccer player Jenni Hermoso, who endured an unwelcome kiss from her federation president Luis Rubiales as they celebrated her World Cup victory. As passionate as the outcry in defense of Hermoso was, Buckner looks at what the effect might be for the player herself, who barely saw the confetti coming before the subject was changed and her celebration stolen.

Buckner writes: "But now, we feel sorry for her; a sentiment that conflicts with her natural character. The unwanted kiss thrust Hermoso into a spotlight not of her choosing and turned her into the woman who had something done to her."

Emily Sohn for Long Lead has a riveting look at iconoclast Virginia Kraft, the first woman to cover a beat for *Sports Illustrated* starting in the 1950s. Kraft traveled the globe to cover big game hunting for the better part of three decades, back when the expense accounts were large and magazines were the industry's prestige jobs. Kraft was a complicated subject, and Sohn brought the era to life again. Here is how Sohn described Kraft's job hunt as a college graduate in 1951:

> The first listing she saw was *Field & Stream*, the preeminent outdoor magazine at the time. She had no real experience relevant to the hunting and fishing publication, but she walked into the office cold and talked to an editor who was "at first somewhat startled at the prospect of a young woman invading his bastion of maledom," Kraft told Siena graduates. He quickly calculated that he could pay her a third of what men earned for the same job, but she would still make three times what she could at fashion magazines. "We both felt we had made a pretty shrewd deal."

We are introduced to some new competitors as well. An NBA daughter, Kami Miner, is playing volleyball at Stanford, and ESPN's Aishwarya Kumar weaves her promise with the professional disappointment of her father, Harold Miner. David Fleming writes a romp of a tale about the search for the Dallas Mavericks–themed Barbie from the NBA collection.

Michael Lee of ESPN follows up with the girls who played with Kobe Bryant's daughter Gianna before they were killed in a helicopter crash in 2020. The loss of the Bryants is still felt in the women's basketball community, but Lee writes of legacy.

Hailey Salvian and Katie Strang detail the awful conditions around Harvard women's ice hockey for The Athletic; an important piece that also highlights the way women who play are demanding changes in the way they are coached. The *Boston Globe*'s Bob Hohler writes about runner Lynn Jennings, who in her 60s has decided to tell her own story about a predatory coach.

For so many years, bullying was ignored if a team or athlete was winning, that you break players to build champions, without knowing whether those athletes could do more if their well-being were centered in the process. It's important those systems are unearthed, whether in hockey, track, gymnastics, or soccer, or elsewhere.

Given these conversations, the story David Alm tells for *Esquire* is incredibly timely. He looks at Rachel Rapinoe's soccer career, in which injury led to addiction. In the wake of that, Rachel has started a CBD oil business looking to use the properties of cannabis to help athletes heal without tripping drug tests. Rachel's sister is soccer star Megan Rapinoe, so to know how different their career trajectories were makes it even more poignant.

You'll still find the Big Three—the NFL, the NBA, and MLB—here, as well as surfing, mountain climbing, and other competitive feats to test the limits of human ability, strength, intellect, and endurance.

Chris Nowinski has been on the forefront of the discussion of the long-term damage that playing football can cause. After playing football at Harvard, Nowinski founded the Concussion Legacy Institute and has been looking into the connection between sports and brain injury. Kent Babb takes a look at that Harvard team for *The Washington Post*, and how Nowinski's work has impacted the nostalgia and camaraderie. Babb's story is a mix of ambitious reporting and great storytelling.

ESPN's Ryan Hockensmith's story of a million-dollar halftime shot back in the era of Michael Jordan's Bulls is all that more vivid after so many watched *The Last Dance* during the pandemic. Steve Rushin of *Sports Illustrated* paints a vivid picture of the Bills fanbase, matches and lighter fluid not included. This is a story about how that power can be utilized to help individuals in need, and I challenge you to leave uninspired.

When my daughter Charlotte, a reader and a rock climber, heard I was editing this collection, she asked if I'd read Michael Levy's piece in *Outside* on free soloist Austin Howell. At that moment, the story was pulled up on my laptop thanks to another recommendation. You'll be able to read it here as well, detailing the limitations of using risk-taking sports as therapy. Mental health is also a topic of Dana O'Neil's search for Delonte West through his former St. Joe's and NBA teammates and coaches for The Athletic.

And I kept coming back to "Casual Luke Rides the Big Wave" by Gabriella Paiella for *GQ*. This gorgeous story of Luke Shephardson, a David conquering a Goliath of a wave, feels like it's from an era before money and betting and the noise of professional sports swept into every other corner of competition.

The power of investigation is on display when Nathan Fenno tells a wild story of an FBI investigation into college basketball for *The Los Angeles Times*, while Don Van Natta Jr. and Seth Wickersham at ESPN offer a tick-tock of the emails that sank former Washington NFL owner Dan Snyder.

Jarrett Bell tackles a difficult topic for *USA TODAY*, and that's Andy Reid's family troubles during the Super Bowl. At the time he struck and severely injured a 5-year-old girl, Britt Reid was working for his father as a coach for the Kansas City Chiefs. After he was sentenced to three years for driving while intoxicated, Britt's sentence was commuted by Missouri governor Mike Parsons. There are plenty of columnists that would avoid this topic, but Bell skillfully handles it, refusing to ignore a tragedy for a young girl and her family. It's hard to imagine the governor would step in to insulate Britt Reid were it not for the NFL and Andy Reid's stature. In some ways, Bell's column gets to the power of sports more than many others.

Mirin Fader gets the 2007 No. 1 NBA pick Greg Oden to open up about his injury-plagued career and his comeback as a coach at Butler in *The Ringer*. Brendan Prunty has a story in *Golf* about a bespoke club-maker whose life is upended by success.

Tom Friend's piece on baseball writer Peter Gammons is so well told in *Sports Business Journal*, and has the effect of introducing audiences to someone they may have thought they knew well. Alex Coffey delves into the alcoholism in Preston Mattingly's home growing up, and his mother Kim's recovery from addiction.

"I love my dad. He's helped me a ton," said the son of Yankees legend Don Mattingly in the piece. "But this is the story I think people should know."

Rounding out the storytelling is Sam Borden's look at the funeral of Pelé for ESPN. What I like about this, and so many of the pieces here, is that the subject is presented as his complicated self. The hagiography is less interesting than the full portrait, even as the soccer great is laid to rest.

Choosing which stories to include in this volume and which to make honorable mention was challenging. There were a few stories that were immersive and multimedia, and unfortunately didn't translate as well into text only. I encourage readers to seek out Tim Layden's piece on a photo of Secretariat for NBC Sports, as he plays sleuth to find the identity of the photographer these decades later. Similarly, John Branch's "Ghosts on the Glacier" for *The New York Times* is a brilliant piece, unraveling the events of a deadly mountain-climbing expedition in a lately unearthed canister of film.

Quinn's piece for ESPN on Griner's release is an epic tale that is worth hunting down and savoring, but space constraints made it difficult to include in full here.

It was an honor to be able to read so much great sports writing. Thanks to everyone who submitted their work for consideration. I also owe a debt of gratitude to Richard Deitsch, the editor of the 2023 edition of this book, for including me on his panel and offering so much advice on how to go about putting together a list like this. J.A. Adande, who edited the 2022 volume, Kavitha Davidson, and Sandy Padwe rounded out my own advisory panel, and they each found gems from outlets across the spectrum. Glenn Stout, who has been associated with this work in its different incarnations over the years, was a terrific sounding board.

Throughout this process, I was reminded again of the power of a good story, well-reported and truthfully told. It's a skill to be practiced and taught, and serves the basis of anything distributed in any medium past, present, and, I'd wager, future.

Enjoy and share.

The Year's Best
Sports Writing
2024

Bitter Rivals. Beloved Friends. Survivors.

SALLY JENKINS

FROM *The Washington Post* • JULY 3, 2023

There is an audible rhythm to a Grand Slam tennis tournament, a *thwock-tock, tock-thwock* of strokes, like beats per minute, that steadily grows fainter as the field diminishes. At first the locker room is a hive of 128 competitors, milling and chattering, but each day their numbers ebb, until just two people are left in that confrontational hush known as the final. For so many years, Chris Evert and Martina Navratilova were almost invariably the last two, left alone in a room so empty yet intimate that they could practically hear what was inside the other's chest. *Thwock-tock.*

They dressed side by side. They waited together, sometimes ate together and entered the arena together. Then they would play a match that seemed like a personal cross-examination, running each other headlong into emotional confessions, concessions. And afterward they would return to that small room of two, where they showered and changed, observing with sidelong glances the other's triumphalism or tears, states beyond mere bare skin. No one else could possibly understand it.

Except for the other.

"She knew me better than I knew me," Navratilova says.

They have known each other for 50 years now, outlasting most marriages. Aside from blood kin, Navratilova points out, "I've known Chris longer than anybody else in my life, and so it is for her." Lately, they have never been closer—a fact they refuse to cheapen with sentimentality. "It's been up and down, the friendship," Evert says. At the ages of 68 and 66, respectively, Evert and Navratilova have found themselves more intertwined than ever, by an unwelcome factor. You want to meet an opponent who draws you nearer in mutual understanding? Try having cancer at the same time.

"It was like, are you *kidding* me?" Evert says.

The shape of the relationship is an hourglass. They first met as teenagers in 1973, became friends and then split apart as each rose to No. 1 in the world at the direct expense of the other. They contested 80 matches—60 of them finals—riveting for their contrasts in tactics and temperament. After a 15-year rivalry, they somehow reached a perfect equipoise of 18 Grand Slam victories each.

On some slow or rainy day, when the tennis at Wimbledon is banging and artless as a metronome or suspended by weather, do yourself a favor. Call up highlights of Evert and Navratilova's match at the 1981 U.S. Open. They are 26 and 24 years old, respectively, honed to fine edges. It's as if they were purposely constructed to test each other—and to whip up intense reactions from their audiences, the adorable blond American middle-class heroine with the frictionless grace against the flurrying Eastern European with sculpted muscles who played like a sword fighter.

Evert played from a restrained conventional demeanor, with ribbons in her hair, earrings in her ears. Yet she was utterly new. Audiences had never seen anything quite like the compressed lethality of this two-fisted young woman, who knocked off the legendary Margaret Court at the age of just 15 in 1970. She was a squinteyed, firm-chinned executioner who delivered strokes like milled steel.

She had mystique. And she refused to be hemmed in. As she held the No. 1 ranking for five straight years, she reserved the right to court romantic danger with a bewildering array of famous men, not all of them suitable for a nice Catholic girl, from the surly Jimmy Connors to superstar actor Burt Reynolds—and to put them second to her career. Her composure cloaked one of the toughest minds in the annals of sport, and her .900 winning percentage remains virtually unrivaled in tennis history.

Navratilova was her inverse, a gustily emotional left-handed serve-and-volleyer who challenged every traditional definition of heroine with an edgy militancy. Her game had an acrobatic suppleness that was also entirely novel—never had a female athlete moved with such airborne ease. Or acted so honestly. Navratilova was as overtly political as Evert was popular. Her defection from communist Czechoslovakia in 1975 was an act of unimaginable bravery, and her struggle to win acceptance from Western crowds was compounded by her defiant inability to censor herself or mask her homosexuality. Advised to put a man in her box at Wimbledon, she refused. Once, when asked whether she was "openly" gay, she shot back, "As opposed to closedly?"

More prideful generations can't comprehend how in the vanguard Navratilova was when she came out in 1981 or the price she paid in lost endorsements. *The New York Times* that year announced that homosexuality was "the most sensitive issue in the sports marketplace, more delicate than drugs, more controversial than violence." Male sportswriters fixated on the veins in her arms. *Newsweek* veered out of its way to accuse her of "accentuating some lifestyle manifesto." She repaid them all by becoming the first female athlete to win a million dollars in prize money in a single year.

Small wonder Evert and Navratilova's matches seemed like such colossal encounters. As they competed, the TV cameras zeroed in on their faces and found mother-of-dragons expressions, a willingness to play to ashes. That too was new.

It once had been considered "unnatural" for a woman to contend with such unembarrassed intensity. As Evert's own agent said in 1981, female sports stars were expected to be "ladylike" and not too "greedy" in their negotiations, while their male counterparts could win "every nickel and feel quite comfortable about it." Not anymore. Evert and Navratilova had established their common right "to go to the ends of the earth, the absolute ends of the earth, to achieve something," Evert says.

By the time Evert and Navratilova retired from singles play, in 1989 and 1994, respectively, they had reached a mutual understanding. Not only were they level with an equal number of major titles, but the rivalry was so transcendent, it had become a kind of joint accomplishment.

After their retirements, they followed strangely similar courses. They were neighbors in Aspen, Colo., and Florida, at times living just minutes from each other. Evert's longtime base is Boca Raton, while Navratilova has a home in Miami Beach as well as a small farm just up the road in Evert's birthplace of Fort Lauderdale, where she keeps a multitude of chickens. "She brings me eggs," Evert says. Each eventually went into tennis broadcasting, which meant they continued to meet at Grand Slam fortnights. "Our lives are so parallel, it's eerie when you think about it," Navratilova says.

They became the kind of friends who talked and texted weekly, sometimes exchanging black-box confidences deep in the night. And who could tease each other with a mischief they wouldn't tolerate from anyone else. On Navratilova's 60th birthday, she received a Cartier box from Evert. Inside was a necklace with three rings of white gold, signifying the two and their long friendship. "I guess I'm kind of the guy in our relationship, giving her jewelry," Evert cracks.

The parallels were funny, until they weren't.

In January 2022, Evert learned that she had Stage 1C ovarian cancer. As Evert embarked on a grueling six cycles of chemotherapy, Navratilova pulled the Cartier necklace from her jewelry box and put it on, a talisman. "I wore it all the time when I wanted her to get well," Navratilova says. For months, she never took it off.

Only one thing made her remove it: radiation. In December 2022, Navratilova received her own diagnosis: She had not one but two early-stage cancers, in her throat and breast.

"I finally had to take it off when I got zapped," Navratilova says.

On a late spring day, Evert and Navratilova sat together in an elegant Miami hotel, both finally cancer-free at the end of long dual sieges. Evert was just a few weeks removed from her fourth surgery in 16 months, a reconstruction following a mastectomy she underwent in late January. Navratilova had just finished the last session of a scorching protocol of radiation and chemo, during which she lost 29 pounds. She toyed with a plate of gluten-free pasta, happy to be able to swallow without pain.

They were finally ready to look over their shoulders and tell some stories. New stories but also some old ones that felt fresh again or came with a new frankness.

Evert recalled the day she phoned Navratilova to tell her she had cancer.

"She was one of the very first people I told," she says.

Wait a second.

Is Evert saying that the rival who dealt her the deepest professional cuts of her life, whose mere body language on the court once made her seethe, was among the very first people she wanted to talk to when she got cancer? It's one thing to share a rich history and be neighbors and swap gifts and teasing, but they are those kinds of confidantes?

And is the same true for Navratilova, that Evert—whose mere existence meant that no matter how much she won, she could never really win, who at one point dominated her with an infuriating superciliousness—was among the first people she called when she got cancer? Is that what they are saying?

Indeed, it is.

"When I called her, it was a feeling of, like, coming home," Evert says.

Hang on, you say.

Go back.

Guts and glory, together and apart

They met Feb. 25, 1973, in the player lounge of a Florida tour stop. Evert, 18, was playing backgammon with a tournament official at a table by a wall. Though she had been a top player for two years by then, she was by nature shy and felt isolated by her fame and the circumscribing stereotype that came with it. *Sports Illustrated* would paint her as a "composite of Sandra Dee, the Carpenters, and yes, apple pie," which she dealt with by cultivating a clamped, sardonic purse of the mouth.

Evert glanced up and saw a new girl approaching, pale and plump as a dumpling, with a guileless face beneath a mop of hair. "Hi, Chris!" she recalls Navratilova blurting.

From the 16-year-old Navratilova's point of view, it was Evert who spoke first, giving her a sweet murmured "Hi" and a small wave. *Oh, my God, Chris Evert said hello to me*, Navratilova thought. Navratilova recognized Evert from the pictures she pored over in *World Tennis* magazine, one of the few subscriptions she could get in her home village of Revnice, outside of Prague.

Let's stipulate that the greetings were simultaneous, the reflexive reactions of two girls who were the antithetical of mean, more sensitive than their other competitors ever realized, "both always underestimated in our empathy," as Navratilova says. And who had the mutual desire to break the "taboo" of competition, as Evert once called it, that inhibited so many girls.

Later in the tournament, Evert spotted Navratilova again. "Picture this," Evert says. Navratilova was walking straight through the grounds in a one-piece bathing suit and flip flops, oblivious to stares at her crisscrossing tan lines. It was Navratilova's first trip to the United States; she was granted an eight-week leave by the communist Czechoslovakian government to try her game against the Western elites', and she was determined to luxuriate in it. *She's got guts*, Evert thought.

Their first match a month later, in Akron, Ohio, on March 22, 1973, is crystal to them both a half-century later. Though Evert won in straight sets, Navratilova pushed her to 7–6 in the first. "Five-four in the tiebreaker," Navratilova says instantly, as soon as it's mentioned, bristling, "And I actually had a set point."

Evert had never faced anything like it. The curving lefty serve caromed away from her, and so did the charging volleys. "She had weapons that I hadn't seen in a young player—ever," Evert says. Two things gave Evert relief: Navratilova's lack of fitness—she had put on 20 pounds in four weeks on American pancakes—and her emotionalism. "She was almost crying on the court in the match, you know, just moaning," Evert says. Nevertheless, Evert had never felt such a formidableness from a new opponent and never would again. "Overwhelming" is the word Evert searches for—and finds. "More than any player coming up in the last 40 years."

To Navratilova, it was equally memorable, for the simple reason that she had nearly taken a set off Evert. "For me, that was unforgettable. But, yeah, I made an impression.... I was pretty confident that I would beat her one day. I just didn't know how long it would take."

Friendship was easy enough at first—so long as Evert was winning. She won 16 of their first 20 matches. In their first Grand Slam final, at the 1975 French Open, she smoked Navratilova 6–2, 6–1 in the second and third sets after casually sharing a lunch of roasted chicken with her.

Evert was so utterly regnant and aloof in those days she seemed to Navratilova like a castle with a moat. She had a for-bidding self-containment, a stony demeanor that one competitor from the 1970s, Lesley Hunt, likened in *Sports Illustrated* to "playing a blank wall."

Navratilova could not fathom how Evert cast such a huge projection with such an unprepossessing figure. "I was like, 'Holy s---, how does she do it?'" Navratilova remembers. Evert stood just 5-foot-6 and weighed a slim-shouldered 125 pounds. But she had a superb economy of motion—and something else. One day Navratilova watched fascinated as Evert practiced against her younger sister Jeanne Evert, who also played on the tour. Both Everts had two-handed backhands, and they wore skirts with no pockets. Which meant that to hit a backhand, someone had to drop the ball she carried in her left hand and it would bounce distractingly around her feet. As Navratilova watched, she realized with growing amusement that Chris was engaged in a subtle contest of will.

"It was kind of a mental fight," Navratilova recalls. "Who was going to hit the first ball? Because whoever didn't hit first would have to drop their ball." Chris never missed the chance to hit first. "It was a small thing, but it took a steely determination," Navratilova says. "And she never missed." It registered. By the end of the session Navratilova understood that Evert's greatest weapon was "her brain."

Navratilova herself was so mentally distractible that she would follow the flight of a bird across the stadium sky. Her thoughts and feelings seemed to blow straight through her, unfiltered. Evert could not help but be disarmed by this openhearted, unconstrained young woman who seemed hungry to experience…everything. Pancakes. Pool time. Freedom. Friendship. Fast cars.

Evert's urge to befriend Navratilova won out over her reserve. Evert invited her to be her doubles partner and even took her on a double date, with Dean Martin Jr., son of the entertainer, and Desi Arnaz Jr., Martin's actor friend and pop-band collaborator. The teen idols squired Evert and Navratilova to a drive-in movie.

Evert and Navratilova traveled together, practiced together, even brunched before they met in finals. "I was a tough nut to crack," Evert observes. "But she was so innocent and almost vulnerable when she was young, I trusted being safe with her."

Over dinners and glasses of wine, Navratilova discovered the mutinous side of Evert, which expressed itself with an unsuspected saltiness. Evert delighted in telling Navratilova scandalously dirty jokes. The outward banality of the girl hurling herself off the pedestal compounded Navratilova's outbursts of laughter. "The curtain would fall," Navratilova says, "and the funny Chris came out. The filter was gone. The walls were gone. And that's when I realized she just kept the cards close to her chest. But she was soooo mischievous underneath it all."

By 1976, however, Navratilova began to score more victories over Evert. In that year's Wimbledon semifinals, it was all Evert could do to hold her off, 6–3, 4–6, 6–4. "I was nipping at her heels," Navratilova says. "I was becoming a threat."

Which is when all the trouble started and they entered the narrowest part of the hourglass. Evert believed she had gotten too close to Navratilova. She broke up their doubles partnership. "She ditched me," Navratilova says.

Evert did it politely, telling Navratilova she would have to find another partner because she wanted to focus on her singles. But it stung. And Navratilova knew the real reason. "Chris, by her own admission, could only be close friends with people who never had a chance of beating her," Navratilova says.

Evert hated to play someone she cared about—hated it. "I thought, 'God, I can't be emotional towards these people,'" Evert says now. "…It was easier not to even know them."

Evert's on-court demeanor was a facade, developed to please her father and coach, Jimmy Evert, a renowned teaching pro at the public Holiday Park in Fort Lauderdale. Jimmy was a man of such rigor and unbending rectitude that he refused to raise his $6 hourly fee for lessons because of his daughter's success. But he was not right about everything. He demanded that Chris commit to tennis to the exclusion of all else—friends were incompatible with rivals, he told her. "I was raised in a house that did not encourage relationships," she says. And he brooked no dissent. "It was a fearful sort of upbringing," she adds. The result was a young woman who beneath her stoicism roiled with insecurity and anxiety.

Navratilova observes that, in its way, Evert's childhood was as stifling as her own had been in Czechoslovakia. "We are much more the same than different, really," she says. "So much of it was imposed on both of us, one way or the other, with her Catholic, proper girl upbringing and me being suppressed by communism."

Evert convinced herself that she and Navratilova had become too familiar with each other and that it cost her an edge.

So "I separated myself from her," Evert says.

It was bad timing for Navratilova, who was feeling doubly cut off. A year earlier, she had defected. Czech authorities had increasingly expressed the ominous sentiment that Navratilova was getting too Americanized—partly thanks to her budding friendship with Evert—and she feared they were about to choke off her career.

Navratilova struggled with homesickness; concern for her family, whom she would not see for almost five years; mastering a new language (she studied English by watching *I Love Lucy* reruns); and the stresses of hiding her homosexuality. As she related in her autobiography, by the time Evert ditched her at the U.S. Open, "I was a walking candidate for a nervous breakdown." She lost in the opening round to a grossly inferior player, Janet Newberry, and dissolved into sobs on national television.

But Navratilova emerged from the catharsis a firmer character. She watched with a mounting, gnawing dissatisfaction as Evert dominated the Grand Slams, challenged only by Evonne Goolagong. At one point, Navratilova heard Evert talk in an interview about how her rivalry with Goolagong was "defining" her.

Navratilova bridled at the statement. "I remember thinking, what about *me*?" Navratilova recalls.

When it finally came, Navratilova's breakthrough—and the role reversal—was breath-snatching. By 1981 she had developed some armor. Training with Nancy Lieberman, the former basketball great, she dropped her body fat to 8 percent. Lieberman told her she had to get "mean" about Evert and showed what she meant by being intentionally rude to Evert in player lounges.

Evert would start to greet them, and Lieberman would turn her back or say frostily, "Are you talking to me?" It quietly infuriated Evert. "They weren't very nice to me," Evert says. "I mean, Nancy taught her to hate me."

From 1982 to 1984, it was Navratilova's turn to be cold. She reached 10 Grand Slam finals—and won eight of them. In that stretch, she beat Evert 14 straight times, with an abbreviating serve-and-volley power that seemed almost dismissive. "She was in the way of me getting to No. 1," Navratilova says. "So I kind of created that distance. She was my carrot when I was training. You know, I would imagine beating Chris. She became the villain, even though she really wasn't."

Evert struggled not to lose heart, especially when Navratilova beat her by 6–1, 6–3 in the 1983 U.S. Open. "It was not a good feeling to know that I wasn't even in the game," Evert says. About to turn 30, she had fallen behind in a variety of ways, from her fitness to the fact that Navratilova was using a graphite racket while she still used wood. She was also trying to sort her personal life and separated from her husband of five years, British player John Lloyd.

Navratilova paraded her triumph by whipping around in a white Rolls-Royce convertible, one of six cars in her garage. She won so much that by 1984 it made her generous again. She now trained with a more amiable tennis tactician named Mike Estep, and her partner, Judy Nelson, a former Texas beauty contestant, liked Evert and worked to repair the relationship. At Wimbledon that July, after beating Evert, 7–6 (7–5), 6–2, to even their all-time match record at 30–30, Navratilova was sensitive to Evert's quiet devastation. Navratilova said sweetly into the victor's microphone, "I wish we could just quit right now and never play each other again because it's not right for one of us to say we're better."

"So does that mean she's retiring now?" Evert said in a news conference afterward, wisecrackery intact.

Navratilova's dominance of Evert that summer made her more of an antiheroine than she had ever been—and resulted in one of the most wounding days of her career. On the afternoon of the 1984 U.S. Open final, they had an interminably tense wait as Pat Cash and Ivan Lendl engaged in a five-set men's semifinal that went to two tiebreakers and lasted nearly four hours. There was nothing to do but stare into space or chat. Evert became starving. Navratilova, who had a bagel, split it and handed her half.

When they finally took the court, they needed a while to find their form—and then they suddenly went into full classic mode. When Evert began to lace the court with passing shots as if she was running out clotheslines, taking the opening set 6–4, the crowd leaped to its feet and roared like jet engines.

But when Navratilova took the second set 6–4, there came a smattering of boos. As Navratilova turned the match in her favor, some grew surly. They began to applaud her errors and cheered when she double-faulted. When she won it with a knifing volley, 4–6, 6–4, 6–4, there was a barely polite ovation.

Navratilova was unstrung by the rejection. As Estep gave her a congratulatory hug, she burst into tears in his arms. "Why were they so against me?" she asked Estep. The answer: Because she had won too much against Evert. It was Navratilova's sixth straight Grand Slam victory—and the most ambivalent feeling she ever had. She buried her head in a towel, shoulders quivering.

One person knew how Navratilova felt that day: Evert. For years she had lived with the "ice maiden" label and frigidness from crowds that considered her too impassive. Goolagong, the wispy, ethereal Australian, had always been more favored by fans, to the point that on one occasion Evert came back into the locker room after a loss and flung her rackets to the floor and spat bitterly, "Now I hope they're happy."

Evert and Navratilova wanted to be appreciated for who they were. But it felt impossible with all the media caricatures of them as princesses, robots, "Chris America" vs. the foreigner, the delicate sweetheart vs. the bulging lesbian. "All that stuff hurt," Navratilova says.

Evert refused to play into any of the tropes that day—or any other day. For which Navratilova felt deeply grateful. "Chris *never* did anything to make it worse, you know?" Navratilova says.

At some point in the wake of that difficult year, they struck a private agreement: They would not respond to the stereotypes or any egging on from the media or their own audiences. If either had a question about something, she would speak directly to the other, "so that we knew where we stand," Navratilova says.

Early in 1985, Evert beat Navratilova for the first time in over two years, at the Virginia Slims of Florida. "Nobody beats Chris Evert 15 times in a row," she deadpanned.

The renewal set up another masterpiece, the 1985 French Open final. The match is a fascinating revisit—and reveal. After they took the court, what's striking is how they had borrowed from each other, forced the other to adapt. It's Navratilova who wins some of the longest baseline rallies and Evert who presses the net first on some points. Navratilova has fully appropriated imperiousness, blond and bejeweled, diamonds in her ears, gold bracelets and rings. Evert is the one who is stripped down—her hair is shorn short, and there is nothing on her wrist but a sweatband. It's clear she had gone back to work, developed ropes of muscle in her arms and stealthily broadened her game over those two seasons of losses.

Right hand against left, they went at each other like flashing sabers.

As their rallies wore on, they played with apparent curiosity. "There had been so many matches. How do you surprise one another?" Navratilova says. "How do you find something new or different? When you know everything already?" Sometimes, as the ball flew, one of them would just nod before it landed and acknowledge that it was too good with a "Yep."

Evert would never be better; she found ways to wrong-foot the charging, slashing Navratilova. She always had been irritated by the shoulder swagger Navratilova could show after a great point, but she was fully capable of her own show of supremacy, and she showed it here, with the head tossing of an empress and a mincy little walk that could only be called a sashay.

A point-blank volley exchange at the net, won by Evert, had broadcaster Bud Collins screaming: "OHHHHHH! Eyeball to eyeball!" On one exchange, the force of Evert's shot knocked the racket from Navratilova's hand and sent her sprawling to the red clay. On match point, she lured Navratilova to the net with a short forehand, then pivoted to deliver an unfurling backhand winner up the line past a diving Navratilova, through an opening as narrow as one of her old hair ribbons. And it was over. Evert had won, 6–3, 6–7 (7–4), 7–5.

The embrace at the net is one of their enduringly favorite pictures. They threw their arms over each other's shoulders, mutually exhausted yet beaming over the quality of the tennis they had just played. "You can't tell who won," Navratilova says.

It seemed as if they no longer were playing against each other so much as *with* each other. And that's how it stayed. From then on, their locker room atmosphere became more than just companionable. It was…consoling. Someone would win and someone would lose, and the loser would sit on a bench, head dangling, and the other, unable to look away, would drift over and sit down. Sometimes, hours afterward, one of them would open her tennis bag and find a sweet note in it.

"We were the last two left standing," Evert says. "…I saw her at her highest and at her lowest. And I think because we saw each other that way, the vulnerable part, that's another level of friendship."

In 1986, Navratilova was scheduled to return to Czechoslovakia for the first time since her defection to play a match for the U.S. Federation Cup team. "Will you come?" she asked Evert. "I don't know how they'll treat me." Evert was nursing a knee injury, but she went. Navratilova was overjoyed to be teammates for a change. "We could be happy at the same time for once," she says. Evert was rewarded with an extraordinary experience: She watched her friend get a standing ovation from crowds standing three deep while Czech officials stared at their shoes.

At Evert's final Wimbledon in 1989, one more remarkable scene played out between them. Evert by then was flagging, her intensity worn thin. In the quarterfinals she was in danger of an undignified loss to unseeded, 87th-ranked Laura Golarsa. She trailed 5–2 in the third set, just two points from defeat. *This isn't how I want to go out*, she thought grimly. Navratilova, watching on TV in the player lounge, stood up and dashed out to courtside. She took a seat in the grandstand.

"*Come on*, Chrissie!" Navratilova's voice rang out.

Evert had just a moment to feel moved. Touched. Just then Golarsa delivered a volley. On a dead run, Evert chased it. Stretched out, pulled nearly into the stands, her backhand fully extended, Evert drove a screaming pass down the alley that curled around the net post and checked the opposite corner, a clean winner. Navratilova shrieked with the thrill of it like a little girl. Evert swept the rest of the set and won it 7–5, arguably the most astonishing comeback of her life.

"She's got my back," Evert says now. "I've got hers."

'Cancer makes you feel alone'

Friendship is arguably the most wholly voluntary relationship. It reflects a mutual decision to keep pasting something back together, no matter how far it gets pulled apart, even when there is no obligatory reason, no justice-of-the-peace vow or chromosomal tie.

Evert and Navratilova just kept finding reasons to hang on to the relationship. To the point that they became hilariously entangled in each other's personal affairs. It's a fact that Navratilova set up Evert with the man who remains the most important one in her life, Andy Mill. Toward the close of Evert's playing career, Navratilova knew Evert was lonely and depressed after her divorce from Lloyd, which caused Jimmy Evert to briefly stop speaking to his daughter. Navratilova invited Evert to spend

Christmas with her in Aspen. She took her skiing and to a New Year's party at the Hotel Jerome, where she knew there would be good-looking men in droves. That night Evert met the impossibly handsome Mill, who the next day gallantly coached Evert down a steep slope, skiing backward and holding her hands.

At the end of the week, as Navratilova packed to leave for the Australian Open, Evert appeared in her doorway. "Do you mind if I stay on for a few days?" Evert asked. Navratilova arched an eyebrow and smiled. "Sure." With the house to herself, Evert had her first tryst with Mill, causing the gentleman to exclaim the next morning, "My God, I'm with Chris Evert in Martina Navratilova's bed." Evert's 1988 wedding to Mill marked the rare occasion when Navratilova wore a skirt. Years later, Navratilova was still teasing Evert. "I should have put that bed on eBay."

In 2014, when Navratilova wed longtime partner Julia Lemigova, she did not have to debate whom to choose as maid of honor. Evert was by her side. "But of course," Navratilova says.

Navratilova had never properly told Evert how much her unwavering support against homophobia had meant. Especially in crucial moments such as 1990, when Australian champion Margaret Court called Navratilova a "bad role model" for being gay. "Martina is a role model to *me*," Evert snapped back publicly. As Navratilova put it, Evert was "gay-friendly before it was okay to be." It made Navratilova's public life incalculably more bearable. "It was more than nice," Navratilova says now of Evert's stance. "It was *huge*." On matters of character, Navratilova says, Evert "underrates herself."

Here's where they stood when the cancers came. Evert had just finished rearing three adored sons to adulthood and was resolutely single again, after a psychological reckoning. Her long emotional containment finally imploded in 2006: She left Mill for former pro golfer Greg Norman; a terrible mistake, the union lasted just 15 months. Determined to know herself better, she went into counseling "to figure out what makes me tick and how I'm wired, why I'm wired the way I am and why I have made mistakes the way I have" and emerged with a piercing self-honesty. She reestablished a closeness with Mill and reinvested herself in her second calling as a mentor to young prodigies at the developmental tennis camp she founded, the Evert Tennis Academy. At over 60, she could still go for two hours on a court with women a third her age.

Just down the freeway from her, Navratilova had found her "anchor" with Lemigova, with whom she step-mothered two daughters and cared for an assortment of animals: donkeys, goats, dogs and exotic birds, including a talkative parrot named Pushkin. One of the most broadly read great athletes who ever lived, she absorbed tomes such as Timothy Snyder's account of encroaching fascism, *The Road to Unfreedom*, with a lightning intelligence that could light up a hillside.

In February 2020, a funeral notice appeared in the Fort Lauderdale papers: Mass for Jeanne Evert Dubin would be said at 10 a.m. at St. Anthony's Church. Evert had watched with mounting grief as her precious younger sister fought ovarian cancer until her arms were bruised by needles and ports and she wasted to less than 80 pounds.

Sitting in a pew was Navratilova, who would spend the next 12 hours by Evert's side. She attended the graveside services, then sat with Evert and her family at home until 10 that night.

Nearly two years after Jeanne's death, in November 2021, Evert got a call out of the blue from the Cleveland Clinic. Genetic testing that Jeanne had undergone during her illness had been reappraised with new study, and she had a BRCA1 variant that was pathogenic. The doctor recommended that Evert get tested immediately. The very next day Evert got a test—and she, too, was positive for the BRCA1 mutation. Her doctor, Joe Cardenas, recommended an immediate hysterectomy.

Evert called Navratilova and told her about the test and that she was scheduled for surgery and further testing. "It's preventive," Evert told her reassuringly. On the other end of the phone, she heard Navratilova exhale, "Ohhhhhhhhh," a long sigh of inarticulate dismay. In 2010, Navratilova had been diagnosed with a noninvasive breast cancer after making the mistake of going four years without a mammogram. Her cancer was contained—but still. Navratilova wouldn't feel comfortable for Evert until all the tests had come back.

"The first thing, the very first thing I thought of was, if I'm going to go through these trenches with anybody, Martina would be the person I'd want to go through them with," Evert says. "Because she's...strong. She doesn't take any nonsense from people. She just gets the job done. And I think that's the mentality I had."

When Evert's pathology report came back after the surgery, however, she felt anything but strong: Surgery revealed high-grade malignancy in her fallopian tubes. Evert would have to undergo a second surgery, to harvest lymph nodes and test fluid in her stomach cavity, to determine what stage she was. Jeanne's cancer had not been discovered until she was Stage 3; "I knew that anything Stage 3 or 4, you don't have a good chance," Evert says.

For three days, Evert waited for the results with the understanding that they were life-or-death. "Humble moment," Evert says. "You know, just because I was No. 1 in the world, it doesn't—I'm just like everyone else."

Evert got unfathomably lucky. The cancer hadn't progressed. Had she waited even three more months to be tested, it probably would have spread. As soon as she was able, Evert would go public with her diagnosis to encourage testing. An estimated 25 million people carry a BRCA mutation, and like her, 90 percent of them have no idea. "I had felt fine, I was working out, and I had cancer in my body," she says.

Evert still had a hard road ahead, with six cycles of chemo, but her chances of recovery were 90 percent. Her eldest son, Alex, moved in to support her daily care and even designed a workout regimen so she could sweat out the poisons. Mill took her to every chemo treatment and held her hand. Her good friend Christiane Amanpour, also diagnosed with ovarian cancer, sent her healing ointments from Paris. Her youngest sister, Clare, flew in monthly to nurse her through the sickish aftereffects, even climbing into bed with her.

But nothing can really make cancer a collective experience; it's an experiential impasse. Everyone responds differently to the treatment and the accompanying dread. Late at night, Evert would be sleepless from the queasiness and a strange sense of small electric shocks biting into her bones. She would have to slip out of bed and walk around the house, by herself with it. "Cancer makes you feel alone," Evert says. "Because it's like, nobody can take that pain from you."

Compounding Evert's sense of aloneness was the abruptness with which she had toppled from a sense of supreme athletic command to feebleness. There was one person who could understand that. "What can I do for you?" Navratilova asked. They were in a room of just two, all over again. "I can tell her my fears," Evert says. "I can be 100 percent honest with her."

Navratilova came by the house and called regularly, but she also knew how to "lay back." Sometimes she would call and Evert would answer right away. And sometimes it would take three or four days before she answered. It felt, in a way, like the old locker room days when she knew Evert was laboring with a loss. "I think because we were there for each other before, we kind of knew what to do or what not to do, instinctively, even though this was a first," Navratilova says.

In the middle of Evert's treatments, a gift arrived from Navratilova. It was a large piece of art. The canvas was lacquered with Evert's favorite playing surface, red clay, and painted with white tennis lines, on which a series of ball marks were embedded, including one that had ticked the white line. The piece was by Navratilova herself, who in retirement took up art. The canvas was really a portrait—of Evert, of the exquisite, measured precision of her game. A tribute. Evert immediately hung it in a primary place in her living room.

After every cycle of treatment, Evert would rebound with a tenacity that astounded Navratilova. She would plead with her doctors, "Can I get on a treadmill?" Just days removed from an IV, she would start power walking again or riding her beloved Peloton bike until she was slick with sweat. She even did light CrossFit workouts with weights. "She's an *animal*," Navratilova observes admiringly.

By the summer 2022, Evert was healthy enough to go back to work as a broadcaster (although with a wig), and in November she joined Navratilova in a public appearance at the season-ending WTA Finals in Fort Worth. The pair went shopping together for cowboy boots and hats, strolling through the Fort Worth Stockyards historic district. And that's when Evert delivered a piece of news that undid Navratilova. "I'm having a double mastectomy," Evert said. She explained that her BRCA mutation meant she was at high risk of developing breast cancer on top of the ovarian.

Navratilova was so affected, she burst into tears. "It was such a shock to me because I thought she was done," she says, and as she retells the story, she weeps again. She had watched Evert go public with her diagnosis and slug her way through chemo, and she hoped she was past it. Now she would face more months of convalescence. "I knew what she was going through publicly and privately," Navratilova says, "and it just knocked me on my ass."

Navratilova was still grappling with Evert's news when she was floored by her own cancer diagnosis. During the Fort Worth trip, Navratilova felt a sore lump in her neck. She wasn't taking any chances and underwent a biopsy when she got home. Evert got a text from Navratilova. *Can you call me as soon as possible? I need to talk to you.* Evert checked her phone and saw that Navratilova had also tried to call her. Evert thought, *Oh, s--t. That's not good.*

Navratilova's sore lump proved to be a cancerous lymph node. Like Evert, she had to undergo multiple lumpectomies and further tests, with a frightening three days waiting for the

results, worried that it had advanced into her organs. "I'm thinking, 'I could be dead in a year,'" she says. She distracted herself by
thinking about her favorite subject, beautiful cars, and browsing
them online.

Which car am I going to drive in the last year of my life, she
asked herself. A Bentley? A Ferrari?

The verdict when the testing came back was a combination
of relief and gut punch. The throat cancer was a highly curable
Stage 1, but the follow-up screening also revealed she had an
early-stage breast cancer, unrelated to her previous bout. She
was so stunned she had a hard time even driving herself home.
But by the time Evert reached her by phone, Navratilova was in
an incredulous, fear-fueled rage. "I sensed that it really pissed
her off more than anything," Evert says. "She was *mad* about it."

"Can you believe it!" Navratilova stormed. "It's in my throat.
And then they found something in my breast."

For a minute, the two of them considered the bizarreness of
both fighting cancer at the same time. Navratilova had always
chased Evert, but she didn't want to chase her in this pursuit.
"Jesus. I guess we're taking this to a whole new level," Navratilova
said.

And then they both started giggling.

"Because it was just so ironic," Evert says.

But then Navratilova grew serious again. She admitted to
Evert, "I'm scared."

It was the same sudden whiff of mortality, the same *you're
not so special after all* jolt that Evert had gotten. "As a top-level
athlete, you think you're going to live to a hundred and that you
can rehab it all," Navratilova says. "And then you realize, 'I can't
rehab this.' So sharing that fear was easy—easier with her than
anybody else."

Navratilova's cancer was not as dangerous as Evert's, but it
was more arduous. It required three cycles of chemo, 15 sessions of targeted proton therapy on her throat, 35 more proton
treatments on the lymph nodes in her neck and five sessions of

conventional radiation on her breast. Navratilova arranged to do it at Memorial Sloan Kettering hospital in New York, hunkering down at a friend's vacant apartment.

Unbelievably, Navratilova chose to undergo most of it alone. She wanted to protect her family from worry over her. "You just keep it in because you don't want to affect the people around you." She also wanted to cultivate her former big-match mentality, to focus on the fight. "Even just answering the question when somebody says, 'Can I get you anything?' it takes energy," Navratilova says now. "And it's just easier to not have to think what you're going to say or to deny help 10 times."

The proton treatments were a series of slow singes. Her sense of taste turned to ashes, and swallowing felt like an acid rinse. As her weight plunged, she shivered on the cold medical tables, unable to get warm, to the point that she wore a ski vest to the hospital. She developed deep circles under her eyes from insomnia.

As the poisons mounted in her, it was as if she aged 50 years overnight. "Everything felt just *wrong*," she says. This was a woman who had trekked up Mount Kilimanjaro at the age of 54, reaching 14,000 feet before she was felled with a case of pulmonary edema. At 65, she could still do 30 push-ups in a row. Now she needed two hands to drink a glass of water.

Evert had an almost intuitive sense of when to check up on Navratilova. Just when she would be near despair, not trusting herself to drink from a glass with one quivering hand, the phone would buzz, and it would be Evert. "What stands out is the timing," Navratilova says. "It was always spot on. Like she knew I was at a low point. I don't know how she knew, but she did. It was like some kind of cosmic connection. Because it was uncanny."

Evert would be briskly sympathetic and to the point. "Don't tough it out," she would say, then just listen. There was no need for question or explanation. There was just understanding. "It was always there," Navratilova says. "So we didn't have to, like, try to find it."

Sometimes the only sound on the line would be two people breathing, wordless with mutual comprehension.

Evert says, "With all the experiences we had, winning and losing and comforting each other, I think we ended up having more compassion for each other than anybody in the world could have."

Their finest rally

As Evert and Navratilova finish picking over lunch salads, their senses of renewal in the Miami sunshine make them seem almost radiant. Life feels clearer, "uncluttered," Evert says. From a distance, they cut the figures of teenagers. Evert is as neatly trim as ever, an impression enhanced by her newly grown pixie-length platinum hair. Navratilova, too, is slender as a youth. Only up close do you see lingering creases of fatigue around their eyes and sense the scars beneath their clothes and the tentativeness of their confidence.

Evert admits she is "hesitant" to say her cancer is really gone. "It could come back. Look, it could come back. It's cancer, right? It's always peripheral." Navratilova agrees. She compares it to waking up on the morning of an important match, a Wimbledon final, with the reverse of anticipation. For the first few seconds of semiconsciousness after opening her eyes she feels peace, and then the awareness of something important and pending seeps in. And then it hits her: *cancer*. "It's always hovering," Navratilova says. "You just put it out of sight. You go on with what you're doing."

The way they go on is as follows. They go public with their diagnoses and accounts of treatment because all those years that they were clashing over trophies, they also had a sense of a larger public responsibility, to "the game or women athletes or women," as Navratilova says. A sense that it wasn't enough just to be great; they also had to be good for something. "To help," Evert says.

They work out as much as the doctors allow, maybe even a little more than they advise, at first provisionally and then with growing defiance, even though each of their bodies is "still fighting the crap that's inside it," as Navratilova says, in her case doing just two push-ups and going skiing before her radiation was done. ("Skiing! During radiation!" Evert crows in disbelief.) They lift weights above their shoulders though the sore scars in their chests aren't entirely healed, and they hit on the tennis court, though in Navratilova's case, the effort to chase a ball even two steps leaves her winded, and in Evert's, it makes her feel clumsy-footed and angry, until she reminds herself, *Chrissie, who do you think are?* And then she calls Navratilova, and they both laugh at themselves in this companionable frailty.

There are statues of Arthur Ashe at the U.S. Open, Fred Perry at Wimbledon, Rod Laver at the Australian Open and Rafael Nadal at the French Open. The blazers who run the major championships have not yet commissioned sculptures of these two women, who so unbound their sport and gave the gift of professional aspiration to so many. Yet who exemplify, perhaps more than any champions in the annals of their sport, the deep internal mutual grace called sportsmanship.

But then, they don't need bronzing. They have something much warmer than that. Each other.

SALLY JENKINS has been a *Washington Post* columnist and feature writer for more than 30 years. She was a finalist for the Pulitzer Prize in 2020, and in 2021 was the winner of the Associated Press Red Smith Award for Outstanding Contributions to Sports Journalism. She has been named Sports Columnist of the Year five times by the Associated Press. She is the author of 12 books of nonfiction including *The Real All Americans*, the story of the Carlisle Indian School and its use of football as a form of resistance following the close of the Indian Wars; *The State of Jones*, about a Unionist militia in Mississippi during the Civil War, co-written with Harvard University historian John Stauffer; and the No. 1 *New York Times* bestseller *Sum It Up*, an account of legendary basketball coach Pat Summitt's battle with Alzheimer's disease, co-written with the late Summitt. Her work for *The Washington Post* has included coverage of 10 Olympic Games. In 2005 she was the first woman to be inducted into the National Sports Media Hall of Fame. She was presented for induction by her father, the late Dan Jenkins, also a Hall of Famer. She is a native of Fort Worth, received her Bachelor of Arts degree from Stanford University in 1982, and resides in New York.

Casual Luke Rides the Big Wave

GABRIELLA PAIELLA

FROM *GQ* • JUNE 13, 2023

The most remarkable day of Luke Shepardson's life started in traffic. So much traffic. An unmoving, unending line of cars tracing the wild blue coast of the North Shore of Oahu.

Crowds had been flocking there all night and all morning, their vehicles jamming up the typically sleepy two-lane road that gets you in and out of these parts. Infrastructure-wise, Waimea Bay isn't exactly meant to host one of the world's most-storied sporting events. But every once in a while, when the waves are just right, it does. The famed Eddie Aikau Big Wave Invitational is the rarest of rare surf contests, one that defies human scheduling and relies instead on the whims of nature. It requires exceptionally specific conditions: Waves in Waimea Bay must reliably reach an awesome, gut-churning height of 40 feet minimum. Even though the contest—named in honor of the legendary Native Hawaiian lifeguard and big-wave surfer Eddie Aikau—has been going since 1985, this was only its 10th run.

The chosen few who are invited to compete will drop everything and fly in from Australia and Tahiti, Brazil and Portugal. So when word got out in January that the contest was on, the world's best surfers began racing to Waimea.

Luke was racing there too. He had to get to work, lifeguarding at the Eddie. His boss called him at 6:30 that morning to tell Luke he was needed on the beach, stat. The drive from his house usually takes all of five minutes. Now he was stalled a half mile away, not getting anywhere anytime soon.

Having grown up here, Luke knew full well the commotion that the Eddie could bring, but he'd never seen anything like this. As he sat idling in his beat-up 2001 Toyota Highlander, he thought about everything that was hanging on him. Up here on the North Shore, good, stable jobs can be hard to come by.

And Luke needed his good, stable job. He was 27 years old, with two small children. His girlfriend, Natalia, was already working three gigs. But no matter how much they hustled, rent always seemed to be due, groceries got pricier, the gas tank needed filling, and the medical bills piled up.

He couldn't be late. Not today.

His family was with him, so Luke made a split-second decision. He kissed Natalia and told her to take the wheel. Said bye to their kids in the back seat. Then he hopped out and took off running for Waimea.

Even on an ordinary day, surfing is imbued with the mystical, every wave hinging on chance and elemental collision—a storm in Japan will create a swell thousands of miles away in Hawaii. But the waves produced during the Eddie are perhaps the most sacred on earth. To be invited to ride them means being one of the 40 most-esteemed surfers in the world, as chosen by a committee of your peers. The Eddie forges champions: Kelly Slater, John John Florence, and Bruce Irons have all won in the past. On the beach and along the cliffs that line Waimea Bay, some 50,000 spectators would soon squeeze together for a chance to see greatness, to witness ineffable bravery, and to take part in the grand human tradition of watching some guys (and a few women) do truly crazy shit.

Once his feet touched the sand, Luke started picking his way through a mass of tightly packed bodies just to get to his station at the lifeguard tower. When he had finally worked past the throng, the bay opened before him and the undulating ocean revealed itself for the first time that day.

Holy shit, he thought. *It's huge.*

He'd barely had time to contemplate the immensity of the waves before one of them crashed onto shore, lifting a log and pinning a young woman underneath. It took 10 people to rescue her. Furious waves rolled in, one after the other, knocking spectators off their feet and sucking in bags and phones, towels and sandals. The crowd started screaming about a baby being swept up, so another lifeguard booked it, returning with what turned out to be a small dog. All morning long, the beach thrummed with nonstop chaos.

As Luke tended to the mayhem, he kept a close eye on the clock. Busy as the day was, he had arranged with his bosses to take two breaks from his lifeguard duties—which required him to cash in some hard-earned vacation hours.

At 11:30 a.m., it was time.

He retreated inside the lifeguard stand, where he slipped out of his work uniform and into his white competition jersey. He was surprised when he started to get a little teary-eyed. Competing in the Eddie was his lifelong dream, this North Shore kid who first got into the ocean at three days old and onto a surfboard at seven months. He grabbed his board and ran down to hug his family, who had arrived to watch.

Then Luke got on his 10-foot gun and paddled out into the raging sea.

FORCES HAD BEEN conspiring for over 2 million years to create that special day. On the island now called Oahu, primordial volcanoes spewed molten magma, slowly constructing a verdant mountain range. Over time, the water carved through those mountains, forming a river valley. Sea levels fell and rose with the ice ages, eventually drowning the low land at the mouth of that river valley, creating the one-of-one crescent that is Waimea Bay, where, in 1957, big-wave surfing was born.

Waimea is uniquely positioned to the northwest, where it apprehends swell energy from winter storms that roil throughout the Pacific. When that energy meets the shallow ocean floor, it alchemizes into those tremendous hollow tubes that contain the possibility of transcendence—and the possibility of death. The powerful riptide can render even the strongest swimmers helpless. For a surfer, wiping out can mean getting dragged across a bed of sharp coral. The violence underwater regularly cracks ribs, tears shoulders from sockets, and breaks backs, as the force of the ocean rag-dolls surfers beneath the waves, sometimes for a minute at a time.

As both a surfer and lifeguard, Luke knows what the ocean is capable of. Just a week before the Eddie, one of his childhood best friends, Kala Grace, had an almost-fatal accident at nearby Pipeline. Luke saw Kala dragged out of the ocean, concussed and bleeding, and it was Luke who put the oxygen mask on his friend's face. Throughout the frenzy, what everyone remembers is Luke remaining calm and focused.

Luke, by the way, is known as "Casual Luke." In *Hawaii*. Which is like being called "Neurotic Matt" on the island of Manhattan. The nickname came to be after a really good day out in the water, when Luke was just shredding wave after wave. The surfer Mason Ho told Luke that he was "casually causing casualties." But any of Luke's friends will tell you that it stuck because he's especially humble and chill. For this reason, sometimes they also call him "Laid-Back Luke."

When Luke became a lifeguard four years ago, the fact that he'd been surfing these waters since childhood gave him an advantage. Conversely, he says that lifeguarding has since made him a better surfer. "I'm more aware of all the other parts of everything else going on around me," Luke says. "Before, when I was just surfing, I was focused solely on myself."

On the North Shore, all lifeguards—and plenty of surfers—are following in the formidable footsteps of Eddie Aikau, the Native Hawaiian who, in 1967, became the area's first lifeguard. Aikau had dropped out of high school to surf by day and work at the local Dole cannery by night. When Eddie wasn't surfing, he was lifeguarding. As the legend goes, he saved more than 500 people, never letting a single person drown.

In 1978, while taking part in a canoe trip reenacting the ancient Polynesian migration between the Hawaiian and Tahitian islands, tragedy struck one night when his group's boat capsized. Eddie mounted his surfboard and paddled out into the pitch-black Pacific for help. His companions were soon rescued. Eddie, just 31, was never seen again.

To honor his brother, Clyde Aikau founded the Eddie Aikau Big Wave Invitational in 1985. The last time they held it, in 2016, Luke wasn't invited. But he paddled out and caught a few waves before and after the competition just to prove that he could do it. He strained his shoulder so bad that morning that he landed himself in the hospital—but later that afternoon, he was back out there.

Luke had already long been a quiet fixture of the local surf scene. Liam McNamara, brother of big-wave pioneer Garrett McNamara, had taken Luke under his wing when he was a child and showed huge promise. He would cover Luke's surf trips and contests all over the world. Liam says he saw something special in the kid. "He had the attitude that even though he probably wasn't the most talented, he wasn't going to back down to anyone who was more talented than him," Liam tells me. There were days at Waimea where the waves were so brutal that even Kelly Slater couldn't make it out past the break. But Luke somehow could.

Luke's peers came to include some of the world's greatest surfers. He had earned their respect and then, in 2017, he earned something else: an invitation to compete in the Eddie the next time those insane, mythical waves ever materialized.

LUKE FLOATED OFF the side of his board, waiting for his first wave of the day.

He was eyeing one, but then watched as big-wave champion Billy Kemper snagged it. *Fine*, Luke thought, *he can have it*. Instead, Luke caught the next one and the one after that in quick succession, probably the biggest waves he'd ridden since he started surfing Waimea as a teenager.

When he got out of the water 45 minutes later, Luke made his way back to the lifeguard stand and resumed his duties. An excited coworker told him that he was crushing it on the scorecards. *Really?* Luke thought. *Fuck. Okay. Yeah, whatever.*

Soon, he slipped back into the distractions of his day job, helping his competitors by bandaging their cuts and tending to sprains. All the better to keep his mind busy. Before Luke paddled out for his next heat, Clyde told him that if he got a 9.5, he could clinch it. It was down to him and a handful of other guys, John John and Billy Kemper among them. Whoever could nab the biggest and most beautiful wave next would walk away the champion.

Winning the Eddie was suddenly a very real possibility. And for someone like Luke, a win could be life-changing.

Luke's parents split when he was four, and he grew up in a working-class household, raised by his mom, Mary. She juggled jobs as a hairdresser, massage therapist, and house cleaner, and the family shuttled between different rental houses every year. Luke's dad, Mark, was priced out of paradise, living in camps he set up outdoors.

Luke dropped out of high school at 15, earned his GED, and taught surf lessons while he tried to make it as a pro. He was traveling the world, hitting competition after competition, without much luck. When he was 22, life made a choice for him. Natalia was pregnant.

So he got a job as an electrician. It was good money that, over the years, would get even better. The available electrician gigs just happened to be stationed at the prison.

He would arrive at 4 a.m. every day and get locked inside until 2:30 p.m. His days mostly consisted of pulling out wires from malfunctioning doors while prisoners heckled him. It was miserable, and he realized something watching his more-senior coworkers who made five times what he did: "If you're not happy, I'd rather be broke and happy."

Then one day, Luke missed a really good swell. "I was locked in the prison, sweating my ass off," he says. "Like, *Fuck. This fucking sucks.*" After that, he never showed up again.

That's when Luke got hired as a lifeguard. He would be spending his days outdoors by his beloved ocean, but the job was hazardous and paid way less than what he was making as an electrician. Until 2020, Luke and Natalia and their first child were squeezed into a two-bedroom unit with his mom and brother.

The dreams that Luke had been harboring in those days were modest ones, the dreams that you tend to have when your life is settled and people are depending on you. They didn't involve winning a legendary surf contest that you couldn't even count on happening.

As Luke got back in the water for his final heat, he pushed what Clyde had told him as far out of his head as he could. A few minutes after settling into the lineup, the biggest and most beautiful wave appeared as a glimmer on the horizon and rolled right up to him.

I guess I gotta go, Luke thought.

The wave roared out of the water, impossibly sized, a prehistoric beast emerging from the abyss. Luke turned his gun toward the shore and paddled hard. He leaped up just before the wave crested and elegantly glided down the face: essentially, a free fall from a four-story building.

Luke disappeared into the tube for a heart-stopping moment, then another, then another. *Please let me get out of this*, he thought. An avalanche of white water exploded. Suddenly, the wave spit him out unscathed. He threw up his arms to claim the ride and tumbled into the water.

Afterward, as he was floating there in the brief calm, something a little weird—something a little magical—happened. A sea turtle suddenly surfaced in front of him. The two creatures stared at each other, transfixed. Luke felt himself getting chills.

Then the turtle returned to the depths of the ocean and Luke returned to shore.

Soon, he was lined up on the beach as the judges announced the knocked-out contestants, one by one. Luke's family and friends rushed down to the staging area, growing anxious, then hopeful, with each name that was called. Improbably, it was soon down to John John Florence—the defending champ, the prodigy, the world's greatest surfer—and Luke.

Then they called John John...for second place. A lifeguard—a lifeguard who was on duty, no less, and not a professional on the circuit—had beaten the world's greatest surfers in the greatest surf contest there is.

Luke started crying. Natalia started crying. His whole family started crying. His bros started crying. They hoisted him up on their shoulders and covered him in beer and handed him his prize of $10,000 and 350,000 Hawaiian Airlines miles.

Then Luke excused himself to go back to the lifeguard tower, where he finished his shift, staying until the crowds had left and the sun had set. At home that night, he ate pizza and watched *The Lion King* with his kids, then went to bed early.

THE CHAMPION RUSTLES around his fridge, bleary-eyed and looking for breakfast. Bagels. Cream cheese. A little smoked salmon. He's slim and unassuming, with a permanent tan and an even more permanent case of shirtlessness. He walks like someone who's perfectly content not to be noticed. His shaggy hair and sparse goatee make him a dead ringer for the actor Pedro Pascal. Everyone says it now, but he first heard it years ago, from a security guard at an MMA fight he was attending.

"What are you talking about?" Luke remembers saying. "You calling me old? You telling me I look like a 50-year-old man?"

When Luke has something to say, he usually punctuates his thoughts with an easy, involuntary laugh. You can tell it pains him a bit, all the talking.

Natalia, petite and model gorgeous, makes coffee. The baby, Wild, babbles in his high chair, wearing a T-shirt that says "Aloha Dudes" and waving around a drooly bite of toast. A skinny black-and-white mutt named Nala scampers in excited circles below, waiting for scraps to fall. Haven, 4, is conked out in the bedroom.

Between Luke's lifeguarding and Natalia's shifts as a wedding caterer, wedding coordinator, and at a shave ice stand, this is their only day off every week. They're tired, partially because they possess the genial low-grade weariness that comes with being parents to two children under five, and partially because they've been spending their nights looking for a new apartment. They currently live at the top of a hairpin hill, all four of them sharing a one-bedroom unit in the back of a larger house. Their decor is mostly: toys. Dinosaurs and bouncy balls and scooters. Luke doesn't have an Eddie trophy to display, but the Hawaiian Lifeguard Association made him a custom wooden surfboard to celebrate the win...only they engraved it with the wrong date. (Luke doesn't mind.)

Luke and Natalia recently got a 60-day notice to vacate because their landlord's daughter is moving back in. Finding an affordable new place on the North Shore is not easy when studios with hot plates are going for $3,000 a month. They were thinking about finally trying to buy, and then skyrocketing interest rates yanked that dream out of reach. "People are like, 'We would love to rent to you,'" Luke says. "But then they're like, 'Oh, you must have money now.'" Next thing Luke and Natalia know, they're getting quoted $4,000 a month.

"That's the only shitty thing: Everybody thinks that he's got this huge cash cow," Natalia adds. She and Luke think the mix-up has to do with everyone seeing Luke hold up a big check with 350,000 written in the box, not realizing the figure was airline miles, not dollars.

But the Eddie win has helped relieve the constant, everyday stressors of being broke. "It always took a really big toll on him," Natalia says. "He tried not to show it to us. Luke has a great poker face, even when everything is going to shit around him."

The morning after Luke won the Eddie, his phone started blowing up. In an instant, the beautiful, anonymous ordinariness of their life had been torpedoed. Press flocked to the North Shore. The mayor of Honolulu visited and gave him a plaque declaring that January 25 would be known, in perpetuity, as Luke Shepardson Day. Tourists chased him down for selfies and handshakes as he worked. Suddenly, everyone wanted a piece of Luke: He filmed ads for Bank of Hawaii and a local Kia dealership (he got a new Kia out of that one). Off-days that were once dedicated to seeing friends and family were now devoted to various attendant responsibilities. The musician Jack Johnson, a fellow North Shore local who made it big, sensed what he was going through and reached out to Luke, offering his help.

"The first week was like, 'Fuck, I just want this to be over and done with.' I don't like the cameras, I don't like the attention," Luke says. He would pull on a hoodie and sunglasses and try to get as far away as possible from everyone on the beach. Now, he's more sanguine about it. Might as well enjoy the ride.

Still. Most athletes, when they reach the pinnacle, do not immediately dream of descending back into obscurity. Most *people* are not content with simply trying to keep on keeping on, uneaten by ambition. Luke feels blessed, to be sure. Before the Eddie, he was waking up at 4 a.m., when the stock market would open in New York, to try to make a few extra bucks day-trading, without much success. His $10,000 prize mostly went toward paying a medical bill that had gone into collections. In years past, winning the Eddie was more financially lucrative. Quiksilver used to sponsor the contest, with a grand prize of

$75,000. Somehow Luke's Venmo handle got out after his win, and he received close to that amount in donations.

He could finally put some money into savings. Breathe a little. Luke gave his old truck to his dad and got himself a new Tacoma, which all the surfer guys around here drive. Natalia ditched her lemon that would leak and turn off unexpectedly midway down the hill for the free Kia.

There were other useful perks. In 2021, Luke tweaked his back lifting a six-foot-four, 400-pound guy out of the water. Which means that not only did he surf the Eddie while working, he surfed the Eddie with a bad back.

He recently got platelet-rich plasma injections at the injury site, which speeds up the healing process. Luke had been trying and trying to get approval for insurance coverage for months, without much luck. But when he finally had a call with a doctor, it turned out his Eddie win was good for something else.

"The doctor was like, 'I know the city. They won't approve it, but I'll do it for free,'" Luke recalls. "And I was like, 'Oh, sick.'"

HAVEN AWAKENS FROM his slumber and stumbles out of the bedroom. The kid is so shy at first that he asks me my name with his face buried in the couch cushions. In a matter of minutes, he warms up enough to commandeer the conversation.

"Did you know my brother loves surfing?" Haven asks me.

"Your brother, Wild?" I reply, incredulous. "But he's a baby! When does he go surfing?"

"My dad took him surfing," Haven says with a shrug, focusing his attention on a container of Play-Doh.

Luke, too, was raised this way, improbably surfing before he could walk. As a kid, he'd sleep with his arms wrapped around a surfboard. He remembers staring out at the ocean, watching all these surfers he admired riding monsters. He thought to himself, *How am I ever going to do it? Everyone in Hawaii surfs big waves. I have to surf big waves.*

His Eddie win may have been big news to the rest of the world, but those who surf in these parts always knew what Luke was capable of.

"He's always been that quiet guy that just paddles out," says John John Florence, "then, all of a sudden, he's on one of the best waves."

Luke thinks he's a horrible competition surfer. Gets too inside his own head. His theory is that he won the Eddie in the first place because he was working all day and couldn't think about it too much. "I always overthink it, stress out, get anxious, make stupid mistakes," Luke says. "I'd just trip over my own feet."

Back when he secured his lifeguarding job and Haven was born, Luke decided that his contest days were over. This was more than fine by him. For starters, the waves on the competition route kind of suck. Plus, all the money had drained out of pro surfing. Titans like Billabong and Quiksilver struggled after the 2008 financial crisis. Only the top guys—the John Johns and Kelly Slaters—were getting sponsorship deals in the millions, while everyone else lived contest to contest and paycheck to paycheck. "It was always the dream and then it kind of wasn't the dream…." Luke says, trailing off. "Seeing it firsthand go from everyone's being paid to nobody's being paid."

One time, not long after Haven was born, Liam McNamara offered to pay for Luke's entrance fee in a local contest, but Luke turned him down, saying that he couldn't take off from his day job.

"I think he still feels he's not a pro surfer," Liam tells me. "But he just won the biggest professional surfing competition in the history of the sport. For him *not* to be considered a pro surfer is just crazy."

Once breakfast is finished, we all pile into the new Tacoma and start cruising down the hill to the coast. Though the North Shore is just an hour north of Honolulu, it might as well be a different country. Luke rarely goes, preferring to stay in what he calls "the North Shore bubble."

This bubble, where Luke was raised, is its own Eden. Ancient green mountains with a halo of clouds on one side, a coast lined with bucket-list surf spots on the other. Waimea, yes, and Pipeline and Rockpiles and Chun's Reef. Wild chickens roam the parking lots and outdoor restaurants, crowing at all hours. Carefree, unsupervised kids pedal their bikes to the beach. If the North Shore had an official shoe, it would be the flip-flop, which is about as formal as it gets. In every situation I find myself in over the course of a week, I am the most-dressed person present. (I'm wearing jorts.) Everyone knows everyone and has known everyone since way, way back. As Luke's mom put it after the Eddie: *I changed first- and second-place's diapers.*

But the North Shore is Eden, until it's not. In recent years, the cost of living exploded, ignited by inflation and the pandemic, until the median home price hit $1 million. Rich folks swept in from the mainland. A house that once housed a local Hawaiian family of 10 is now owned by a celebrity or tech CEO who drops in a couple of weeks a year. Food is so expensive that most people drive down to the Costco in Honolulu. Meth addiction runs rampant under the surface.

For Luke, this contest win means more than just extra cash for groceries. It means that there is hope that he can preserve a disappearing way of life for his family, in a place where it's getting harder and harder to do just that. I meet Luke's dad, Mark, one evening on Sunset Beach, right around sunset. Mark is leathery, wearing camo swim trunks and a homemade shell necklace, with a tattoo of an intertwined shark and dolphin on his leg. He could be a character in a tropical Bruce Springsteen song.

He used to surf too. Loved it so much that, at 19, he flew from California to Hawaii with $50 in his pocket to start a new life—arriving, as chance would have it, on the same day that Eddie Aikau disappeared forever. Mark ended up giving up big-wave surfing after a gnarly near-death accident, shortly after meeting Luke's mother. He was saved by a lifeguard.

"He was one of them that never was unhappy in the water," Mark tells me about Luke. "He's more merman than human." A UFO enthusiast, Mark believes it was an early sighting here that father and son had together that rendered Luke preternaturally chill.

I ask Mark what he wants for his son.

"I hope he can live a happy, calm, healthy life with his beautiful woman and his beautiful sons. And that he gets to save a lot of people," he says. "I hope he gets to be the first one to win two Eddies in a row, is what I really hope."

LUKE HAS NO plans of entering another contest besides the Eddie. Instead, he's been daydreaming about what it would be like to buy a house. Maybe even another house that he can rent out. He wants to pass the test at work that will allow him to operate the Jet Ski, which means an automatic pay bump. Planting a garden with some avocado trees and orange trees sounds pretty nice too.

He fulfilled his childhood dreams, even if he didn't take the most direct route. In a way, isn't that more satisfying? To have a dream and to shelve that dream because life gets in the way. To think that it's too late, only to have life surprise you.

Luke has surfed waves in Tahiti and Fiji, chased swells in Japan and Chile. But he wants to stay on the North Shore forever. He wants his kids to be able to stay here, and maybe even their kids. "It's better to struggle in paradise," Luke tells me, "than to be unhappy and rich somewhere else."

As Luke drives us to the beach, he realizes he's forgotten something. He has an event that night—the Marines want to honor him—but he has yet to book a babysitter.

"You can watch us, Auntie!" Haven proposes to me. "Because tomorrow you're coming back to Hawaii to watch us?"

I assure Haven that I will return someday.

"And stay here?"

Luke's winning has permanently tied him to the story of the island. In fact, when Clyde Aikau won the Eddie in '86, two sea turtles guided him toward his waves. Clyde can't let that cosmic coincidence between him and Luke go: "The turtle was actually showing Luke, 'You're the one, you're the one.' I don't know if it's appropriate to say that Luke was the chosen one. But he actually *was* the chosen one."

Luke's win means something to the people around here, especially the people who love and miss Eddie. "It was the first time we've had someone like that, who actually *lived* here and didn't follow the circuit," Linda Ipsen, Eddie's former wife tells me. "He really has the spirit of Eddie."

At the beach, Haven gets zipped into a small burgundy wetsuit. Natalia and I relax on the sand with Wild, as Luke and Haven paddle out on the same board, catching wave after wave.

"I love watching them surf," Natalia says, staring out at the water, "seeing how much Haven totally trusts his dad."

When Haven and Luke emerge, Wild keeps trying to toddle into the shore break.

"Brother wants to catch a wave," Luke tells Haven.

No way, I think. *No way*.

And then Luke takes his 14-month-old baby, plops him onto his board, and together they catch a wave.

After surfing, Dad and his two boys get in the impossible blue-green water. The sun glints off the surface in a way that should only be possible in a postcard. Luke holds Wild, who splashes his chubby arms. Haven floats happily nearby. As I sit on the sand watching, I realize what's really extraordinary about Luke.

Most other people, if they accomplished what he did, would want more. They would be greedier for fame. Maybe a little bitter that it didn't all happen sooner. They would have tried to get far, far away from where they are. Isn't that the most human of human impulses? To look at what you have right in front of you and to think that it could all be so much better?

But Casual Luke has it figured out. He recognizes that here on the North Shore, where he's always been, he has everything he could possibly want or need. He wants to hold onto the life he's built. A beautiful family. A job that fills his days with purpose. An endless supply of perfect waves.

GABRIELLA PAIELLA is a writer based in New York City. She works as a senior staff writer at *GQ*, where she covers culture in all forms. Yes, her name rhymes.

The $1 Million Shot That Changed Sports Contests Forever

RYAN HOCKENSMITH

FROM ESPN • APRIL 11, 2023

Right before he heaved the million-dollar shot, the one that would launch an era of sports contests and change his life forever, Don Calhoun took a long look at his shoes.

He was only out here standing on the floor of Chicago Stadium on April 14, 1993, 15 feet from Michael Jordan and the Bulls, because of his shoes. "Those won't scuff the court," an arena worker said as she signed Calhoun up for a $1 million, three-quarter-court contest shot that the Bulls had been running every night.

As he stared at his feet, waiting to be told it was his turn to take the shot, he was warned, "Whatever you do, don't step over the free throw line." Calhoun, a 23-year-old office supply salesman from the Chicago area, darted his eyes from his non-scuffing sneakers to the free throw line about 80 feet from the hoop he needed to make.

The impossibility of the shot was settling in. He wasn't going to be able to shoot it with both hands; he'd have to throw it like a quarterback. The Bulls had held the promotion 19 times that year already. Two people clunked the backboard. Another clanged the rim. The other 16 were air balls. Nobody came close. The best estimate of someone like Calhoun making that shot? Less than 1%.

But then, a calm came over him. He thought about his brother Clarence, who had told him five years earlier, just before he died, that Michael Jordan would soon be the best player in the NBA and the Bulls would be a dynasty. He thought about his bittersweet feelings toward the sport of basketball—he loved the game and was good at it, but he never made his high school team.

It might sound ridiculous, but as Calhoun stood there and heard his name announced, he became sure—*100% certain*—that the shot was going to go in. The last thing he remembers is the steady hum of 18,600 people rising to cheer for him. As the Bulls huddled up nearby, Calhoun palmed the ball in one hand. The free throw line warning was bouncing around inside his head, and for a second, he felt his flow get disrupted.

But the flow came back as he stepped past the end line. He took one fast dribble, thought to himself, "This is for Clarence," and then threw a high-arching rocket.

As the ball sailed toward the hoop, Calhoun's eyes again turned toward his feet and he saw that he was *very* close to the free throw line—but a few inches behind. Whew. When he looked up again, he had a moment of panic. He'd thrown it too far and too hard.

"It looked like it was going to hit the shot clock," he says.

But then the ball began to sink. It dropped, and dropped, and dropped, and...*swish*. Right through the net. Calhoun threw his arms toward the rafters, and the crowd let out one of those levels of cheers that aggravates the arena neighbors.

Then the real mayhem began.

The ensuing 30 seconds might be the most joyous footage of that Bulls team ever. Seriously, watch the most celebratory moments from *The Last Dance*, and compare those with the clips you will inevitably see this April 14 on social media on the 30th anniversary of Calhoun's heave. John Paxson and Scott Williams go wild. Some player just off-camera slaps Calhoun's ass over and over again, and even one of the game refs comes over, hits him on the back and hands him the ball from the shot. Phil Jackson stands there with an incredulous grin, looking like he just won the $1 million.

Suddenly, Calhoun found himself bumped and butt-slapped directly into the middle of the Bulls huddle, where the other players parted and there stood Scottie Pippen and Michael Jordan. Calhoun was the team's 13th man at that moment. Calhoun was in there for a good 10 seconds when he felt Jordan slap him on the back and lean into his ear.

"Great shot, kid," Jordan said.

Calhoun says he can still hear the way Jordan was yelling "Woo!" behind him the entire time. After the game, Michael Wilbon, then at *The Washington Post*, wrote, "Jordan, smiling in a child-like way I've never seen on the court, threw both arms around his neck and squeezed." As the celebration exploded around him, Calhoun felt as if his life was going to change. He was the toast of Chicago for the next 24 hours, with the shot going viral by 1993 standards, with newscasts and newspapers all showing the clip so much that Calhoun's shot is now referenced as the beginning of a boom in contests at sporting events. And best of all, Calhoun was about to become a millionaire.

Or so he thought.

BY THE TIME Don Calhoun made his shot, in-game contests had begun to pop up here and there across the country. But Calhoun's make caused an eruption in popularity. Chris Hamman, VP at industry leader SCA Promotions, thinks "The Calhoun Shot," as it's become known in the business, might have doubled or even tripled the number of contests.

"These types of contests grew quite a bit, and a lot of NBA teams started doing similar contests," says Hamman, whose dad, Bob, founded SCA Promotions, which has been insuring sports contests since the mid-1980s. Chris compares Calhoun's make with the impact Chris Moneymaker had on poker in 2003 when he went from an $86 online qualifier to winning the World Series of Poker (and $2.5 million).

The contests took off afterward. They were the perfect way to keep 15,000-plus people engaged during TV timeouts and between quarters. They were wildly popular crowd-pleasers back then, and remain slam dunk #ViralContent in the social media era. SCA Promotions has insured billions of dollars of sports contests since the mid-1980s, paying out something like $250 million in winnings over the years, according to Bob Hamman. (SCA was not the insurer of the Calhoun Shot.)

As the Hammans note, the perfect contest is like the most tempting carnival game: just feasible enough to make people think they can do it while actually being extremely difficult. Everybody at the Bulls game that night in 1993 probably had sunk a long shot or two at some point in their life. In reality, Jordan himself might not have made one if you gave him 100 tries. "With the shot that Don Calhoun made, you could have Steph Curry out there and still make money," Chris Hamman says.

But, as was the case with Calhoun, people do win enough to keep contest dreams alive. SCA Promotions insures more than $100 million in sports contests every year, and the Hammans love telling stories of paying off winners…because the vast majority of holes-in-one and half-court shots never happen. It's a little like when sportsbooks leak out those betting slips of the fan who hit a 12-team parlay that cost $40 and pays out $250,000. The good news fuels the delusion of it happening to you.

One of the Hammans' favorite winners was a Diamondbacks fan, Gylene Hoyle, who won a 1999 radio contest where she had to pick one Arizona player and an inning. If that player hit a home run in that exact inning during a specific game, she'd win $1 million.

Seems doable, right? The math is actually obscene. She picked Jay Bell, who was in the middle of a monster year (38 home runs and 112 RBIs). She had about a 1-in-2,916 chance. And yet, Bell came to the plate in the sixth inning with the bases loaded. He fouled off two straight two-strike pitches, then hit a home run on a pitch that could have been ball four. Afterward, he acknowledged that he knew about the contest and swung hoping to get someone $1 million. "That one stung," Bob Hamman says.

The math on insuring high-stakes contests generally works the same way. Brokers come up with a likelihood that a random contestant could win—the Hammans say a three-quarter-court shot is less than 1%, for example—and divide it into the prize amount, then charge about twice that to insure it. For a $1 million contest with a 1% success rate, that means it'd cost the team $20,000 every time they run it.

Once the details are ironed out, insurance companies come up with all the fine print. Contestants usually must be randomly selected from the crowd. If it's one shot, there's no warmup toss or second attempt. If it's three makes in 30 seconds, three makes in 30.1 seconds is close but no money. For something like a hockey shot that must go through a tiny plywood cutout and into a goal, the shot has to be entirely through. Not mostly through. Not on the line. *Entirely* through.

Insurance companies are unforgiving with teams that don't explain the rules right, and it's not unusual for franchises to end up paying out the contest themselves if there are any issues. The PR hit of stiffing a middle school geometry teacher out of $25,000 generally isn't worth it.

But lawsuits and disagreements happen, and that's what almost happened to Don Calhoun. One key stipulation in most insurance policies is that the contestant can't have played an "organized" version of the sport in question for a certain time period before the contest—usually, five years.

Calhoun grew up in Chicago playing hoops on the playground with Clarence. Both had trouble making it onto junior high and varsity teams despite what seemed to be a worthy skill set. They were tough guards who loved dogging opposing ball handlers on defense. But they also played a brand of streetball that didn't always translate well to high school hoops.

They certainly had talent, though. Clarence graduated and played at a junior college for his freshman year, then transferred to DePaul to walk onto the basketball team as a sophomore. Don, then a senior in high school, drew inspiration from Clarence's unwillingness to quit basketball despite a high school career that didn't pan out—he, too, planned to go to a small school to play hoops before transferring to a bigger school.

But one weekend, Clarence was on his way home from school to hang out with his family for a few days when the Calhouns got a dreaded phone call. He had gotten tired on the drive home, pulled over to rest, and been struck and killed by another car. He was 20.

Don was devastated. He didn't graduate that spring on time as he grieved. But he went back to school in the fall and got his diploma. He slowly landed in a headspace where he wanted to use his brother's memory as fuel. He bounced around at two community colleges and walked on with both basketball teams. One newspaper account from the time says he was 3-for-12 shooting in 11 career games.

But Don eventually walked away from school and from any formal basketball. He found out his longtime girlfriend was pregnant, so he got a job as an office supply salesman. Binders, notebooks, day planners, you name it, Don Calhoun was the guy to talk to. He was making a decent living, and he eventually had a son. The little boy's name? Clarence Calhoun II.

When Clarence was 3, Don hugged him and told him to watch the Bulls game that night because Dad might be on TV. Clarence remembers his mom letting him stay up, although he's not sure he saw the actual shot. He just recalls yelling and pointing at the screen as he watched his dad leap up and down with Michael Jordan and the Chicago Bulls. Then he went to bed.

Calhoun says that he marked on the forms that he had played some college basketball three years earlier and that the contest people shrugged about it. The insurance company disagreed, and the weekend after he had won, local news media began to report that Calhoun might not be getting the money. That prompted the

Bulls to hold a news conference, where Calhoun sat beside Jerry Reinsdorf and several contest sponsors.

"It is unclear at this time whether the company that insured the event will pay on the policy," a joint statement read. "However, regardless of its decision, [restaurant group] Lettuce Entertain You, Coca-Cola (Foundation) and the Chicago Bulls will honor the $1 million award and ensure that this event has a happy ending."

Calhoun left that day knowing that the win was, in fact, going to be a win. He would immediately receive his first of 20 annual $50,000 payments. In the coming weeks, he appeared on *The Tonight Show with Jay Leno* and got a cup of coffee as a member of the Harlem Globetrotters. He was, unbelievably, the unofficial mayor of Chicago for a brief period. When Wilbon called Calhoun's company for his story, someone answered by saying, "Reliable Office Superstore. This is the home of one-shot Don Calhoun, the million-dollar man."

He never got many details about how the sponsors and insurance company worked it out. He just took yes as an answer. It wasn't until a few weeks later that he found out that he might have needed a key assist from a secret source: Michael Jordan himself.

AFTER CALHOUN MADE the shot, he was asked to stay on the floor and do an endless string of TV hits and print interviews. As he bounced from camera setup to camera setup near the Chicago locker room, Bulls players kept leaving and spotting him on their way out. Almost every player came over, said congratulations and signed his basketball. "It took me three years to make a million dollars, and it took him five seconds," Horace Grant joked afterward.

Calhoun got signatures from Grant, Scottie Pippen, John Paxson and B.J. Armstrong, plus two Heat players who swung by, Rony Seikaly and Steve Smith. And then, as he got ready to do another live hit, Calhoun saw Jordan and a Bulls staffer come out and stand nearby. Calhoun made eye contact with Jordan, who smiled back at him and was clearly there waiting to say hello to him. Calhoun wanted to run over and ditch whatever TV interview he was about to do, but producers kept telling him they were about to go live any second now.

When the lights went on, Calhoun did the best interview he could as he watched in dismay what was happening on the other side of the camera. Jordan said something to the Bulls staffer and left. Calhoun wasn't going to meet MJ, after all, and it crushed him. The Bulls worker said he could leave the ball behind and they'd try to get Jordan to sign it.

But Calhoun had other plans. He didn't want to leave the building without that ball, so he took it. He thought there was a chance he might run into Jordan somewhere down the road, then he could get an autograph.

Over the next few days, news broke all over the country that Calhoun's winnings seemed to be in jeopardy. Calhoun clung to that ball, and it provided him hope. He had made the shot. The crowd had gone completely wild. The Bulls had pulled him into their huddle. He had left with the ball. That was all real, and he would have it forever. The $1 million? He sure hoped it was coming his way. But he also felt an odd peace about the money. The experience alone certainly wouldn't pay for Clarence's school clothes. But it wasn't nothing, either. It was priceless.

As reports swirled, fan outrage was palpable in Chicago, which created enough heat on the franchise to figure out some way to pay the local office supply salesman his damn money. That led to the news conference and the first $50,000 check.

But what to do about his beloved basketball? The next school year, he had heard from a friend that Jordan always attended one of his kid's home games at a specific school in the area. So he showed up that night—with his ball and two magazines—and tried to walk up to Jordan. The Bulls star had his own section away from the crowd, complete with security that kept people from doing exactly what Calhoun was trying to do.

Calhoun was stopped on his approach by a Jordan security guy, who said Jordan had a firm policy of no autographs at his kids' events. Calhoun explained who he was and that Jordan had seemed to really want to meet him back in April. The security guy wouldn't budge. "No autographs at his kids' stuff," the guy repeated.

But Calhoun had a funny feeling that he shouldn't give up. He asked the security to *pretty-pretty-pretty please* tell Jordan that the guy who made The Calhoun Shot had come to the game hoping for his signature. The security guy shook his head. Calhoun was even willing to just hand the guy the ball to take to Jordan. No luck.

"Michael doesn't do anything when he's at one of his kid's games," Calhoun was told.

An unlikely thing happened near the end of the game, though. The security guard came to Calhoun in the stands and told him he could walk with Jordan to his car after the game. So Calhoun got his ball and Sharpie ready, then met up with the Jordan crew as he left the high school.

The first thing out of Jordan's mouth? "Did you get your money?" Jordan asked.

Calhoun said yes, and Jordan told him something that caught him off guard. "We made them give it to you," Jordan said. "We were upset that they were trying to not pay you."

Calhoun was stunned. He had heard rumors that the Bulls players were agitated at the thought of him getting stiffed. But this was confirmation that Michael Jordan himself helped make him a millionaire. (Jordan declined an interview request for this story; the Bulls also passed on participating.)

As they got to a set of doors, Calhoun knew Jordan's car was waiting for him on the other side. He asked whether Jordan would sign his ball, and MJ said no, that he had to stick to his principle of no autographs at his kids' stuff. "Bring it down to my steakhouse and drop it off, then I'll sign it," he said.

Calhoun waved goodbye that night and thanked Jordan once more for advocating on his behalf. But as he left later, he felt a pang as he considered just pulling up to Jordan's restaurant, dropping off the ball and hoping for the best.

The ball had grown to mean so much to him. It wasn't the signatures, or that he thought the ball might be worth something like $20,000. Its actual worth was beyond what someone could pay. It represented the agony of losing Clarence and trying to carry his brother's message with his own son. It represented the end of the bitter, unfulfilled taste that "organized" basketball had left in his mouth. It represented closing that chapter of his life when he had to fight and claw to pay every bill for his family, opening up 20 years where he knew he had a financial backstop each year.

Was he really going to hand the ball to some random steak-house assistant manager and cross his fingers, hoping he'd see it again?

The answer was...yes, he was going to do exactly that. He felt as if Jordan's signature was too important as the coda to the story of the ball. So he drove over there one day and implored the person he handed it to for help, saying that this ball meant so much to him, that MJ's signature was the last missing component of an artifact from the most important moment of his life.

It must have worked. A few weeks later, he got a call to pick up the ball. "Michael signed it, and he wishes you well," Calhoun was told.

The ball became a family heirloom over the next three decades. But not in the way you'd expect. Calhoun never locked it up in a vault or even put it in a protective case in the house. He left it in the basement of his house, and Clarence and Calhoun's other three kids would dribble it and throw it around. He wanted his kids to be able to touch and feel something that had altered the trajectory of their family. "I'll always keep it for you," Don told Clarence.

For the next 20 years, Calhoun would get a check for $50,000 every year. Of that money, he'd have to set aside around $12,000 for taxes. He kept his office sales job for a few more years, and the other $38,000 (about $79,000 in 2023 dollars) was a very nice supplemental living. But, as Calhoun says, it was more like a bump up within the middle class. "In reality, you're not rich," he says. "You're not a millionaire."

Maybe he didn't have generational wealth. But he was about to experience a generational breakthrough.

As the 30th anniversary of the shot approaches, Calhoun takes a few weeks to decide whether he will talk about the shot, the money or any of it. He hasn't done many interviews over the years. Eventually, he agreed to one but asked that his current location and occupation be left out of the story. Let's say he's living within a few hours of Chicago in the Midwest, and he works the second shift at a solid job.

He's not hesitant because he's a particularly shy person—once he gets rolling on the phone, he's funny and unafraid to argue, and he comes off as very open and honest as he talks. Toward the end of an hourlong interview, he asks, "How can I get to the Hall of Fame?"

When the answer is a surprised chuckle, he says, "Don't you laugh. I want to be in the Hall of Fame. I think I deserve it."

He seems to be goofing around, but Calhoun changes lanes easily between being confident and reserved. He talks about the shot like he knew it was going in the entire time, yet it never sounds particularly braggy. He seems as if he had his 15 minutes and is content with that...but also thinks it'd be nice to have a small shrine to it.

Calhoun is 53 now. He catches the video only every few years, when somebody will show him a tweet or video link to a clip that you will most likely see every April 14 for the rest of eternity.

Calhoun is neither rich nor poor, at least in the traditional sense of the word. He does, however, feel wealthy when he talks about his four kids. The Calhoun Shot gave them all a better life. His youngest, Terrelle, is 20 and lives in Austin, Texas. Naomi, 22, is in nursing school. Gabriela, 28, is a teacher. And Clarence II, 33, is living out something beyond his own wildest dreams— and his dad's.

Don Calhoun's oldest son became a good prep basketball player at East Aurora High School and graduated in 2008. With five years of $50,000 checks left, Don encouraged Clarence to finish the job he and his brother had started years earlier: graduating from college. Clarence loved that idea. What a cool way to pay tribute to the uncle he never met but was named after. The problem was, he still didn't know what he wanted to be when he grew up.

For the first few years after high school, he bounced between community colleges before getting into Wiley College, an HBCU in Marshall, Texas. He had developed an interest in the human body, especially biology. But college was no joke. Clarence Calhoun II limped to a 1.6 GPA in his first semester. It wasn't that he couldn't handle the coursework or the social life or the amount of work it took. It was the totality of doing all of those things all at once. He didn't know a single person who had experience at this level of education. He was a rookie, surrounded by rookies.

That's when he met a Ukrainian physician named Dr. Valentyn Siniak. Siniak was at Wiley teaching while he took mandatory tests to begin practicing medicine in the U.S. Calhoun was blown away by the level of support Siniak provided. Calhoun isn't sure exactly what Siniak saw in him, but he saw something.

In emails to Calhoun, Siniak began calling him "Dr. Clarence Calhoun." When Calhoun asked him for guidance on how he could get his grades up, Siniak made him laugh out loud. "I think you should start tutoring other students," Siniak said.

"Tutoring?" Calhoun said. "I'm struggling to learn everything myself. How can I teach others?" Siniak thought this would give Calhoun an extra nudge to learn the material and boost his own command.

Siniak was *exactly* right. So right, in fact, that Calhoun sighs and shakes his head on a Zoom describing this section of his life. He still can't fathom the way Siniak manifested belief into Calhoun's life. His grades soared, and he liked working with other students. He had to work his ass off to get there—at one point, campus security officers would close up the science building for the night, knowing Calhoun was still in there. He'd study most of the night, inflate a mattress for a few hours and wake up the next day ready to do it again. "I found out I was smarter than I thought I was," Calhoun says now.

And so in 2013, Calhoun graduated from college just as his dad's $50,000 annual checks ended. He was the first in his family to get a college degree, and he battled and scrapped every day to get it.

He also had found out that his girlfriend was pregnant and that they were having a boy. When he told Don, he said, "Know what we're going to name him, Dad?"

Don began to think about it for a second…and then it hit him. He didn't say a word, and his son didn't either. They laughed, hugged and celebrated the upcoming birth of Clarence Calhoun III.

Clarence Calhoun II started to chart a course for the next phase of his life, which had come into focus for him. "I want to be a doctor," he told his dad, and he began to try to get into medical school. He worked jobs at Jiffy Lube, a toxicology lab and other places before he finally passed his labs and got accepted. This was happening. Not only was a Calhoun going to earn his degree but he felt as if he might actually become the Dr. Clarence Calhoun his instructor, Dr. Siniak, had predicted in his emails.

That's why it breaks the younger Calhoun's heart to tell this next part of the story. Siniak didn't get to see Calhoun get his degree. In January 2013, Siniak was struck and killed while riding a motorcycle in Texas. "Having him believe in me helped me believe in myself," Calhoun says. "My biggest downfall that was keeping me from excelling was my confidence. I just didn't think I could. I didn't have anybody around me who had done it."

Over the next eight years, he passed his boards and did his residency, and an envelope arrived in May 2021 that he couldn't wait to open. The piece of paper inside made it official: He was now Dr. Clarence Calhoun.

He went to his dad's house to show him in person, and they had a long embrace. Don couldn't stop smiling. After a minute, he walked out of the room and came back holding two things he was giving to his son.

One was the shoes he had worn during The Calhoun Shot. Clarence noticed they had a signature on them. They were autographed by…none other than Don Calhoun, which makes Clarence laugh to this day when he holds them up. His dad can be a goofball—an inspiring goofball. "He drops spiritual motivation all the time, and that's always needed," Clarence says. "In moments when it feels like life is too difficult, he helps you figure out how you can do it."

For the second item, Don Calhoun didn't hand it to him. He reared back and threw a push pass at his son's chest.

"Here, I want you to have this," and he chucked an old basketball at his son. Clarence Calhoun II hadn't seen the ball from The Calhoun Shot in 10-15 years, and now it was going to live with him and his son. The two older Calhouns, Don and Clarence, hugged once more. And as Dr. Clarence Calhoun left that day, with a basketball under one arm and some old shoes under the other, his whole life felt like sinking a less than 1% three-quarter-court shot.

After graduating from Penn State in 2001 with a journalism degree, **RYAN HOCKENSMITH** got an internship at *ESPN The Magazine* and has never left. He transitioned from writing into editing in the mid-2000s as part of the magazine's award-winning run in New York City. When the magazine relocated to ESPN headquarters in Bristol, Ct., in 2011, Hockensmith served as a senior editor before taking a job as a deputy editor at espnW from 2014–16, then with the ESPN.com college football team from 2016–18 before moving back to the magazine. From 2018, he gradually wrote more and more, culminating in moving full time to a writer role in March 2022. Hockensmith is a survivor of bacterial meningitis, which caused him to have amputations on both feet. During his 20-plus years at ESPN, he has emerged as a proud advocate for coverage of those with disabilities and addiction issues. He and his wife, Lori, have three daughters.

Jenni Hermoso Is a Giant. Only an Unjust System Reduces Her to Victim.

CANDACE BUCKNER

FROM *The Washington Post* • SEPTEMBER 8, 2023

Jenni Hermoso isn't a helpless woman who was pulled into an unwanted kiss. She's the prolific scorer who propelled Spain through the 2023 World Cup bracket. She's much more than the summoned plaintiff seeking an investigation from the Spanish attorney general's office on whether that act rises to a "crime of sexual assault." She's the swaggering player who broke down in tears after helping her team make history by winning the whole thing.

The identities assigned to Hermoso now threaten to overwhelm and diminish everything she accomplished before Luis Rubiales, the president of the Spanish soccer federation, placed his greasy paws on her face and pulled her into that kiss. She didn't consent to Rubiales's act. She never asked for this role. Hermoso had to define herself as a complainant in court because Spanish authorities can investigate a sexual assault only if the victim reports the case herself. Justice might arrive, eventually, but only if cloaked in unfair irony.

Among the most disheartening twists to the ongoing saga that has toppled the Spanish soccer's power structure—and eclipsed every other storyline of the World Cup—is that Hermoso must take on a new identity. One that never should have belonged to her: "Victim."

In the weeks since the championship match and the celebration that soiled Spain's defining moment, the fallout has offered a glimpse into why it's so hard for some alleged victims to seek justice. Hermoso has been called a "liar" and has been lied about by her own federation, the bullying boys' club that went with the tired play of blaming the woman to defend their guy. As the days go by, evidence of her career achievements in soccer can be scarcely found on search engines. For instance, try Googling broad terms such as *Jennifer Hermoso soccer*, or something a bit more specific such as *how many minutes did Jenni Hermoso play in the World Cup*. Hermoso's accolades are buried beneath an avalanche of stories documenting the fallout from the unwanted kiss. And, of course, *his* mug. A face synonymous with morally corrupt men in charge who wield their power like weapons. And because Rubiales couldn't merely celebrate the players and saddle his privilege for two seconds, her face has become synonymous with victimhood.

"I felt vulnerable and a victim of an impulse-driven, sexist, out of place act, without any consent on my part," Hermoso said in a statement. "Simply put, I was not respected."

If victims ever feel hesitation in reporting crimes of verbal, physical and sexual abuse, it might be because they don't want to acknowledge what Hermoso had to publicly admit.

When the U.S. Soccer Federation released the investigative findings into mistreatment in the domestic women's professional league, Sally Q. Yates wrote: "The verbal and emotional abuse players describe in the NWSL is not merely 'tough' coaching. And the players affected are not shrinking violets. They are among the best athletes in the world." Many of those players endured seasons worth of misconduct from their coaches before reporting them to the league—and sometimes it took years for the league to stop ignoring their claims. Hermoso had the benefit of video evidence and a public rallying to her side (*Contigo Jenni!* they have screamed in the streets of Madrid and worn on their wrists in the NWSL), and yet she still needed several days to pass before making her first public comments.

The Spanish soccer star, the all-time goal scorer and a world-class *campeona*, or champion. This is who admitted to feeling "vulnerable" and disrespected. Imagine how complicated that must be for a professional athlete who has made a career of commanding the stage or powering through obstacles.

In a sport that exalts toughness, Hermoso plays the part. No woman in the history of Spain's national team has scored more goals. During the World Cup held in Australia and New Zealand, although she's 33 years old, Hermoso still applied more ball pressure and covered more ground than any of her teammates. Past her prime? Nope. Hermoso's too spicy for that.

"The age thing is just a f---ing number that people want to put on everything," she said after her team defeated Sweden in the semifinal round.

But before she was running all over the place—and putting any critics in their place—she was speaking up. Last September, Hermoso was one of three players to hold a news conference to explain the "general unease" felt by the national team. This happened before the majority of the team sent an email to the Royal Spanish Football Federation to say they would not suit up if Jorge Vilda remained as coach. The federation (RFEF) stood by their boy, retaliated with silly threats and tried to strong-arm apologies from the players. Despite the RFEF stooping to new levels of petty, Hermoso, like her teammates, represented her homeland anyway.

In a world that expects women to grit it out and persist, Hermoso performs that role just as well.

She has covered her left arm in a sleeve of tattoos and lets profanities fly freely from her lips. In Australia, my only up-close moment with the leader of La Roja was when she bounced through the media zone following the semifinals—and not giving a single

care about the reporter's microphones nor the broken hearts of
the Swedish players who had just lost—she yelled triumphantly
in Spanish: "We're in the f---ing finals!"

With that little peek into her personality, Hermoso appeared
carefree, equally a jubilant victor and a cheeky agitator. She would
make no apologies for her presence. There she was. All of her.
And tough if you didn't like it. In Spain, you might say *que ella
no se amilana*. She's not intimidated. Around here, we would just
look at her and go *that girl's baaaad!*

But now, we feel sorry for her; a sentiment that conflicts with
her natural character. The unwanted kiss thrust Hermoso into a
spotlight not of her choosing and turned her into the woman who
had something done *to* her. Judging by her statements and her
decision to request an investigation, however, it seems Hermoso
is determined to flip that identity.

After her fight, maybe she won't just be the plaintiff but the
willing advocate who stood up against sexism. It's up to the world
to recognize this difference. Considering Hermoso's background
as a fearless goal scorer, emboldened speaker and all-around *jefa*,
she may not give us a choice.

Beatriz Rios contributed to this report.

CANDACE BUCKNER has written sports criticism for *The Washington Post*
since 2021. She graduated from the University of Missouri and calls St. Louis
"home." She currently resides in Washington, D.C.

How an FBI Agent's Wild Vegas Weekend Stained an Investigation into NCAA Basketball Corruption

NATHAN FENNO

FROM *The Los Angeles Times* • MARCH 9, 2023

The FBI agents arrived in Las Vegas with $135,000 and a plan.

They took over a sprawling penthouse at the Cosmopolitan, filled the in-room safe with government cash and stocked the wet bar with alcohol. Hidden cameras—including one installed near a crystal-encrusted wall in the living room—recorded visitors.

In the heart of a city known for heists and hangovers, the four agents were running an undercover operation as part of their probe into college basketball corruption that investigators code-named Ballerz.

One of the agents was posing as a deep-pocketed business-man wanting to bribe coaches to persuade their players to retain a particular sports management company when they turned professional. He distributed more than $40,000 in cash to a procession of coaches invited to the penthouse. The sting concluded at a poolside cabana on a blistering afternoon in July 2017 with a final envelope of cash passed to one last coach.

After that transaction, the lead case agent, Scott Carpenter, joined the undercover operative and the two other agents in eating and drinking their way through the $1,500 food and beverage minimum to rent the cabana.

Carpenter had consumed nearly a fifth of vodka and at least six beers by the time he returned to the penthouse to shower and change clothes before a night out.

He grabbed $10,000 in undercover cash from the penthouse safe, then headed to a high-limit lounge at the casino next door. What happened next would ultimately stain the investigation like a cocktail spilled on a white tablecloth.

THE INVESTIGATION WAS hailed as a watershed moment in men's college basketball. But in an extensive reassessment, *The Times* examined thousands of pages of court testimony, intercepted phone calls, text messages, emails and performance reviews. The records provide a detailed look inside the high-profile investigation, led by a veteran FBI agent whose conduct on a vodka-soaked day in Las Vegas landed him on the wrong side of the law.

Ballerz was the top priority for the New York FBI's public corruption squad for almost a year, according to Carpenter's performance review in 2017, and included two undercover agents, operations in at least eight states, dozens of grand jury subpoenas and thousands of wiretapped phone calls.

The performance review and other court records offer new details about the lead case agent's role and provide the most comprehensive account to date of the FBI's handling of an investigation that, for all its hype, focused on lesser-known coaches and middlemen, most of them Black.

The weight of the federal government crashed down on college basketball at a livestreamed news conference in Manhattan when authorities unveiled the investigation in September 2017. The assistant director in charge of the New York FBI office warned potential cheaters that "we have your playbook."

FBI agents, some with weapons drawn, had arrested 10 men, including assistant coaches from USC, Arizona, Auburn and Oklahoma State. Prosecutors alleged that the coaches took bribes and, in a related scheme, that Adidas representatives funneled money to lure players to colleges the company sponsored.

Major universities and shoe companies were deluged with subpoenas. Coaches retained attorneys, even if they hadn't been charged, and rumors swirled about the government's next target in its crusade to clean up the sport.

Carpenter's performance review said the "takedown has already had a major national impact and…is likely to continue to have major impact." Prosecutors characterized the effort in a court filing as "arguably the biggest and most significant federal investigation and prosecution of corruption in college athletics."

But almost six years later, the operation that was supposed to expose college basketball's "dark underbelly" didn't transform the sport. No head coaches or administrators were charged. There wasn't a public outcry.

Instead, the meandering government effort seemed at times like an investigation searching for a crime, marshaling vast resources to ultimately round up an assortment of low-level figures for alleged wrongdoing—particularly the coach bribery scheme—that people involved in the sport said wasn't a common practice until the FBI started handing out envelopes of cash.

"This was a massive waste of time on everybody's part," said Jonathan Bradley Augustine, a former Florida youth basketball coach who was among those charged, though the charges were later dismissed. "It was a sexy case. This was big news. It was everywhere…. A lot of money wasted. A lot of people's lives turned upside down."

The saga started more than a decade ago with a Pittsburgh financial advisor and two ill-fated movie projects.

Louis Martin Blazer III, whose clients included professional athletes, had pumped money into two minor films. *A Resurrection*, which was about a youngster who thinks his brother is returning from the dead, earned just $10,730 at the box office. The other movie, *Mafia*, went straight to DVD with the tagline: "He crossed the wrong cop."

To bankroll the investments along with funding a music management company, the Securities and Exchange Commission later alleged, Blazer misappropriated $2.3 million from five clients between 2010 and 2012, forging documents, making "Ponzi-like payments" to hide the theft, faking a client's signature and lying to investigators.

Seeking leniency, Blazer met with federal prosecutors and the SEC in New York in June 2014. He came clean about the fraud—and volunteered details about an unrelated scheme prosecutors didn't know about in which he had paid about two dozen college athletes to use his financial services firm when they turned professional. This could have rendered the players ineligible under NCAA rules and left their schools vulnerable to sanctions.

That fall, prosecutors put Blazer to work as a cooperating witness posing as a financial advisor trying to sign up college athletes as clients. He traveled the country to meet with agents, coaches, athletes and their family members, while recording conversations.

Blazer's undercover operation had stalled by the time the FBI took over in November 2016, though the bureau saw "major unrealized potential" in the case, according to Carpenter's performance review. Carpenter was transferred from the Eurasian organized crime squad to take over as the lead case agent on the basketball probe.

Raised in New Jersey as the son of a municipal judge and lawyer, Carpenter graduated from Wake Forest in the top of his ROTC class and served in Iraq as an officer with the 82nd Airborne. Carpenter's annual officer evaluation in 2008 described his performance during 15 months in Baghdad as "absolutely phenomenal" with an "ability to turn chaos into order." He left the Army that year as a captain, lived on the family's sailboat and joined the FBI.

But signs of trouble began to emerge.

"He had started to become reliant on vodka," his father, Frank Carpenter, would later write in a letter filed in court. "Whenever I saw him, he either had a drink or I could smell it on his breath. I still did not connect this to bigger mental health issues or the symptoms of PTSD that I learned about later."

A court filing blamed his heavy drinking on the emotional toll from the lengthy deployment in Iraq and an improvised explosive device destroying the Humvee behind his vehicle.

At work, however, the complexities of the basketball probe appeared to be an ideal match for the skills of Scott Carpenter, who had worked on the high-profile investigation into global soccer corruption. His performance review said Blazer had previously been "unsuccessful in developing evidence," but became "highly productive" under Carpenter's direction.

Without Carpenter, the performance review said, "it is likely there would have been minimal if any investigative results."

JEFF D'ANGELO HAD money and wanted to invest it in a sports management company. The exact source of his wealth wasn't clear. Real estate? Restaurants? Family? Wherever it came from, he talked like someone who orchestrated major deals.

The thirty-something slicked back his hair, liked to mention he served in the military and had the thick biceps of a workout fiend.

One person who met D'Angelo described him as a "mix between a hedge fund baby and Jersey Shore Italian."

In fact, "D'Angelo" was a pseudonym. He was an undercover FBI agent. Carpenter served as D'Angelo's handler. The lead case agent's performance review lauded the work, saying that the undercover agent "had the resources and guidance to significantly expand this investigation" thanks to Carpenter.

In mid-May 2017, D'Angelo was introduced at a Manhattan restaurant to Christian Dawkins, an ambitious 24-year-old attempting to start a sports management firm.

"If it makes sense…I'll invest," D'Angelo said. "I would put down some capital."

Dawkins had grown up in Saginaw, Mich., the son of a basketball coach and middle school principal, and hoped to become a sports agent or college coach. As a teenager, he started a high school basketball scouting service called "Best of the Best" and peddled it to college coaches for $600 a year. He was a relentless self-promoter, mentioning himself in prospect updates, adding inches to his true height and listing himself among "standout campers" at a clinic run by his father.

After the 2009 death of his younger brother Dorian from a heart ailment while playing basketball, Dawkins helped start a youth travel team named Dorian's Pride. He created an event company called Living Out Your Dreams—LOYD for short—named himself chief executive and organized basketball camps.

Just shy of 21, Dawkins joined a Cleveland financial advisory firm working with NBA players. He later moved to New Jersey–based ASM Sports, recruiting clients for the powerhouse sports agency.

Dawkins continued to pursue the goal of leading his own sports management company. He connected with Blazer through a bespoke suit maker with deep links to professional basketball. Dawkins outlined his ambition in an email to Blazer and another associate in April 2016 that, like secret recordings of their meetings, ended up in the hands of authorities: "I want to have my own support system, and I want to be able to facilitate things on my own, independent of ASM…. I just have to have the resources to continue."

After the SEC accused Blazer of defrauding professional athletes in a news release the following month, Blazer testified that Dawkins "didn't want to be around" him for almost a year.

In the meantime, Dawkins paid players and their families to retain ASM, according to his court testimony and exhibits, used two phones to stay in touch with some of the biggest names in the sport and relaxed in the green room at the NBA draft as players waited to be selected. When an associate joked in a text message that Dawkins seemed to be everywhere, he responded with apparent pride, "But never seen."

ON A WINDY afternoon in June 2017, Dawkins boarded a large yacht moored at the North Cove Marina in Manhattan's Battery Park.

He expected to finalize the launch of his sports management company. In reality, the gathering was a setup. Everything was recorded. Among those in attendance were Blazer and D'Angelo, who introduced Dawkins to a wealthy friend named Jill Bailey. She was another undercover FBI agent.

In the agreement signed that day, D'Angelo pledged to lend $185,000 to the company in exchange for a minority stake. Dawkins got 50% of the firm called Loyd Inc. and would be president. The company didn't have a licensed NBA player agent, formal structure or even an office. D'Angelo—whose name was misspelled in the contract—handed out $25,000 in cash for the company's start-up expenses.

D'Angelo wanted to pay college coaches to direct their players to use the new company when they became professionals, saying if the firm had "X amount of coaches that are on board with our business plan…that's just that many more kids we're gonna have access to essentially every month." Dawkins was skeptical. If the investor insisted on paying coaches, he argued, only "elite level dudes" should get money. Still, Dawkins offered to introduce D'Angelo to several coaches the following month when they flooded Las Vegas for a huge youth basketball tournament.

In the days and weeks that followed, Dawkins complained to associates in recorded conversations that bribing coaches was nonsensical. The best players usually spent less than a year on campus before leaving and had limited time with coaches. Parents, close relatives, youth coaches or middlemen, like Dawkins, exerted the real influence in the daily lives of many top-level players.

A system built around the NCAA's ban on paying players and their families was lucrative for everyone but the people on the court. The NCAA brought in $761 million from the March Madness tournament in 2017. Multinational shoe companies paid universities to wear their gear. Top head coaches earned $4 million or more a year. It all helped to nurture a thriving underground economy with bidding wars for top players to attend universities, retain agents, sign with financial advisors.

The distribution of aboveboard money reflected only part of the power imbalance. While 81% of Division I athletic directors and 70% of men's basketball head coaches were white in 2017, 56% of their players were Black. If the 47% of assistant coaches who were Black had a prayer of landing a head coaching job—or remaining employed—they needed to land top-level players.

The four college assistant coaches charged in Ballerz—and eight of the 10 initial defendants, including Dawkins—are Black. The four Black coaches all worked for white head coaches.

"When you're a Black assistant coach, man, you've got the world on your shoulders," said Merl Code, a former college basketball player who worked for Adidas and Nike and became a target of the sting. "If you don't get kids, then you don't keep your job. But if you don't do what's necessary to get kids, you're not going to be successful, and what's necessary to get the kids is to help the family."

In conversations with D'Angelo, who is white, Dawkins maintained that paying coaches to influence their athletes wasn't "the end-all be-all."

"I'm more powerful," Dawkins told him, "than any coach you're going to meet."

The dispute came to a head during another recorded phone call a few weeks after the yacht meeting.

"If you just want to be Santa Claus and just give people money, well f—, let's just take that money and just go to the strip club and just buy hookers," Dawkins told D'Angelo. "But just to pay guys just for the sake of paying a guy just because he's at a school, that doesn't make common sense to me."

D'Angelo wasn't swayed. The investigation was built around ensnaring coaches.

"Here, here, here, here's the model," D'Angelo stammered.

He had the money, he said. They would pay coaches.

"I respect that…you don't think that's the best approach, but that's what I'm doing," D'Angelo said in the call. "That's just what it's going to be."

Afterward, Dawkins vented to Code in a wiretapped phone call that throwing cash at a slew of coaches meant spending lots of money for no discernible purpose.

"We're just going to take these fools' money," Code said.

"Exactly," Dawkins replied. "Because it doesn't make sense…. I've tried to explain to them multiple f— times. This is not the way you wanna go."

During a call with an associate in early July, Dawkins wondered aloud if he should find someone to pay back the money D'Angelo had invested in Loyd and end their relationship. The investor's odd requests, like wanting to meet players and their parents, unnerved Dawkins. He wondered why D'Angelo cared so much.

"People are gonna think that honestly they're being set up," Dawkins said in the recorded call.

But he still wanted D'Angelo's cash. A few days after the call, Dawkins and Code faced a problem. Prosecutors alleged they had agreed to help funnel cash from an Adidas company employee to the family of a touted high school prospect who had agreed to play for an Adidas-sponsored university. An installment had been delayed. D'Angelo agreed to provide a loan of $25,000.

The payment came at a critical point in the investigation, according to Carpenter's performance review. He pushed for it to preserve D'Angelo's "bona fides as a high roller" and "set in motion events which would widely expand the case from addressing bribery by NCAA coaches to incorporating the illegal conduct of officials at a major international sportswear company."

As the Las Vegas trip approached, Code and Dawkins brainstormed which coaches could meet D'Angelo, but Code's unease about the investor was growing.

"I'm looking up Jeff D'Angelo and I can't find nothing on him," Code told Dawkins in a phone call on July 24, 2017, "and that s— is really concerning to me."

CARPENTER FLEW TO Las Vegas on July 27, 2017, accompanied by a supervisor, junior agent and the undercover operative—and having "serious misgivings" about whether he had enough personnel to run the operation.

Over three days, D'Angelo, Dawkins and Blazer met with 11 coaches—10 college assistants and one youth coach, all in town for the youth tournament—at the Cosmopolitan. The trendy hotel that advertised "Just the right amount of wrong" seemed to be the ideal setting.

Augustine, the Florida youth coach, recalled that Blazer fixed him a vodka water when he stopped by the penthouse on the first night. The opulent surroundings staggered the coach. His players were jammed into rooms at a budget-friendly hotel. The penthouse appeared to be a different world. Black marble and dark wood. Enough seating—bar stools, couches, easy chairs—for a full team. Master bathrooms that rivaled the size of some hotel rooms. A huge balcony. Quirky art around every corner, like the enormous photo of a golden-hued woman dancing underwater in a swirl of purple fabric.

Augustine received an envelope from D'Angelo stuffed with $12,700, according to the complaint. The next day, Augustine said he deposited much of the cash at a nearby bank and, since his players had flown to Las Vegas on one-way tickets, used some of the windfall to pay their way home. Augustine said he used the remainder to pay down debt he had accumulated while running the team. (He was later charged with four felonies, but all counts were dropped.)

The hidden agendas at play in the penthouse seemed tailor-made for Sin City. D'Angelo distributed envelopes of bribe money as cameras recorded each transaction. But Dawkins later claimed he had arranged for three of the coaches to give him their would-be bribe money so he could run the company his way.

Dawkins pleaded with Preston Murphy, then a Creighton University assistant coach and longtime family friend, to meet with D'Angelo in the penthouse, saying he would be forced to move in with his parents if the financial backers didn't support him, according to Murphy's attorney.

"I needed him to basically help me, you know, continue to get funding," Dawkins testified.

NCAA investigators said in reports that Murphy and TCU assistant coach Corey Barker knew before their meetings in the penthouse on July 28 that they would be paid and had agreed to give all of the money to Dawkins. Prosecutors alleged Murphy and Barker each received $6,000 from D'Angelo. Murphy handed the cash over to Dawkins in a bathroom off the main casino floor, while Barker did the same near the hotel's valet parking stand, according to accounts they gave to the NCAA. The same day, Dawkins deposited $5,000 in cash into the Loyd bank account. (Neither Barker nor Murphy was charged.)

Shortly after midnight on July 29, Tony Bland, a USC assistant coach, sank into a couch in the penthouse. He had arrived from L.A. that afternoon and looked tired. The conversation sounded like the others—boasts about influence over college players, banter about prospects with a shot at the NBA.

"I have some guys that I bring in that I can just say, this is what you're f— doing," Bland said. "And there's other guys who we'll have to work a little harder for, but we'll still have a heavy influence on what they do."

Hidden-camera footage shows Dawkins, not Bland, pick up an envelope of cash from the coffee table. The federal criminal complaint alleged Bland—making more than $300,000 a year at USC—got the $13,000 in the envelope. But bank records show Dawkins deposited $8,900 at an ATM later that day. Bland eventually pleaded guilty to receiving $4,100, the difference between the $13,000 and the deposit.

Dawkins testified that the actual amount Bland received was less because he only gave Bland "between $1,000 and $2,000" to spend at a bachelor party that night.

For the final undercover meeting, the FBI team had rented a poolside cabana at the Cosmopolitan. Afterwards, the agents decided to use the cabana for themselves when they learned the $1,500 they paid for the space was actually a food and beverage minimum, according to a court filing.

"Despite the obstacles, all of the undercover meetings were very successful," Carpenter's attorney wrote in a court filing. "At the same time, there is no doubt that the intensity, anxiety, elation and exhaustion of the weekend's activities left Mr. Carpenter in an even more precarious position."

AFTER SHOWERING AND changing clothes in the penthouse following the alcohol-filled afternoon at the cabana, the four FBI agents walked next door to the Bellagio Hotel and Casino and ended up at a high-limit lounge.

Carpenter bought $10,000 in gambling chips with the government cash he had taken from the penthouse safe and started playing blackjack. The three other agents—including Carpenter's supervisor—watched him gamble from an adjacent bar and took turns visiting, according to court testimony and a filing by his attorney, as Carpenter gulped free drinks and lost.

"They at least had to have a decent idea it was undercover FBI money and nobody took the keys to the car," Carpenter's attorney Paul Fishman said in court.

Carpenter churned through the $10,000, then pressed the undercover agent—D'Angelo—for additional government cash. He handed it over.

According to a court filing, Carpenter played for two to three hours, placed an average bet of $721 and, by the time he walked away, had lost $13,500.

As the alcohol wore off in the early hours of July 30, Carpenter paced around the penthouse. According to a document read in court, one of the agents told an investigator that Carpenter was brainstorming how to make it right and asked if they could say the gambling was part of the operation. The agent refused.

The undercover agent alleged that the four agents met early that morning and "there was a discussion…to just take care of it," Assistant U.S. Atty. Daniel Schiess said in court. The supervisor and junior agent, Schiess said, "hotly contest" that such a meeting occurred.

In a court filing, Carpenter's attorney wrote that his client "vehemently disagrees" that he "intended in any way to conceal his conduct or evade responsibility."

After returning to New York and taking a scheduled day off, Schiess said, Carpenter met with his supervisor about the missing money and, afterward, told the undercover agent and the junior agent he was going to try to pay it back and asked if they could split the cost. The other agents and Carpenter's supervisor who was in Las Vegas aren't identified in court records.

Two days later, Carpenter was transferred from the public corruption squad and college basketball investigation. He checked into an inpatient alcohol treatment program the following week, according to a court filing.

D'Angelo was also pulled from the case. He told Dawkins in a phone call Aug. 8 that he was traveling to care for his ailing mother in Italy.

Carpenter's performance review from 2017 devoted one paragraph to the incident: "Carpenter appeared to have displayed poor judgment in some of his operational security practices and behavior…(he) did not immediately or in a timely manner report events constituting potential misuse of funds to his chain of command."

Nevertheless, the review rated Carpenter's overall performance as "successful."

HEAVY FOOTSTEPS WOKE Bland almost two months later in Tampa, Fla., early on the morning of Sept. 26. Someone pounded on the door of his hotel room. The USC assistant coach had stayed out late the night before to celebrate the commitment of a recruit to play for the school. Bland got out of bed and opened the door. A team of FBI agents with weapons drawn burst into the room. One of them twisted his right arm behind his back—the arm still doesn't feel right today, Bland said—and shoved him against a wall. Bland told them they had the wrong man.

Around the same time, Code answered the door at his home in Greer, S.C., in his underwear. He counted at least 20 FBI agents, some brandishing pistols and assault-style rifles, and 15 vehicles lined up on his block.

Augustine, the Florida youth coach, had planned to meet Dawkins that morning at a New York hotel. He checked his phone on the walk over and found scores of tweets mentioning him, then scrolled through the criminal complaint against him while standing in Times Square. He thought it was some kind of elaborate, twisted joke. Then the FBI called and, a half-hour later, arrested him.

Similar scenes played out across the country. At the news conference in Manhattan the same day, the acting U.S. attorney for the Southern District of New York alleged the defendants had circled "blue chip prospects like coyotes."

The four college assistant coaches who were charged lost their jobs. Augustine resigned from the youth team and swept floors in his father-in-law's warehouse to make ends meet.

Carpenter kept his badge, service weapon and security clearance after returning from the alcohol treatment program. But he was exiled to a facilities squad to help manage a remodeling project at the FBI office in New York.

Judges in the two Ballerz trials barred defense attorneys from questioning witnesses about alleged misconduct by agents during the Las Vegas trip. One of the judges ruled that it "did not occur while the agents were conducting investigative activities" and was "irrelevant to this case."

Though Carpenter and the agents posing as D'Angelo and Bailey were subpoenaed, they didn't testify. In the first trial, Code, Dawkins and a former Adidas employee were convicted of using payments to steer players to attend three universities sponsored by the sportswear giant. Then Code and Dawkins were found guilty during the second trial, which focused on the alleged scheme to bribe coaches to persuade their players to use the sports management company that the undercover agent had helped finance.

The investigation led to 10 men being convicted of felonies at trial or by taking plea deals. Five were sentenced to prison. Dawkins got the longest combined term—18 months and a day.

After Dawkins' sentencing, prosecutors released a statement warning that the outcome "should make crystal clear to other members of the basketball underground exposed during the various prosecutions brought by this Office that bribery is still a crime, even if the recipient is a college basketball coach, and one that will result in [a] term of incarceration."

Bland had been placed on administrative leave by USC after being arrested, then was terminated about four months later. He pleaded guilty in 2019 to a felony, conspiracy to commit bribery, and was sentenced to probation for admitting to receiving $4,100. Prosecutors argued that USC faced "significant potential penalties from the NCAA" because of his conduct, echoing claims they made in sentencing memorandums for other defendants.

The cases were built around the theory that universities were the victims. Prosecutors argued the schools had been deceived into issuing scholarships to athletes who would be ineligible under NCAA rules barring payments to players or their families. They also argued the schools had been exposed to penalties from the organization for other rule-breaking, including a prohibition on coaches and other employees benefiting from introducing athletes to agents, financial advisors or their representatives.

In a victim impact statement filed in court, USC said the school, "its student athletes, and college athletics as a whole have suffered greatly because of what Mr. Bland and his co-conspirators did." The school's statement came at a time when USC was already reeling from its involvement in the Varsity Blues college admissions scandal and allegations that a campus gynecologist had sexually abused hundreds of students.

In the years since Ballerz became public, several universities have been sanctioned by the NCAA in connection with the investigation, but the penalties have largely been lighter than the "significant" punishments prosecutors warned about in sentencing memorandums for the defendants. USC, for example, received two years of probation and was fined $5,000 plus 1% of the men's basketball budget.

More significantly, some long-standing NCAA rules have shifted. College athletes can now profit from their name, image and likeness, known as NIL. Last year, Adidas unveiled a nationwide NIL program for athletes at schools sponsored by the sportswear giant.

Jay Bilas, a former Duke basketball player who is an attorney and ESPN television analyst, called the investigation a waste of time and resources.

"It seemed like bringing in the National Guard to deal with jaywalkers," Bilas said. "It damaged people's lives over nothing.... At the end of the day, all it did is make a lot of noise without a lot of result."

The FBI declined to comment for this story.

Blazer, who originally told prosecutors he could expose college sports corruption, pleaded guilty to five charges—for misappropriating money from five clients and paying college football players to retain his financial advisory firm—and was sentenced to one year of probation in February 2020. He admitted misappropriating $2.35 million from clients—much more than all the bribes combined in Ballerz.

Today, Bland coaches basketball at St. Bernard High School in Playa del Rey. He said he loves working with young players, but is eager to return to coaching in college when a three-year penalty imposed by the NCAA as punishment for the bribe expires in April 2024.

He struggles to sleep in hotel rooms, his heart pounds if there's an unexpected noise in a hallway, and he can't get past the allegations against the lead case agent in Las Vegas.

"It's like, OK, [the FBI] can mess up…and still run you over," Bland said. "It doesn't even matter."

Code wrote a book about college basketball's underbelly called *Black Market* before serving five months and nine days in prison.

"If anyone thinks that there is such a thing as a clean big-time program, they need to wake up and smell the donkey s—," he wrote in the book.

Book Richardson, a former University of Arizona assistant coach, was sentenced to three months in prison in the case. He now makes $3,000 a month working with youth basketball players in New York. He has kidney disease and sometimes struggles with the person he sees in the mirror. He said he contemplated suicide on two occasions in the years following his arrest—once when he put a pistol in his mouth but was interrupted by a phone call from a friend.

"Your mind starts messing with you, man," Richardson said. "'Maybe I am the scum of the earth. Maybe I am the worst coach ever. I threw my life away for $20,000. I should be dead.'"

CARPENTER WAS TRANSFERRED to a counterintelligence squad in October 2020, the same month he and his wife bought a home listed at 3,200 square feet with a swimming pool in suburban New Jersey. In a letter from his wife later filed in court, she wrote that the couple had assumed Carpenter's construction assignment had been the extent of his punishment.

On Dec. 13, 2021, the Supreme Court denied the final appeal related to the Ballerz investigation. Four days later, Carpenter signed an agreement to plead guilty to a misdemeanor charge of conversion of government money for gambling away the $13,500. The agreement and his presentencing memo detail the events surrounding his misconduct in Las Vegas. The FBI suspended Carpenter after he pleaded guilty, then terminated him in May.

Steve Haney, the attorney for Dawkins, learned about Carpenter's plea in a news release and moved for a new trial for his client. But a judge rejected the motion, finding the "misconduct did not concern the defendants."

Last August, Carpenter returned to Las Vegas to be sentenced. He was contrite during brief remarks at the hearing: "Five years ago, I made a terrible and stupid mistake…. While there isn't an excuse for what I did, there's an explanation: The combination of job stress, alcohol and lingering issues from my military service."

Fishman, Carpenter's attorney, characterized the blackjack episode as an isolated error in an otherwise exemplary life. He told U.S. District Judge Gloria M. Navarro that Carpenter returned from Iraq "not quite right" and has been "hellbent" on righting his wrong. The judge interjected during Fishman's argument that his client had not been diagnosed with post-traumatic stress disorder.

Navarro told Carpenter he had "already received a lot of lenience." He wasn't immediately fired, hadn't been arrested, kept being paid—he and his wife reported an income of $411,000 on their 2020 tax return, the judge said—and wasn't even on pretrial supervision, something the judge couldn't recall for a defendant in her courtroom. She sentenced him to three months of home confinement and ordered him to repay the government money. Carpenter declined to comment.

The status of the three FBI agents who accompanied him to Las Vegas is unclear.

The Department of Justice Office of the Inspector General, which investigated the Las Vegas misconduct along with the U.S. attorney's office in Nevada, has declined to comment on the case and refused to turn over any records in response to Freedom of Information Act requests, saying to do so could interfere with enforcement proceedings.

Meanwhile, Dawkins is serving his sentence at a low-security federal prison in North Carolina and is scheduled for release in May.

Before reporting to prison, Dawkins founded another company. Unlike the ill-fated venture backed by undercover FBI agents, Par-Lay Sports and Entertainment has a veteran management team that includes his defense attorney. A teenage phenom named Scoot Henderson, projected to be the second overall pick in June's NBA draft, is one of the firm's clients.

The draft will be held in Brooklyn, N.Y., some three miles from the courthouse where Dawkins' life was upended and the room where the FBI boasted they had the "playbook" for college basketball corruption. Dawkins, his attorney said, is expected to attend.

NATHAN FENNO is an investigative reporter for *The Los Angeles Times*. A Seattle native, he previously wrote for the *Washington Times*, the *Ann Arbor (Mich.) News*, and the *King County (Wash.) Journal*.

The Free Soloist Who Fell to Earth

MICHAEL LEVY

FROM Outside • AUGUST 8, 2023

The footage is shaky, but there's no doubt what's in the frame: a man climbing a section of shining white rock. "What in the world," the guy filming says. "This guy's fucking insane. He's soloing, climbing this route, naked, without a rope. He's out of his damn mind."

As the camera zooms out, it becomes clear that the soloist is hundreds of feet off the deck. Aside from eschewing clothes and a rope, the climber is also barefoot. All he's got on is a gray newsboy cap. A twangy guitar lick comes in, followed by the lyrics: *You can't kill me / I will not die / Not now, not ever / No never/ I'm gonna live a long, long time / My soul raves on forever.*

The clip, just 1 minute 56 seconds long, ends with a still frame of the climber looking back at the camera and flipping the bird.

Titled "Free Soloing with a Hat," the video enjoyed a viral moment in the climbing corners of the internet when its subject, Austin Howell, shared it on Vimeo in April 2015. Howell, then 27, was a sinewy string bean with a permanent dirtbag scruff of a beard. His frizzy shoulder-length locks and the hat, which he was rarely without, belied the quickly thinning hair atop his head.

I remember seeing the clip when it came out. I'd been climbing for five years and was then preparing to take a crack at the 3,000-foot Nose route on El Capitan in Yosemite. I was blown away by the absurdity of the video, which struck me as one part *Free Solo*, one part *Jackass*. But I was also unsettled, filled with a kind of macabre awe. I began following Howell on Instagram, where he went by @freesoloist.

Howell was an enigmatic character, and I found it difficult to look away from his antics. His death-defying behavior was complemented by a fun-loving temperament. When he went out soloing, for example, he kept mini Snickers in his puppy-dog-shaped chalk bag. If he came upon a roped party, he'd toss a candy bar in their direction.

I followed along as he soloed 19 different 5.12's, a grade that many people spend their lives trying to climb *with* a rope on. Many of the routes were in Kentucky's Red River Gorge and had little margin for error—an overhanging 5.12 could be as steep as the underside of a church dome; a vertical 5.12 might have grips the width of a dime's edge. One time he free-soloed over a mile of technical terrain in a single day. The number of people in the world soloing that volume at that difficulty can likely be counted on one hand.

Howell saw his free soloing as the product of careful, sober analysis. He spent hours ahead of each hard climb satisfying what he called his "preflight checklist," making sure he'd accounted and planned for all the variables that could go wrong. But the annals of climbing, like other extreme sports, are littered with stories of risk-takers who convinced themselves that they could reason their way out of catastrophe.

HOWELL FIRST WENT climbing as a 19-year-old freshman at the University of Houston, in 2006, and from the get-go he felt like he was onto something special. His newfound obsession, however, nearly came to an abrupt end in 2008, when he was climbing at the university's indoor rock wall. Thirty-five feet up, he attempted a tricky move but couldn't hold on. He started to fall. At the same moment, Howell's belayer let go of the brake strand of the rope, a careless mistake. The rope hissed through the belayer's safety device, and Howell smashed into the ground, fracturing three vertebrae and several bones in both feet. He spent four months convalescing in a back brace. But there were invisible injuries, too.

Terri Zinke Jackson, Howell's mother, recalled an evening not long after his accident when he came to her and said that he'd gone to the top of a ten-story building in Houston and peered over the edge at the concrete below, intending to throw himself off. He told his mom that he'd been crying so hard, he was too exhausted to follow through. "That's when we got him in to start seeing someone, and learned the full scope of the head injury," Zinke Jackson said.

According to Zinke Jackson and Austin's father, David Howell, who divorced in 1991, doctors said that Austin suffered a "slow brain bleed" caused by the impact of the fall, which could lead to personality and emotional changes. It could take up to five years for Howell's brain to recover from being rattled as violently as it had, they were told. Austin began seeing a psychiatrist for the first time after his accident, something he would continue on and off over the following decade.

Depression, David said, was new in the post-fall Austin—at least that's what he believed. He suspected the brain trauma was to blame. "I changed Austin's first diaper when he was born," David said. "I know him better than he knows himself. Me and his mom discussed it, and we never saw that in him. I think a lot of it was that first accident he had."

Austin saw things differently. In blog and social media posts years later, he wrote that his depression was an innate, lifelong condition. He recalled imagining different ways he might kill himself as a near constant part of his adolescence. He eventually received a more specific diagnosis in early 2018: bipolar II, a variant of the disorder that manifests itself in prolonged bouts of depression interspersed with shorter periods of mania. Initial symptoms and diagnoses commonly occur in the late teens to early twenties.

As Howell's physical injuries healed, climbing became his polestar, the animating principle around which the rest of his life revolved. It was in this period, too, that he started to free-solo.

His first foray without a rope was unplanned. He had just floated up Texas Crude, a moderate 40-foot crack at Enchanted Rock, in the Hill Country, while holding a conversation with friends and absent-mindedly placing safety gear. Back on the ground, he gave his partner a camera and said, "I'm about to do something so incredibly stupid that obviously I'm never going to do it again."

The next weekend, Howell soloed 32 different routes, some 2,200 vertical feet of rock. Soon after, in his junior year, he dropped out of college to climb full-time.

IN THE YEARS after Howell's accident at the university rock wall, he came into his own as a climber. From 2009 through 2015, he developed his own philosophy of soloing, replete with maxims for any occasion, many borrowed from others: "Life is an inherently dangerous sport" or "Thinking is the best form of life insurance." He liked to repeat a favorite adage of "Hollywood" Hans Florine, who has climbed El Capitan more than anyone else: "The only thing better than climbing is more climbing."

But soloing was more than a feat of bravado for Howell. "Freesoloing isn't a death wish, it's a life wish," he later wrote on Instagram, paraphrasing the late Michael Reardon, an outspoken free soloist who died in 2007 when he was swept away by a rogue wave at the base of a cliff he'd been climbing. Reardon, with his punk-rock attitude and no-fucks-given approach to soloing, was Howell's biggest climbing influence.

"[Soloing is] the single best therapy I've ever found for calming my tumultuous mind," Howell wrote. "The control that I've developed on the wall transfers into my daily life. This is important, because I'm not the guy who 'beat depression.' I don't get to be that guy. I've got to manage this for my entire life."

Through climbing and therapy, Howell made significant progress toward finding emotional balance. After school he moved to Atlanta, where he built a community. But on Mother's Day 2015, "it started all over again," said Zinke Jackson.

Howell, now 27, was in Yosemite, trying to make an ascent of El Capitan. He was climbing with a partner, using ropes, but even still, Zinke Jackson tried to stay busy to avoid thinking of the different ways Howell could get hurt up on the massive wall. She works as a real estate agent, and had driven down to Galveston to lead a home tour. Partway through the showing, she got a call from the Yosemite Parks Department. Austin had been in an accident.

He'd been climbing the first pitch of the Nose, the iconic route that splits the monolith right down the center. "A piece of aid gear pulled out under body weight," Howell later told *Blue Ridge Outdoors* magazine. "Then, an additional piece probably pulled out as well. Then I hit the ledge." He fell around 20 feet and landed on his head. He was airlifted to a hospital in nearby Modesto, where the news was grim: He'd fractured his wrist, his right shoulder blade, five vertebrae, and his skull, which resulted in another traumatic brain injury. He'd also obliterated his left ear drum and would never hear out of that side again.

Doctors kept Howell in an induced coma for over ten days. When his mother arrived, doctors explained that he was in no shape to travel. But when Howell awoke, he wanted out of there. Zinke Jackson rented a Suburban, plopped a mattress down in the back, and drove Howell to his childhood home in Friendsville, Texas, over the course of a week.

But Howell could think of nothing except returning to the rock.

"About ten or twelve weeks into his healing, he just cut off his casts, took off his neck brace, and said he was leaving," Zinke Jackson remembers. "And we had a big fight. I was like, 'No, you're not!' But he's a grown man, he can do what he wants to do." Howell's father came and took him to Lucedale, Mississippi, where he lived.

Zinke Jackson was incredulous. Howell was still recovering from his injuries, and doctors had told him that, due to his hearing loss and its effect on his balance, he'd have trouble walking and would never be able to climb again at a high level. He'd be unable to remain steady on his feet, let alone on the wall.

"It put a wedge between us for a little while," Zinke Jackson says. "He wanted me to be more supportive, but I didn't want him to get hurt again." Howell didn't talk to his mother for a year and a half after he left Texas for Mississippi.

"In Austin's world, if you weren't going to be cool with his soloing, he wasn't interested," says Brandon White, a 32-year-old Marine veteran who was one of Howell's closest friends. "It was a hard line for him. If I pushed him too hard, he'd never talk to me again. Meanwhile he had herds of people cheering him on."

Through his Instagram and Facebook accounts, Vimeo videos, blog, and a podcast he created called *The Process*, Howell developed a following. He posted mind-bending photos and videos of dangling by his fingertips high in the air, and wrote uncommonly candid reflections about his mental health. "For me, climbing is the one time where my mind shuts down. There is no me, no depression, no elation, just the next move, the hold I'm on, the feet I'm using for balance, and the core tension keeping it all together," he wrote in a 2015 blog post. Thousands watched, read, and hit the like button on his content.

I was one of them. Mine was more than a passing fascination with Howell's stunts: Though I've been a climber for over a decade now, I've suffered from depression for far longer. My lowest point followed a major depressive episode after college in 2012; my high school sweetheart had dumped me, I hated my job, and my social network felt paper-thin. My memories of that time are ones of deep loneliness. Of wandering snow-covered streets around Cambridge, Massachusetts, until 4 A.M. Of nights spent drinking alone. Rock climbing became a refuge, an escape from a brain that felt like it needed a reboot. The physical problem-solving—being forced to think about nothing but the moves, the thrill of executing a sequence just right—helped to temper the darkest darkness. I had never free-soloed, but Howell's pronouncements about how climbing helped him deal with his demons felt like they spoke directly to me.

In fact, there are a growing number of studies that have examined how rock climbing can be an effective therapeutic tool in battling depression. Although no studies have yet looked at possible links between free soloing and mental health (researchers I spoke with pointed to the ethical problems inherent in studying people who participate in extreme sports), prominent examples of depressed climbers using free soloing as therapy— or at least as a coping mechanism or release valve—are easy to find.

In Alison Osius's *Rock and Ice* profile of Earl Wiggins, a prolific free soloist, Wiggins's sister, Lynda, describes her brother's battle with depression and how climbing helped him manage it. "I do think that climbing took care of his problems for years," Lynda said. Yet in the end, he couldn't escape his anguish even through free soloing. Wiggins died by suicide in 2002.

In *Free Solo*, the filmmakers ask Alex Honnold, "Are you depressed?" He deflects. But in a separate interview with podcaster Tim Ferris, Honnold addressed it head-on: "I think I kind of gravitate toward being a somewhat depressed person," he said. "Or—I don't know, actually. I'm sort of just flat... I feel like I don't have any of the highs. I kind of go from level, to slightly below level, to back. Sometimes you just feel useless, you know? But in some ways I embrace that as part of the process, because you kind of have to feel like a worthless piece of poop in order to get motivated enough to go do something that makes you feel less useless. But then, ultimately, that still doesn't make you feel any less useless, so you just have to keep doing more."

Honnold's explanation exposes one of the core pitfalls of free soloing as a potential tool of self-medication. The highs can start to feel addictive, and getting your fix can become more difficult. I've noticed this in my own reliance on climbing as a therapeutic tool. Gym climbing and clipping bolts on small cliffs satisfied the itch at the start, but I soon needed other ways to get my kicks. Within a few years I was seeking out longer, scarier routes.

And then I started free soloing.

In 2017, as I crested the top of the 700-foot Redgarden Wall, in Colorado's Eldorado Canyon, after my first proper free solo, I felt like I had leveled up. Things had a different sheen. My self-worth felt higher. I told friends about my adventure afterward, and they responded with awe. After years of in-person therapy and on SSRIs, I was going without either; I'd come a long way since that year in Boston and felt I could manage the depression on my own. I was climbing more than ever, and the dopamine boosts kept me afloat—and Redgarden was the biggest jolt I'd had yet.

Like Howell, I had convinced myself that the solo was a one-off; that I just wanted to taste that rarified air. But sure enough, a week later, as would happen with each progressively harder solo going forward, I was already thinking about the next step. My solos were easy compared to Howell's, but I still found myself fixated on how I could one-up my last climb and find that high anew.

So it was with Howell. In the back of his truck, he kept an expensive bottle of whiskey. He told friends, "I only drink from this when I've done something radder in my life than I've done previously." At the beginning of his soloing career, he was drinking from it often. Later on, it became harder and harder to earn his sips.

HOWELL'S SOLOING REACHED new levels when he started climbing again after the Yosemite accident. He'd always trained, but now he was maniacal about it. Despite the doctors' predictions, he had learned how to cope with his balance issues.

In April 2016, he free-soloed his first 5.12. He soloed three more that same weekend. Once he broke that barrier, adding to his tally became extremely important to him. That fall he completed what he called the "Mile of Mojo," at Shortoff Mountain, North Carolina, which involved free-soloing 5,700 vertical feet via 15 different routes. It took him ten hours.

Meanwhile, his depression surged in mid-2017. Howell had moved to Chicago for a new job with the telecommunications company Ericsson, training their engineers in rope-access work. His relationship with his girlfriend in Atlanta had ended, and he was farther away from his favorite climbing areas in the Southeast. Boxes of belongings, still packed, lay strewn around his apartment, and he'd spend nights sitting on the floor with his laptop, getting drunk. Sunny, his pet sun parakeet, was his primary company. Climbing was the only thing that sustained him.

Susan Hill, a close friend of Howell's who he'd met climbing in 2014, lived a few hours away in Minneapolis. "He came up one day and hung out with me and stayed overnight at our house," she said. "I could see the darkness in his eyes at that point and just asked him, 'Are you OK?' We had a big heart-to-heart. He wasn't taking care of himself."

He smelled bad and was cutting himself on the inside of his leg, where no one could see. With assistance from Howell's former girlfriend in Atlanta, Hill helped get Howell back into therapy. He started taking medication, which he later called "the best thing that ever happened to me."

As he adjusted to life in Chicago, Howell made more friends and became part of the local climbing scene. He was a frequent sight at the Vertical Endeavors climbing gym, where he was stoked to talk climbing with anyone from a first-timer top-roping easy routes to elite athletes. That was where he met Brandon White, then a neophyte climber flailing on beginner boulder problems. Howell came up and started offering advice.

The two were soon spending days out climbing together at Devil's Lake, in Wisconsin, another place where Howell developed an extensive free-solo circuit. Some days Howell showed White the finer points of trad climbing—where the climber places his own pieces of protective gear, called cams and chocks, on the way up. Other days they'd just sit on top of nearby West Bluff, looking over the pine trees and blue water, talking about high-energy physics, meditation, or folk music.

More often than not, though, Howell was doing his free-solo thing. He liked to say that after his Yosemite accident, he climbed more pitches each year without a rope than with one.

His first free solo of autumn 2018 was a 5.12 route in the Red River Gorge called Twinkie.

The night before, he and a friend, Bones Rangel, were at Miguel's Pizza, a popular climber hangout. They ran into some folks from Vertical Endeavors and joined them at a table. Over pizza and beers, Howell filled them in on his plans for soloing Twinkie the next morning and invited them to come watch, unable to contain his enthusiasm.

The next morning, everyone met up at Fantasia crag. "He was holding a cup of coffee," said Alicia Legowski, one of the climbers from Chicago. "And he stumbled over his own feet, and the coffee went up in the air and got all over him. And we were like, This is the guy we're going to watch solo?"

Conditions were abysmal. Ninety-degree heat and 85 percent humidity had turned the air thick. Howell tied into a rope so he could lead climb Twinkie and re-familiarize himself with the route, which he had sussed out in the spring. As he led up, the sandstone edges felt like they were covered in grease. He hung on the rope five times before lowering from the top, dejected. Half an hour later, he climbed the route with a rope again. Conditions had improved slightly, and he didn't need to weight the rope. He top-roped the route once more, then decided it was time to solo it. Over the next hour, he and Rangel rigged up some ropes so Rangel could film the feat.

By the time Howell was ready to climb, two other guys were getting ready to head up Twinkie with a rope. Howell asked them if they'd mind if he went first. He always made sure to ask permission before starting up a hard solo at a crag if others were around; he didn't want to make anyone uncomfortable. The other climbers obliged. Howell laced up his shoes, tied his chalk bag around his waist, and started up the route.

"I was really nervous," Legowski said. "But a few seconds in, I could tell he was super comfortable up on the wall and very confident in himself. And it almost put me at ease." Everyone kept silent as they watched. One of Legowski's friends, unwilling to witness a tragedy, turned his back on the spectacle.

Some minutes later, Howell reached the top. As everyone waited for him to hike down, the other two men who planned to climb Twinkie began gearing up. One of them realized that his shoes were missing. Howell, who wore the same model, had put on the other climber's shoes by mistake.

THE TWINKIE SOLO encapsulated many idiosyncrasies of Howell's free soloing: climbing hard, steep routes that had awkward descents; a tendency to climb with his shoes untied, or without chalk; always sandbagging himself on rehearsal climbs; an undercurrent of recklessness, despite his claims to the opposite.

And then there was the performative quality. He invited others to come watch the Twinkie solo in person, and he went to elaborate lengths to document it. With other solos, if he couldn't get a photographer friend to join, he'd rig up an iPhone or a GoPro himself. He'd then post the clip and stories about his ascents on Facebook and Instagram. He detailed his solos in blog posts that became the blueprints for his podcast episodes. This side of his soloing—publicizing or bragging about his ascents—is probably the thing for which Howell received more criticism than anything else.

"I don't mind people soloing and posting videos and all that," read a typical post in a thread on the climbing website Mountain Project about Howell's soloing. "What galls me about this guy in particular is he tries to claim like he's just out there doing it for the pureness of the climbing... then sprays to anyone and everyone and pays to advertise his podcast and shit. At least be honest about your intentions and motivations."

Lindsey Marie Vetter, an ex-girlfriend of Howell's, told me, "I used to kind of bust his balls a little bit about that. He was so humble, but he was so self-promoting all the time. I was like, 'Give it a rest, chill out. We all know the story.' But he was just so excited about it all the time. I just don't think he could contain it."

Howell refuted that sharing his achievements had anything to do with ego. "A narcissistic craving for attention isn't driving this show," he wrote on Instagram, "because I don't get a bump off of praise like most people. Instead, it feels foul, and false, because my mind tells me it 'knows better.'"

The apparent disconnect between Howell's actions and his words made me start to wonder about the provenance of the naked-soloing video. I tracked down Lohan Lizin, the film's videographer, who Howell listed in the credits. Lizin's narration makes it seem like he's a random unwitting climber who happened upon this bizarre scene by chance. It turns out he'd met Howell a couple years before the video, which took place on a climb called Dopey Duck, but Lizin hadn't seen him again until running into him at Shortoff Mountain that day. After getting reacquainted and climbing some together, Howell mentioned his idea of climbing Dopey Duck naked. And he asked Lizin to film it for him.

"He said it would be cool if I acted like I was some tourist or something and not much of a climber," Lizin told me. "Austin said, 'Just say some goofy shit, pretend like you just stumbled upon it and pulled your cell phone out and started recording.'"

I was taken aback to learn that the video had been staged, but not totally surprised. It revealed the complicated motivations behind Howell's actions and, more than anything, it made me sad. Taken all together—free-soloing ever more, ever harder, and seemingly for the attention—there was only one way it was going to end, as several of those closest to Howell told me.

"One day after he admitted to free-soloing," said his father, "I told him, 'Son, you know what's going to happen if you keep doing this, right?'"

"Yeah, Dad, I've thought it all through," Howell told him, "and I'm willing to take the consequences of my actions."

DRIVING DOWN NORTH Carolina State Highway 126 in early December 2021, stands of leafless oaks betrayed the hills beyond. There was not a cloud in sight. After months of immersing myself in Howell's life, talking with those who knew him, listening to his podcast, and combing through his social media, I'd convinced myself that the only way to understand him was to follow in his footsteps. My plan was simple: I would make a pilgrimage to Shortoff and free-solo Dopey Duck. I thought there was some nebulous gonzo-journalism value to be had, perhaps some final epiphany to be gleaned.

I prepared as best I could, using the Shawangunks, a climbing area above New Paltz, New York, and close to my home in New York City, as a training ground. The Traprock architecture is similar to that of the cliffs at Shortoff Mountain: big, horizontal bands, with jutting overhangs separated by sweeping faces. On one of the last days of summer in 2021, I started up the first pitch of the 250-foot High Exposure, the Gunks' most famous route, without a rope. At a monstrous ledge halfway up, I stopped to bask in the morning rays and took a couple selfies on my iPhone.

The second pitch begins with one of the most famous sequences in modern rock climbing. To gain a headwall, you have to surmount a gigantic roof by stepping on a polished chip of rock hovering over the void. The second you commit to it, there's nothing but air beneath you.

I positioned my right foot on the chip, took a breath, and reached around for a good side pull. As I grabbed it, the cobbles smooth beneath my fingers, I imagined, just for a second, what would happen if I released the tension in my core. That's all it would take for my foot to wiggle a millimeter to the side and skate off that chip. I'd plummet more than a hundred feet to the ground. I cleared my head, pulled through the move, and stood up onto the face, now in more secure territory. I listened to my heartbeat. I calmed my breath. I closed my eyes. A few minutes later, I scampered over the top of the cliff.

A few months later, in North Carolina, I turned onto a dirt road and drove through a forest of red maples. My commitment to soloing Dopey Duck had wavered. I was no longer sure exactly what I hoped to gain from this exercise. And I was scared.

At a dead end, I threw the rental car in park, shouldered my pack, and started up the trail. l was alone, as Howell often was here, and I walked slowly up the switchbacks, admiring the views of Lake James off to my left and the Appalachian Mountains in every direction. I listened to the haunting lyrics of one of Howell's favorite songs, "Wolves," by Down Like Silver: *When I die / Let the wolves enjoy my bones / When I die/ Let me go.*

It was a song Howell listened to during one of his hard solos, and it prompted thoughts of risk, danger, and mortality.

"Rather than shirk the discomfort of these thoughts mid-route, I instead stayed with them and used them as a focus for meditation of sorts, while exploring the inner recesses of my mind, managing my heart rate," Howell said on a December 2018 episode of his podcast. "I allowed irrational anxieties to float across the sky of my mind, like clouds drifting across the sun in an otherwise empty firmament. They did not carry my attention away, but rather, they simply just were. And I allowed them their own space to be. Beside my attention, rather than competing for it."

I passed a crew of trail workers and imagined how Howell would have stopped to chat with this jovial bunch of sweaty retirees armed with pickaxes and hoes, how he would strike up a conversation about the beautiful day and gush about his climbing plans.

At the descent gully, I stared across at an overhanging wall hundreds of feet above the ground that held some of Howell's favorite routes. It was from this magnificent wall that Howell fell 200 feet to his death, on June 30, 2019.

That day he went to Shortoff with photographer Ben Wu. Howell free-soloed a handful of climbs while Wu snapped away. After getting some good material, Wu headed back to the parking lot while Howell continued soloing around.

Later, two climbers, Riley Collins and Jay Massey, were making their way down the Shortoff Mountain descent gully. They were planning on climbing Dopey Duck. Eighty feet from the bottom, Collins looked to his left and saw Howell soloing in the steepest part of the face's roof, only 30 feet or so from topping out.

"I knew it was him because I followed him on Instagram, and he always wore that same tie-dyed shirt and that cap," Collins told me. He watched Howell make a big lunge to the left to a flake. But something went wrong. He heard Howell yell, "No!"

"That was the only thing he said," Collins said. "He didn't scream or anything on the way down. He kind of knew it, I guess."

Collins and Massey scrambled back to the top of the cliff, and Massey rappelled down to Howell's body and saw him take his last breaths.

I descended that same dark gully of rotting leaves from which Collins and Massey had seen Howell fall. Once at the bottom, I walked over and stood beneath Dopey Duck. The gleaming stone was cool to the touch. I thought one final time about saying, Fuck it, and just starting up.

I liked to believe that what I derived from my own free soloing wasn't a matter of ego, but in truth, I'm not sure it's that simple.

I lay down on top of a large boulder. I chewed on sassafras twigs, letting the root-beer flavor coat my mouth. The Linville River shined silver at the bottom of the gorge.

Howell was resourceful and clear-eyed about his mental health—free soloing was just one part of a therapeutic tool kit that by the end included counseling and medication. But the epiphany I wish he could have had is this: That if you can't find enough of the peace and mindfulness you need with a rope on, you'll never find enough of it without it. That the hungry hole at the center of things only grows larger. That the whiskey bottle is bottomless.

THOSE CLOSEST TO Howell still carry pieces of him around, some of them literal. His mother mailed snipped lockets of his hair to several of his best friends before he was buried. Howell had made his wish to be cremated known to her and others, but his father insisted that his son be buried in the family plot in Lucedale. In lieu of ashes, his mother hoped friends would let his hair loose in the wind.

After the funeral, Brandon White asked David if he could have a piece of Austin's climbing gear as a memento. Maybe just a cam or something, he figured. David sent him Austin's entire rack.

"I place those pieces when I get scared, and it's like double confidence," White said.

The upper edge of Howell's black marble headstone is cut to look like jagged peaks. On the front is a picture of him reclining on some rocks atop Shortoff Mountain, wearing his newsboy hat and a tie-dyed shirt. "The mountains are calling and I must go," the famous John Muir quote, is etched along the bottom.

The back is similar. "NO FEAR OF FLYING / AUSTIN, FREE SOLOIST," it reads. And above the inscription, another photo from the same day: Austin, high on the wall, smiling at the camera.

MICHAEL LEVY is the editor of *Summit Journal*, an American rock climbing magazine founded in 1955. His work has appeared in *The New York Times*, *Men's Journal*, and *Sierra*, among other publications. He lives in New York City.

Peter Gammons: Diamond Vision

TOM FRIEND

FROM *Sports Business Journal* • JUNE 19, 2023

She fell from heaven and landed in Mashpee. That's where this starts, and exactly where it ends, in a wind-whipped, low-fog Cape Cod village where a retired nurse parked in front of a Stop N' Shop ATM and noticed a pair of spindly legs dangling from the backseat of a four-door Lexus.

Good thing she was nosy, because it could've been another stinking drunk sleeping off the whiskey, bourbon and wine. Summer in the Cape attracts all kinds—grunge bands, neophyte ballplayers and weary baseball scouts, to name three—but if someone's white patchy legs are strewn out of an open car at around 7 a.m., nine times out of 10 there's booze on their breath from a dive bar the night before.

But the 76-year-old nurse took a peek anyway because that's what her servant's heart told her to do, and as she approached the Lexus she saw the shock of white hair, a look of unconsciousness and a driver's license left strategically on the stricken man's chest.

She took his pulse like she'd done a trillion times—locating a faint beat—and dutifully dialed 911, knowing the Mashpee fire department was a convenient two blocks away. She waited there gritting her teeth, monitoring his vital signs, and took a closer, squinted glance at the driver's license.

She had no idea who this was. This man named Peter Gammons.

IF ONLY SHE could've asked Roger Maris. That would've shed some light. Long before this Peter Gammons was the greatest baseball writer who ever lived—indirectly responsible for the Red Sox's first World Series win in 86 years, for the Cubs' first World Series win in 108 years and for furthering the careers of ballplayers, singers, executives and journalists all over the planet—he was just a 15-year-old boy with a frayed autograph book trying not to stare into Maris' baby blue eyes.

It was summer of '61, the summer of the Maris-Mantle home-run chase, and he and his parents—Ned and Betty—had driven the 45 miles from their home in Groton, Mass., to Boston for the Red Sox–Yankees series. They were making a long cultural July weekend out of it, spending Thursday night at the theater, Friday night at Fenway Park, Saturday and Sunday afternoon again at Fenway and Saturday night at a concert. Of course, a concert. Ned Gammons was the music teacher at the prestigious Groton School and had passed his sense of rhythm down to his second son, Peter.

Not that Peter was in love with classical music. Rather, he was an aspiring Chuck Berry who could pick a guitar and capably sing the blues or rock 'n' roll. In later years he and his high school buds started a band called The Fabulous Penetrations—"We almost didn't graduate because of that," he jokes—but he had reverence for his father and dutifully sat through the night at the Boston Symphony Orchestra.

There was a beyond-his-years duality to Peter. If his father hadn't taught at the elitist Groton School—a blue-blood Harvard and Yale pipeline in a quaint town of just 4,000 people—the family never could've afforded to send him there, and, for that reason, Peter related to both the preppies and townies. He played Little League baseball with Bill Shaughnessy, who attended the peasant-like public school and whose prodigious younger brother

Dan Shaughnessy was a sports encyclopedia. Dan will say the difference between public school and Groton School was that if a Groton player hit a foul ball into the woods, they'd simply grab a new ball. "We'd want to hop over to get 'em," Dan says.

Peter took the sophistication of Groton and the humanistic spirit of Ned and melded them together. Refined, yet self-aware. Add in his affinity for baseball—which he inherited from his mother, Betty, who suffered through every Red Sox game on the radio—and he was ready to politely ask any Red Sox or Yankee for an autograph that July '61 weekend.

During Friday night's series opener, Maris hit his 36th home run, and Mantle smashed his 37th. A magical Fenway evening. The next morning, the Gammons family casually ate breakfast at their hotel, the extravagant Park Plaza where the Yankees also happened to be staying. Minutes into the meal, Betty noticed Maris eating alone at an adjacent table and urged Peter to request his signature. Peter had his autograph book ready, but, on second thought, told Betty he'd rather not bother Maris while he was dining.

Later, as the Gammons were exiting, Peter heard someone from behind say, "Son…" It was Maris, with a gleam in his eye.

"I heard what you said," Maris told Peter. "And I appreciate that you respected my privacy. Would you like me to sign something?"

Maris autographed Peter's book, then asked when he was leaving for Fenway that day. "About 11," Peter said. Sure enough, at the stroke of 11, Maris was waiting for 15-year-old Peter in the lobby.

"Here son," Maris said, handing him a signed piece of paper. It was Mantle's autograph. Chills shot down Peter's spine, a wave of sensibility gushed to his head.

Roger Maris had become the first Major League player, not the last, to be enthralled by Peter Gammons.

IF ONLY SHE could've asked Dean Smith. In the mid-1960s, Peter enrolled at the University of North Carolina and became a curious reporter for the campus's *Daily Tar Heel*. Taught by Ned Gammons to be inclusive, Peter was especially drawn to the burgeoning head basketball coach Smith, who was about to make Charlie Scott the first Black athlete at the university. On the infamous 1965 day Smith was hung in effigy after a brutal loss to Wake Forest, Peter was sitting near Smith on the team bus and couldn't believe how stoic the coach remained. Peter had already befriended several players, particularly future All-America forward Larry Miller, who told him how altruistic Smith was. Peter was fascinated.

Smith, sharp as a tack, noticed how the players related to Peter and occasionally let Peter watch his sacred closed practices. "He just took a liking to me," Peter says. "Dean reminded me a lot of my father. I always thought he was a schoolteacher who was a basketball coach. And sometimes, I think because my father was a schoolteacher, that enabled the relationship to go farther."

It went so far that Smith gave Peter this firm career advice: "You're a good listener. You could write for a living." Not long after—perhaps on a day Peter's college band, "Little Gam and the Athletes" had just finished a jam session—Peter received an urgent message at his frat house to see Smith. "Figured I'd written something he's really pissed about," Peter says. Instead, Smith told him *Sports Illustrated*'s vaunted storyteller Frank Deford was arriving to do a profile on him, that Peter should observe "how a giant in the industry" conducts an interview. So Peter sat in, riveted and now certain of his calling.

Dean Smith—perhaps because his servant heart told him to—had turned Peter into a sportswriter.

IF ONLY SHE could've asked Bill Lee. On June 10, 1968, just days after RFK's assassination, senior-to-be Peter started a summer internship at the *Boston Globe* sports department. On that first day, he and another intern—a garrulous Boston College grad named Bob Ryan—were assigned to chronicle how MLB was planning to honor Kennedy. Peter called each American League team, while Ryan dialed every National League club. Their dual byline ran on 1A of the stocks edition that afternoon, and buddies already, they went to Boston's Eire Pub to grab a beer and dream about careers as "ink-stained wretches." Peter was hooked.

Peter impressed *Globe* editors with his whimsical writing style. At Carolina, his Journalism 41 teacher once passed out a cookie-cutter exam saying, "If you all write the same lead, I'll be successful as a teacher." Peter, trying not to be "a smart ass," raised his hand to say, "That's not going to work, sir." Peter felt badly, but also felt journalism should be about "your curiosity," how you "related" to your subject matter. "I didn't want to be the byline," he says, "I wanted to be the story."

The irreverent *Globe* was on the same page as Peter. "Forget the five W's of journalism: who, what, when, where, why," Ryan says. "The *Globe* let us run wild." So the winter following Peter's internship, in February 1969, they contacted him during mid-terms to say, "Can you come to Boston next Monday and start full time?" He dropped out to drive north.

That summer he first laid eyes on Red Sox rookie pitcher Bill "Spaceman" Lee, a mercurial lefty out of USC who had the guts to throw a slow, rainbow Eephus pitch—or "Space Ball"—to big-league hitters. Peter loved it. As legend has it, Peter once threw an Eephus pitch himself at Groton School to a stud hitter from Boston Latin named Bobby Guindon. Guindon, who wound up playing five games for the Red Sox in '64, smashed it 300-some feet into an art department window.

Either way, Spaceman and Gam (Peter's nickname) had a pitch in common, and they became fast friends the same way Peter had buddied up to Larry Miller at Carolina. With his floppy head of hair, walrus mustache, windbreakers and sandals, Peter was becoming a welcome sight at Fenway, or the Fens, as he called it. By the summer of '71, Peter was a backup Red Sox writer doing sidebars and asked morning sports editor Fran Rosa if he could

.

pen a weekly column about the Red Sox farm system. He'd model it slightly after Dick Young's three-dot column in the *New York Daily News* and call it "Majoring in the Minors." Baseball's first notes column was born.

The *Globe's* Will McDonough was already writing notes on the NFL, and Ryan the same for the NBA. But what Peter began churning out every Sunday—especially once he took over the Red Sox beat full time in '72—became baseball gospel. He was majoring in the majors now. These were nuanced, 2,000-word joyrides through the game. "He was like a gonzo journalist in sports and baseball," says Dan Shaughnessy, who'd eventually join the *Globe*.

Peter's single-minded routine made it possible. He'd wake up as early as 5 a.m. to exercise and read the papers. Then, he'd phone as many scouts, agents and GMs as he could conjure up. He'd get to Fenway, or wherever the Red Sox were, as early as noon to watch early BP or, better yet, shag fly balls himself.

That's where the real intel came from. By '75, bench coach Johnny Pesky was hitting him pregame fungos, or Carl Yastrzemski was purposely smacking BP line drives to Peter in the gap. Through it all, he'd pick up nuggets and backstories. He'd then shower, visit the opposing manager and produce original copy full of trade chatter, clubhouse mischief and future stars. "I don't know anybody who loves anything as much as Peter Gammons loves baseball," Ryan says.

That Sunday notes column was so rich, *Globe* sports editor Vince Doria says editors from other cities had him airmail it to them every Monday. GMs would pick Peter's brain as much as he'd pick theirs. One year, he campaigned in print for the Red Sox to hire Orioles manager Earl Weaver. When Weaver got inundated with phone calls, he said, "What did that [bleeping] Gammons write this time?" Someone answered, "That the Red Sox need you and even if it's $1 million a year, they gotta pay it." Weaver responded, "I've always liked that Gammons."

Peter's music references made the column hip. In season previews, he'd give every MLB franchise a team song (Baltimore's being "Duke of Earl"), and, inspired by the Warren Zevon tune, he'd allude to Lee in print as "Excitable Boy." John Curtis and the 300,000 college students in Boston applauded Peter. He brought his guitar on the road, taught *Globe* writer Lesley Visser about a blues singer named Bonnie Raitt. "Peter was talking about Bonnie Raitt before anybody else was talking about Bonnie Raitt," Shaughnessy says.

His copy was littered with music, sarcasm and New England nuance, and Doria's philosophy was he wouldn't edit Peter if one out of five readers "got it." To describe a disjointed Red Sox team, Peter wrote: "25 guys, 25 cabs." When the Red Sox blew a key game on network TV in August of '74, Peter wrote: "Like Richard Nixon, the Red Sox went on national television to announce their resignations from the race."

But his game stories showcased his lyrical genius most of all, and nothing put him on the map more than the 1975 World Series between the Reds and Red Sox. As the baseball world descended on Boston for Game 6—the Sox trailing three games to two—Peter ended up producing arguably the greatest game story ever written on deadline, a piece crafted on a typewriter in 55 minutes that stands the test of time for every New Englander with a pulse.

At first, it was a blah game. The Sox looked dead in the eighth inning until Bernie Carbo hit a missile three-run home run—"There was this whoosh," Peter remembers—to tie it up at 6. Peter was taking copious notes in the press box and prioritizing all the signature moments of the game. Dwight Evans' circus catch in the 11th. Third base coach Don Zimmer saying "No, no, no" to base-runner Denny Doyle in the ninth, and Doyle thinking Zimmer said "Go, go, go" before being nailed at the plate. But in the 12th inning, Carlton Fisk trumped it all with a drifting game-winning homer down the left-field line that he waved fair with hands extended wildly over his head. Peter's first three paragraphs were silk:

> And all of a sudden the ball was there, like the Mystic River Bridge, suspended out in the black of the morning.

When it finally crashed off the mesh attached to the left field foul pole, one step after another the reaction unfolded: from Carlton Fisk's convulsive leap to John Kiley's booming of the "Hallelujah Chorus" to the wearing off of the numbness to the outcry that echoed across the cold New England morning.

At 12:34 a.m., in the 12th inning, Fisk's histrionic home run brought a 7–6 end to a game that will be the pride of historians in the year 2525, a game won and lost what seemed like a dozen times, and a game that brings back summertime one more day. For the seventh game of the World Series.

Ever since that night, Bostonians young and old have treated Peter's Game 6 lead as local legend. "Like the Midnight Ride of Paul Revere," says former *Globe* and *Herald* sportswriter Jeff Horrigan. If Peter and Lee went out anywhere in Boston—from Faneuil Hall to Southie to Cambridge—locals would first say hello to Spaceman and then recite the Game 6 lead out loud to Peter's face.

"Hey Petuh!...*And all of a sudden the ball was there, like the Mystic River Bridge, suspended out in the black of the morning....* You're a wicked pissuh, Petuh!"

What he'd told his Carolina journalism professor had finally come true. Peter Gammons was the story.

IF ONLY SHE could've asked Ted Williams. Peter's star shined so bright that even the Splendid Splinter, chronically annoyed at ink-stained wretches, would wave Peter over to tell stories over a bourbon and tonic. Did you know in 1941 Ted used to get updates on Joe DiMaggio's 56-game hitting streak from a Fenway scoreboard operator in left field and shout them over to Dom DiMaggio, Joe's brother, in center? Peter knew. But then, suddenly, baseball was over for Gam. Done.

He'd become too prolific for his own good. *Sports Illustrated*— Frank Deford's *Sports Illustrated*!—offered him its NHL job in 1976, and Peter took it thinking he'd eventually scoot over to baseball. He knew hockey well enough and bonded with Bruins Hall of Famer Bobby Orr. But *SI* made him move to New York, and Peter says he pined for "the frenetic fandom of New England" and the scent of tobacco chew. While in Toronto for a Maple Leafs story, he moseyed over to the first-ever Blue Jays game. He showed up out of the blue at Brooks Robinson Night in Baltimore. He lasted two years on hockey.

Back to the *Globe* he went, and with new perspective on life, he began to pay sportswriting forward. He was his father's son; Dean Smith's protégé. He'd help the next person in line. He told his homie Dan Shaughnessy the Orioles beat job was open at the *Baltimore Evening Sun*; shared his Sunday notes with the *Philadelphia Inquirer's* Jayson Stark; got 23-year-old John Lowe an interview with the *Chicago Tribune*.

Probably 100 writers had similar tales. When Dale Murphy shooed the *Globe's* Lesley Visser from the Braves' clubhouse, Peter waited outside with her. When Rangers beat writer Tim Kurkjian sensed the team was making a trade, he called Peter, who told him, "Yeah, you guys are dealing for Cliff Johnson." He kindly alerted *Baltimore Sun* beat writer Richard Justice that the Orioles were signing Don Aase and Fred Lynn. Justice dialed Orioles exec Larry Lucchino, who said, "Where'd you hear that?" Gammons, Justice said. "Well," Lucchino said, "Gammons isn't wrong very often."

An entire generation of baseball writers wanted to be him. Justice wore the same New Balance sneakers Peter wore; bought the same brand steno pad. Peter was the envy of them all. Baltimore all-star Eddie Murray famously spurned the media, but Gammons would still waltz up to Murray's locker to chat him up. When Justice later told Murray, "Hey, I thought you aren't speaking to the press," Murray blurted, "That ain't the press, that's Gammons."

Fenway was Peter's second home, and he and his wife, Gloria—whom he'd met teaching Sunday school at church— bought a house at 46 Glen Road in Brookline, just 1.1 miles away from the Fens. Peter wanted to walk to games. His new next-door neighbors, the Kennedys, had an admiring young son named Sam who watched Peter leave for night games at 10 or 11 a.m.—"I borderline stalked him," Sam says—and overheard Peter's top-secret chats with GMs across a backyard screen. Peter's access to powerbrokers was unprecedented, and trade deadlines were his personal Christmas Day. He had a pulse on every impending trade, and GMs had the good sense to take his calls. "He was really a special assistant to about 30 teams," says A's GM Billy Beane, soon to be a Gammons confidant.

By then, Tigers pitcher Jack Morris had nicknamed him "The Commissioner," and Peter says three or four MLB teams offered him front office jobs. Legend has it Peter once laid out a three-way trade proposal to Red Sox GM Lou Gorman, who responded, "I haven't thought of anything like that." To which Peter said, "Well, by God, you better start thinking of things like that."

But the epitome of his bandwidth came during the '85 World Series. It was Game 7, Cardinals-Royals, and tense St. Louis manager Whitey Herzog had locked himself in his clubhouse office beforehand. Ah, but Peter knew Whitey's secret code. So he knocked, paused, knock-knocked, paused again and knock-knock-knocked. Whitey let him in.

Peter was too big now to stay local, and *SI*—Frank Deford's *SI*—came calling again in '86, this time with the baseball beat. Managing Editor Mark Mulvoy promised Peter he could still live in Brookline or his other home on the Cape and urged him to buy Red Sox season tickets so he wouldn't have pangs for Fenway. Peter found a pair of seats just seven rows behind home plate, next to the scouts, and accepted the *SI* job. He would write an "Inside Baseball" column and dive into the human interest stories he craved. He visited Yankee Don Mattingly's hometown of Evansville, Ind., and discovered Donnie Baseball learned to hit the ball the other way because the Wiffle ball field in his yard had a massive tree blocking fly balls to right.

Mattingly respected Peter—just like an earlier Yankee great, Maris—and agreed to do a three-sided chat about hitting with Ted Williams and Wade Boggs. Peter chronicled it all. When Williams hosted a fundraiser for the Jimmy Fund in Boston, which included Joe DiMaggio, Peter asked Ted if he could write about the Williams-DiMaggio relationship for *SI*. Ted said sure. But when DiMaggio arrived, Joe said, "I don't talk to *Sports Illustrated.*"

Williams bared his teeth at DiMaggio and then growled what needed to be growled, the ultimate tribute to Peter Gammons:

"This is my event, this is my city, and it's my f***** friend," Ted Williams said. "And you're going to talk to him."

So Joe DiMaggio talked.

IF ONLY SHE could've asked Theo Epstein. Theo happened to play Little League and then high school ball in Brookline with a certain Sam Kennedy, Peter's industrious next-door neighbor. But under the instructions of Sam's father Tom, a minister who had grown close to Peter, Sam had to be wary of inviting over friends who might eavesdrop on Gam's backyard GM calls.

So as the years passed, Theo Epstein was someone Peter knew in name only. Sam would tell him Theo is at Yale. Sam would tell him Theo is an intern for the Orioles. "I'd always say, 'Keep an eye on this guy,'" Sam says. Peter would file it away in that baseball brain of his.

Sam wanted a baseball internship himself and asked Peter for advice. Peter urged him to write to every big league club, and, in the spring of '93, Sam finally heard back from a team: Mattingly's Yankees. The Yanks asked Sam to provide three references. "My first was Peter Gammons," Sam says. "So that was pretty good."

If *SI* made Gammons a literary star, ESPN made him a national sensation. The network, under the wise leadership of John Walsh, had entered the information age. No more tractor-pull shows or fluff. Walsh wanted to put sportswriters on *SportsCenter*, no matter how they looked or dressed, and if Peter was the spitting image of 19th century president Andrew Jackson, the cover of the $20 bill, so be it. Walsh hired him away from *SI* in 1990, the first sportswriter ESPN ever put on-air.

At first, Peter's peers guffawed, considering Gam himself used to call local TV guys "barking dogs and frauds." But he was paving the way for them all. That is, unless he flopped. The genius of Walsh was he understood Peter was a man of the people. So, at Peter's first ESPN spring training, Walsh had him filmed interacting with fans. "Hey, Petuh! How the Sox gonna be, you wicked pissuh?" Peter would charm them all. Once back at ESPN, Walsh shoved in a tape of the fan exchanges and told Peter, "See, that's your job. It's no different from people coming up and talking to you. Only now you just look in the camera and do it."

That was the breakthrough, and in Peter's ESPN years, he had exclusives with problem players (A-Rod and Albert Belle), elegant players (Bernie Williams and Derek Jeter) and rock stars (Johnny Ramone and Huey Lewis). President George W. Bush called him "Petey." He went to Cuba with his trusty producer Julie Chrisco Andrews, saw teenagers Kendrys Morales and Yuli Gurriel and decided they were future big leaguers. Filed it away in his baseball brain.

His scout friend Billy Beane had just become the A's GM in '98, and Peter suggested he select lefty pitcher Mark Mulder with the second overall pick. "The first guy who told me about Mulder was Peter Gammons," says Beane, who ended up drafting the kid. Fact is, Peter spent parts of every summer at the Cape Cod League and had seen Mulder pitch for the Bourne Braves in 1997. Peter was royalty at the Cape, from his home in Cataumet to his favorite gym in Mashpee, and his baseball brain had catalogued every prospect up there.

His ESPN duties included *SportsCenter*, *Baseball Tonight* and Diamond Notes for ESPN.com. "He was a volume guy, and ESPN and *SportsCenter* was a volume place," Walsh says. But Peter eventually needed help, and channeling his father and Dean Smith, Peter told Walsh, "Get Tim Kurkjian." Later he said, "Get Jayson

Stark." Later he said, "There's this young guy who just went to the *New York Times*, Buster Olney."

At around the same time, Peter set his sights on none other than Theo Epstein, who had ascended to director of player development for the Padres. During Game 3 of the '98 Yankees-Padres World Series, Theo was in his usual post behind home plate, using a speed gun to input the velocity and pitch type up on the scoreboard. When suddenly, he says, Peter "appeared out of the ether."

Every other writer was in the press box, but Peter was behind the batter's box, picking Theo's brain. He'd earlier filed Epstein's name away in his baseball mind, and now they were finally meeting. Throughout the game, Theo was uncannily predicting which pitches Padre pitchers would throw and their locations. He saw Trevor Hoffman warm up for a save opportunity and told Peter, just from watching Hoffman's arm speed, that Trevor was going to struggle. Sure enough, Hoffman blew the game.

From that day on, Peter kept writing about the savant Theo Epstein. Peter felt the same about Beane, whose "Moneyball" theorem was revolutionizing the sport. When the Red Sox offered Beane $12.5 million to become their GM in 2002, Beane drove to the Cape with his daughter Casey to consult with Peter. It was a brilliant, no-fog day in Cataumet, and Beane decided he could get used to New England. It's the scene that didn't make the *Moneyball* movie—Billy and Peter roaming the Cape, riffing on Jason Varitek. "Peter may be responsible a little bit for my flirtation with the Boston Red Sox," Beane admits. "The whole ordeal: my going, not going. Peter very much was a confidant for me. He wasn't a writer, a journalist. He was a friend."

When Beane turned the job down for family reasons, Epstein ultimately got it, buoyed by Peter's endless endorsements. "Peter became a huge advocate for me in the way he's done for countless others," Theo says. "I'm sure that he made my path smoother when I got to Boston, both as assistant GM and when I got the GM job."

When the Red Sox broke the 86-year Curse of the Bambino in 2004, Peter probably deserved a ring. He helped create Theo.

Actually, Peter was creating a lot of things, including music. Along with Horrigan in 2000, he had started the antithesis of a charity golf event—a charity rock 'n' roll concert called "Hot Stove Cool Music" that initially featured two bands named "Thurman Munson" and "Carlton Fisk." Through the years, Peter brought in Paul Barrere from his favorite band Little Feat, Kay Hanley from Letters to Cleo and Eddie Vedder from Pearl Jam. "How could that be?" Kurkjian laughs. "He covered Eddie Murray and played with Eddie Vedder."

Pitcher Bronson Arroyo made his musical debut for Peter. Bernie Williams, Peter and Buddy Guy jammed on-stage together. Before long, Theo and his twin brother Paul merged their charity, "The Foundation To Be Named Later" with Hot Stove Cool Music, raising thousands to send kids to college through a platform they dubbed "Peter Gammons Scholars."

A force of nature, Peter—who'd named his dog after Bonnie Raitt—was not only writing original music, he was releasing an album in the summer of 2006 called "Never Slow Down, Never Grow Old." The album was legit and included self-deprecating songs such as "Bad Teeth" and "NyQuil Blues." But the song that perhaps resonated most was a ditty about a girl who's raised to be perfect and learns a little imperfection can go a long way.

The title: "She Fell From Heaven and Landed on Her Face."

DAYS BEFORE THE album's release, on June 26, 2006, that retired 76-year-old nurse Agnes Rockett-Bolduc landed from heaven, all right. Not on her face, but in the Mashpee parking lot alongside a dying stranger named—what did the driver's license say?—Peter Gammons.

Just back from a weekend White Sox–Astros series in Chicago, he had driven solo to his favorite gym early that morning to speedread four different sports pages on the StairMaster. But, along the way, his head began to throb and pulsate in a way that disarmed him. This was beyond a headache. While he could still see straight, he pulled erratically into that Stop N' Shop lot, parked crooked across two spaces and staggered to his backseat to lay down—never closing the door. Somehow, he thought to lay his driver's license on his sternum. "I remember nothing about that," Peter says. "It was just one of those inexplicable things that humans do."

The closest hospital was 11 miles away in Falmouth. But once the EMTs realized in the ambulance this was a brain aneurysm, not a heart attack, an order went out for Peter to be airlifted to Boston's Brigham and Women's Hospital. Then the fates got involved again.

Dr. Arthur Day, chief of medicine at the hospital, was supposed to be playing golf that day, but was conveniently accessible because his golfing partner never showed. An utterly confident brain surgeon, Dr. Day explained to Gloria the aneurysm was a "two-percenter," meaning Peter had a 2% chance of a clean, good-as-new recovery. The Red Sox once had a zero percent chance of ever winning a World Series before Theo arrived—so she took the 2%.

Because doctors don't do post-surgery interviews, what happened next is chatter among Peter's close friends such as his ESPN producer Andrews and Cape Cod buddies Keith Carroll and John Keenan. But apparently the minute Dr. Day opened Peter's skull, the aneurysm burst. If Nurse Agnes had never fallen from heaven, if the doctor had played 18 holes, if Falmouth Hospital had not rushed an airlift, the best baseball writer of a generation would've been gone.

Dr. Day finished the repair, but word was it was touch and go. Doria, who was now an executive at ESPN, called Kurkjian that night to say in a hushed voice, "Tim, I need you to write Peter's obit. Just in case." Kurkjian, who worked at ESPN all because of Peter, fell apart. "I wrote Peter Gammons' obituary in full tears," Kurkjian says. "I mean, I was weeping as I was writing. Hardest story I've ever written in my life."

Peter wasn't allowed any visitors at first. Bobby Orr showed up and was turned away. No one could tell Peter it was the trade deadline, for fear he'd get overexcited. Soon, Theo arrived with Sam Kennedy—who would eventually become Red Sox president—and the visit shook both of them up. Peter would talk about baseball from the '40s, the '90s, the '70s, incongruent stories that made it seem the catalog in his baseball brain had been tipped over.

"Peter wasn't Peter for those few days," Sam says. "The file cabinets in his brain, I think, were shuffled a bit. I remember Theo and I walked back up Brookline Avenue to Fenway from Brigham and Women's Hospital and talked about 'Oh my God, Peter might never be the same.'"

One day, a FedEx package arrived. From Don Mattingly. Gloria opened it to find a gaudy, gargantuan rapper's-style cross. Peter smiled, slipped it around his neck.

He wouldn't take it off.

THREE MONTHS LATER, Peter was back. It's miracle material, but Andrews knew he was cogent when he was recovering at Mashpee's Rehabilitation Hospital of the Cape and Islands and spied a baseball game on the TV. "Wait a minute," Peter asked, "when did Austin Kearns become a National?"

Andrews had to spill the beans then: "Peter, you missed the trade deadline. That's when the Reds sent Kearns to Washington." Ah, he said. The card catalog in his brain was firing on all cylinders. Dr. Day urged him to drive alone to Fenway for a September Red Sox–White Sox game to prove to himself he was healed. He could visit Chicago manager Ozzie Guillen, chat up Theo and Sam.

Peter was sketchy about it, but he handled the Route 128 traffic and glided into the Fens. He sat in his seats seven rows behind home plate. The Commissioner was back. In the weeks and months that followed, he returned to ESPN, ran a 5K and walked five miles a day all over the Cape wearing headphones, talking to Beane and other GMs.

Kurkjian finally confided, "You know, Peter, I wrote your obituary," and Gam answered, "Yeah, I should read that sometime, I guess." Eventually, he left ESPN for MLB Network because, according to Doria, Peter felt ESPN was prioritizing football. "He wasn't incorrect in that assessment," Doria says.

MLB Network was a more natural fit and built a studio for him on the second floor of his Cape home, overlooking the choppy water. They sent him to the 2016 World Series to see the Cubs—and new GM Theo—win their first title in 108 years. Peter's Theo.

If Peter was upbeat before the aneurysm, he had even more of a servant's heart now. He and Gloria never had children, but "sons" of Peter were scattered through baseball. For instance, his friend Scott Bradley, a fellow Tar Heel and the head coach at Princeton, asked him to help his former player Mike Hazen find a job. Peter had Hazen scout the Cape Cod League, and Hazen's reports were so detailed Peter disseminated them across MLB. Cleveland hired Hazen on the spot, then Theo scooped him up in Boston. Now Hazen's GM of the Diamondbacks.

"Peter lives his life with this incredible sense of justice," Theo says. And does so even though there's new injustice in his. For the past three years, Peter's been stricken with multiple myeloma—a blood and bone disease—and needs a periodic form of chemo. "I tell people I'm like a 1995 Volvo with 160,000 miles," Peter says. "I have to be maintained the rest of my life."

But he still does essays for MLB Network, still writes for The Athletic, still has half a million followers on Twitter. He still thinks about returning to Carolina at age 78 to finish his journalism degree. He still defends Bill Buckner, still wears Mattingly's cross, still is close with today's players such as Bo Bichette, still sings Pearl Jam, still signs autographs on Andrew Jackson $20 bills, still hears, "*And all of a sudden the ball was there, like the Mystic River Bridge, suspended out in the black of the morning. Petuh, you're a wicked pissuh!*"

Eventually, the nurse who fell from heaven, Agnes Rockett-Bolduc, figured it out. Not from Roger Maris or Dean Smith or Bill Lee or Ted Williams or Theo. She figured it out from her husband a few months after the aneurysm. He had been chiding her for walking up to a mysterious man in an empty low-fog parking lot when the guy could've been a mugger.

And just as he was saying this, Peter's picture flashed onto their TV.

"That's him," said Nurse Agnes.

"Peter Gammons!" her husband howled. "Thank God you stopped!"

TOM FRIEND is a two-time Emmy-nominated writer, author, columnist, documentary director, and producer who, over a 40-year career, has worked at ESPN, *ESPN The Magazine*, *The New York Times*, *The Washington Post*, *The Los Angeles Times*, the *Kansas City Star*, the *San Jose Mercury News*, *The National Sports Daily*, and now *Sports Business Journal*. He co-produced Showtime documentaries on Mahmoud Abdul-Rauf (*Stand*) and Ron Artest (Emmy-nominated *Quiet Storm*); co-directed ESPN Films' documentary on Sam Bowie (Headliner Award-winning *Going Big*); and turned the story "The Chicken Runs at Midnight" into both an Emmy-nominated feature for ESPN and a book that was a CASEY Award finalist for best baseball book of 2018. A native of Washington, D.C., and a graduate of the University of Missouri, he is currently based in Southern California.

Football Bonded Them. Its Violence Tore Them Apart.

KENT BABB

FROM *The Washington Post* • MAY 14, 2023

About a year ago, a bunch of old college roommates met up at a tavern in rural Nebraska. Most of them had played football at Harvard in the late 1990s. Now they were in their mid-40s, their broad shoulders rounded, their hairlines giving way to the beach erosion of time. But the same nonsense made them laugh: the teammate from California who wet the bed, the kid whose family ran a traveling carnival, the time a traffic cone mysteriously appeared in their living room after a night of drinking.

Old roommates keep certain memories locked away, untouched until they're together again. If football teams are sports' biggest tribe and produce unbreakable bonds, the friendships grow that much tighter when they involve sharing a refrigerator and toilet.

The carnival kid is Harvard's defensive coordinator now. Another ex-roommate has written jokes for Jimmy Kimmel. One was a federal air marshal until he couldn't stand the boredom. And over there, near the Herbie Husker mural, was the nation's leading voice on sports-related brain trauma, the man CNN called when Tua Tagovailoa suited up after a concussion last season and *Newsweek* interviewed after Aaron Hernandez killed himself in prison.

On this night in Nebraska, the friends broke the seal. Stories and beer flowed. Mostly they reminisced about the roommate they had come to bury. He had been their team captain, the best of an illustrious collection of Harvard men, an almost comic assemblage of genes and charm. He had been the soft-spoken roommate. The clean(ish) one. They tried to square it with what he had become. How had he kept it all secret, even from them?

When the bartender went to fetch another case, someone pointed out the paradox of meeting at a bar to honor a man who had drunk himself to death. Some social rituals just are, and remaining a member of the tribe means never challenging its code.

"It's just what we do," says one of the old teammates, Brian Daigle. "At tailgates, at a wedding or party or, in this case, for a funeral."

The bartender returned and passed out fresh cans. A little before closing time, Daigle posed a question to the group: If you had known then what you know now about football, the game that had brought them all together, would you play? Knowing it could be you in the next casket, would you still?

CHRIS NOWINSKI WAS driving with his family in Florida recently, about a year after his old roommate's funeral, when his phone rang. The father of an Olympic ice dancer was calling to discuss the ongoing symptoms of his daughter's concussion. Then another call: A kid who had played seven years of football needed a psychiatrist. Another: the parents of a Division I women's basketball player whose coach insisted on playing her despite lingering concussion symptoms.

"Almost every car ride we take, we get these calls," says Nowinski's wife, Nicole. "A child, a wife, a mother, asking Chris, '*Please* help.' He has this in his head 24-7."

Nowinski played defensive tackle for the Crimson and still counts his old roommates as his closest friends. He lives in South Florida with Nicole and their daughter and son, 4 and 2, but he will never stop caring about what the Harvard guys think— and where he fits into a decades-old hierarchy. Several of the friends are lawyers or executives or venture capitalists, but the Crimson football team produced only one 6-foot-5 canary in the sports coal mine, constantly chirping about the dangers of his old sport. Nowinski is why most American sports fans have even *heard* of chronic traumatic encephalopathy (CTE), and his personality and bona fides are a major reason the NFL grudgingly began inching its concussion protocols beyond the dark ages. When Boston University's CTE Center wants grieving relatives to donate a former athlete's brain, it's often Nowinski who suggests they make the phone call.

CTE can be confirmed only posthumously, so Nowinski's primary objective is connecting those who *suspect* they have the disease with the vast network of resources maintained by the Concussion Legacy Foundation, the advocacy group he founded in 2007 alongside neurosurgeon Robert Cantu. Some need an appointment with a neurologist; others require addiction specialists and support groups. Many are just looking for someone who understands.

"You can't always fix it," Nowinski says. "But if I'm able to talk to them, there's almost always a happy ending."

If his phone stops ringing long enough, sometimes Nowinski calls the old Harvard guys to check in. Scott Larkee in Cambridge, Mass.; Isaiah Kacyvenski in Boston; Daigle in North Carolina. They catch up, talk about the Crimson's chances next season, do what you do for a taste of that fleeting magic of being 20.

No one can explain this now, but for a long time and probably for many reasons, there was one topic they never discussed.

WHENEVER THE APARTMENT door opened back then, the polyphony of funk included hints of day-old pizza, mangled chicken parts and sweat. *So* much sweat. One summer, they had to lay down cardboard in Nowinski's car so they wouldn't soak through the upholstery.

Nowinski was 285 pounds. Tight end Chris Eitzmann was a sturdy 250. The runt, Larkee, was 225. Some years a dozen football players piled into the same suite, competing for microwave space and arguing over whose turn it was to empty the trash, which was usually overflowing with beer cans and animal bones.

"They weren't barbarians," says Mikaela Eitzmann, the tight end's college girlfriend and eventual wife. "But the whole place was definitely like a closet door that had shut some socks inside for a while."

This being Harvard, football players weren't exactly NFL-or-bust meatheads. Sure, they would deliberately eat foods they knew wouldn't agree with them just to wage gastrointestinal war on the others. And, yes, survival and acceptance meant an onslaught of insults. Daigle was the great Texas pontificator. Alex Garcia was the slovenly Californian who showed affection to friends by choking them. Nowinski was the suburban Chicagoan who serenaded his roommates, whether they liked it or not, with favorites from when he played Diesel in his high school performance of *West Side Story.*

When you're a Jet
If the spit hits the fan
You got brothers around
You're a family man.

Eitzmann mostly rolled his eyes. The roommates never had much ammo on him, other than him being a slow-talking plowboy. He had grown up alongside the corn stalks and milo husks of Hardy, Neb., population 179, contemplating a future beyond the plains.

He was tall and blond, with piercing blue eyes and a layer of wide-eyed innocence the other players couldn't crack. Eitzmann tutored classmates and rarely missed Sunday services at University Lutheran on Harvard Square. He turned down a roster spot with the mighty Nebraska Cornhuskers to become the first graduate of his high school to enroll at an Ivy League school. This made him a local celebrity and heartthrob, so when Mikaela graduated from high school a year after Eitzmann, she moved east to enroll at Boston College.

"I was young and had a crush," she says, "probably like all girls did within a 100-mile radius."

He drank beer, but nobody remembers him losing control or puking on the sofa. Other roommates, sure. But Eitz? He had too many things he wanted to accomplish, this spit-shined drive that pushed away temptation and muffled the pressure of being the first Nebraskan to suit up for the Crimson varsity since the 1960s.

"Even his swear words were wholesome," says Will Burke, Eitzmann's first Harvard roommate. "It was like Superman landed on Earth and was like, 'I've got to figure out these Earthlings,' and he just crushes it."

The practice field is where he went into Cyborg Mode, blasting into defenders at every turn. Nobody thought much about concussions then, and there was nobody to warn players about long-term effects or urging them to sit out. Getting your bell rung was a badge of honor, every hit part of a daily competition for masculinity and bragging rights.

"If I didn't come off the line as fast and strong as I could, I was losing," says Daigle, a defensive end who often squared off against Eitzmann. "I was hitting people with the front of my head as often as I could."

Two days after Yale beat Harvard in 1998, the team gathered in Boston for its annual postseason banquet. Among Harvard's many traditions is a particularly sacred one: Since 1873, football players have voted on one teammate as captain, the locker room's leader and a symbol representing more than just talent. Joe Azelby, Dan Jiggetts and Ryan Fitzpatrick are among the luminaries.

The underclassmen wrote names on slips of paper and passed them to the coaches. That night Coach Tim Murphy announced

Christopher John Eitzmann as captain of the 1999 Harvard Crimson.

"First of all, how in the world did I ever get to Harvard?" Eitzmann told a Nebraska newspaper reporter later. "I never could have dreamed all this would have happened to me."

There was no honorary kegger or roommates-only whiskey toast—not for Eitz. All anyone remembers is the pride that one of them, the obvious one, had made it. It was a feeling they knew they would be talking about—and probably ribbing him about—when they returned to campus as old men, their bond everlasting and shatterproof.

When you're a Jet
You're a Jet all the way
From your first cigarette
To your last dyin' day.

THE FRIENDS SCATTERED after graduation: Larkee to Paris to play for a club football team, Burke to Hollywood to try comedy, Daigle back home to guard the Texas-Mexico line for the Border Patrol.

Eitzmann did what they all expected: overachieved and earned a roster spot with the New England Patriots. He moved in with two new roommates not far from Foxboro Stadium. Defensive end David Nugent was all right, but what a stiff the other guy was. When Burke visited, he pleaded with Eitzmann to keep their plans secret from Tom Brady, a robotic and humorless rookie quarterback.

"Let's ditch this f---ing loser," Burke says he insisted more than once. "God, he was boring."

A thousand miles south, Nowinski was searching for a place of his own. He had worked for a pharmaceutical consulting firm in Boston his senior year, but he wasn't passionate about it. A colleague suggested that with his size, athleticism and big personality, he would make a great pro wrestler. Before Harvard, he had never followed the sport. But his roommates did, and during wrestling's late-1990s golden age, Monday nights belonged not to the NFL's weekly prime-time game but to Stone Cold Steve Austin, D-Generation X and the New World Order.

Nowinski enrolled in wrestling school in Atlanta and landed a spot on a reality show in which the winner received a contract with WWE. Two contestants were named Chris, so producers called Nowinski "Chris Harvard." He finished second but earned a spot anyway and made his televised debut in 2002, playing the role of an elitist pretty boy in a Harvard letterman's jacket.

He insulted the audience's intelligence, thrashed competitors with a book of quotes, delighted in the crowd's chants of "Har-vard sucks! Har-vard sucks!"

"He got a taste of being the bad guy and just loved it," says Kacyvenski, a former Crimson linebacker who was the only former roommate drafted by an NFL team.

Nowinski got his buddies free tickets and backstage passes. They watched as he took a "Singapore cane" to the face, a power bomb from the Undertaker, a beatdown from Scott Steiner after Nowinski criticized the Iraq War during an in-ring political debate. It was all scripted, of course, but Nowinski occasionally took real bumps and bruises with him to the bar afterward. Still, as he greeted fans and signed autographs, a few longtime friends believed he had never been happier.

During a match in 2003, Nowinski charged toward an opponent named Bubba Ray Dudley, expecting the painless kick they had rehearsed. But he reached the corner an instant early, catching Dudley's boot just under his chin. He crumpled to the mat and felt pain ripping through his head. He's still not sure what happened next.

A trainer asked whether he was okay, and Nowinski lied and said he was fine. Later, he lay on the locker room floor for a half-hour and again told the trainer he was okay. Days passed. WWE's next show was in New York, and he was still experiencing nausea and memory loss. There were no concussion protocols then, in wrestling or anywhere. Nowinski planned to report his symptoms to WWE's medical team, but upon arriving and seeing wrestlers being treated for "real injuries," he says of knee and back and shoulder problems, he left, kept silent and prepared for the night's match, which he lost after being dropped through a table.

He just lived with it because that's just what you did. Wrestling legends didn't complain; they jumped off cages and spit out cracked teeth. Football players didn't sit out because they saw stars after a big hit; they modeled their games after Jack Tatum's and Ronnie Lott's because that earned you a spot on highlight montages and a bust in Canton, Ohio. A *man* didn't tell his bosses or even his friends that he was in agony because that meant he was soft.

"I'm not going to tell them I had a headache," he says. "I just didn't want to say anything."

One night in 2003, Nowinski was in Indianapolis when he saw his then-girlfriend falling and leaped forward to catch her. But Nowinski was actually asleep, acting out a dream in a hotel room. His brain was so injured it was conjuring visions without waking him. When his eyes opened, he had no idea why there was broken glass on the floor, why the nightstand was busted, why he had been clawing at the wall as his girlfriend sat on the bed crying, horrified by what she had seen.

FOR YEARS AFTER they graduated, the roommates would return to Cambridge each fall. A few would pound beers at Harvard football tailgates, do shots, sip from a flask. Never Eitzmann. He was the Golden Boy, just sickeningly perfect. Even after a hip injury ended his NFL career in 2002, he came out on top.

He married Mikaela, completed his master's requirements at Dartmouth, got a job as a hedge fund manager in Boston. The couple had their first son, and three more children would follow, all healthy and beautiful. They adopted a Vizsla, went on ski trips to New Hampshire, bought a six-bedroom house in Wellesley, Mass., and a cabin overlooking New Hampshire's Squam Lake. Eitzmann raced bicycles on weekends, went elk hunting in Colorado, kept Mikaela laughing and never feeling unsafe, a live-action postcard from a utopian life.

"The dream couple," Nicole Nowinski says. "These beautiful people with the beautiful love story, and they were both so humble and lovely. They really were these Harvard Barbies."

Chris Nowinski's path had become rockier. He never wrestled again. He had nightmares and dizziness, and if his heart rate increased, a wave of nausea would hit. He became sensitive to bright lights and friends who asked when he would return to the ring. Doctor visits alternated between confusing and pointless, with Nowinski being assured his symptoms would disappear. Weeks, though, became months. Depression set in.

Eventually, in 2003, a friend with WWE got him an appointment with Cantu, the renowned Boston-area neurosurgeon whose analysis of a concussion was different from that of the NFL. The league office at the time considered it a singular, "trauma-induced" event. Cantu, though, believed a concussion was less an injury than the first link in a longer chain of mental malfunction—a continuing process in which cells experience an outage and hastily attempt to rewire themselves and get back online as quickly as possible. This can take weeks or even months. When the new connection is made, the injured neurons and nerve cells are abandoned, left to die by the brain's own survival blueprint. With enough injuries, the brain can become a graveyard of scar tissue that can cause chronic symptoms and dramatically alter judgment and behavior.

Cantu asked Nowinski how many concussions he had had. He had no idea. Zero? He had never been formally diagnosed, neither at Harvard nor by WWE. So Cantu asked whether he had ever blacked out, had double vision, felt dizziness after a hit, gotten his bell rung? Nowinski thought back and counted more than a half-dozen such instances. Potentially far more.

"I had been banging my head for 19 years without any real consideration for what it could be doing to me," Nowinski says. Cantu diagnosed Nowinski with post-concussion syndrome, and

Nowinski says some effects never went away. He and Cantu kept talking.

"Shouldn't athletes know about this?" Nowinski asked.

"People don't listen to doctors," Cantu said.

"Maybe I'll take a crack."

Now set adrift professionally, Nowinski spent his newfound free time reading concussion studies and interviewing athletes and doctors. He analyzed the work of Bennet Omalu, the controversial pathologist who discovered unusual protein buildup in NFL legend Mike Webster's brain, the first link between football and CTE. Nowinski compiled his findings into what would become a book titled *Head Games*.

As he wrote, Nowinski called his former Harvard teammates to share his discoveries and ask for their experiences. Some were intrigued. Others, not so much. The NFL disputed Omalu's findings, with a league-appointed neurologist saying Webster died not because of brain trauma but because he had been a smoker, suffered from depression and been in generally poor health. Omalu also found evidence of CTE in the brains of former NFL players Justin Strzelczyk, Terry Long and Andre Waters, the latter two of whom died by suicide.

"Just because [suicide] happened to a few football players," the league's top concussion expert, neurologist Ira Casson, said in 2007, "doesn't mean it's linked to football."

So, Nowinski's old roommates wondered, why was he attacking the game? Was he so bitter that he hadn't gotten a shot at the NFL that he was going to bring down the entire sport? Or was this just Nowinski the heel, an attempt to regain his bygone WWE attention?

"To put it bluntly," Mikaela says, "I think everybody thought it was bulls--t."

One former roommate refused to read an early draft of his manuscript. Another accepted a copy but never opened it. Larkee, by then a coach at Harvard, had no interest. So when he and

Nowinski talked, they just avoided the topic and suppressed their feelings. If Nowinski brought it up, Larkee walked away.

"I'm right there with these young college-aged kids, putting them through tackling reps, so we *could* have had that conversation: 'What are we doing? What's the best thing for these guys?'" Larkee says now. "But I think we both know we would disagree on pretty much everything."

At the Harvard tailgate in 2006, not long after *Head Games* was published, Nowinski brought books to give friends gathered around a fire. Many rolled their eyes at Nowinski being Nowinski, proselytizing about the evils of football at a football tailgate to a bunch of ex-football players.

"He was screaming," Daigle says. "But nobody was listening."

Daigle had helped Nowinski edit chapters of his manuscript and grown curious about his former roommate's conclusions. Daigle's father and grandfather both played college football; his grandpa died of Alzheimer's disease, and his father is 72 and has dementia, Daigle says.

"How much of that is genetic? How much of that is football?" Daigle says. "My future is definitely clouded by, what have I done to myself?"

He would regret this later, but Daigle climbed into the bed of a pickup during the Harvard tailgate. Emboldened by a few beers and the promise of a laugh from his ex-teammates, he raised a copy of Nowinski's book. Has anyone here suffered a concussion? he asked. Should any of this spell the end of football?

Then Daigle climbed down, took another long pull off his beer and tossed the book into the fire.

THE EITZMANNS LOVED Halloween. One year they dressed as a 1920s gangster and flapper, Mikaela in a dark suit and fedora, Chris in a sequined dress and heels. Mikaela carefully applied his mascara. Another year, he was Wilt Chamberlain, short-shorts challenging the limits of comfort and decency.

In 2008, Chris dressed as Axl Rose, but because Mikaela had to watch Coen, their infant son, before her nursing shift the next morning, she skipped the Halloween party at a bar in Boston. At 3 a.m., Chris still wasn't home. He didn't answer Mikaela's calls. She called hospitals and police departments, eventually learning her husband had been arrested for drunken driving.

When he got home, Chris made excuses. He hadn't had *that* much. The officer was just a jerk. All he had really done was roll through a stop sign.

Chris was a social drinker, Mikaela says now, but he was always in control. He had never put himself or anyone else in danger. But was that true? Had she spent years ignoring signs of a worsening problem?

"He was so good at telling me, 'I'm all right, I'm all right,'" she says.

Now on alert, Mikaela began to notice lipstick on his shirt and charges for $500-a-night hotel rooms. He would disappear to the lake house sometimes, claiming he needed to focus on work. Why couldn't Mikaela understand that? Why wouldn't she give him space? He couldn't be reached for hours or days, again saying he needed to work late.

"He was slowly unraveling," she says, "and I just didn't see it."

She ignored evidence Chris had been with another woman because, she says, it wasn't worth the explosion. She waited until after he had coached Coen's flag football game one morning to tell Chris his breath was a thick fog of rum. He calmly walked into their baby daughter's room that day, gave her a hug and drove away. An hour later, Chris called and said he was in a hotel in Woburn, a half-hour north, about to kill himself.

"I was paralyzed," Mikaela says. "I had no idea what to do. No one would believe me. Who *would* believe me?"

She called the police, who took him into custody and tested his blood alcohol concentration. It was 0.44, Mikaela says. When a taxi later dropped him off, Chris apologized, hugged Mikaela and begged her not to tell anyone. When she agreed, he put on his suit and left for work carrying a bottle of wine. A gift for his assistant, he assured his wife.

"I didn't really believe that, but I was so terrified of making him mad," Mikaela says. "I feel like this major wuss, and I'm really not like that. But I just loved him so much, so I wanted our marriage to be okay and I wanted *him* to be okay, so I just talked myself into believing him and believing it was all going to be okay."

Months could pass without arguments or threats, a sign Chris was improving. Mikaela kept telling herself that. Their life was peaceful, loving, as perfect as everyone believed. She told herself that, too. They went to Harvard alumni events and socialized with old friends. If Chris had alcohol on his breath, Mikaela just smiled and kept their secret. Then one day in 2016, when Chris was 39, he came home and announced that he was planning to drive off a bridge. Another time he said he was going to Colorado to veer off an embankment.

After Mikaela's father died in 2017, they agreed to go home to Nebraska and take over the family farm. A change would be good for them. Then, in 2019, Chris got drunk and buckled the kids into the car to go boating, and Mikaela stopped him. She insisted he enter rehab, and he agreed to report to a facility in Arizona. They flew there together, Chris in the window seat and Mikaela on the aisle, and soon after takeoff, Chris fell asleep as the two held hands.

Fighting tears, Mikaela unlocked her phone and took a picture. This, of their clasped hands, would be the "before" photo, back when things got crazy that one time. She told herself a dream life built once could also be rebuilt. Soon Chris would be sober and recalibrated, and they would be smiling in their next picture together, their bond stronger for this, and looking happy, just as they always had.

REHAB DOESN'T ALWAYS work the first time, and for Eitzmann it didn't work the second, third or fourth times, either. He would commit to it, get on a plane, then discharge himself or escape after a few days and go looking for a bar. Then he would come home.

As a way to cope, Mikaela and their preteen son, Coen, developed a code for when Chris was drunk. It wasn't Dad who would come through the door. It was "Earl." And they must tread carefully because Earl might get loaded and go driving. He might threaten suicide or slide a pan of fish sticks into the oven and pass out.

"Earl still had Chris's memories, and he still had Chris's desire to be part of a family. Chris was still in there, so we had to protect Chris," Mikaela says. "We couldn't make him upset, because then Earl might leave for good and Chris might never come back."

Mikaela and Coen hid Earl's credit cards and keys, but he always found them. He accumulated five DWIs and would later fly to Boston to meet up with a woman he had met in rehab. He would spend $6,000 on a vacation to Costa Rica but never go, or he would disappear without announcement and sleep in a camper near the Kansas line.

CTE had by then become ubiquitous, and an alarming number of former NFL players—Dave Duerson, Junior Seau, Aaron Hernandez—had taken their lives after unexplained behavioral changes. The NFL had implemented new rules to protect players from the most devastating hits, but for families across the country, the damage was done. Mikaela read about their symptoms, about the mysterious spirals that now felt familiar, and didn't Chris complain years earlier of headaches and dizziness? Had he been experiencing depression when he refused to get out of bed all day? Had she ignored these signs, too?

One evening on the sofa, Mikaela told her husband they could get through this—whatever this was—together. She suggested they call Nowinski, his old roommate. By then he had a doctoral degree in behavioral neuroscience and had testified before Congress; he had been nominated for *Sports Illustrated*'s sportsperson of the year in 2010 and ultimately pressured the

NFL into acknowledging, for the first time in 2016, the connection between football and CTE.

Nowinski was also a longtime family friend, so obviously he would be willing to—

"I've taken care of it," he said.

But this was Earl, not Chris, and this is how fiendish he could be. Mikaela wanted to believe him when he said he already had spoken with Nowinski, and so she did. As she did when her husband claimed he had visited Nowinski in Boston and been put through a battery of tests and even an MRI exam. Nowinski had assured him, he insisted, that all of it had come back clean.

THERE WERE TWO dozen former teammates on the group text, but when it came down it, only three could make it to Nebraska on short notice. So one day in January 2021, Larkee, Joe Mattson and Ryan Kauppila formed what they playfully called "The Extraction Team." Their all-too-serious mission: Get Eitzmann to his fifth—and hopefully final—stint in rehab.

Mikaela had finally broken. She could no longer believe her husband's lies—or the ones she had told herself. But a side effect of covering for Eitzmann all these years was that now nobody believed how bad things really were. His work friends in Boston distanced themselves. Eitzmann's parents and siblings accused Mikaela of giving up too early. Chris was gaining weight, looking good, getting better.

"No, he's not; he's really bad," Mikaela says she told them.

"Because I had kept it a secret for so long, there was just no way I was ever going to get him the help he needed," she says.

So when Eitzmann needed one final assist, it was the old roommates who came through. One picked up the tab for the treatment. Another, a lawyer, checked state laws and arranged for Eitzmann to be admitted to the facility. Others chipped in money for gas and food, and a few more plotted the quickest route from Omaha to Boston.

The evening before the Extraction Team deployed, the room-mates remained skeptical that things were as dire as Mikaela had indicated. "I was completely in the dark," Burke says, "because he wanted me to be."

When Eitzmann emerged from a restaurant alongside his parents, the trio almost didn't recognize him. The muscular tight end was gone. In his place was a gaunt and pale figure wearing clothes that swallowed him.

"A bag of bones," Larkee says.

They set off in a rented Tahoe, toward Des Moines and Chicago. The plan was to stop only for essentials. But the rehab place said that someone with Eitzmann's level of dependency couldn't just go 24 hours with zero alcohol. So, counterintuitive as it seemed, the friends were advised to limit him—but to let him drink.

The friends talked trash, laughed at old stories, pointed out how fat and bald and gray they had become. Eitzmann alter-nated between grand proclamations about getting his family back and questions about his friends' children and jobs. He talked to Larkee about the Crimson's hopes against Yale the following season.

"The exact normal Chris," Mattson says. "There was some joy of being together and feeling the real love that existed between all of us."

They were somewhere in Ohio when Eitzmann fell quiet. He was sweating, and a tremor in his hand spread throughout his body. The Tahoe parked at a store, and Larkee had to phys-ically block Eitzmann from going inside. Instead, Mattson and Kauppila went in and returned with cans of high-test hard lem-onade. Eitzmann drained them, his tremor eased, and eventually he went to sleep.

"We were all thinking: Just f---ing keep driving," Mattson says. "Take a deep breath, keep the doors locked and see what happens when he wakes up."

After 24 intense hours, the SUV stopped outside a hospital in Brighton, Mass., just three miles from their old Harvard apartment. Someone came to help Eitz inside, and the three ex-roommates watched him disappear from within the idling SUV. They waited a while, the three of them, in case their friend tried to make a run for it, joking about who was still athletic enough to make a tackle.

THE 126TH CAPTAIN of Harvard football died alone, surrounded by bottles, on the couch of his $3,500-a-month apartment in South Boston. The medical examiner determined that Eitzmann's heart and liver gave out, no longer able to defend against a daily assault of alcohol.

Mikaela had last heard his voice five days earlier, when the kids called him on Christmas Eve. Eitzmann was slurring and unintelligible, and he ended the call after speaking with only two of his four children. That fifth rehab stint had ended almost immediately, after Eitzmann tested positive for the coronavirus and was discharged. The detox place in Millbury couldn't hold him, and neither could the halfway house in Chestnut Hill. One night Mikaela got an alert that Eitzmann was trying to use his credit card at a restaurant in Boston, and Larkee agreed to go looking for him. He found his ex-roommate on Boylston Street, having a steak dinner and an old-fashioned.

He drove him to a facility in Worcester but feared it was pointless. "He's going to have to do it on his own," Larkee remembers thinking.

After Eitzmann's death, his friends began looking for something to blame. Some of his hedge fund friends decided he had suffered from mental illness. A few relatives pointed to a family history of addiction. His brother wondered whether decades of seeming so put together, of trying to be the hero of every story, had gradually ripped him apart.

"It looked like he was so good at everything, that it all came easy," Nate Eitzmann says. "But he must've put an intense amount of pressure on himself to succeed, and what he was feeling inside versus what we were seeing on the outside were probably two different things."

During a Zoom call with the Harvard roommates later, Nowinski said Eitzmann's family had donated his brain to be analyzed for CTE. The response startled Nowinski. A few of the men issued unequivocal rejections that football could be responsible, a vigorous defense of a game that remains a precious ingredient to both identity and social matrix.

"Just look at the evidence: We've been playing football for a hundred-plus years. What are we talking about here?" Larkee says. "He had a drinking problem for other reasons, some classic reasons. Some childhood stuff, high-pressure job, just general depression and personality issues and those type of things, like any normal person in their mid-40s would become an alcoholic and lose their family. Football player or not, that classic horrible, tragic story."

He continues a moment later.

"For his loved ones, if it makes them feel better that that was his problem, that it wasn't his fault, then that's fine. I think it was Eitzmann's fault."

For more than a decade now, this tension has coursed through the friend group as Nowinski insisted that CTE would eventually "get one of us." In response, friends say, the former roommates established a separate text thread that doesn't include Nowinski. That's where they sometimes call him an "opportunist," one ex-teammate says, and compare him to an ambulance-chasing attorney.

"There's still so much unknown," says a different friend, speaking on the condition of anonymity to protect his privacy and relationship with Nowinski. "Genetics and trauma, the effect of alcohol on the brain—it probably *is* a blend. That's not a good enough story for him."

Some are willing to concede Nowinski's contributions to accountability and football player safety, which one friend calls a "blessing." The NFL reported a 30 percent reduction in concussions from 2015 to 2020, and the National Institutes of Health acknowledged for the first time last fall that repetitive traumatic brain injuries cause CTE.

For the most part, though, they do what men their age do: They just don't talk about it.

"We are sort of beating around the bush of directly asking each other: Where do you fall on this?" Daigle says. "Chris sees CTE everywhere he looks because that's his life. Scott sees a lack of evidence of CTE because he sees hundreds of football players a year.

"If we were skewing, it would probably be to Chris's side but with a bias toward saying we are not ideologues like Chris is on this. If he could ban football, he would."

LAST SEPTEMBER, NOWINSKI traveled past the Overtime Grill and Lounge, where, over beers that night, he had been one of the only friends to say he regrets playing football. He continued past the cemetery where Eitzmann's remains are buried, alongside dense cornfields, eventually turning off the paved road.

When families donate a loved one's brain, the neuropathologist who studies it conducts a virtual meeting to explain the results. Nowinski doesn't usually sit in, but this time he did.

"I didn't want to treat Chris as another research case," he says.

Nowinski and Mikaela sat on the family's L-shaped sofa, and Ann McKee, director of the brain bank at Boston University, appeared on a laptop screen. Coen, who turned 15 last month, watched from the cushion between them, while the other children were at school. Coen is looking more like his father each day. He stands like him, shoulders back, and has the same jaw line and curiosity Eitzmann once brought from Nebraska to Cambridge.

Coen witnessed many of his father's worst moments, so Mikaela believed he had earned the right to know their source. McKee explained that she had found severe Stage 2 CTE, or a considerable amount of scar tissue in his brain. It could have been the cause of his alcohol abuse and impulsive behavior, along with Eitzmann's deteriorating cognitive function. Eitzmann's fried circuit board had become a wasteland.

"There was nothing we could've done," Mikaela says. At first this was a relief, she says. But as she processed McKee's diagnosis, Mikaela realized she had actually lost her husband long ago. She believed that photo she had taken of their hands in 2019, just before dropping him off at the rehab place in Arizona, documented their true end.

"Looking back now," she says, "I never really had my real Chris back. He was just never himself ever again. I don't think he was himself for a really long time."

After McKee signed off, Nowinski turned to Coen. The boy just stared. His father had been a great man, Nowinski said, and Eitzmann's death had shattered him. They all had idolized him at Harvard, where everyone was a big shot but none as big as Chris Eitzmann. He had just been born into a town, a state, a country in love with a violent game, as addictive and culturally important as it is brutal.

But what happened, Nowinski continued, wasn't inevitable for Coen or his three younger siblings, and neither did it suggest either of them would—

Mikaela interjected. She thanked Nowinski for coming, for bringing understanding and closure, for retelling a few stories from happier times. But it was getting late, and Coen needed to head out soon. It was fall in Middle America, and the young man had a football game that night.

NOWINSKI AND NICOLE were coming back from a beach trip with friends recently, their kids asleep in the back seat. The topic of Chris Eitzmann came up. Nicole saw her husband's face tighten, his skin turn red, that common sight of a middle-aged man using everything within him to avoid crying.

"It just hits so close to home," Nowinski said once the wave passed.

He had felt many emotions after Eitzmann's death: sadness, regret, guilt. He talked about none of them. It wasn't just that Superman was dead; it was that helping people is Nowinski's job, and even he couldn't save him. If only Eitzmann or Mikaela had asked. Or if Nowinski had checked in more frequently. Or paid closer attention.

"It broke Chris, and he's still very, very, very broken," Nicole says. "He kind of just handled it like, unfortunately, like you guys tend to do: just crawled into a hole."

By the time Nowinski emerged, so had a different emotion: fear. Two decades after his last wrestling match, Nowinski still takes prescription medication to ease headaches that can last all day. Though he discontinued his sleepwalking medication a few years ago, he still has vivid, disturbing dreams. Still, if he wakes in the night or feels foggy or forgets something, this is evidence, Nowinski says, that he has CTE. Be it soon or years from now, a fate similar to Eitzmann's—and his family's—is inevitable.

"I've seen this pattern," he says, "over and over and over again."

Mikaela admits she enabled Eitzmann, lied for him, helped him keep his secret. "I protected him for a really long time," she says. It's a regret she will live with forever.

Nicole says Nowinski rarely drinks and has never been aggressive or menacing. She says she watches and "charts" her husband's every move, comparing them with those from 15 years ago, when they first met in Boston.

"I run my little science experiments all the time," she says. "How has Chris changed? If he gets angry about something, is this just typical Chris behavior or is this a new type of anger? Or if he just forgets something, is this something he *normally* forgets? The headaches scare me, the sleep scares me, but that's also been an issue since Day 1."

But what if Nowinski were to hide the severity of his symptoms, as Eitzmann did? If he knows how to address them, it stands to reason he also knows how to conceal them.

"Chris is the love of my life and my best friend," she says. "But I have to put my children first. His connections in the science field, they're my connections as well. I've always been, in the back of my head, prepared for that, if it's pretty or not. That's my plan, just kind of go to his people—"

She pauses, considering what it would mean to actually do what she's describing.

"—behind his back," she continues, "and just ask for help."

For now, Nicole says, her objective is to listen and be supportive, even if Nowinski doesn't want to talk. It's to make him feel safe, she says, when he feels insecure or afraid and assure him they're in this—whatever *this* is—together. On this late afternoon, Nowinski turned off the interstate as twilight approached. Nicole sat in the passenger seat of their SUV and leaned over. She looked at the sky and pointed out the orange and pink and purple streaks emerging.

She gripped his hand as they drove, and Nowinski seemed calmer now as they listened to music and searched for new colors. Nicole squeezed tighter, a gentle reminder to her husband that she was there, would stay there, and that a day's earlier moments don't necessarily foretell how vibrant and lovely the sunset can sometimes be.

KENT BABB is a sports features writer at *The Washington Post* and is the author of two books. He lives in the Washington, D.C., area with his wife and two daughters.

The Catch

EMILY SOHN

FROM Long Lead • DECEMBER 2023

PART 1: TOURNAMENT DAY

> "By mail and telephone we get many strange questions about sports and sportsmen. A man called here a few days ago wanting to know what kind of after-shave lotion the big-game hunters on our staff prefer. We were able to answer that one pretty easily. The only big-game hunter on our staff is Writer Virginia Kraft, and she doesn't use the stuff. She does occasionally carry Chanel No. 5 on hunts…"

Letter from the Publisher
Sports Illustrated
February 22, 1965

A streak of fiery pink brightened the horizon, lighting up a line of clouds that towered like smokestacks over the bayou. It was 5:30 a.m. on a Monday in early June, and although the full moon had not yet set, the marina in the tiny outpost of Venice, Louisiana, was already awake. A pickup truck backed a boat to the edge of the water alongside a fleet of vessels lining an L-shaped dock. The smell of gas infused the salty air while captains filled tanks for a nine-hour day on the water. And from every direction arrived anglers—all of them women.

It was tournament day, the first of a three-day event hosted by the International Women's Fishing Association (IWFA). Competitors, many of them longtime friends and all carrying fishing rods, greeted each other with exuberant hugs, cheek kisses, and selfies in front of the sunrise. They scanned the dock for the guides and partners they had been paired with for the day. Mary Weingart, a 65-year-old competitor from North Carolina, had risen at 4:30 a.m., eaten an egg-and-sausage biscuit with grits, and gulped a cup of coffee. Now she was out by the dock, where she couldn't find her guide, Jack. The night before they had agreed on a 5:30 meetup. "If you tell me to be here at 5:30," she grumbled, "I'm here at 5:30."

An all-women's fishing tournament is nothing new in 2023, but the concept was revolutionary back in 1955, when a group of women decided to leave their husbands at home and start the IWFA—a history I knew about because of Virginia Kraft. In 1960, Kraft first wrote about the IWFA for *Sports Illustrated* (*SI*), making her—at the time and for a long time after—one of the only women writing the kinds of in-depth stories the magazine became known for.

Over a 26-year career at *SI*, Kraft wrote deeply reported and immersive features, just like her male colleagues. All the while, she quietly racked up an unrivaled collection of firsts. She was the first woman to race in a major dogsled event in Alaska, the first woman and first foreign journalist to hunt with General Francisco Franco of Spain, and likely the only mother of four to traverse six continents to take down all of the Big Five trophy animals. Yet despite the enduring reputation enjoyed by her male contemporaries at *SI*—including George Plimpton, Frank Deford, and Roy Blount Jr.—her work has since faded into obscurity.

Despite more than 100 *SI* bylines and significant accolades and attention in her time, Kraft is absent from lists of pioneering women in journalism, and her articles are excluded from discussions of notable *SI* stories. Her work isn't covered in journalism schools, and when asked, none of my peers was even familiar with her name. Virginia Kraft might be the most influential sports journalist nobody has ever heard of. Why?

The more I learned about her, the more compelled I was to answer this question. My start in adventure-based journalism came in 2001, more than 50 years after Kraft's, when I joined a mostly male expedition team to write about animals and the environment in the Peruvian Amazon, Turkey, Cuba, and other remote places where I was always outnumbered by men and sometimes the only woman. Since then, I have hiked up mountains, trekked through jungles, and even skateboarded down ramps for my work—never considering whether I could or should do it, even when I left my children behind. In fact, more often I was motivated to demonstrate, through my work, that women can achieve whatever they want.

When I first heard about Virginia Kraft, she seemed to be a classic overlooked hero, a woman who had chiseled early cracks into a male-dominated world that would eventually open enough to make way for my own writing career. Delving into her life and writing in the context of 1950s New York, however, revealed a complicated story of a woman who did not fit into simple boxes, and whose career challenged my expectations of what it means to be a pioneer.

To figure out why she had been forgotten, I scoured Kraft's words for clues about what it was like to be one of the first. This research led me to the women of the modern-day IWFA. In 1960, Kraft covered the group's fifth annual sailfish tournament. It was "perhaps the most unusual fishing contest in America," she wrote, drawing competitors from around the continent "to show the male world, which has long excluded women from fishing competition, that the International Women's Fishing Association was ready to compete with anyone."

Eager to see how that description held up 63 years later, I contacted IWFA President Denise Freihofer and asked to watch the group's upcoming tournament. She tried to talk me out of it. It would be hot, she said, adding that everyone would be too busy fishing to talk to me during the day, and afterward they might be too tired. And, she piled on, boat captains are secretive about their fishing spots and would likely not want me following them.

"We would hate to think of you traveling with your guide and not be able to find any of us," she wrote in an email. "How disappointing that would be for you."

Virginia Kraft would have been undeterred by Freihofer's discouraging words. Stories of her confidence were legendary among those who remember her best. During a trip to Cuba in 1956, she knocked on Ernest Hemingway's front door without any notice. He answered wearing yellow pajamas. She told him her name, which he recognized from her work, and he invited her in. They spent the morning drinking together. "I mean, who does that?" recalled family friend Christian Erickson, who is also the trustee of her estate. "She was not afraid to take risks, and she did. Nine times out of 10, it worked out."

Channeling Kraft—or, at least, who I thought she was—I replied to Freihofer that I was willing to get hot and I'd take my chances with getting ditched.

"OK," she wrote back. "I can see you are going to Venice!"

PART 2: THE SHREWD DEAL

"Although it surprises some people, we do not consider it unusual that our big-game expert is a lady who has taken trophies on five continents and has fallen down the sides of a few mountains in the process. There are something like 18 million licensed hunters in this country. The Winchester gun manufacturers estimate that about one million of these are women. Winchester admits that this estimate is little better than a wild guess, but it seems reasonable to us because wherever hunting guns are fired today, in local bogs or on distant scarps, we find a growing proportion of women."

Letter from the Publisher
Sports Illustrated
February 22, 1965

Virginia Kraft was born in Astoria, New York—a neighborhood in Queens, across the East River from the Upper East Side of Manhattan—on February 19, 1930. Her Canadian mother Mary Flora Gillis, known to most as Jean, was the daughter of a prominent Nova Scotian builder who also ran a bottling plant. Jean was a housewife who had dinner on the table every night at 6 p.m. Kraft's father George John Kraft, born to working-class German immigrants, became a successful sales executive, first for a printing company and later for Johnson & Johnson.

As a kid, Kraft loved spending time outside during the day and listening to the radio at night. She owned her first horse at age 8 and played polo as a young child. She and her younger sister Jacqueline spent summers with their family on Long Island. After excelling in high school, she went on to attend Barnard, an all-women's college in Manhattan, where she majored in English and participated in extracurriculars like the student newspaper, the junior class play, the Newman Club, and other social committees.

Kraft was also the subject of a 1949 college newspaper story about a coed European tour she was organizing at Eastern colleges to take place the following year. For $1,148—the equivalent of nearly $15,000 today—students on the all-inclusive trip would visit England, Holland, Belgium, Switzerland, Italy, and France. "This is a tour I have arranged for myself and students like myself," she told the paper, "who would otherwise go to Europe alone, with *no* experience arranging accommodations and travel."

After graduating in 1951, Kraft wanted to work in magazines but wasn't content with the typical roles open to women as secretaries or on staff at women's publications. She had been raised to do something different. When she was just 5 or 6 years old, Kraft recounted in a speech to Siena College graduates in 2012, her father lifted her onto a windowsill on a clear night and pointed to the full moon, which looked close enough to touch. "You can go there someday," he told her, decades before space travel was a reality. "You can do anything you want as long as you want it and work for it. The whole universe is out there waiting for you."

What she wanted was excitement and something other than writing about hemlines. So she opened the phone book and started searching for outdoor publications. The first listing she saw was *Field & Stream*, the preeminent outdoor magazine at the time. She had no real experience relevant to the hunting and fishing publication, but she walked into the office cold and talked to an editor who was "at first somewhat startled at the prospect of a young woman invading his bastion of maledom," Kraft told Siena graduates. He quickly calculated that he could pay her a third of what men earned for the same job, but she would still make three times what she could at fashion magazines. "We both felt we had made a pretty shrewd deal."

Over the years, articles written about Kraft provided various accounts on how and when she learned to hunt. Among them: she started as a child, she taught herself to shoot in order to land her first job, she learned from her first husband, and she learned while at *SI*. In her speech to Siena graduates, she said she learned to fish and hunt—first with a bow and arrow, then with a gun—on weekends while at *Field & Stream*. However it started, she was seemingly willing to fake it until she made it. "She kind of bull-shitted her way into the job," says Erickson, citing the version he was told. "She'd never hunted in her life."

Kraft soon got her first introduction to what it was going to take to succeed in a heavily male space. Forgoing recognition was part of the deal. While there, she wrote for the magazine under a male pseudonym: Seth Briggs.

As Briggs, Kraft appears to have been responsible for writing a one-page running feature called "Outdoor Questions." Briggs—or Kraft—addressed reader questions, mostly about animals, hunting, and camping: how to keep butter fresh on a camping trip, why whales die when they're beached, how long venison can last in a freezer before it spoils, if a black bear can run at 50 miles per hour, and whether a lion or tiger was the superior beast.

Although Kraft's name never appeared in the magazine, reading the column with her in mind conjures an image of a young, ambitious writer, collecting knowledge, accumulating experience, and patiently observing men in the workplace. Briggs' answers, assuming they were written by Kraft, reveal occasional hints of an emerging voice and a hardening point of view. In July 1953, an amateur fisherman told "Outdoor Questions" about the guilt he felt every time he hooked a fish. "Actually, I don't think there is much pain at all," answered Briggs/Kraft. "The low state of development of the nervous system apparently explains why a fish is relatively insensible to the pain caused by a hook."

Briggs, not Kraft, appeared on the masthead as an associate editor when she started at *Field & Stream*, becoming "department editor" at the end of 1953. But the name actually preceded her, first appearing in the magazine starting in 1927 and remaining there for years after Kraft moved to *SI*. It suggests "Briggs" was a placeholder name for staffers who hadn't yet made a name for themselves—a regular practice in many magazines and newspapers at the time.

At *Field & Stream*, Kraft worked hard. Whereas the rest of the staff left at 5 p.m., even if they were mid-sentence, she stayed at least until 7, sometimes later, studying the archives from A to Z. Over a year and a half, she "gained a Masters-worth of knowledge about the outdoors," she said, and she used that knowledge to hone her outdoor skills. Still, there didn't seem to be much in the way of additional writing opportunities for Kraft at *Field & Stream*. Although a female byline occasionally appeared on the publication's pages in the early 1950s, those stories tended to follow entrenched gender stereotypes, like a complaint-filled essay entitled "I Married a Fisherman."

How Kraft felt about her work appearing under a male name remains a matter of speculation. It's possible she was unbothered, happy to get valuable experience. But if she was like every other writer I know, she wanted to write under her own name. As she bided her time and practiced writing convincingly as a man, she could have studied her male colleagues and their confidence. It didn't take long for her to get her shot.

PART 3: A CLEAR HIERARCHY

"For the first time since I had stepped from the cab at the palace gates, the guards, soldiers and servants mysteriously vanished, and I found myself entering the imperial reception room alone. Before I realized what had happened, a gray haired man in a double-breasted suit was striding toward me with the long, smooth steps of an athlete, his hand outstretched and a broad smile on his surprisingly young face, fixing his warm brown eyes directly on mine, the Shah of Iran said in a soft, low voice, 'I have been waiting a long time for your visit.'"

Virginia Kraft
"A Lady Hunts with the Shah"
Sports Illustrated
December 24, 1962

The early '50s, when Kraft started in journalism, was the *Mad Men* era, and according to Michael MacCambridge, author of *The Franchise: A History of Sports Illustrated Magazine*, Time Inc. was "*Mad Men* on steroids." The company, based in midtown Manhattan, already published *Time*, *Life*, and *Fortune* magazines. Looking to add to their portfolio, discussions began about relaunching *SI*, reviving the title of two previously failed publications by other publishers.

Conversations about the third iteration of the magazine involved booze, crude conversations, and jokes about whorehouses. To hash out the details, 67 male executives from Time Inc. met at a country club in South Carolina in 1954. There was golf. But, likely, no women.

Kraft left *Field & Stream* and joined the new *SI* staff as a reporter. Like most of the other women hires, she would have a supporting role for the heavily male writing and editing staff. But she didn't see why her gender should get in the way of her ambitions. "The magazine was brand new, the beats were up for grabs, and advancement was based on performance and competition—being male or female had nothing to do with it," she told a reporter for Copley News Service in 1975. "So I ended up on what is considered the most 'masculine' beat—hunting."

The first issue of the relaunched *SI* hit newsstands on August 16, 1954. From cover to cover, more than half of its 148 pages were advertisements, heralding Ford Thunderbirds, Chryslers, Goodyear tires, Seagram's gin, a new automatic shotgun produced by Winchester, and Skyway luggage "geared to the needs of a man who gets around." Only a handful depicted women or women's goods: the department store Bonwit Teller, Keepsake engagement rings, Vassarette shapewear, and Samsonite suitcases.

Every story was written by a man and all were about men, animals, or both. Features covered Roger Bannister, who had recently run the first sub-4-minute mile; a court battle between bubble gum manufacturers over baseball trading cards; and an appreciation of the important role that beavers play in protecting forests. Although no stories were about women, they appeared in photographs, including a "pretty, well-tanned" 15-year-old golfer, Betsy Cullen, who would later become a professional.

A woman did show up, sort of, in a cheeky one-page feature department called "Hotbox," which asked readers to respond to the question, "What sport provokes the most arguments in your home?" *Golf* was the response given by Warren Austin Jr., an attorney from Burlington, Vermont, whose wife remained nameless and faceless in his answer even as he praised her skills. "My wife was afraid of becoming a golf widow," he wrote. "I didn't want her to tag along, but she would trail me to the country club against my orders. There she'd take golf lessons. Now she teaches me. It's downright humiliating. But the arguments are not so frequent. She's won."

The women, including Kraft, who helped make that first issue happen worked behind the scenes as assistants and reporters. From the get-go, they conducted interviews, got quotes, checked facts, and did all the grunt work for writers. The job was a place to prove your worth. If you were good, you might work your way up to a writer position, says Curry Kirkpatrick, who joined *SI* as a reporter in 1966 and transitioned to writing during his 27 years there.

There was a clear hierarchy. After Time Inc. relocated its offices within midtown Manhattan to the 20th floor of a 48-story skyscraper in 1959, reporters toiled away in cubicles in a large room called the bullpen, whereas writers and editors worked at the other end of the hallway. By the time Kirkpatrick arrived, Kraft's door was down that hall.

Although Kraft has been described as the first woman on staff at *SI*, she wasn't the only woman reporter on the masthead in the early months, nor was she the first to become a staff writer. But she was the only one who soon moved into a steady writing job that involved major adventure.

In 1954, Kraft joined a pheasant hunt with other members of the *SI* staff at a preserve in upstate New York. Also on the trip was Red Smith, a *New York Herald Tribune* columnist and frequent *SI* contributor whose later work for *The New York Times* was syndicated in nearly 300 papers nationwide and earned him a Pulitzer. Smith noticed Kraft, who showed up the night before the other staffers, went out early the next morning, and shot a buck with a brand-new shotgun. Smith's column about the hunt, which appeared in December that year, described Kraft as a "pretty gun moll" who "smiled with cool composure" but confessed that the sport was new to her. "It was the first deer I ever saw," said Kraft, who told Siena graduates that the hunt is how she landed the *SI* job. A few months later she wrote her first story.

On May 2, 1955, less than a year after starting with the magazine, Kraft's debut bylined article appeared, an ambitious feature about joining General Francisco Franco's hunting party. The over-the-top expedition was a massacre: 92 hunters and 350 servants downed 34 boars and 82 bucks, including a 20-point stag. Even though Kraft never fired a shot, raising her gun only once, it was a dramatic opener. The story set the template for her career at *SI*.

How Kraft managed to land this first assignment is uncertain—it was likely part of a press junket organized in partnership with other Time Inc. publications, says MacCambridge—but she would go on to write dozens of similar stories about hunting and fishing in exotic locales, often with notable, wealthy, and sometimes controversial men. There is no sign that she or *SI* were bothered by Franco's fascist and dictatorial regime—or by the carnage of the hunt.

Not long after starting at *SI*, Kraft met her first husband, Robert Grimm, at a cocktail party in New York City, says her oldest daughter Tana Aurland. Wealthy and 10 years older than Kraft, Grimm had done his share of traveling before they met, once spending two months in Cannes, France. He eventually owned an advertising agency and marketed his own inventions, including a cigarette holder. After they married in 1955, Kraft moved in with him at the Gipsy Trail Club, a private membership community in Carmel, New York. "It's 60 miles to midtown Manhattan but may as well be 600," Kraft told a newspaper reporter. The enclave, still active today, includes a clubhouse, a horse stable, tennis courts, and space for trap shooting. With easy access to hunting near home, Kraft honed her stalking skills, cultivating both an obsession and a path toward career advancement and notoriety.

PART 4: STONE-COLD KILLER

"Marion Rice Hart, the pilot, is indeed a little old lady, though at 83 the description makes her cringe almost as much as when she is called 'Widow Hart' or a 'flying grandmother'. She is quick to point out that she is neither. While she has no objections to motherhood other than that it leads to grandmotherhood, she has never been a mother, and she was divorced, not widowed, from a fellow named Hart whom she did object to because he insisted on asking her why she could not act like other women."

Virginia Kraft
"Flying in the Face of Age"
Sports Illustrated
January 13, 1975

Sports Illustrated was already covering hunting and fishing sporadically, but Kraft soon staked claim to the beat. Before long she was regularly striking out on harrowing adventures in wild places. In November 1957, for example, she wrote of her travels to the Bob Marshall Wilderness, a vast roadless area in Montana. Taking along a single pair of pants, six pairs of socks, camping gear, a variety of warm layers, and perfume in lieu of deodorant, she set out on horseback at around 5 a.m. with three guides—two state game rangers and a game biologist, all male—in pursuit of elk and skittish mountain goats.

After six miles on horseback, the quartet started to hike, scrambling on hands and feet over shale slides. Navigating wide crevasses, they climbed to the top of a 9,000-foot mountain, where they spotted five mountain goats on the other side of a boulder-strewn canyon. Then came nearly an hour of tiptoeing, crawling, and zigzagging to stay downwind. Once Kraft had crept close enough, she aimed and shot, bringing down the biggest of the five.

The story's multipage spread features a photo of Kraft, then 27, crouching behind her trophy goat, holding up its horned head, smiling as though there were nowhere else she would rather be. In a larger photo, she holds a rifle and beams over another trophy: a 400-pound black bear that wandered into camp. "It was quickly converted," she wrote, "into a long-desired bearskin rug."

Stories written about Kraft in the 1950s and '60s often dwelled on her looks and femininity. She was a "brunette beauty with sparkling eyes" that shone with the ruddy glow that comes from time spent outdoors. On her travels, she styled her hair, packed a full set of perfumes and face creams, and wore bespoke hunting pants, boots, and gloves with leather backs and corduroy fingers. As fit as Kraft was—5'4" and maybe 120 lbs.—she didn't look it. One female reporter noted, "Despite the fact that Virginia's athletic abilities are such that she could outclimb the Shah's own Master of the Hunt in the rugged 20,000-foot Iranian mountains, Virginia Kraft gives no hint of muscles in her looks or delightful manner."

Writers who covered her accomplishments also marveled at how such a beautiful woman could hunt so well. "When pretty Virginia Kraft talks about outdoor sports, the men perk up their ears and listen, and when she writes, the men read every word," reads a 1959 United Press International article about a lecture Kraft gave to an all-male audience. "The reason—simply that Virginia Kraft, or Mrs. Robert Grimm in private life—really speaks man language on the subject of hunting or fishing."

For her part, Kraft argued that women's patience made them particularly good hunters. She may have spoken with the accent of a New Yorker and looked enough like an all-American model to once appear in an ad for *Family Circle* magazine, but in the wilderness of men, she moved with stealth.

Kraft came up with many of her own story ideas, Aurland says, and they often involved exotic places and notable people. Apart from Franco, she hunted with the Shah of Iran, the king and queen of Nepal, and King Hussein of Jordan. Grimm accompanied her on some expeditions, doubling as photographer and companion in places where it was considered culturally inappropriate for a woman to travel alone. Accommodations could be lavish. To prepare for the hunt in Nepal, 1,100 locals spent two months clearing trails and landing strips in the jungle. The hunting party included at least two dozen jeeps.

Diving into Kraft's life and work, I found a lot to admire. But her decision to go all-in on hunting as a beat planted seeds of discomfort in me. My writing about animals, conservation, and the environment in the 21st century tends to focus on saving species, not killing them. I haven't eaten meat since I was 19. But Kraft—whom Erickson affectionately described as a "stone-cold killer"—slaughtered just about every major charismatic creature on earth, detailing the drama of her hunts in the pages of a major national magazine. Then, after filing her stories, she kept and displayed their heads, tusks, and bodies as trophies. How could I look to her as a hero when so many of the stories she told made me wince in pain?

PART 5: IN HER SIGHTS

"At first I did not see it, so perfectly did it blend into the blacks and grays and golds of the jungle's filtered sunlight. It watched me with fierce, amber eyes, as if it had known of this meeting all along and had been waiting for me to arrive. This was the big cat, the king of the New World, the prize at the end of a search that had begun almost 10 years before. Ten years of plotting and planning, and more than 10,000 miles of traveling, had led me finally to the base of this tree in the Mato Grosso (Great Forest) of Brazil, deep in the interior of South America."

Virginia Kraft
"A Meeting in the Mato Grosso"
Sports Illustrated
February 22, 1965

In 2011, while in the jungle of Costa Rica's Osa Peninsula, I interviewed a jaguar researcher, a woman who had been studying the elusive and increasingly rare animals for eight years but had never seen one in the wild. I thought of that biologist again when I read about Kraft's own encounter with a jaguar.

She had already taken several fruitless trips in search of the wild cats in Mexico, Colombia, and Venezuela. In October 1964, she made another attempt, this time to the Brazilian Mato Grosso, a vast, hard-to-get-to tropical forest full of swamps created by thousands of tributaries of the Paraguay River.

Kraft spent nearly three weeks in her element, sleeping in camps, waking before sunrise, and riding horses through the spectacular landscape, sometimes getting lost but always finding her way. "These days were some of the best I have ever known," she wrote. Several times her group thought they were close to seeing a jaguar, but they were repeatedly stymied by thick brush, bitten by fire ants, and stung by wasps.

Finally they saw one. The scene erupted in chaos. Dogs barked. Men shouted. Kraft heard two gunshots and thought someone had killed it. But no, there it was. A spotted feline, black and gold, perfectly still, camouflaged by the speckled sunlight of the forest.

This moment in Kraft's story gripped me with recognition of the rare kind of joy that comes when nature shows you its cards. It is a glimpse of what the world would be without people, something I had experienced just a handful of times, including once while on assignment in Peru.

Years ago, sitting in an inflatable raft on a tributary of the Amazon River, I also saw a jaguar. Like Kraft's journey, our trip had become a survival story, filled with venomous stingrays, killer bees, vampire bats, excruciatingly itchy insect bites, dwindling food supplies, and agonizingly slow progress through a river that was not deep enough to paddle through. Then, suddenly, the majestic cat was standing shin deep in water downstream from me. It stood still and silent, not 100 feet away, seemingly relaying the message that my hardships were not the center of the tale. For a long and precious minute, it stared directly into my eyes.

Kraft must have seen this look in the cat's eyes, too—how could she not? But after finally setting her gaze on the animal that had eluded her for nearly a decade, she raised her rifle, took aim, and shot it dead. In the *SI* photo spread, she proudly holds the cat's limp carcass. A caption below boasts of its size as the seventh largest jaguar trophy on record.

Lost in the reverie of my own memory, I should have seen a violent ending. I had already learned to expect this kind of heartbreaking conclusion in Kraft's work. But it still pained me each time. She wrote about nature with the lyricism of a poet. Her stories included rich characters and revealing quotes. They brimmed with sensory details and suspense. And, too often, they ended with the deafening crack of a gun.

After a trip to Alaskan sea ice with scientists for a 1968 story on concerns about polar bear populations, she hired a guide and killed one. On a canoe trip down the wild Serpent River through the Tehuantepec jungles in Mexico, the group slayed javelinas and tapirs. By 1970, she had taken down a tiger, an elephant, a rhino, a polar bear, an ibex, a caribou, and a moose.

She was, unapologetically, both an adventuress and a conqueress. *SI* senior writer William Leggett called her, in 1981, "one of the best shots that ever lived—male or female."

PART 6: THE GALS WERE GAME

"If her husband is not a fisherman, angling offers a woman even broader horizons. It is her entree to new adventures and new alliances. It is a thoroughly aboveboard excuse to get away from home and hubby as frequently as she wishes, to whip off to the islands or the interior or to one of a dozen resorts and spas where, alone, she might be viewed with suspicion, but where as an angler she is never alone. Her travels are always complete with rods, reels, boat and crew—a most respectable and businesslike combination. The fact that the captains and mates on the top sports-fishing boats are frequently young and handsome and that the husbands of women who can afford to fish such boats are more often than not old and faded though rich, is not entirely coincidental."

Virginia Kraft
"Scourge of the Seven Seas"
Sports Illustrated
July 10, 1967

The Venice Marina is about as close as you can get to the southern tip of Louisiana, a maze of waterways and marshes that separates the Mississippi River from the Gulf of Mexico and is ideal habitat for sea trout, flounder, snapper, marlin, and other big game. Angling is so important to the region's economy that Venice dubs itself "The Fishing Capital of the World."

The day before the tournament began provided a chance to hang out, warm up, and scope out where the fish might be biting. Unlike on tournament days, competitors were more relaxed about bringing along a guest. As the boat left the dock at 6:30 a.m., Weingart, the 65-year-old competitor from North Carolina who would be looking for her guide Jack the next morning, marveled that she had made it there at all. A cancer survivor, she had developed a 103°F fever and blistered lips a few days earlier. She was taking six medications and relying on the other women, now some of her best friends, to help her out. "This is where I feel most alive," she said. "Even when I don't feel well, I feel good out here."

In some ways, the modern version of the group echoes the IWFA's early years, when Kraft chronicled a mix of competition and fun that defined the organization's beginnings. Back then the women were fabulous. During the first IWFA billfish tournament in 1956 in Florida, Kraft detailed some of the atypical fishing attire worn by the event's 66 competitors: silk pants, Chanel sweaters, gold lamé pants, a full-length mink, hairdos adorned with ribbons and lace, and hazardous footwear, although no high heels.

They were also fearless. In 10-foot waves and chilly temperatures during one tournament, competitors puked over the side of the boats. Yet soon after, the women of the IWFA were beating men at their own game, crushing world records and winning coed tournaments. They changed the sport, too, insisting that fish be thrown back alive into the sea to count for points. And they were fierce. At a competition in Cuba, the IWFA team beat Fidel Castro, who didn't catch a single fish. "Even the most begrudging captain had to admit that, if nothing else, the gals were game,"

Kraft wrote. "Before long the captains were also admitting, reluctantly or not, that there was nothing more formidable than a female who has learned how to fish."

Kraft's writing style hints at the way *SI* reflected society's view of women in the '60s. It is unclear how much of that culture Kraft embodied, how much was pushed upon her by a male editorial staff, or how much of it she intentionally included to satisfy the expectations of her editors and readers. But she scoffed at the women's unconventional attire and embedded insults throughout the story that diminished their accomplishments. "The lady may have trouble figuring out the phone bill," she wrote in 1967, "but give her one glimpse of a leaping sailfish at 200 yards and with computer speed she will come up with a pretty accurate estimate of its length, weight and girth."

In writing about the first big-game fishing organization created for women only, Kraft dwelled on the question of why women might want or need such a group. In her view, most of those reasons revolved around men. Women with fishing husbands cast their lines because of jealousy, curiosity, or competitiveness. Even when they won major prizes, there was no sign—at least in Kraft's writing—that the women did it for pleasure, joy, or love for the sport.

For those whose husbands didn't fish, the sport offered opportunities to get away from home and have relatively respectable adventures without arousing suspicion about what they were up to. But as a bonus, Kraft noted, they could spend time on fishing boats with male captains. Good captains were in such demand for their ability to help even mediocre anglers win tournaments, Kraft wrote in 1963, that prospective employers sometimes bribed them with extravagant gifts: split-level homes, sports cars, even marriage proposals.

For these female anglers, Kraft made it clear that catching men was still as much of a sport as hauling in fish, and maybe even more important. Kraft ended her 1967 story not with the women or with the marine life, but with the line, "Men, we still need you!"

During my day with the women of the IWFA, I noticed something Kraft didn't acknowledge: the strong sense of community. These women clearly adore one another. As they fished, they took breaks to drink beer, eat snacks, and pee off the side of the boat together. "When I am out on the water, it's almost like a religious experience because I am so thankful to be able to be out there and to be with such a great group of women who love me like a sister," Weingart told me before the trip. "They don't expect anything out of me other than just be kind, go fishing, and have fun." At the tournament launch party, nine of the competitors dressed up in shark costumes and performed a choreographed dance for a room full of women who whooped and cheered.

The women fish to win, but the long game goes deeper. "We come for fishing, friendship, and fun," says Kathy Gillen, past IWFA president. "A lot of people stay members until they die."

By the end of my time at the tournament, I felt so moved by the connections I saw that I found myself reflecting on the importance of these kinds of enduring friendships in my own life. Kraft did not. She probably knew her male audience wouldn't have wanted to read about women bonding with women, even if her editors had let it through. "Within the lush though limited captain market, trading is always brisk," she wrote. "The rules are simple: every gal for herself—and the stakes are high."

Nobody at the Louisiana tournament had heard of Kraft or read her stories about the IWFA before my visit, nor had they heard her views on the motivations of their predecessors. When I read this excerpt to the women while they fished, they laughed hard, especially after the part about catching men. A few female fishing guides are available now—although not many, said IFWA board member Connie O'Day. They still hear from male guides that women are better clients because they actually listen, something Kraft noted, too. All agreed that fishing with one another is different, and still preferable, to fishing with their husbands.

Caught in the middle of the exchange given the small size of the boat, Brent Ballay, the captain, smirked while the women hooted. "I'll keep my mouth shut," he said. "I'd rather fish with women."

PART 7: MRS. ROBERT GRIMM

"Virginia Kraft has a full personal life; privately, she is Mrs. Robert D. Grimm, wife of an advertising executive and mother of four. She is also our hunter-writer because she fills the two major requirements of the job. The first of these requirements is an obvious one. She likes to hunt. She relishes the ordeal, enjoys the laughs and appreciates the challenges of the sport."

Letter from the Publisher
Sports Illustrated
February 22, 1965

When she returned home from reporting trips, Kraft wrote in her third-floor office of the Carmel house, which was filled with trophies from her hunting trips: the heads and skins of caribou, buffalo, polar bear, and other animals. "When other kids came to our house, they said it was like a museum of natural history," says Aurland. "To us, that was totally natural."

Kraft was disciplined about her work, and she depended on live-in nannies and caretakers for her kids and home. "We run a tight ship around here," she told a newspaper reporter in 1968. "When I'm working, it's just like normal office hours and I'm not disturbed." At the end of the workday, she played with her kids and spent a lot of time outdoors—riding horses, skin diving, fishing, sailing, and playing tennis, which she wrote a book about (one of five she penned during her career). Not knowing what else to do with the mandatory six-month leave of absence forced on her during her pregnancies, she wrote a book during each one. She took many of her activities to extremes. A finalist in several world championship fishing tournaments, she skied competitively, raced sailboats, earned trophies for winning a national hot-air balloon race, and, according to some accounts, was inducted into the Underwater Hall of Fame for diving.

Although Kraft was often away from her kids, she took each one on adventures. Aurland remembers a month-long journey to Africa in 1972. In Ethiopia, they met Emperor Haile Selassie. When they arrived at his palace, Aurland presented him with a rifle. Then she played with the emperor's Chihuahuas while her mother met with Selassie. After returning home, she was surprised to receive a gift of one of the dogs' puppies—sent all the way to New York from the emperor.

For weeks, mother and daughter camped in the rainforest with their Ethiopian guides, waking at 3 a.m. to sit in a blind and wait for nyala, a spiral-horned antelope, to show up. Kraft never appeared bothered about being the only woman in these situations, Aurland says, equally comfortable in a five-star hotel or a pup tent. She espoused flexibility. "Let's play it by ear," was her favorite phrase. That kind of confidence got her ahead but could also be intimidating—a judgment that women who work in predominately male spaces continue to face.

Kraft did face her share of struggles as a working mother of four in the 1970s, Aurland says, especially after she and Grimm separated in 1970 and divorced the next year because of "irreconcilable differences," according to her nephew Jon Wickers. After the split, the kids, ages 7 to 12, lived with Kraft in the house and regularly saw their dad, who lived nearby. Kraft did her best to keep things normal. She made Halloween costumes, cooked dinners, and cultivated silly traditions at home. Whenever one of their eight cats had a birthday, the pet was allowed to sit on a special stool at the table.

I wonder whether other suburban stay-at-home moms of the era judged Kraft for her commitment to work. Even if they did, she didn't let them get in her way.

As she traveled the world and churned out stories—moving into a staff writing position at *SI* in 1959 and an associate editor role in 1966—other women at Time Inc. struggled to land the same kinds of opportunities. Men were more quickly promoted from reporter to writer positions, according to MacCambridge, and women were less likely to get plum field reporting assignments. During the 1967 Masters golf tournament in Augusta, Georgia, *SI* sent a team of reporters that included just one woman, journalist Sarah Ballard. After a day of watching golf and conducting interviews, Ballard was also expected to cook dinner.

Nobody said women couldn't do the work of writing, but the culture of the place implied it. André Laguerre, the magazine's managing editor from 1960 to 1974, regularly worked until 3 a.m., then returned a few hours later at 9 or 10. He expected his staff to do the same, whether male or female, parents or childless. After-work drinking sessions were also part of the deal. "*Sports Illustrated* made nearly impossible demands on people's personal lives," MacCambridge says. "It was that kind of remorseless place that Virginia Kraft would have had to make her way in."

Kraft did more than just make her way. She won journalism awards, gave talks, appeared on television, and garnered media attention for her successes as a woman in both hunting and writing. But from the perspective of history, Kraft stayed strangely under the radar. Despite her pioneering status, MacCambridge didn't mention her once in his 400-plus-page book about the history of the magazine; her name didn't come up in his research. Although he regrets the omission, he says he didn't have anything to work with. "She was a trailblazer and an important figure, and I feel bad," he says. "But I don't even have an anecdote."

Kraft's erasure from the history of sports writing may have something to do with her general absence from the offices of *SI* during her career there. Distancing herself from the boys-will-be-boys, hard-drinking culture based at the Time & Life Building in Rockefeller Center, Kraft lived in a world of her own. She spent about a third of each year traveling on assignment, making the outlandish claim that she covered 200,000 miles annually. And although that number is hard to believe, she was clearly prolific: In 1967 alone, she published 10 major features, including one of her stories on the IWFA. (That year she also wrote about hunting in Jordan, hunting in the Grand Canyon, fishing in Australia, and racing in a dogsled competition in Alaska.) When not in the field on assignment, she generally went to the office only a couple of times a week, staying in an apartment in the city as needed. More often, like some of the other senior writers, she wrote from home.

Kraft was something of an enigma to her colleagues. When Kirkpatrick arrived at the magazine in the mid-1960s, Kraft was already both well established and scarce in the office. On the days she did come in, she kept to her end of the hallway, less social than the writers who invited reporters to their offices or even dropped by the bullpen to chat. Kirkpatrick rarely saw Kraft, whom many called Ginny. On the handful of times he spotted or even exchanged words with her, she seemed aristocratic and classy, on another level. "I remember her having an office way down the hall at the other end, with the editors and writers and me thinking that she was like a big, big deal," Kirkpatrick says. "I remember being very intimidated."

He wasn't the only one. Around the same time, Carolyn Keith started working as a summer intern at the magazine. On the only occasion she recalls interacting with Kraft, the writer emerged from her office as Keith walked by. Kraft complimented Keith's clothing, which surprised the young intern. "At that point, she was very well known, very upper crusty," and "she was dressed like somebody that had the money to do it properly," Keith says. "She looked stunning."

In fact, Kraft was so elusive at *SI* that every other staffer I talked with for this story who overlapped with her responded that they didn't have anything of substance to say about her because she was either gone a lot or too important to interact with them, although she was pleasant if you managed to get a minute with her.

Beyond *SI* alumni, Kraft is otherwise unknown among many who do parallel work today. I talked to a number of journalists and experts on women in sports journalism for this story. None knew who she was before I told them about her.

It is no surprise, then, that Kraft also appears to have been invisible when, in the spring of 1970—a few months before an estimated 50,000 people walked down Fifth Avenue as part of the Women's Strike for Equality March—the New York Attorney General's office filed charges on behalf of more than 100 women at Time Inc. who complained of gender-based discrimination at *Time*, *Life*, *Fortune*, and *SI*, in violation of state law. The move followed a similar action at *Newsweek*, where 46 women had filed a gender discrimination suit not long before.

Although 60 women were employed at Time Inc. as researchers at the time of the lawsuit, men held all the highest-paid positions and women made only a fraction of the income. Women averaged $15,000 year to the men's $35,000, according to journalist Ann Crittenden, who wrote a 2020 article about the conflict and its own near erasure from history. In 1970, after three years of working as a researcher at *Fortune*, Crittenden tried to move up to a writer position, but her male editors insisted she was too valuable as researcher. Other women felt similarly blocked from promotions. Time Inc. denied the charges. But soon after the filing, 23 women at *SI* signed a petition to support the cause. According to lore, Laguerre heard about the suit and asked, "Do we have 23 women at *Sports Illustrated*?"

At all the Time Inc. publications, men dominated leadership roles. At *Time* magazine, all 12 senior editors and 19 of the 20 associate editors were men. These kinds of gender disparities may have been acceptable in the Roaring '20s, the women of Time Inc. said in support of the lawsuit, according to news coverage at the time. But in 1970, the obstacles they faced were humiliating and illegal. There was a similar gender breakdown at *SI*, where the masthead from May 1970 reveals one woman editor camouflaged in a field of male counterparts: Virginia Kraft.

After the case settled in 1971, improvements came grudgingly, and then only for women who hadn't signed the petition, according to MacCambridge. When Laguerre promoted Pat Ryan to a senior editor position that year, he offered her a raise of $3,000, which would up her salary to $21,000 a year. She insisted he match what men in the same position were making. Reluctantly, he gave her $28,000. "Every woman who fought through the glass ceiling was fiercely self-reliant," MacCambridge says. "You had to be really willful and resilient to succeed there."

From her perch as senior member of the staff with four children—three daughters and a son, born between 1959 and 1964—Kraft left no evidence of any involvement in the lawsuit and no public comments about it. Maybe she was in Carmel with her kids. After all, family was very important to her, says Adrienne White, 94, a college classmate and longtime friend of Kraft's. Perhaps she faced financial stress as a divorced mother with a full house of young children. Or maybe she was away on reporting trips when other women were fighting to catch a break.

Still, her apparent absence from the struggle is notable. I found it unsettling. She had been doing men's work for well over a decade, and she had the potential to influence a generation of women behind her. Instead, it seems, she made a deliberate decision in 1970 to pursue her own interests rather than fighting for other women. "I don't remember her saying, 'Listen girls, let's have lunch together and talk about it,'" Keith says. "She was not part of the daily or weekly scene."

There is another possibility. Maybe Kraft saw that choice as a different way of fighting the fight. Her contribution to women's lib, she told a reporter in 1972, was that she "wanted to cover hunting and fishing and the editors had no objections." She didn't consider herself a feminist, Aurland says, so much as motivated to do what the men were doing. She was an individualist, Wickers adds: industrious, independent, and always busy.

Whatever she thought about the lawsuit and women's struggle, Kraft had, it seems, fully embraced her role as a huntress, tending to her own pack while stalking her ambitions. This contrast, more than anything else, may have set her up to be overlooked. To make it at *SI* as a woman in a field of men, she'd had to become a kind of apex predator, determined and willing to take what she wanted. But leaning in to an ambitious male persona actually made her harder to recognize as a role model later, especially through a contemporary lens in a world where so much wildlife is now at risk and women are supposed to have power independent of men.

Kraft's views on nature, in particular, have since proved controversial. In the pages of *SI* in 1963, she criticized Rachel Carson's *Silent Spring*, citing sources who argued that pesticides were good for wildlife. To this day, multiple books point out her critical take of Carson, while her role as a woman journalist remains largely unmentioned. Her passion for hunting wasn't always popular, either; today the beat no longer has a place in major sports publications. She could have been remembered forever as a trailblazer. Instead, the very thing she needed to do to be a pioneer—hunting—may be what prevented her from gaining that recognition.

Even at the peak of her journalistic success, Kraft felt like many people didn't understand her. She appeared on *The David Frost Show* in 1971, described only as a "big game huntress" rather than a writer or even an angler. In the interview, Frost ambushed Kraft. "He told her he would ask about stories but attacked her," Aurland says.

Still, with her persona well established by then, Kraft did not back down in the interview. Wickers, who was 5 or 6 years old when it aired, watched it on a black-and-white TV. "She kept her composure perfectly, and she explained that if everything's utilized and recycled properly, it's the healthiest way, it's the way of nature," he says. "She boxed her way out of a corner, and it was extremely, extremely impressive. I never forgot it."

In her mind, Kraft was an animal lover, no matter how many creatures she killed. The family had many pets: horses, cats, dogs. Wickers, who lived with Kraft and her children for a summer when he was 16, once watched her, nearly in tears, carefully pull a rodent out of the mouth of one of the cats. Another time she scolded a hunter for improperly taking down a game animal, causing it to suffer. In multiple stories, she reported on conservation efforts that fought for kangaroos, white rhinos, the Arabian oryx, white crowned pigeons, and others.

"Big game hunters are often misunderstood," she told *The Tennessee Sun* in 1970. Illegal poaching was the problem, not licensed hunters. Hunters, she said, "don't simply destroy animals, but they replace them and are deeply concerned with ecology."

I found myself facing a paradox in both the life of Virginia Kraft and the way I thought of her. Just as she simultaneously adored animals and killed them, I both detest the idea of hunting and admit she had a point. Like Kraft, I have written about counterintuitive environmental efforts that sacrifice living things for the sake of a bigger picture. I have covered conservation projects that kill invasive animals to save native ones. And I have documented the way that hunting groups, in order to preserve the animals they want to shoot down, have allocated billions of dollars to protect vast habitats. Those efforts have, among other benefits, allowed wetland fowl to thrive amid global declines of other kinds of birds. Although some of Kraft's views seem misguided now, someday mine may, too.

Kraft may have continued killing animals and pursuing her dreams while other women vocally fought the patriarchy. But in her life and through her words, I started to see something more subtle, and possibly more subversive. Given the obstacles that stood between her and success in the context of her time, she was willing to stand behind her belief that two opposing concepts could coexist. The courage required for her to do that highlights how far we've come over the past 50 years.

PART 8: UNEQUAL OPPORTUNITIES

"DuBois' answer arrived the next day: 'Women don't sled-dog-race with men for much the same reason they don't play football with them—too rough.' But he was enthusiastic, anyway, about the idea of my entering and he soon managed to arrange for a team of dogs.... Busy in New York on other assignments, I undertook to prepare myself physically by lifting weights, doing sit-ups and knee bends, running along crowded sidewalks past startled doormen, riding stationary bicycles and not-so-stationary horses and by jogging several times a day up and down the 16 flights of stairs to my apartment. On the day I was to leave for Alaska, I was a regular female Jack Armstrong."

Virginia Kraft
"Belle of the Mushers"
Sports Illustrated
January 23, 1967

With an insatiable appetite for adventure and new experiences, Kraft made it clear through her actions that women could do anything men did. With that approach, she laid out a kind of playbook for how to follow in her footsteps: Act without hesitation and display only confidence. Equity, her stories seem to say, was there for the taking.

But Kraft was not the beginning of the end of gender imbalances in sports, outdoor, and adventure journalism—far from it. Although women now outnumber men in journalism schools and programs in the U.S., sports journalism remains stubbornly male. According to data from more than 100 websites and newspapers compiled by Richard Lapchick, director of the Institute for Diversity and Ethics in Sport at the University of Central Florida, in 2021, fewer than 15% of sports reporters were female, up from 10% in 2006. Just under 17% of sports editors were female, compared with 5% in 2006. Nearly 70 years after Kraft joined *SI* in 1954, men continue to dominate the most important jobs: editors, columnists, executive management positions, long-form feature writers. The situation is even worse for people of color, particularly women. The survey didn't mention nonbinary or trans people.

When Vicki Michaelis, director of the Carmical Sports Media Institute at the University of Georgia in Athens, started covering high school sports for *The Palm Beach Post* right out of college in the early 1990s, coaches called her "honey" and offered to explain the sports to her. Still, given the pivotal gains women had made in the previous decades, Michaelis was sure things were heading in the right direction.

Some of the first equitable inroads into sport journalism came in the 1940s, when sportswriter Mary Garber broke into the male-dominated newsroom and paved the way for Kraft. Then in 1978, *SI* writer Melissa Ludtke earned women reporters access to locker rooms by prevailing in a lawsuit against Major League Baseball. In 1981, Christine Brennan became the first woman sports reporter at the *Miami Herald*; in 1988, she was named the first president of the Association for Women in Sports Media. Soon after women took on more roles in the industry, covering big-time sports. "If you would have asked young me in the 1990s if [the work] would be done by 2023, I'd be like, 'For sure,'" Michaelis says. "There were other women, and we were young, so we were like, 'Man, think about what we can do in the next 20 to 30 years—this is all going to be solved!'"

But an uptick in major opportunities for women in sports journalism has occurred only recently. It wasn't until 2017 that *Outside* magazine, one of today's top adventure publications, announced efforts to improve diversity in who it covered and who did the writing. The next year, Latria Graham wrote a story for the magazine debunking stereotypes about Black people in the outdoors. I started reporting my first *Outside* feature story—about a female psychologist for a female editor—the year after that.

In a post-MeToo world it's hard to explain, even to myself, how I could have not consciously recognized that my gender might have been one of the reasons it took me 20 years to achieve one of my career goals, even as I saw younger male writers breaking in. And I'm not the only female journalist who feels this way.

In 2018, Kim Cross wrote a series of articles for *Outside* about equity in sports. As an athlete and journalist, Cross has long been familiar with being one of the only Asian-American women she knew doing everything she has done: competitive waterskiing, mountain bike coaching, award-winning sports journalism, and more.

Recently Cross started reflecting on the complicated ways that gender has played out in her career. In both sports and writing, she has noticed that women become less collaborative as they reach higher levels, where there are fewer spots for them. Women, and especially women of color, she says, have to work harder and be better to reach the same positions and achieve the same pay levels as men. "I honestly didn't feel like being a woman was a disadvantage until the last few years, when I started thinking, 'Oh, yeah, sometimes women are kind of treated like Junior Varsity in the sports writing world,'" Cross says. "Maybe I was just really naive."

In accepting the way things were because there didn't appear to be another choice, how we thought—or didn't think—may have been similar to how Kraft viewed her world. By the time the women at Time Inc. filed their 1970 lawsuit, Kraft may have already realized that she was going to advance in the very male world surrounding her only if she beat the men at their own game *and* became one of the best shots who ever lived. Maybe she had come to see herself as something different from the women who came after her. They were taking collective action, but she'd had to do it on her own. It's hard to be a role model, after all, when you're busy doing the hard work of being first.

Even if Kraft didn't act the part of a new wave feminist, marching in protest parades or signing petitions, it's possible her byline filled that role for an unknown number of women who read *SI* early on, giving them a chance to see themselves reflected in its pages. "Let's say you're a young girl reading *Sports Illustrated* in the '60s and you see Virginia as a name and a byline," says Michaelis. "That's incredibly powerful if that's something that you think you want to do."

All the currently working women journalists I spoke with said they wished they'd known of Virginia Kraft before now. Given the challenges I encountered while excavating her life in search of a hero, this sentiment struck me. Back when I'd channeled Kraft to get invited to the fishing tournament, I had wanted to see myself in her—and in many ways I did. Even as I found differences between her life and mine, I came to identify with her, including the parts I had initially viewed as shortcomings. Working, traveling, and raising kids already makes it hard to find time for anything else. I can only imagine how much harder life would be if chasing your ambitions also required ignoring society's rules. Put in the same position at the same time, I wonder how many women journalists of my generation would have turned down the opportunities Kraft seized. Or, unlike her, would we have been too timid or uncertain to seize what we wanted?

But Kraft never quit, and in that trait alone I found inspiration. Revisiting her literary legacy prompted me to think about my own career and what I want to leave behind, given the different set of circumstances I started with. I kept thinking about the day she walked into the offices of *Field & Stream* for the very first time, saw only men, and talked her way into a job anyway. Kraft did so without role models, but I have always seen women writing and women in leadership roles. She spent hours immersed in old magazines, teaching herself the language. I received mentorship from more experienced writers. Kraft may not have deliberately shown other women journalists the way forward, but with the trail women before me blazed—and an understanding of Kraft's lonesome climb—I'm now motivated to make that journey easier for the next generation of women journalists.

PART 9: HUNTER AND PREY

"For a man who owns a spread on the coast of Maine, a horse farm in Kentucky, a 100-acre estate on Long Island, a house at Saratoga, an apartment on Fifth Avenue and a Hobe Sound mansion on Florida's Gold Coast, deciding on any given day where to rest his head could be perplexing. But for Charles

Shipman Payson, the owner of all of the above as well as a
yacht and a plane, the decision is simple."

Virginia Kraft
"At Payson's Place, He's Just Plain Charlie"
Sports Illustrated
April 18, 1977

More than two decades after she started working at *SI*, Kraft
traveled to South Central Florida to hunt with Charles Shipman
Payson, the owner of the New York Mets, who was then in his late
70s. She had interviewed him before, but this time was different.
Aurland was 17 years old and, as she remembers it, got a call
from her mother while she was on that reporting trip. "You won't
believe what happened," Kraft confided in her oldest daughter.
"We were out in the buggy, and he suddenly turned to me and
kissed me."

"I always could see something like that coming, and I knew
how to fend it off without causing bad feelings," Kraft told
Newsday in 1987. "But with this man, my guard was down. I mean
he was seventy-eight years old, he had already been married to a
woman for fifty years, he was old. I didn't see him as a man. He
was simply a story."

Kraft was 47, by then an associate editor at the magazine.
Payson's health, according to some sources, was ailing, and he had
four grown children from his previous marriage to Joan Whitney
Payson, the extremely wealthy original owner of the Mets, art
collector, and horse breeder. Payson's children were older than
Kraft was. It seemed crazy.

The kiss, which was neither friendly nor fatherly, threw her
for a loop. Payson was persistent, throwing one of Kraft's trade-
mark traits back at her. "I said, 'Mom, you know what? If you
like him, it's not crazy,'" says Aurland.

Kraft's feature about Payson ran in *SI* in April 1977. In
December that year, the two were married at the Episcopal
Church of St. Mary the Virgin in Falmouth Foreside, Maine, with

around 54 guests in attendance, mostly family. Virginia Kraft became Virginia Kraft Payson.

Her new husband's children were not enthusiastic about the May-December match, complaining openly that Kraft was in it only for the money. After Payson died in 1985, they sued her for fraud, claiming she had tricked him into rewriting his will at least 16 times in the seven years they were together. The final version left most of his liquid wealth to her, including an $18 million estate and the interest on a $30 million trust fund to be split among the children after her death. To them, he bequeathed only a collection of art—albeit expensive art. Kraft argued that their love was real, that his children didn't know her, and that she was a fighter who did whatever it took to preserve his reputation and achieve her own vindication.

She won, like she usually did, although sour feelings persisted, bubbling over in 1987 news coverage of the $53.9 million sale of the Van Gogh painting "Irises," which the Payson family owned. At the time, it was an art auction record. One of Payson's daughters reportedly told *Forbes* that Kraft was "a big-game hunter and my father was the prey." (Payson's one surviving child from his first marriage to Joan Whitney declined to be interviewed for this story.) A quarter of the sale price went to charity, and the rest was put in a trust for Payson's children.

Soon after her marriage to Payson, Kraft left *SI* and said goodbye to journalism. Her last story for the magazine, on December 11, 1978, was about the invention of a machine to match tennis players with rackets—an oddly mundane service piece to finish on after more than two decades of writing wild feature stories. The couple bought a thoroughbred horse in Kentucky on a whim and a winter training facility in Florida. For a time, they owned the house on Long Island that some believe inspired the mansion F. Scott Fitzgerald described in *The Great Gatsby*. Like everything else she did, Kraft dove completely into the horse business and worked twice as hard as anyone else.

"When she decided to do something," Aurland says, "she went all the way."

The marriage and the horses appear to mark the end of Kraft's major hunting expeditions. She was too busy learning the ropes of her new obsession. Besides, the pursuit of big game had served its purpose and given her a career as a journalist—a career she didn't need anymore, just like she no longer needed to preserve her original last name for the purpose of a byline. With her departure from the field just a few years before the next generation of women entered sports writing, her impact faded into the magazine's archives.

In the meantime, she turned her full attention toward horses. And just as her immersion into journalism had led rapidly to adventure and achievement, success in horses came quickly, ultimately bringing in a lot more money than journalism. Dozens of the farm's horses placed well in major races, and Kraft continued breeding and racing horses after Payson's death. One stallion, St. Jovite, was named the European Horse of the Year in 1992 and later sired eight winning horses that went on to earn more than $7.5 million.

Kraft continued to gain accolades and honors, earning Breeder of the Year from the Thoroughbred Owners and Breeders Association in 1997. In her later years, she appeared in an ad for a private jet business. She married twice more, first to thoroughbred owner Jesse M. Henley, Jr., and after he died, David Libby Cole, a real estate broker. Her life, she often said, was a "magic carpet ride." Kraft died from complications of Parkinson's disease in January 2023 at age 92.

Only after Kraft transitioned out of the media and into horses did profiles written about her start to probe on her journalistic impact beyond the big animals she killed or the beauty products she carried on safari. That's when she, too, finally appeared willing to reflect on what she had done. In both her careers, she told Siena College graduates, it took "long hours and determination to try and do everything just a little bit better and sometimes a little bit differently than it had been done before." In 2015, she said *SI* took her in because of her background in the outdoors, but her position was not secure, especially in the beginning. "Every guy who was hired looked around and figured, 'I can knock her off first,'" Kraft said. "I just did my job and created the opportunities."

Friends and family described Kraft as loyal, generous, energetic, and fun. But even with the people she loved, she didn't want to hear about your aching back, says Diana Kaylor, 83, who had been friends with Kraft since 1989. "She was not somebody who lived with delusions," Kaylor says. She didn't brag about accomplishments. She preferred to blaze her own trail instead of waiting to be shown the way or making a big deal out of what she had done.

By the time the *SI* era was behind her, Kraft acknowledged that she had developed some skills she treasured and that there were some downsides to journalism, including its transience. In 1992 she told an equine magazine that the horse business was like journalism, only more enduring. As a journalist, she had been criticized for over-researching, she said. But that tendency to dive deep into her interests paid off in horse breeding. "With the magazine, you did all this research and wrote a story, but a week later, aside from Mom and the scrapbook, it was old, outdated," she said. "With horses, you do the research, and then the result is part of your life. You live with it for years."

PART 10: A NEW KIND OF REVOLUTION

"I tried my hand at it, too, and I was surprised. In three days of continuous fishing I lost six sails on 10-pound line before bringing my first alongside. All six might have been caught by an experienced angler, and with each mistake my respect increased for the women fishing the tournament. When finally the seventh sail was officially caught and released, I was soaking wet, there was a foot of water in the cockpit, a callus across my left palm and an ounce of salt water in the works of my watch. But the important fact was that I had whipped this fish, not by luck or strength but by careful manipulation of a wisp of monofilament."

Virginia Kraft
"The Ladies and the Sailfish"
Sports Illustrated
February 1, 1960

Rising before dawn on the first morning of the IWFA tournament, I wondered if Kraft had trouble sleeping on reporting trips, like I sometimes did. And after drinking coffee to sharpen my senses for the reporting hunt ahead, I marveled at the chasm created by history over the decades since she first started writing, alone, and these women arrived to go fishing together. At 6 a.m., boats started zooming away from the docks, scattering across the delta past oil rigs and squawking gulls, each guide motoring off to secret spots for eight hours of fighting fish.

Waters were calm through the morning, with some rain dousing competitors in the early afternoon. By 3 p.m. the participants were back on the dock in Venice, Louisiana, where they handed in their score sheets for tallying. Weingart, the cancer survivor from North Carolina, won an award for making the competition's first catch, recovering from her early struggles to find her guide. Prizes also went to daily wins, top teams, and other achievements like reeling in the fish with the most spots. Connie O'Day, a longtime member in her 70s who organized the shark-dancing performance, won the whole thing, taking home a coveted gold disc. Over the three-day event, the IWFA anglers caught nearly 1,600 fish, a record.

When Kraft wrote about the women of the IWFA in 1967, her words spooled out under an ominous headline: "Scourge of the Seven Seas." And although *SI*'s first female adventure writer might have marveled at how joyful—and uninterested in seducing their fishing guides—the group's members are today, she would have been unsurprised by their impressive haul. "By the time the IWFA was 5 years old, 23 of its members accounted for

27 of the world-record catches," she wrote then, lauding them for their win over Castro in Cuba. "The IWFA victory was, as one Havana daily put it, 'a new kind of revolution.'"

Perhaps the wildest thing about Kraft's wild tale is that, despite her remarkable ability to shape-shift—mimicking male writing, staying downwind from mountain goats, dressing the part of a blue-blooded Manhattanite—she didn't promote herself or her achievements as revolutionary. Yet she blazed a new path, leaving in her wake both accomplishments and casualties, building a life that was unimaginable for just about any other woman at the time. Virginia Kraft hunted and fished alone. In later generations, we don't have to.

The women of the IWFA stick together and wouldn't have it any other way. When I joined them, O'Day—who helps run the organization's junior angling program—handed me a fishing rod baited with frozen squid. Just as Kraft did in her 1960 story, I gave it my best shot. First I dropped the hook to the bottom and almost immediately felt a tug. But when I started to reel in, it was too late. The squid was gone and so was the fish. The same thing happened on my second try. The third time, I started cranking the reel more quickly and soon was locked in a tug-of-war with the fish.

I braced the end of the rod against my stomach, my hip, my thigh. I couldn't get leverage. O'Day reached over and held the pole while I struggled, likely so I wouldn't drop the rod in the water altogether. My back and arm aching, we pulled a foot-long snapper out of the water. I didn't get splashed with seawater as Kraft had, although I was soaked in sweat.

I pictured Kraft, armed with her notebook, standing on the back of the boat taking in the scene, searching for the right words, just as I was. I thought about what I might have asked her if she were there, but in the excitement of the moment my questions floated away.

As for my catch, I was surprised by the size of it, the satisfaction I felt, and the women cheering my first fish like it was their own.

It was harder than they had made it look.

EMILY SOHN is a journalist in Minneapolis who covers mostly science, health, and adventure. Her work has appeared in *National Geographic*, *Outside*, *The New York Times*, and many other publications.

'You Just Feel Hopeless': Twenty Years after St. Joe's Historic Hoops Run, an Absence Haunts the Team

DANA O'NEIL

FROM The Athletic • OCTOBER 13, 2023

Editor's note: This story addresses mental health and addiction and may be difficult to read or emotionally upsetting.

AVALON, N.J.—Phil Martelli eases back into his chair and sighs. He has been scrolling through his phone, reading text messages that span a two-year window. It is a one-sided conversation, all black and white from the sender, no blue responses from him.

It is a beautiful sunny day in New Jersey and just a week ago, Martelli and his wife, Judy, enjoyed an idyllic Jersey Shore weekend, their home stuffed with children and grandchildren as the kids' exuberance ricocheted off the ceilings.

But on this August afternoon it is pin-drop quiet in the house. The kids have left and the mood is heavy as Martelli pages through the texts from a person he always considered part of his family. The messages all follow the same pattern: a desperate request for help, a pressing need for money—to pay the dope man, the bartender, or, to get off the streets and find safety.

Martelli used to answer, even send the money as requested. But then counselors advised him he wasn't helping; that, in fact, he was hurting. Then the messages stopped, the last one coming more than a year ago now—in April of last year. "I'm really sad" is how it ends.

Martelli is sad, too. Crushed with guilt, overwhelmed with helplessness, devastated that there is nothing he can do. The coach known for his quick wit stops and starts during an hour-long conversation, struggling to find the right words where there are really no words at all.

Twenty years ago, Martelli and his Saint Joseph's Hawks captivated college basketball, the team from a tiny Catholic school rolling to a 27–0 start and eventually into the 2004 Elite Eight. Two players from that team were drafted in the first round, a feat nearly as improbable as the Hawks' run.

One, Jameer Nelson, played 14 years in the NBA and is now the assistant general manager with the Philadelphia 76ers G League team, the Delaware Blue Coats.

The other, Delonte West, has been, the last anyone's heard, living outside of a 7-11 in Alexandria, Va. He sent the texts to Martelli.

A host of people, people with means and contacts—Martelli, Nelson, Mark Cuban, Jayson Williams—have tried to help West. Save him, really. They are basketball people, after all. In the business of getting results. It is what coaches and athletes live for, why team owners buy into the allure of sports—the thirst for a win, the ecstasy of victory.

Except this one they can't effort into success, or buy their way to a solution. Instead, they have found what too many other families already know: that the vicious storm of mental illness, drug addiction and desperation stewing inside West cares little about work ethic or money; it swallows everything and everyone whole.

"Everyone has someone going through something similar and those who have the means to help, or create a barrier to protect their loved ones, that's what you do," Cuban says. "I thought I could help. And I tried. I really did. We all did. It's just, you just feel hopeless."

MARTELLI REWINDS THE story, going all the way back to a tennis court at the College of New Jersey on a summer day in 2000. Rob Kennedy ran a Hoop Group event there, and West and a collection of teammates from suburban Maryland were running in a game. Most coaches went to see Eddie Basden, who eventually would land a scholarship to Charlotte. Martelli, admittedly, was mostly curious about Basden, too.

Then he watched a kid he'd never heard of get clipped from underneath while driving to the basket. The entire crowd groaned as he banged back-first into the portable stanchion. The kid jumped up, hustled down the court and started playing defense.

Martelli told his staff, "Forget Basden. I want Delonte West." It wasn't too much of an ask. West only had a handful of mid-major suitors—Siena, Manhattan, Towson. He once half-jokingly told a reporter that he opted for the Hawks because they were on TV the most.

During his three years on campus, West played with the same single-minded devotion that he showed on that tennis court. He did not merely devote himself to basketball; he devoured it.

Following West's freshman season, assistant coach Matt Brady suggested he tinker with his jumper. Many nights that summer, Martelli would see the lights on in the gym as he rode down City Avenue. West, he knew, was working. As a freshman, West connected 11.8 percent from the 3-point line. By the end of his junior season, West shot 49 percent from the floor and 41 from the arc.

It's not that he was all basketball. What started out as doodling in the margins of high school assignments blossomed into a passion. West majored in art at St. Joe's, and if he wasn't in the gym, he was in the art room. Martelli still has some of West's artwork back home in Philly.

West also was savvy. He once changed out the radio in a teammate's car for a CD player, offering to trick it out so lights flashed every time the bass bumped.

He could be funny, glib, introspective and deep all in the course of one conversation. His teammate Brian Jesiolowski used to drive West around in the summers, the two earning cash at area basketball camps. One night they passed a guy walking who was Philly famous—a long-haired, berobed preacher who traversed the city barefoot. Jesiolowski mentioned him to West as they drove past, and West insisted they go back and offer him a ride. "I mean, he's barefoot, he probably wants a lift," West reasoned.

The preacher naturally was reluctant at first, but they reassured him that they were college students headed back to campus, nothing sinister. The preacher hopped in the backseat and as Jesiolowski drove, West earnestly asked how he might be able to achieve his dreams—to play pro ball, help his family. He explained that he prayed regularly, went to church, but wanted to know what else he could do. The preacher assured him that he was on the right path. The dialogue, serious and intense, continued until they pulled up to Larry's Steaks across from campus. Just before the preacher exited the back seat, West said, "Man, I have one more question for you. What the f— happened to the dinosaurs?"

As he retells the story, Jesiolowski bursts out laughing. "I nearly crashed the car," he says. "But he didn't even crack a smile." The two commemorated the night by dashing into a nearby convenience store to buy disposable cameras, each posing with the preacher. Jesiolowski still has it somewhere.

"He was absolutely hilarious," Jesiolowski says. "But he also, once you cracked the shell, he was really this very kind, profound person. Honestly, I think he was misunderstood. You see him, you think he's just this great basketball player from a tough neighborhood who made himself great. That's all true, but he was so much more than that."

Upon learning that he had been chosen for the cover of *Sports Illustrated*, Nelson had a question: Could West appear alongside him? Nelson didn't love the spotlight, and spent the bulk of the Hawks' 2003–04 season making sure all of his team-mates were showcased.

It also was an acknowledgement that, without West, Nelson would have been special, but together, they were magical. The year before The Year (West's sophomore season), the Hawks finished 23–7, and had West not suffered a late-season stress fracture, who knows what might have happened? As it was, they lost to Auburn by two in overtime in the first round of the NCAA Tournament. That year Nelson averaged 19.7 points, 5.1 rebounds and 4.7 assists to West's 17.3, 4.3 and 3.2. A year later, as they rolled to near perfection, they were an extension of each other—Nelson the savvy, quick point guard and West his fearless, aggressive backcourt mate.

West opted to turn pro following his junior year—he mem-orably spent the day he declared riding around campus in a golf cart, tossing water balloons at unsuspecting classmates—and wound up a first-round pick, selected by Boston four spots after Nelson went to Orlando via a trade from Denver.

"Delonte made himself into a pro because of his work ethic, his determination and his will to be good," Nelson says. "He had an amazing basketball IQ. He was unorthodox because he was left-handed, but really, he just had this grit in him. That's what made the difference."

Martelli recalls how West worked all hours and refused to lose at drills—even if it meant he had to bend the rules a little bit. But he also can't help but reconsider what he then wrote off as a fierce commitment to basketball as something more, maybe an obsession more than a passion.

They all do this now, reconsider moments that they chalked up to West's ultra competitiveness and burning desire to play. There was the game against Xavier in the Atlantic 10 tournament. Just days before, Saint Joseph's had reached the pinnacle, the tiny school sitting atop the AP rankings. But that game, it was like the Hawks' sneakers were stuck in quicksand. The Musketeers led by 22 at halftime and won by 20. With a few minutes left, Martelli waved the white flag. He took Nelson out of the game, and a few minutes later, yanked West.

Except West wouldn't sit down. He begged the coach for a few more seconds, insisting he could win the game by himself. When Martelli told him no, that they had to surrender this one, West bowed up to his head coach. Nelson came over and defused the situation.

Or when athletic trainer Bill Lukasiewicz intervened during practice to tend to a cut on West's hand. Itching to get back to action, West fussed while Lukasiewicz put an ointment to stop the bleeding, growing so impatient that he slapped Lukasiewicz's hand away. When Lukasiewicz continued to apply the ointment, Martelli and his former players say West charged at him.

Or the time that Jesiolowski recalls, when West threatened to mess up his teammate who had been defending him hard in practice, or lost his cool when they went out at night. "He'd just sort of snap over something not that serious," Jesiolowski says. "I just always thought, he's a tough kid from a tough neighborhood."

West went public with his diagnosis as bipolar in 2008, only four years after he left Philly, and everyone who has a story now questions if they missed a clue, if they should have known, could have helped or intervened.

The guilt eats at all of them, knowing what they now do about bipolar disorder; how it can worsen over time if left untreated, or lead to harmful coping mechanisms like substance abuse. West is so young, still only 40 years old. What if he had been guided toward treatment, and was open enough then to accept it? "You want to go backward," Nelson says. "But you can't. It's not how it works."

Twenty years ago, mental health didn't have much space inside of a locker room. St. Joe's had a sports psychologist, Joel Fish, but people who sought him out usually needed him to navigate basketball-related questions—how to focus better on their foul shooting; how to stay motivated when their playing time diminished.

"As athletes, we're conditioned to be the tough guys, like superheroes almost," Nelson says. "To say you have a problem? That you need to talk about it to someone? Nah. You can't do that."

Yet just three years after he turned pro, Nelson himself discovered the fragility of the line between muscling through and needing help when he lost his dad, Floyd, in a drowning accident. He remembers sitting at his locker after a game sobbing uncontrollably.

Only at the insistence of general manager Otis Smith and coach Stan Van Gundy did he speak with a sports psychologist. He went reluctantly. "I was fortunate that I had people who saw what was going on, and I was at least open-minded enough to get the help," Nelson says. "If not, who knows what happens to me, right? To my career? To my life? I understand how this happens. The Delonte I knew was resilient, strong-minded, but when you're talking about mental health, it can get the best of anybody."

THE FIRST TIME Martelli stepped in was in 2016. West was seen panhandling on the streets in Houston, wearing a hospital gown and no shoes. There had been other scary moments—in 2009, he was arrested on a three-wheel motorcycle for a minor traffic violation and found to be carting three guns and a knife.

He always had an explanation. He was transporting the firearms, helping a homeless person, not homeless himself. By 2016, West's NBA career had long since run its course. He'd had good years and good moments—most memorably a game-winner in a playoff game for the Cavaliers—but he also had a reputation of being difficult, and bounced from team to team. The last straw came in 2012, when West was twice suspended by the Mavericks for conduct detrimental to the team. He tried to hang on, find some run overseas and in the G League. The search ended in 2015.

So when Martelli saw the video a year later, he was alarmed enough that he reached out to former NBA coach John Lucas, who runs a substance abuse facility for athletes. Lucas thought he could help. Martelli was optimistic. It worked until it didn't, beginning a pattern that lasted for years. West would leave treatment with big dreams, usually about resuscitating his basketball career, but no real plan. When the dream fizzled, he'd wind up right back where he started.

His NBA earnings depleted—at one point, West signed a $12.8 million deal with Cleveland—he'd ask his former coach and teammates for money, usually just a few hundred dollars here or there. If they declined, he'd stop answering texts for a spell. Martelli tried to help financially; Nelson preferred to find him safe harbor, or see if he could help get West medications. It went on like that for years, back and forth, West in and out of their lives.

Then in January 2020, another viral video showed West badly beaten after an altercation in D.C. Quietly, the NBA Players Association tried to help, as did Cuban. He footed the bill to send West to Rebound Institute, an outdoor therapy clinic created by former NBA player Jayson Williams, who had his own struggles with substance abuse.

Soon Martelli, Cuban and Nelson, hell-bent on helping West, connected on conference calls, talking to the counselors at the facility. Tough love, the counselors preached. Let him get on his own two feet. Don't foot the bill. Don't send the money.

It seemed to be working. At the rehab facility, West went skydiving and canoeing, worked on a boat, acquiescing to the facility's mantra to surrender and trust. Jesiolowski got the address from Martelli and sent a care package, including a hoodie he'd won in a hoops tournament and a book by ultramarathoner David Goggins. He added his name and number but never heard back.

West wound up leaving the clinic. In September 2020, another video surfaced, this time showing West panhandling in Dallas. Cuban drove to the gas station and picked him up, sending him again to Rebound. A month later, he posted a picture of West on horseback on Twitter. "A long, long way to go but he has taken the first steps," Cuban wrote. West talked about getting a job at the clinic after he was done with his own rehab. He sounded hopeful.

Less than a year after leaving the rehab facility—in October 2021—West was arrested after banging on police officers' doors in Florida. During the arrest, he ranted about being better than LeBron James and claimed he was both Jesus Christ and the president. Attempts by The Athletic to reach West via text message to his last known cell phone number went unanswered.

"It's just, disappointing is what it is. Or frustrating, I guess," Cuban says. "Delonte sabotages himself.... I don't know what else to say. It is what it is. I tried."

He sounds resigned and exhausted. And he is. They all are. When they step back from it, they see it for what it is—a semi-famous person caught in the crisis that torpedoes so many families. He's not special or immune just because he could play basketball.

"It brings me to tears," Nelson says. "He has so many people who love him, who want to help him, but he has to want to help himself.... I am here for him. I will always be here for him. I tried, and I will continue to try if I can, but he has to meet us halfway. He has to want the help."

THE HAIRLINES HUNG back a little, and the waistlines pushed forward, but the stories? Unlike the tales told at most reunion gatherings, these stories—of a small Jesuit school, led by a Philly lifer, a diminutive point guard and an unheralded two-guard threatening to end Indiana's reign as the last team to go undefeated in college basketball—didn't have to be embellished.

In September, the 2003–04 Saint Joseph's Hawks gathered at a local country club for a reunion. Not everyone could make it, but everyone was invited. Including West. Martelli emailed his mother, Delphina, inviting her as well as her son.

The last time he spoke with Delphina she begged the coach to help her find some hope for her son. "He's got nothing to look forward to," he says she told him. Martelli thought maybe the reunion could do that. Neither came. Martelli didn't expect them to; a part of him worried what would happen if they did.

But West's name came up often, as the stories flowed from the 4 p.m. cocktail hour and long past the dinner service, pushing toward 11 at night. "It felt like a piece was missing," Jesiolowski says. "Like the whole family wasn't there."

Martelli last texted with West on April 25, 2022. West told him he was living outside of a 7-11 in Alexandria, Va. Martelli pressed him for the address and then called a coaching friend in the area. He asked his friend if he knew a cop. Maybe they could arrest West, charge him with vagrancy and get him off the streets and into rehab. Martelli shakes his head. "Think about that," he says. "I was going to get my own player arrested, and I thought it was a good idea."

Six months later, West was arrested outside of the same convenience store on four charges: vehicle trespassing, entering a vehicle, fleeing from law enforcement and public intoxication. Martelli fielded another text, this time for a plane ticket so that, if the charges were dropped, West could get to Texas, where his two children are, and try to find a fresh start.

Martelli didn't send the money. He hasn't heard from West since. Neither has anyone else.

DANA O'NEIL, a senior writer for The Athletic, has worked for more than 25 years as a sportswriter, covering the Final Four, the Super Bowl, World Series, NBA Finals, and NHL playoffs. She has worked previously at ESPN and the *Philadelphia Daily News*. She is the author of three books, including *The Big East: Inside the Most Entertaining and Influential Conference in College Basketball History*.

'He Was Free and Clear': How the Leak of Jon Gruden's Email Led to the Fall of Commanders Owner Dan Snyder

DON VAN NATTA JR.
AND SETH WICKERSHAM

FROM ESPN • JULY 12, 2023

As he hopped on a call with Roger Goodell, Las Vegas Raiders owner Mark Davis had no plans to fire his head coach.

It was the afternoon of Friday, Oct. 8, 2021. A few hours earlier, *The Wall Street Journal* had published a blockbuster story about an email Raiders coach Jon Gruden had sent 10 years earlier, when he worked as a color analyst for ESPN's *Monday Night Football*. Gruden, in an exchange with Washington's general manager Bruce Allen, had called NFLPA executive director DeMaurice Smith "Dumboriss" and described him using a racist trope. To most observers, Gruden's dismissal seemed like a matter of when, not if. But Davis hoped to—at the very least—slow down a hurricane from the center of the storm.

According to sources familiar with his thinking, Davis found the story's timing suspicious. Why were emails coming out now? Who had leaked them? And who had the most to gain?

"It felt like a setup," Davis would later tell an associate.

Even though league officials in New York and a few team owners had known about the Gruden emails for months, as part of the investigation into Commanders owner Dan Snyder and the toxic workplace culture inside his franchise, Davis had learned of them only the day before the *Journal*'s exclusive, when Raiders president Dan Ventrelle told him: "We've got a problem."

After the *Journal* story, Davis polled current and former Raiders players and staff on how they felt about Gruden. Some wanted him gone; others didn't. Davis knew Gruden could be crass and profane, the sources said, but in a relationship spanning more than two decades, he had no reason to believe Gruden was racist.

So when Davis and Ventrelle took the conference call with Goodell and NFL general counsel Jeff Pash, Davis leaned toward sticking by Gruden. But Davis felt immediate pressure. According to sources with direct knowledge of the call, Goodell repeatedly told Davis, "You have to do something."

"What are you going to do?" Pash asked.

The statements and questions incensed Davis. He believed the league office had no purview to pressure an owner to fire a head coach, regardless of the circumstance.

"There's more emails coming," Goodell told Davis. "Something has to be done."

When the call ended, Davis turned to Ventrelle.

"Motherf---er," Davis said in exasperation.

On Monday, Oct. 11, *The New York Times* published a story revealing new emails in which Gruden wrote that Goodell was "clueless" and "anti-football" and described him in anti-gay and misogynistic terms. That evening, Gruden resigned, pushed by Davis. Gruden would soon file a lawsuit against the NFL and Goodell that accused the commissioner of "directly leaking" his emails to harm his reputation and force him out, something league officials have repeatedly denied.

What angered Davis more than anything, he later said, was being surprised by the emails months after Goodell, Pash and other owners, including Snyder, knew about them. It seemed to

Davis as if he and the Raiders were collateral damage in what he saw as Goodell's yearslong effort to protect Dan Snyder, of all owners, at all costs.

"F--- the NFL," Davis later told Gruden. "And f--- Dan Snyder."

'A major miscalculation'

Fifteen days after Gruden resigned under pressure, Goodell denied in a closed-door, owners-only meeting in midtown Manhattan that he or anyone in the league office had leaked the damning emails. The focus of speculation around the league turned to Snyder. In October 2022, ESPN reported that the league believed Snyder was behind the leaks. A congressional report last December contained testimony that also pointed toward the Commanders as the source of the leak.

Months of interviews with executives, lawyers, agents, and league and team officials, most of whom requested anonymity, reveal that a larger cast of people might have played a role in the leaking. Those accused by the sources include:

- Top NFL executives, including Goodell. Sources, including one in ownership, told ESPN that NFL executives approved the release of some emails. Four owners told ESPN they believe Goodell was personally involved. NFL spokesperson Brian McCarthy repeated the league's denial, in public and in legal responses, that it was responsible. "Neither the NFL nor the commissioner leaked Coach Gruden's offensive emails," McCarthy told ESPN. In a statement to ESPN, Gruden said, "it's ridiculous the league thought they could cherry-pick emails from years ago, when I wasn't even a coach and try to end my career." He added: "At a minimum, I deserved the opportunity to respond and receive some due process."
- NFL Players Association chief DeMaurice Smith. Smith bragged that he was responsible for leaking the racist email referring to him, an associate with direct knowledge told ESPN. The leaked email was published on the same day

Smith faced a union vote to retain his job. Smith declined to comment through union spokesperson George Atallah.

- Snyder, in an operation run by his New York law firm Reed Smith and with help from Desiree Perez, the CEO of Roc Nation, which has a $25 million contract to help the NFL on social justice issues. A Reed Smith lawyer told one source, before and after the leaks, about the firm's involvement and Perez's alleged role, which the source did not define. Lawyers with direct knowledge of Reed Smith operations and Perez's dual role—as an influential NFL consultant and a Snyder confidant—told ESPN the group dusted off tactics it had used in Alex Rodriguez's lawsuit against Major League Baseball years ago.

But Jordan Siev, a partner at Reed Smith, said that the firm "never leaked any" of the emails and that "neither Dan Snyder nor anyone on his or the team's behalf ever requested or authorized that Reed Smith do so. Any assertion to the contrary is false." Perez declined repeated opportunities to speak with an ESPN reporter. An attorney representing her said in a letter to an ESPN attorney that "Ms. Perez had no role whatsoever in the leaking of any emails, or in any discussion or decision to leak any emails."

Sources said Snyder, who was serving a punishment after a league investigation had exposed a toxic workplace culture at the team, hoped the emails would deflect blame for workplace issues to Allen while currying favor with Goodell by giving the commissioner a chance to eliminate Gruden, a longtime antagonist. Commanders spokesperson Jean Medina declined to answer any questions about the leaks but issued a statement that "ownership is working constructively with the League to finalize the sale of the Washington Commanders to the Josh Harris Group and will continue to support the organization through the transition process."

The actual leakers' identities remain unknown as lawyers and executives point to each other like a circular firing squad, with plenty of smoke but no smoking gun. Everyone who knew about the emails had apparent motives to leak.

No matter how the leaks were engineered, multiple sources draw a direct line from emails that trickled out over a few days in October 2021 to Snyder's crash and his imminent $6.05 billion sale of the Commanders. Within days of the leaks, a congressional committee launched a wide-ranging investigation of the Commanders and the NFL that forced Goodell, Allen and Snyder to testify under oath. The congressional inquiry would lead to a federal criminal investigation into alleged financial misconduct by Snyder and the team. As pressure mounted, Snyder bragged to associates that he had collected dirt on his fellow owners and Goodell that could "blow up" the league. Unfazed, owners finally all but forced Snyder to sell his beloved franchise.

Although multiple people paid a price—or still could—for a series of leaks that continue to threaten the NFL in the Nevada courts, no one suffered greater blowback than Snyder.

"He was free and clear that October—he just had to wait out his suspension and let everything blow over," a source close to Snyder said. "A major miscalculation. Without the leaks, he might just have survived."

'Dictating his punishment'

In June 2021, Dan Snyder's legal team and select league executives gathered at NFL headquarters in Manhattan. In survival mode, Snyder's team of lawyers prepared a defense against the findings from attorney Beth Wilkinson's investigation into the franchise. The previous summer, he had hired Wilkinson to look into the team, a move to keep the league office at arm's distance. But the league quickly had assumed control of Wilkinson's inquiry and quietly struck an accord with Snyder's team—"a common interest agreement" that the owner and the league would share all evidence and material collected and that neither the NFL nor

Snyder would release any information from the inquiry without the other's consent.

Although it appeared to owners and executives that the league and Snyder had worked together to minimize the investigation's impact, palpable tension existed. In league circles, Goodell appeared to be growing weary of Snyder. During the pandemic, it became a running joke among some owners and executives that when Snyder spoke on videoconference calls, Goodell looked irritated or distracted. But now, Snyder moved beyond simply annoying the league office to causing serious problems.

When Snyder's lawyers—famed defense attorney Joe Tacopina, assisted by Reed Smith partners Siev and James McCarroll—began to show a series of slides, those in the room were stunned, according to sources. What was presented was not a defense against any of Wilkinson's findings made against Snyder; it was a series of screenshots of potentially embarrassing emails and texts from several top league executives, including Goodell's top lieutenant, Pash. The rationale, according to a source with firsthand knowledge, was to argue the hypocrisy of league officials judging Snyder. The tactics were so ruthless that some attorneys felt uncomfortable. Although none of the content was sexist, anti-gay or graphic, the signal was clear: If Goodell didn't do what Snyder wanted in terms of handling the Wilkinson report and punishment, these emails and texts would be leaked.

It became known in league circles as the "Blackmail PowerPoint."

League executives and others involved in the case were angry when they were informed of Snyder's tactics, multiple sources told ESPN. From that point on, any direct communication from the league office to Snyder had to be legally vetted. But Snyder's PowerPoint proved effective. A few top NFL executives had persuaded Goodell to give Snyder a stiff and lengthy punishment. But as the time for announcing Snyder's punishment neared, Goodell began to reconsider.

By late June, Snyder was "dictating his punishment" down to every detail, according to a source with knowledge of the deliberations. Legal sources said that Snyder and his lawyers were consulted by NFL executives in the drafting of the news release, with Snyder weighing in on word choices. It was an atypical and collaborative process, as compared with the way the league typically metes out punishment—notably in the one-sided judgments after Bountygate and Deflategate. Snyder and his team were pleased with the results, later bragging that the discipline was surprisingly light.

In the late afternoon of Thursday, July 1, before holiday weekend, the league announced Snyder's punishment. He would step away from day-to-day operations "for at least the next several months" and pay a $10 million fine—with proceeds benefiting Washington, D.C., area nonprofit organizations. The word "suspension" was never used. In a news release, the NFL praised Snyder for having "recognized the need for change" and "undertaken important steps" to improve the team's culture. None of Wilkinson's specific findings were released, despite assurances she had given witnesses, including former team cheerleaders, that the full report would be public. The drafted recommendations urging the NFL to force Snyder to sell his team had effectively been buried. A Washington radio station reported that it had obtained screenshots of the recommendations from Wilkinson's draft report that included urging the NFL to force Snyder to sell his team. But the NFL insists no written document ever existed.

Her work now complete, Wilkinson turned an estimated 650,000 Commanders emails over to the league. A handful of senior league executives oversaw IT consultants who culled Gruden's offensive emails. Apart from Snyder's lawyers at Reed Smith, only a handful of league staff, mostly in the legal department, had access to the emails. For months after that, sources said, the emails were the source of gossip among owners and executives—until summaries of the emails were shown to Roger Goodell in early October.

'We need your help'

Long before any leaked emails, the NFL enlisted Jay-Z's entertainment company, Roc Nation, to help solve a big problem. The league in 2018 remained on defense from the fallout of then-President Donald Trump targeting the NFL over former 49ers quarterback Colin Kaepernick and a small group of players kneeling in protest during the national anthem. The silent protest of police brutality and the political reaction to it contributed to eroding TV ratings and strained relationships with sponsors. Goodell had lengthy discussions with various groups of players about systemic racism and social justice, but the NFL was now struggling to find ways to be proactive. New England Patriots owner Robert Kraft, among other owners, thought the league needed outside help. Kraft consulted Jay-Z, who had called out the NFL after ESPN reported that then-Texans owner Bob McNair had said of players in a closed-door meeting: "We can't have the inmates running the prison."

According to sources, Kraft told Jay-Z, "The NFL isn't picking up on these social issues. We need your help."

Kraft connected Jay-Z and Roc Nation to Goodell. Soon, sources told ESPN, the league partnered with Roc Nation in a $25 million, five-year deal to reshape the Super Bowl halftime show, produce music tied to the season, amplify the league's social justice agenda and, perhaps most importantly, move beyond the controversy around teams' unwillingness to sign Kaepernick. At an August 2019 news conference at NFL headquarters announcing Roc Nation's partnership with the league, Jay-Z told reporters, with Goodell sitting nearby, "I think we've moved past kneeling."

Top league executives and at least a few owners believe the alliance has worked, beyond the more than $250 million the league has raised to commit toward social justice causes. Executives believe that Roc Nation has raised the bar with Super Bowl halftime shows the past few years. The affiliation with Jay-Z has helped the NFL improve its image on race with fans, according to an executive outside the NFL with knowledge of the league's internal data.

The partnership also gave Perez, the Roc Nation CEO, an open door to the league office. Perez had overcome a criminal past to build a reputation as one of entertainment's most powerful executives. In 1994, she had been arrested for conspiracy to distribute cocaine, later working as a DEA informant and serving nine months in prison for a probation violation. She was among the dozens of convicted felons Trump pardoned a day before he left office.

Some in the league office believed Roc Nation had essentially appointed itself as the league's marketing arm. And some league officials believed Roc Nation employees treated NFL staff dismissively, angering those who sincerely wanted to help find solutions to the league's social justice problem.

Goodell refused to back his staff when tension arose between the league and Roc Nation in 2020, instead telling his charges to just work it out. Roc Nation owned all the leverage. The NFL couldn't afford to suffer a fallout with Jay-Z, not after the Kaepernick controversy, and not after how much it had publicized their partnership. Plus, Goodell seemed to appreciate and trust Perez, inviting her to key meetings, an action that mystified some owners and executives. "The NFL became afraid of Roc," said a former NFL official, who adds that the partnership has been "a mess."

Perez became a trusted confidant to Dan and Tanya Snyder and, according to a letter from a team lawyer to ESPN last December, sits on the board of the Commanders. Jason Wright, the first Black team president in NFL history for Washington in 2020, hired Greg Resh, a former Roc Nation chief financial officer, to be his CFO and, eventually, chief operating officer. Roc Nation and Snyder are both clients of Reed Smith, a firm with a reputation for taking an aggressive approach on behalf of famous clients. Previously, Perez and Reed Smith were allegedly involved in leaking documents to reporters and putting private investigators on now-MLB commissioner Rob Manfred to help Rodriguez's lawsuit against Major League Baseball.

Reed Smith's brass-knuckles reputation appealed to Dan Snyder, who in the fall of 2021 was impatient to return to his team.

Snyder believed that his banishment was supposed to last only a month and that he should have been able to return to normal, sources said. He attended every game during his vague banishment, even if he wasn't seen on the field as usual. As the 2021 regular season neared its midpoint, Snyder considered his punishment served and expected a full return to visibility and attendance at league meetings.

"He didn't think that was part of the terms he had worked out," a source close to Snyder said.

ESPN later reported that Snyder's lawyer, John Brownlee of Holland & Knight, believed that Snyder's punishment was over as of Nov. 1, 2021. But Goodell refused to allow him back to league meetings. If Snyder could have lain low until the end of the season, owners and executives told ESPN, he might just have retained his team.

But Snyder couldn't resist. Sources said they were told Snyder and the NFL saw opportunity in publicizing racist and anti-gay emails from one of the league's most prominent head coaches.

The hope, one source said, was that the leaks would "divert attention from this situation with Snyder and give room for everybody to lay down their swords.... This was a hatchet job—a gift wrapped by Snyder for Goodell, to get back into Goodell's good graces on the suspension."

The source was told by an attorney involved that Perez, meanwhile, saw the chance to help the commissioner: "Goodell and the league wanted to off Gruden and seem like they were tough on racism.

"This was a gift."

'Don't go with this story'

Early in the week of Oct. 4, senior league executives provided summaries of some of the worst Gruden emails to Goodell. Senior league sources insisted that the emails shared with Goodell were to remain confidential.

That plan lasted until late Thursday afternoon, Oct. 7. Gruden was walking off the practice field when he got a call from Davis that *The Wall Street Journal* had obtained one email he had sent a decade earlier. Gruden immediately called his longtime agent, Bob LaMonte. "He could barely talk," LaMonte recalled. LaMonte then called Andrew Beaton, the *Journal* reporter. "Have you talked to Jon?" LaMonte said he asked Beaton. The answer was not yet. "You should talk to Jon."

Gruden immediately assumed the league was responsible for the leak, a final "blackballing" by Goodell, he told associates.

The Gruden email disparaging Smith in racist terms was about to be published within a few days of Goodell's review—a coincidence that was hard to miss, league officials privately acknowledged. League sources declined to say whether Goodell had shared the emails with anyone.

Raiders officials called the league office, trying to understand what had happened. The league immediately sent 11 of Gruden's emails to the Raiders for review, in care of Dan Ventrelle, then the team president and general counsel, the sources said.

Later Thursday night, Beaton called Gruden, who was out to dinner with his wife, Cindy, in the Southern Highlands neighborhood of Las Vegas.

Gruden told an associate he pleaded with Beaton, "Don't go with this story…. You are going to destroy people's lives," and Beaton replied, "This is the tip of the iceberg."

Also on Thursday, Goodell gave Smith a heads-up that a *Journal* reporter had the Gruden email about him, a league source said.

On Friday afternoon, Oct. 8, the *Journal* published its story, and Gruden instantly became the face of racism in the NFL. Race was a subtext of Smith's 14-year tenure—players elected retired business executive Lloyd Howell to replace Smith on June 28—as he was often the only Black man in the room while negotiating against mostly white owners and executives.

At the time, the NFL reacted to the leak without acknowledging that it had prior knowledge of the emails or that there were any league communications with the Raiders or Smith. "The email from Jon Gruden denigrating DeMaurice Smith is appalling, abhorrent and wholly contrary to the NFL's values," McCarthy, the league spokesperson, said in a statement.

The leak came just as Smith was in danger of being voted out of his job by team player representatives. A committee vote on his future ended in a 7–7 tie, triggering a full vote of player reps. For years, Smith had faced stiff criticism among members over the perception that the league had outmaneuvered him on two consecutive collective bargaining agreements. Owners and league executives viewed him as an asset—and wanted him to continue as executive director. Goodell and Smith also have become closer in the past few years since they found a way to have a season played during the pandemic. An owner told an associate that the league hoped the emails would help Smith survive.

A lawyer who frequently works with the league said the timing of the leak was "suspicious because clearly it appeared to anyone paying attention that someone was trying to help De. Who had the incentive for De to keep his job? The NFL."

Within hours of the *Journal* story, Smith was reelected as NFLPA executive director to a fifth term—by a single vote. Smith later bragged that the leak had worked, a source told ESPN.

The *Journal*'s scoop shook the league, with owners and executives wondering who was responsible for the leak and pointing fingers. Bruce Allen, from his home in Arizona, called the league office to complain that his email with Gruden had been leaked. Senior vice president and special counsel for investigations Lisa Friel told Allen that Snyder's team had leaked. "We didn't do it at the league office," Friel told Allen, as he would later testify before Congress. "It came out of their side."

A source who spoke to Pash, the NFL's general counsel, on the day of the *Journal* story said he "was furious about the leak" and insisted it had not come from the league office. Pash, who declined an interview request through a league spokesperson, told the source he believed it had come "from Snyder's law firm and Desiree Perez."

Later that day, the NFL shared server access to thousands more emails with the Raiders, a league source said. The source said that only the NFL, key Washington officials and, by that point, the Raiders had access to the server.

At *The New York Times*, veteran NFL reporter Ken Belson was covering Smith's reelection bid when the *Journal*'s story dropped. He went to work trying to find more emails. It was the same afternoon that Goodell told Davis on the conference call that more emails were coming. Three days later, Belson would drop a scoop—co-bylined by Metro section reporter Katherine Rosman—that revealed a new batch of Gruden emails. Some of them were not among the 11 emails shared with the Raiders by the NFL, suggesting another source provided them to the *Times*, a league source said. A *Times* spokesperson said that, "as a matter of policy, *The New York Times* does not discuss its sourcing."

Despite a furious outcry against Gruden on social media, and Davis believing that the league was tacitly pressuring him to dismiss Gruden, by Friday night the coach believed he would survive. He addressed the team. As he reread his old emails, he thought some were funny—"email chains where six or seven guys are trying to make each other laugh saying stupid s---"—excluding the racist trope he had used to describe Smith. The coach believed the organization knew who he was, at heart. Davis seemed to agree.

Both men were unaware that another bomb was about to drop—in another story containing leaked emails.

'We've got a problem'

On Sunday afternoon, Oct. 10, Gruden was back on the Raiders' sideline, coaching the team to its second straight loss, this time to the Bears 20–9. The coach's emails overshadowed the game, but he still believed his self-inflicted wounds were survivable. By the next night, when he spoke to Davis, the tone had shifted.

"I got an email from *The New York Times*," Davis said. A story was being prepared about Gruden's anti-gay emails about Goodell. Davis told friends he had now been backed into a corner. He wasn't just the owner of the Raiders, who had defensive end Carl Nassib, the first active NFL player to come out as gay, on its roster; Davis also owned the WNBA's Las Vegas Aces, with lesbian players, staff and fans.

"We've got a problem," Davis told Gruden.

Gruden knew it was over. He resigned, ending a 27-year coaching career in disgrace. Later, he reached an undisclosed settlement with the team for the remaining seven years of his 10-year, $100 million contract.

Back in Manhattan, the scandal seemed far from over. Yet more emails were coming out in the *Times*, this time also targeting Pash—some of the same emails Snyder's lawyers had shared with league officials during their June PowerPoint presentation. On Thursday, Oct. 14, the *Times* published another story detailing friendly and casual emails between Pash and Allen, a story people close to Snyder told ESPN was intended to pin the team's toxic culture problems on Allen and show that the league was complicit and cozy with him. "Dan wanted to kill Pash," an ownership source with knowledge of the leaks told ESPN.

Over the years, Goodell has responded to leaks from inside the league office by assembling his top staff and saying the league would be searching its phones and computers for communications with reporters. But after the Gruden leaks, league sources said, Goodell didn't hold that type of meeting; it's unclear why not.

Lawyers close to the NFL and to Gruden said the choice to leak to the *Times* over *The Washington Post*, a newspaper Snyder hates, was a dead giveaway that Snyder and those around him were behind the leaks. Two sources told ESPN that the same "playbook" that was used in the A-Rod lawsuit against MLB was used to leak the emails published by the *Times*.

"The same crew that helped Alex go after Manfred helped Snyder with the leaks," said another source who was briefed on how the Gruden leaks were engineered.

Gruden's legal team went as far as to research prior work by the reporters who received the leaks and found what it saw as favorable stories previously written about Dan and Tanya Snyder and Roc Nation. The *Times'* Rosman wrote a piece in February 2020 about Roc Nation's partnership with the NFL. The *Journal's* Beaton wrote in June 2021 about Dan and Tanya Snyder's efforts to reform the team's culture, including a rare on-the-record interview with Dan Snyder. *The Wall Street Journal* declined to comment.

"How stupid can you be?" said a source close to Snyder who was aware of the previous stories done by the reporters who reported on the leaked emails. "They left a trail in the dirt."

But another source who knows Perez disputed her involvement. The source said she had no reason to help Snyder and had distanced herself from him during her time on the Commanders' board. And Perez "had no knowledge that it [leaking] was even being contemplated," her attorney wrote to ESPN's counsel.

After Gruden was gone, Snyder had hoped to be welcomed back into the league for good. But his plan backfired. Goodell still refused to allow Snyder to attend league meetings.

In fact, the league said in its response to Gruden's lawsuit, the commissioner had no vendetta against Gruden and the email leak "was unequivocally against the NFL's best interests."

"The emails not only dampened the NFL's historic season, but also stood in stark contrast with the significant progress the League had made in recent years on diversity, equity and inclusion initiatives, and resulted in negative media coverage for the League," the NFL filing says.

Within days of the leaks, Congress opened an investigation into Snyder, the allegations of sexual harassment and financial improprieties, and into Goodell's handling of the Wilkinson investigation. A source close to the committee told ESPN that, although congressional staff and some lawmakers were already interested in issues around the Commanders and Snyder, the string of leaks moved them to act. Their thinking was, if the leaks showed the kind of material Snyder was weaponizing against his enemies, what else might be out there?

The congressional inquiry thrust the Snyder allegations that had been dormant since July back into the spotlight. In February 2022, several former Washington employees spoke at a congressional roundtable, and one woman, Tiffani Johnston, alleged she had been sexually harassed by Snyder at a team dinner. That revelation caused the NFL to hire Mary Jo White, the former U.S. attorney and head of the Securities and Exchange Commission, to conduct a new inquiry of Snyder. White's report, the findings of which Goodell has pledged repeatedly to release publicly, is expected soon. In June 2022, Goodell testified but Snyder evaded testimony and cruised the Mediterranean on his superyacht. Snyder and Allen also testified under oath before the committee.

A month after his departure, Gruden filed a lawsuit against the NFL, naming Goodell as a defendant and arguing that the league sought to ruin his career by greenlighting the leaked emails, an act LaMonte calls "disgraceful" and "the worst hit job that I've ever seen."

"For the league to exist, it has to be neutral," said Gruden's attorney, Adam Hosmer-Henner. "If it favors or disfavors owners, teams or coaches, then all bets are off with respect to civil liability, antitrust protection and competitive integrity. The league was not neutral or fair with Jon, and our lawsuit is proving there are consequences."

Gruden's enemies list

Gruden had his reasons to believe Goodell and the league office had it out for him. The reasons were planted by Al Davis, who taught Gruden to hate the NFL office from the moment he hired the coach in 1998, eight years before Goodell became commissioner. Davis often told Gruden that the executives at 345 Park Avenue played favorites—classic Raiders paranoia. But it also stemmed from Davis suing the league for antitrust violations. Davis also was convinced that commissioner Pete Rozelle had personally killed a trade before the 1983 draft that would have sent John Elway to the Raiders, refusing to allow a generational quarterback to play for a renegade franchise.

But after becoming one of the game's best and most celebrated coaches, Gruden saw examples that the old man was right. How else to explain the since-eliminated Tuck Rule—a rule Gruden had never heard of before—that led to a Patriots playoff victory at the Raiders' expense in 2002? As the years passed, and Gruden won a Super Bowl with the Tampa Bay Buccaneers and eventually moved to the *Monday Night Football* booth in 2009, his hatred of the league office grew. In 2011, Gruden was in an especially bad headspace, he later told friends, furious over the owners' lockout that offseason and that clubs had voted in 2009 to give teams the option to eliminate pension plans for assistant coaches and other employees.

His frustration came to a boil during a December 2011 Monday night game between the Falcons and the Saints. Atlanta linebacker Curtis Lofton delivered a helmet-to-helmet hit on receiver Marques Colston over the middle and was flagged for unnecessary roughness. To a national TV audience, Gruden stated his displeasure with the call. "I just don't understand how games are being officiated," Gruden said after a play on the next possession.

Gruden's commentary earned him a call from the league's Park Avenue headquarters. Over the phone, Goodell asked Gruden to come to the league office to meet with John Madden and Jeff Fisher. The purpose, as the commissioner explained, was for Gruden to get a lesson on player safety.

"You've got to be s---ting me," Gruden told Goodell.

Gruden wondered whether it was a joke, he later told associates. He needed a player safety lesson from Madden and Fisher, two coaches whose players had delivered some of the ugliest hits in NFL history? Gruden later told friends he felt that Goodell was treating him like a "stooge" who had "never coached in the league, like I don't study football day in and day out...like I didn't know a damn thing about player safety."

Gruden never went to the league office for that meeting. The only time he ever met Goodell was years later, when he went to the league office to promote youth football, one of Gruden's passions. He expected to sit down with Goodell and plan a way to increase participation rates. Instead, Gruden met with an assistant of the commissioner. At the end of the session, Goodell entered a conference room, thanked Gruden for coming and left. Gruden fumed; after that brief meeting, Gruden never spoke again with Goodell.

Gruden burned with suspicion when Mark Davis was elbowed out of the three-team derby to relocate to Los Angeles in 2016 despite owning the most popular team in the market by far. Those feelings intensified in 2020 when Gruden was in his third year back as the Raiders' head coach. The league fined the Raiders $500,000, fined Gruden $150,000 and stripped the team of a sixth-round draft pick for COVID-19 violations—and that was after the league had fined the team and Gruden a total of $350,000 for violations earlier in the season. (Davis offered to pay Gruden's $150,000 fine, but league officials insisted Gruden pay it personally, which he did.) Livid, Gruden appealed the fines but ended up writing the checks. After he did, his friend Sean Payton, then the Saints' coach and who also had been fined for COVID-19 violations, called him and laughed.

"I never paid the fine," Payton told Gruden, adding that other coaches also refused to pay. "You're the only dumbf--- that paid the fine."

Gruden continued coaching, disenchanted by what he saw as incompetence and overreach from NFL headquarters, from poor and inconsistent officiating to league office executives pressuring him to hire diverse coaches. Like many coaches, Gruden believed there was a massive disconnect between the dictates of 345 Park Avenue and the way the game is played on the field. In quiet moments, Gruden had designs on one day becoming commissioner. But at heart he knew he was a coach, and he never gave much thought to the offensive language that cost him his job. He knows he'll probably never be a head coach again; he's consulting now for the Saints, helping tutor veteran quarterback Derek Carr.

Gruden recently wondered aloud to associates why Dan Snyder would have had it out for him. He knew that Snyder hated Bruce Allen; Snyder had fired Allen in 2019, and the two were fighting over whether Snyder needed to pay the remainder of Allen's contract, sources said. And Gruden knew his brother Jay had shared some unsavory stories earlier in 2021 about working for Snyder, including telling the *Post* that the owner would "come in off his yacht" and pick players on the first day of the draft and override his coaches, scouts, everyone. Gruden thought back to an exchange with Snyder years earlier, when he had bumped into Snyder at a restaurant. Gruden believed Snyder was drunk, and he and Gruden started playfully trash-talking, with Snyder calling Gruden fat and Gruden saying he might "dribble his head into the asphalt." Both men laughed, but Gruden wondered if Snyder had taken offense.

Although the league initially expressed confidence that Gruden's lawsuit would be dismissed, Gruden has won every court motion against the NFL. The league has tried to move the case to arbitration, its venue of choice, where league-friendly lawyers are in charge and discovery, including communications between league officials and others, is not made public. Gruden's case is now on appeal by the NFL before the Nevada Supreme Court. A ruling is expected late this year.

League officials told ESPN that regardless of any bad blood between Goodell and Gruden, the commissioner wouldn't have approved leaking the emails, despite their racist tone. "He still wouldn't do it," a league source said. In NFL circles, it's believed that if not for the leaks, those emails would have remained buried in what owners and executives commonly refer to as "Jeff Pash's black box."

Gruden persists in believing that Goodell "pushed the code red" against him, he told associates, adding that the commissioner executed the "kill shot" on his career, "a bullet to the head." Gruden insists he won't settle his lawsuit for any amount, intending "to burn the house down" to reveal the truth about who ordered the leaks. "This was a massive hit job," Gruden recently told an associate, often saying Allen had told him the 650,000 emails "incriminate everyone in the league."

"Why would these people want to come and get me?" The only explanation, he said, is that he had led a leaguewide whispering campaign of "F--- Roger Goodell. And I'm not the only one, by the way.... Deep down, I knew he—Goodell—had me by the balls."

The way things go

In late May 2023, in a suburban Twin Cities hotel, Mark Davis and Roger Goodell head to league meetings. Goodell enters early. Davis is behind, one of the last owners to enter the closed-door session. For the third straight year, Snyder is not present, but for the third straight year, his presence hovers over the proceedings. The sale of the Commanders to Harris isn't complete, but owners are making clear that it's a matter of when, not if. In the hotel lobby, Jerry Jones is telling reporters the sale will get done because owners want it to get done.

Privately, owners still expect Snyder to fight until the sale is complete, as he has all along. Sources said that in October 2022—a full year after the email leak and days after the ESPN report that he had threatened to "blow up" the league and Goodell with "dirt" he had collected—word spread that Snyder planned to show up at owners meetings in lower Manhattan. Goodell insisted that he still was not allowed to do so despite the vague terms of his punishment. Owners enlisted Jones, the only one of them with influence over Snyder, to implore Snyder not to attend. The next day, the Colts' Jim Irsay told reporters that his fellow owners needed to look into removing Snyder, based on his behavior. Two weeks later, Snyder announced that he was exploring a sale of the team, expected to be approved by owners July 20.

As Davis enters the 2023 spring meeting, he smiles, pleased to be here, as usual. It's been a tough time since Gruden resigned. The Raiders made the playoffs in 2021 but are 13–18 overall since the emails were leaked. The team is now in the midst of another rebuild and in search of a new franchise quarterback, a reminder of how fragile success is in the NFL. Davis recently brought on a new limited partner: Tom Brady. And despite the league and owners awarding Las Vegas the draft in 2022 and Super Bowl LVIII next February, Davis is still seething over the way he was treated by Goodell, especially compared with how the commissioner treated Snyder. In Goodell's NFL, almost always, the commissioner grants an owner far greater leniency than any head coach or star player. But even the owners aren't treated equally. Davis knows it's the way things go for his family, and for the Raiders.

And as the owners in that exclusive room yearn to finally push the league to a post-Snyder world, for this moment Dan Snyder is still one of them.

ESPN senior writer Tisha Thompson and researcher John Mastroberardino contributed to this report.

DON VAN NATTA JR. is a Senior Writer at ESPN. He joined ESPN in 2012 after 16 years as a *New York Times* investigative correspondent based in Washington, London, Miami, and New York. A member of three Pulitzer Prize–winning teams, Van Natta is the *New York Times* bestselling author of *First Off the Tee*, *Her Way* (with Jeff Gerth), and *Wonder Girl*. He's now writing a biography of Cowboys owner and general manager Jerry Jones, which will be published in 2026 by Avid Reader Press/Simon & Schuster. He lives in Miami with his wife, the award-winning journalist Lizette Alvarez, and they have two daughters. SETH WICKERSHAM is a Senior Writer at ESPN, where he has worked since graduating from the Missouri School of Journalism, and the author of the *New York Times* bestseller *It's Better to Be Feared*. His next book, on quarterbacks, will be published in 2025. He lives in Connecticut with his wife and two children.

The Other Rapinoe

DAVID ALM

FROM *GQ* • APRIL 12, 2023

The house was dark. Rachael Rapinoe walked into the kitchen and turned on the light. She sliced a banana in half, placed a pint of vanilla ice cream on the counter to thaw, and scooped a pat of butter into a sauté pan. The pat morphed into a puddle and began to bubble. Rachael added cinnamon, brown sugar, and brandy, stirring the mixture slowly over low heat. As the sweet, nutty fragrance of bananas Foster filled the kitchen, Rachael's loneliness began to melt away. Her nightly Vicodin was just kicking in.

She was at her parents' home in Redding, California, recovering from yet another surgery. Her twin sister, Megan, had been drafted by the Chicago Red Stars, in the Women's Professional Soccer league, and was living large more than 2,000 miles away. Rachael, meanwhile, spent her days in physical rehab, her nights in a fog of painkillers. With recurring injuries came recurring opioid prescriptions. Percocet at first, but it was too heavy. "I felt like a zombie," she says. She preferred Vicodin.

It was 8:30 p.m., maybe 9. Rachael's mother, Denise, was nearing the end of her shift at Jack's Bar & Grill, the steakhouse in town where she'd waited tables for 22 years. Her father, Jim, was already asleep, to be up at 5 a.m. for his job as a general contractor. Her older brother, Brian, was at Pelican Bay State Prison, doing time for residential burglary and manufacturing weapons—crimes he committed, in part, to feed his heroin addiction.

Rachael took her dessert to the kitchen table, sat down, and began to eat. It was 2009, and doctors were doling out opioids with abandon—driving an epidemic that had already hit Redding especially hard. According to data gathered by *The Washington Post*, between 2006 and 2014 more oxycodone and hydrocodone were flowing into Shasta County, where Redding is located, than almost anywhere west of Kansas—a rate of 96 pills per resident annually. For Rachael, one pill at a time became two. Getting more was easy.

Just a few years prior, Rachael had been on the same path to soccer stardom as Megan, now one of the most accomplished players in American history. "I always remember Rachael being the best athlete that I knew, certainly the best in our household," Megan says. When the twins were young, Denise says that Rachael was the "stronger, faster, better" athlete. She was taller, too, Megan slower to develop. Once Megan caught up, in high school, they both played club soccer with the elite Elk Grove Pride, in Sacramento, made the state and regional Olympic Development Program teams, and got recruited by numerous Division-I schools.

Megan would go on to win Olympic gold and two World Cups, and become an LGBTQIA+ icon. Rachael would find herself back in Redding, making bananas Foster every night for over a year. "I didn't want to just give myself a scoop of ice cream; that would take two seconds," she says. "I wanted something that was more of a process." The Vicodin added a warm layer of comfort. She got her first prescription at 21. By 24, she was addicted.

At 37, Rachael is only now beginning to publicly reckon with the ways she's struggled with her drug use and her mental health—an ordeal that she says even her immediate family and closest friends didn't fully understand. "I have experienced a lot of pain and suffering, as we all have," she says, "but I never wanted to show that."

She spent years wrestling with that pain, and contemplating better ways to treat it. In 2019, Rachael co-founded a CBD wellness brand, Mendi, for athletes seeking an alternative to opioids. Cannabis is hardly a panacea, but studies have indicated that in many cases it can be a viable replacement for pharmaceuticals like Vicodin and Percocet. She hopes her niche will set Mendi apart in a $5 billion industry where it can be tough to find a foothold.

But Rachael's intentions transcend the success or failure of yet another CBD company. Alongside her investors, who include Olympic gold medalists, several members of the U.S. Women's National Soccer Team, and a co-owner of the Seattle Storm, she wants to usher in nothing less than a paradigm shift in how we deal with pain. They are responding to an urgent crisis—a sports culture that valorizes serious injuries, and normalizes the prescription of opioids. But as Rachael's experience shows, physical injury often gives way to psychic anguish. And a few Vicodin can numb far more than broken bones or torn ligaments.

REDDING IS A modest logging hub of 94,000 in California's densely forested northern interior, two hours south of the Oregon state line. By the early 1980s, when the Rapinoes moved to the area, deforestation jobs were largely being replaced by machines and the poverty rate had begun to rise. The family settled on a rural property eight miles east and a world away from the hardscrabble city, in the town of Palo Cedro, where Rachael and Megan were born on July 5th, 1985. Growing up the twins liked to kick a ball around their four-acre yard. Rachael also loved spending time with their chickens, fishing for crawdads, and building forts out of branches and leaves. "I appreciated the quietness of what our yard provided," she says. "What the trees provided."

Home, by contrast, was chaos: a revolving door of half-siblings, grandparents, cousins, aunts, and uncles. "My family unit is like, 'If you're blood, you're family, and if you're family, anyone can live in this house,'" Rachael says. Brian was in and out, too, between stints in juvenile detention facilities and drug rehabs across the country. He first got arrested at 16, for bringing meth to school. By 18 he was using heroin. "There was a lot of shuffling and substance abuse in the family," Rachael says. "I could tell it was serious, and kind of scary, but we didn't really talk about it."

Brian had a son who became Rachael and Megan's de facto little brother, joining the household along with Denise's two children from a previous marriage, and her youngest sister, who effectively became Rachael and Megan's big sister. Their mother meant well, but her attention was fractured. She was "going to take care of anyone in our family that needed help," Rachael says. "No questions asked, and definitely not checking in on, you know, how it was affecting us kids." It was indeed affecting them: By the time Rachael was in high school, she began having panic attacks. Denise would find her in the middle of the night, wide awake, lying on the kitchen floor, and just tell her to go back to bed. "We didn't have the tools to deal with anxiety," Rachael says.

Denise Rapinoe, née Kimball, was born in Texas, the second oldest of eight children. When she was seven, the family moved to San Bernardino, California. She says that her father, a Korean War veteran, may have been bipolar, and was definitely an alcoholic. At 18, she left home to get married and moved to San Diego. By 23, when she met Jim, then a 29-year-old commercial fisherman, Denise was a divorced mother of two. "She sort of had to learn to roll up her sleeves and just keep moving forward," Rachael says.

Rachael and Megan inherited their mother's tenacity; nowhere did it manifest more clearly than athletics. From an early age, they knew that sports would be their way out of Redding, which by the mid-2000s had become a conservative stronghold in the otherwise blue state, with militias and secessionists dotting the countryside. Rachael initially didn't want to go to college with Megan, who got some big offers that Rachael didn't. But Megan was still so shy that Rachael didn't want to leave her. They started telling schools that if a program wasn't recruiting both of them, they weren't interested.

And so, in 2004, the Rapinoe twins accepted offers from the University of Portland. That fall, Megan was invited to play in the FIFA U-19 World Championship, in Thailand, and deferred her entry to UP until spring. Rachael went alone to Portland, where intense practices, dining hall food, and a genetic predisposition to anemia sent her iron levels so low that she could barely run, let alone play soccer. When Megan arrived in January 2005, she came out and embraced the city's thriving LGBTQIA+ scene. Rachael, struggling with far more than low iron, embraced the church.

Rachael had begun secretly dating another woman on the UP soccer team, and it tortured her. "It was very confusing, because I was raised Christian and I didn't really have a lot of language around gay and lesbianism and same-sex [relationships]," she says. When they were together, Rachael was happy; when they were apart, she "just had a lot of shame." She began attending a charismatic church in Portland where congregants gathered to help her "pray the gay away." The church became a refuge for Rachael during her "more intense bouts of sadness or confusion," she says. "They thought they were praying the sadness away for me, protecting me from my demons."

Rachael told Megan about her girlfriend their sophomore year. Her efforts to alter her sexuality through prayer weren't working and she didn't know what to do. Denise, sensing something was wrong, went to Portland to check on her daughters. She arrived on a cold, wet night in January 2006. When Rachael arrived at Denise's hotel, around 10:30 p.m., she felt like she'd walked into an ambush. Sitting on the bed, Megan had told their mother she was gay, and outed Rachael too. Denise says now that she wasn't "that surprised" about Megan, but "with Rachael, I was kinda taken aback. I really didn't see it." Rachael felt blindsided and betrayed. "I had no idea that Megan was planning on talking to our mom about this," she says. She felt angry, too. She wasn't gay, she thought. She was lost, that's all.

IN RETROSPECT, MEGAN regrets outing her sister to their mom. "It was not my thing to say and irresponsible to do so, and a little bit reckless," she says. But at the time, she says, she felt so confident in her own sexuality that she didn't see why it was a big deal. "I knew that I'm gay and I knew there was nothing wrong with it," she says, but "I kind of threw Rachael into that, and I don't think she was ready."

In the spring of 2006, Rachael received the last of 35 iron infusions—an amount so high that she was getting her treatment along with chemotherapy patients in the hematology and oncology wing of the hospital—and that fall, her junior year, she began playing the best soccer of her life. She resumed her position as a forward, was named team captain, and won All-West Coast Conference Second Team. "She was unbelievable," says Lauren Hanson, then a UP women's soccer assistant coach.

Then, midway through a game against Purdue in the fall of 2007, Rachael planted her left foot to strike the ball with her right and heard a pop. She'd blown out her left ACL, and would spend the next month fighting a bacterial infection, and the six weeks after that back in Redding, convalescing from surgery, high on Vicodin. She made a comeback for the 2008 season, only to blow out the same ACL again. Back to Redding for reconstructive surgery. More rehab, more Vicodin. "I was devastated," she says. Rachael doesn't recall anyone asking her about a history of drug abuse in her family, nor did her parents connect the dots. "I don't even know if they understood what these pills were in relation to my brother's heroin use," she says.

Around that time, Shasta County saw a 600-percent increase in heroin overdoses, largely a result of people getting hooked on opioids and then turning to the cheaper, more readily available street drug. Rachael never went down that road, but that doesn't mean she wasn't at high risk of doing so. One study has shown that student athletes who are prescribed opioids for sports-related injuries are at increased risk for non-prescription abuse, while another suggests that unemployment, depression, and feelings of isolation further exacerbate that risk. Rachael was saddled with all three. "Part of the reason I was in so much pain is that it was the height of me coming to grips with my sexuality," she says. "I was very sad and depressed and alone. I felt so alone."

Rachael started going to Bethel Church, a megachurch in Redding with reportedly more than 11,000 members that throws its weight behind conservative politicians and staunchly defends its gay conversion therapy practices. She told her mother what she'd been telling herself for years: Maybe she was bi, or just hadn't found the right guy yet. Denise saw Rachael's confusion as an opportunity to steer her back to dating men and gave her evangelical Christian books on how not to be gay. "I wish that I had handled it a little differently," Denise says. "I could have been more open to her and encouraged her to talk freely about it." To 24-year-old Rachael, though, "it was a constant reminder of her not really accepting me." The Vicodin helped to numb that pain, too, a secret Rachael kept carefully guarded. "I didn't know the sort of depth or level that mentally she was struggling," Megan says. "What she was really going through."

Rachael began to wean herself off Vicodin in the winter of 2010. She started swimming laps at the local community college, cycling, and even running. By spring, she was competing in triathlons. She'd also reconnected with a couple of high school friends who recognized that Rachael was gay even if she continued to fight it, and with their support she felt emboldened to finally come out. "I had to be comfortable in my sexuality, because there was so much shame," she says. She stopped going to Bethel and told her parents, unequivocally, that she was gay.

She returned to soccer again, too, first coaching at a UCLA summer camp and training with the varsity team, and then playing with an Icelandic professional outfit. The following summer she was back in LA, preparing to join another professional team, in Sweden, when she got tackled in a co-ed match and fractured her ankle. She was just about to turn 26: Game over. She was tired of getting injured, of rehab, of the endless cycle of opioids.

"I decided to hang up the cleats," she says. She took a job as an executive assistant in Fredericksburg, Texas, in the heart of Hill Country. It reminded Rachael of home. "It's a really pretty area, very remote," she says. It gave her space to think. She began to imagine a career in business and working with athletes, but it would take her several years to realize her true mission: fighting the culture that had so limited and frustrated her as a young woman, and that prevented her from figuring out who she was and who she wanted to be.

RACHAEL AND MEGAN were born in the midst of the Just Say No era, when anti-drug propaganda equated cannabis with heroin and crack cocaine. This messaging helped to normalize policies like California's three-strikes law of 1994, which mandated stiff sentences for third offenses, however minor they might be, and overwhelmingly ensnared people for marijuana possession. More colloquially, the era cemented pot as the first step along a dangerous path. "I definitely believed cannabis was a gateway drug," Rachael says.

But by 2015, the year Oregon legalized recreational cannabis use for adults over 21, Rachael was back in Portland and working as a performance coach, and athletes started telling her they were using the drug to mitigate the everyday aches and pains of training at a high level. Scientific studies corroborate their experience: In 2017 the National Academies of Sciences, Engineering, and Medicine reported that adults with chronic pain who are treated with cannabis or cannabinoids experience a "significant reduction" in symptoms.

Rachael did some research and started microdosing THC, the cannabinoid that gets you high—a single hit off a joint, a fraction of an edible—and experimenting with CBD, a non-psychoactive cannabinoid known for aiding sleep and inflammation. She found that together they helped her manage her anxiety and ongoing knee and ankle pain without the downsides of Vicodin.

"Not that it fully goes away," she says, but cannabis "just took the edge off."

In 2018, Rachael teamed up with two cannabis entrepreneurs, Kendra Freeman and Britt Price, and a commercial designer named Brett Schwager to develop a business plan for a CBD brand for athletes. Most professional sports leagues in the U.S., as well as the U.S. Anti-Doping Agency and the World Anti-Doping Agency, still had bans on all cannabinoids at the time, but they were slowly coming around on products that used CBD without a trace of THC. Rachael and her team had a vision for a line of CBD-infused gummies, tinctures, balms, and bath salts to help athletes with everything from physical pain to insomnia. Pretty much every other CBD brand in the market was promising the same, but Rachael wanted to prioritize purity in a way that her competition wasn't. She knew her target customers couldn't take any chances. Even if a progressive league like the WNBA were to lift its ban on THC, a positive test could still lead to disqualification from an international event, like the Olympics.

Mendi, which launched in September 2019, hasn't been without its setbacks. Freeman, Price, and Schwager have since left the company. Rachael, the only elite athlete among the four, says they simply didn't agree on how to best grow the company. Some saw it as "a race to the finish," she says, while she wanted to take a more measured approach. Freeman declined an interview request, stating that she could not legally discuss the terms of her departure from the company. The other co-founders could not be reached for comment.

Now Mendi is just Rachael, two full-time employees, and two part-timers. Despite its small size, the company has sponsored two women's pro soccer teams, the North Carolina Courage and the Utah Royals, and enlisted dozens of investors, most of them women, and many from the LGBTQIA+ and BIPOC communities. "Rachael could be opening a zoo and I probably would wanna invest in it," says five-time Olympic gold medalist Sue Bird, who began dating Megan in 2016 and has become like another sister to Rachael. "I just believe in her as a person; she's really intentional in how she approaches things."

Bird underwent more than 10 sports-related surgeries during her 20-year career in the WNBA, and says that most athletes she knows always "had an extra bottle" of opioids in the cupboard. Bird never abused the pills, but their abundance in the professional sports world has led to some tragic outcomes. In 2019, a 27-year-old pitcher for the Los Angeles Angels named Tyler Skaggs died of an overdose of fentanyl-laced painkillers given to him by the team's communications director. This dependency doesn't always stop when athletes retire, either. According to a 2011 study, former NFL players reportedly use opioids at a rate four times that of the general population, often to battle lifelong afflictions that began on the field.

Consider the case of Ryan O'Callaghan, a former offensive tackle for the New England Patriots and Kansas City Chiefs—and, like Rachael, a product of '80s Redding who was closeted well into his twenties. For years he secretly managed his pain with cannabis until a coach caught him smoking pot and he was forced to switch to opioids. He became addicted, fell into a severe depression, and planned to kill himself as soon as his NFL career was over. Were it not for his trainer noticing O'Callaghan's downward spiral, as he writes in his 2019 memoir, he would have followed through with it. He'd even written a suicide note to his parents.

Now that some professional leagues, like the NFL, are loosening their restrictions on THC, while others, like the NBA and MLB, are suspending random in-season testing or lifting their bans altogether, Bird sees the sports world at a turning point. "With weed being legal now in a bunch of states, people are able to use it more, and use it more effectively," she says.

In 2021, Rachael partnered with NFL Hall of Famer Calvin Johnson (aka Megatron) to sell Mendi products out of his Michigan dispensary, Primitiv. Johnson had been prescribed opioids throughout his career, and he never liked how they made him feel. "My whole sense of balance, of proprioception, is just awful when I take those things," Johnson says. "It just never did well on me." Instead, starting in college, Johnson secretly managed his pain with cannabis, and launched Primitiv in 2021 with his former Detroit Lions teammate Rob Sims to serve other retired football players. He met Rachael at a cannabis conference in San Francisco, and immediately felt their values were aligned.

The same year, Kyle Harrison, a now-retired lacrosse star who played for the U.S. in two World Lacrosse Championships, became a Mendi ambassador. He was in his late 30s and not recovering as well as he used to, he says, and Mendi products helped him to bounce back faster. He decided to invest in the company. "She's exactly who she says she is," Harrison says of Rachael, and as a Black lacrosse player in a predominantly white sport, he says he's inspired by her willingness to advocate for marginalized groups. "I'm not sure if she gets enough credit for that," he says. "I know it's not easy."

As of February this year, Rachael says that Mendi had raised $2.3 million, mostly from friends and family. But growth comes slowly and is never guaranteed. Rachael says she's been approached by every major sports league in the country about sponsorship opportunities, but since the pandemic, the cost of sponsoring a team has become prohibitive—$25,000 and up for a National Women's Soccer League team, and often upwards of $10 million per year for a men's major league team. "We don't have deep enough pockets," she says. For now, she's focusing on "owning our backyard," the Pacific Northwest, and pivoting from elite athletes only to the broader endurance sports community. Ex-linemen and pitchers might have the most intense ailments, but Rachael's experience has taught her that all kinds of athletes—from weekend joggers and rock climbers to sub-elite marathoners—are no more immune to the tolls of testing their bodily limits.

DENISE RAPINOE, WHO turns 70 this year, still works at Jack's Bar & Grill. After nearly five decades as a waitress, she suffers from knee aches and arthritis in her fingers. Pain in her back, from a fall when she was 40, has grown worse with age. For years, she accepted chronic discomfort as part of life. Now she's using Rachael's balm and bath salts, and it's brought some relief. "I take a lot of soaking baths," she says. "I love that. It feels so good for my joints."

A few months ago, on Christmas Eve, she invited close to 30 people to a big house in Redding that Rachael, Megan, and Sue Bird had rented to accommodate the whole Rapinoe clan, along with partners and friends. It was the first time the extended family had been together for the holiday in more than 20 years. "Some people would probably like it a little bit smaller, but that's not how my mom rolls," Megan says with a laugh.

Brian was there, too. He's nearly two-and-a-half years off heroin and meth, living back home with Denise and Jim, and working as a general contractor while taking classes in computer science. He was released from prison in January 2022, and after spending the majority of his adult life in correctional institutions, he says he's ready to straighten out. Not that it's been easy. "I have pain issues," he says. "I have anxiety, I have, you know, eating, sleeping issues, all this stuff." But spending the holidays with his "little sisters" again was restorative, even if their relationship had changed. "They looked up to me growing up," he says, "and now I definitely look up to them."

On Christmas day, the three Rapinoe siblings did a workout together and then drove to their parents' house. Denise and Jim live in a suburb now, but they still have a huge yard. Rachael brought her dog and the family took a walk around the property. It felt a lot like those long childhood afternoons among the chickens, crawdads, and trees. Only this time Rachael wasn't seeking escape. "I think in the past there was a lot of pain, and then a lot of resentment, and then frustration," she says. "Now we're grateful that we could just be together."

After five days in Redding, Rachael went back to Portland, where she lives with her pitbull-boxer-plott hound mix and sits on the advisory board of the University of Portland women's soccer team. In the months since Christmas, she has continued to reflect on her path from elite athlete to addict to wellness entrepreneur. She's told people parts of her story over the years—the painkillers, the megachurches, the emotional turmoil—but is just starting to see how it all fits together. "It's taken me a long time to get here," she says, adding, "There's still so much struggle in unraveling things." But for the first time in Rachael Rapinoe's life, she feels strong enough to be fully herself. The pain is starting to go away.

DAVID ALM is a Brooklyn-based writer and editor whose longform journalism has appeared in *GQ*, *Runner's World*, and *Mother Jones*, among other publications. His 2021 story for *GQ*, "The Marathon Men Who Can't Go Home," received a notable mention in *The Year's Best Sports Writing 2022* and was named one of the Best Features of 2021 by Longreads. He teaches journalism at Hunter College–CUNY.

A Mother's Vow to Find a Dallas Mavericks Barbie Leads to a Worldwide Chase

DAVID FLEMING

FROM ESPN • JULY 21, 2023

Five years into her NBA Barbie quest, a frustrated Marilyn Harvey stood up in the closing moments of her 2004 family reunion in Alabama. She grabbed the microphone and prepared to issue her loved ones an ultimatum. Out of respect for Harvey, a prep basketball pioneer in Alabama, a longtime nurse and the family matriarch, the raucous room of nearly 100 family members from across the country fell silent. Most of them knew that for years Harvey, a hoops junkie with a force-of-nature personality, had been on a mission to secure the entire NBA Barbie doll collection for her Barbie-obsessed daughter, Candice, who was then 13.

In 1999, the NBA and Mattel teamed up to sell a one-time, leaguewide collab featuring Black and white Barbies outfitted in each franchise's authentic uniform and warmup top. The dolls also came with white high-tops, knee braces, an official NBA basketball the size of a marble and a large hairbrush that, proportionately, was the size of a cello. Barbie's sartorial timing on the collab was rather impeccable, since nearly half the teams during this NBA era incorporated some kind of funky variation of purple or teal in their outfits, starting with Detroit's horrifically awesome teal horsehead jerseys. That memorable Pistons logo and the other 28 NBA team logos were featured on the back of every NBA Barbie doll box near a special 888 number for more info on the dolls and the phrase: Own all 29 NBA Barbie dolls and have the coolest collection in the world!

The challenge was especially powerful for the Harveys: Marilyn was a Michael Jordan fanatic and a starter on the first women's basketball team at Pike County High in Brundidge, Alabama; Candice, as a kid, slept in Barbie sheets, sent Santa a complaint letter for not bringing her a Barbie Jeep and, for a short time, dreamed of dental school after seeing a dentist Barbie.

"For me, the connection with Barbie was representation, first, and of course her ultimate fabulosity," says Candice, 32, who was her high school valedictorian, went the business Barbie route in earning her MBA and now works for the USDA in Atlanta. "More than anything else, though, this is one of my connections to my momma. She loves the NBA. Sports wasn't my thing. But I loved Barbie. And I'll never forget how very intentional she was about finding a complete collection of dolls from a sport she loved that looked just like me."

Although the majority of their growing collection was made up of Black NBA Barbies, the ultimate goal for Marilyn and Candice was to complete the set. "I was bananas for Barbie by then," Candice says. "She could have been any color or race and we still would love her just as much."

In the internet days of the early 2000s, searching still meant logging countless hours on the phone and in the car. And after months of searching every toy store within 100 miles of her home, Marilyn had managed to locate 28 of the 29 NBA Barbie dolls— which seems impossible, at first, until you meet Marilyn.

"You don't mess with a momma on a mission," she says.

All they needed was one stubborn holdout:

The Dallas Mavericks Barbie.

More than a billion Barbies have been produced since her debut in New York City on March 9, 1959. But Marilyn has never found concrete proof that the Dallas Mavs Barbie was ever a part of that group.

Marilyn tried everything. She checked stores while on business trips and vacations. She harassed nieces in Texas. She asked co-workers at the hospital to help search. She even called the Mattel customer service number on the Barbie box to ask if they had somehow made a mistake and just forgotten to make one. The doll is out there, somewhere, a company rep promised. Her epic search even caught the attention of the local *Troy Messenger* newspaper. Birthdays passed. Christmases came and went. The futile search for the elusive Mavs Barbie waned on until Marilyn's last-ditch plea at the 2004 family reunion.

"I want to talk about something really important!" she shouted into the mic. "Look: I don't ask ya'll for anything. But by golly, there's enough of us that live across this country, and you all now have one mission and one mission only between now and our next reunion: Find me this missing Dallas Mavericks doll!"

No one ever did.

Twenty years later, as the world braces for Barbiemania with the opening of the *Barbie* movie, the search continues and the mystery has only deepened surrounding the missing Dallas dolls.

Theories abound, of course, in the collectible's world about the lost Mavs Barbies. Marilyn, for one, has begun to wonder if the dolls ever existed in the first place and Mattel is just covering up a colossal Barbie blunder. Because, while the white Mavs Barbies are extremely scarce, there is at least proof of their existence floating around the internet. But when it comes to the Black Dallas Mavs Barbie, not a single one of the nearly 50 Barbie collectors from around the globe contacted by ESPN could ever recall laying eyes on one in person. "The NBA Barbies are the most beautiful collection I've ever seen," says Wade Lewis, a collector from the Bronx, New York, who's been on the hunt since 1999. "I've got all of 'em, except for one. You know which one. Dallas Mavericks Barbie. That thing is a true needle in a haystack."

After all this time, the Harveys are now hoping the movie will finally do the trick and shake the elusive Mavs doll loose from someone's toy chest, attic or storage unit. The new goal, when ESPN first reached out to the Harveys this spring, was to locate the missing doll before a big family wedding in New Orleans just a few days before the *Barbie* movie premiere. And when we offered to help with their latest quest, or, at least get to the bottom of this mystery once and for all, the Harveys were happy to team up.

Just as long as we knew who's boss.

"I want my collection to be complete, OK?" says Marilyn, who gave her son the middle name Xavier after the "X-Man," Xavier McDaniel. "Right now, it's incomplete and I can't think of anything in my life I haven't completed."

Adds Candice, "I was raised to go after what I want and see it through to the end. No one's told me we're at the end yet. First, it was 'We'll find it for your 10th birthday.' Then, it was for graduation, then before college ends, then, when you get your first house. And the older I get the more, I think this is important to finish. So, yeah, I'm just not going to be OK until our collection is complete."

Barbie has no idea who she's messing with.

Dallas

Our hunt begins here, with a hard-target search of more than a dozen Dallas area toy, collectible and memorabilia stores along with a handful of Goodwill and thrift stores. Todd's Toys has a decent Barbie collection featuring a NASCAR Barbie and a Destiny Child Barbie but no Mavs Barbies. (It's too bad we're not looking for a Darth Nowitzki doll because even with the *Barbie* movie opening soon, Star Wars dominates the vintage toy game.) Nearby, there are Mia Hamm Barbies, Rebecca Lobo Barbies and Dallas Cowboys Cheerleader Barbies inside the crowded, museum-like Dallas Vintage Toys but, again, a quick electronic check of the store's entire inventory comes back with zero Mavs dolls.

Passing time during the inventory search, an employee mentions the recent controversy over the Luka Dončić mural painted in the Deep Ellum neighborhood. The painting depicted the sad-faced Mavs superstar holding a sign that read "Please send help," a clear message that fans have grown frustrated with the 38–44 Mavs and the seemingly slow search for talent to build around Dončić.

The team's search for its own Barbie goes pretty much the same way.

In 2021, when the Mavs made Cynthia Marshall the NBA's first Black woman to be a CEO, Candice called the team store in Dallas hoping the move would inspire the franchise to produce the missing Barbies. "They had no idea whatsoever what I was talking about," Candice laughs. Just before the recent July Fourth holiday, a Mavericks team rep reached out to former assistant GM Keith Grant, who had just retired after 42 years with the team, and actually had two Barbie-loving daughters who grew up in the 1990s.

Six days later, Grant reported back: He's not familiar with the "elusive Mavs Barbie" and neither are his daughters.

Maybe a new mural is in order, one with our lost Mavs Barbie holding the "Please send help" sign.

The current Mavs struggles are nothing compared to what the franchise looked like in 1998–99, however, when even the perpetually upbeat Barbie herself might have refused to rep a Mavs uni. At that point, Dallas had gone eight straight seasons without making the playoffs while averaging 60 losses each campaign. (By the way, the 1998–99 roster was impressive with future MVPs Dirk Nowitzki and Steve Nash sharing the floor with Shawn Bradley, Michael Finley, John "Hot Rod" Williams and current UNC coach Hubert Davis.) "It was kind of sad, though, honestly," says current Oklahoma City Thunder broadcaster Matt Pinto, who was on the Mavs' radio team that season. "It had started to seem like one of those endless stretches in pro sports where there's just a cloud over the organization."

The future was definitely bright in Dallas with the selection of Nowitzki, a new arena on the horizon and the sale to Mark Cuban. But one working theory about the missing Mavs Barbie is that the whole thing was, well, kind of Shawn Bradley's fault. In 1998, the Mavs were near the bottom of the league in wins and attendance and after the lockout that year, even their die-hard fans had lost interest. So, the theory goes, Mattel decided to manufacture a bare minimum of Mavs dolls as part of their NBA Barbie collection. In other words, while the six-time NBA champion Chicago Bulls might have gotten as many as 40,000 Barbies in the collection, 10,000 or fewer Mavs dolls likely found their way into circulation.

All we had to do was find one.

How hard could that be?

Dusseldorf, Germany

As the Guinness world-record holder for the largest Barbie collection on Earth (currently somewhere north of 18,500) surely, Dusseldorf's Bettina Dorfman, 62, will have a Mavs dolly or, at least, know where to locate one.

As an only child, Bettina started collecting (or, perhaps hoarding is a more accurate term) Barbie dolls when she was 10. Now, wobbly stacks of collectibles fill every nook and cranny of her jam-packed basement/museum.

With dramatic, silver Barbie-replica bangs (she cuts herself), Bettina has become a bit of a rock star in the Barbie collector world, so much so that fans have even started leaving dolls on her doorstep. She's considered an expert at repairing and appraising Barbies, has published several Barbie books, developed a worldwide network online and often shows her exquisite vintage "Flower Power" Barbie collection from the 1960s at shows all over Europe.

Her current exhibit, titled "Busy Girl," is a retrospective of the 250 or so jobs Barbie has held since 1959, from astronaut to zookeeper. "Barbie shows that women can do all the jobs, from the babysits to the presidents," Bettina says, after her delightful Zoom quirk of pausing for a moment and turning her head to the side to practice/scream the sentence in German first.

When I inquire about Barbie's employment stint with the Dallas Mavericks in the late 1990s, Bettina actually seems, well, hopeful. It turns out her daughter, Melissa Dorfmann, is a national level table tennis player and instructor at the renowned Borussia Dusseldorf Club, home to four-time Olympic medalist and eight-time European champion Timo Boll. And Bettina believes Melissa might have "the dolls of basketball." Although it worries me a little that when she promises to search her collection and online sources for the doll and get right back to me, Bettina keeps referring to the NBA as the NNBA.

A few days later, though, the email update arrives:

I have not find this doll in my collection. I have asked the other collectors but they don't have this doll, too. I will have a look to find the Barbie. I will inform you!

Best whishes

Bettina

When the inform never comes, I decide to stop messing around and go directly to the source.

El Segundo, California

Bill Greening began collecting Barbies in 1988 when he was 16. A decade later, he started at Mattel and now he's the principal designer on the Barbie Signature team and de facto company historian. "But this is probably the first time I've been asked about Barbie's history with sports," he says. "I had to study for this."

Originally, Barbie was the brainchild of Mattel co-founder Ruth Handler. In the 1950s, the legend goes, after watching her daughter Barbara projecting her dreams of adulthood fabulosity onto a flimsy paper doll, Ruth decided to produce a 3D doll worthy of a young girl's highest aspirations. Barbie was introduced on March 9, 1959, at the American Toy Fair in New York City. Mattel sold 300,000 tiny-waisted, busty Barbie dolls in the first year. In 2021, the number was 86 million. Ken came along in 1961. Christie, the first Black doll in the Barbie line, was introduced in 1968. A Black doll with the name Barbie wouldn't come out until 1980.

Along the way, Barbie has dealt with her fair share of controversy, mostly about her narrow and unrealistic beauty and body standards. "Everybody has a Barbie story to tell," Greening says. "That's my philosophy, whether you love her or hate her, everyone has an opinion on Barbie, everyone has a story to share."

In the 1960s, Barbie's story with sports was mostly recreational. In the 1970s, Mattel produced an Olympic Barbie. "Of course she came with a gold medal," Greening says. "She's Barbie." More recently, the trend with sports Barbies has been to collab with famous athletes, including Billie Jean King, Mia Hamm, Gabby Douglas and Olympic fencer Ibtihaj Muhammad. (The NBA Barbies went on sale in 1999 for $24.99 and celebrity antique appraiser Dr. Lori Verderame tells me they could be worth up to $300 each today, which is still relatively cheap in a world where the diamond-studded Stefano Canturi Barbie went for $300,000 in 2010.)

Before our chat, Greening double-checked with Mattel's archive team and confirmed that the Dallas Mavs Barbie dolls were indeed produced and copyrighted in 1998, then scanned into the company's digital catalogue/database before officially going on sale with the other 57 dolls in the NBA collection in 1999.

Greening agrees with the low-production-numbers theory based on Dallas's struggles on the court and plummeting fan base. But he added a twist: The Mavs NBA title in 2011 might have also contributed to the scarcity of the dolls. Whatever limited numbers of Barbies did manage to hit the market in 1999 probably got scooped up in a buying frenzy after the Mavs won their only title.

Mattel's official stance, then, is that there was no mistake and definitely no cover-up. More than likely the missing Mavs

Barbie doll is just a quirk of the collectible's world, the whims of little girls and the equally irrefutable laws of supply and demand.

But, in a way, that only makes them seem even more precious.

"It happens a lot and it's really, really powerful: You've got sports fans who are also Barbie fans and it's like all your loves rolled up into one collection," Greening says. "My guess with the Mavs Barbie is it was just a very small run that sold out super-duper quick."

Greening throws out one last possibility: If all else fails, there's an upcoming Barbie Collectors Convention in Orlando, Florida, featuring more than 1,000 attendees from around the world.

"We will all keep a lookout for that doll in Orlando," he promises. "And if I see one when I get to the convention, I will say 'Please hold this for Dave.' That's what Barbie's all about. Teamwork."

Singapore
Named Singapore's "Most Eligible Bachelor" by CLEO Singapore, Jian Yang has the largest Barbie collection in Asia (over 12,000), a substantial enough following on social media to be considered a Barbie "influencer" and is the author of—I swear to God—*Flushable Fashion*, a travelogue and collection of stunning Barbie dresses he constructed out of…toilet paper from around the globe. (We are now at the part of the search where things have turned wonderfully, epically weird.) Truth be told, though, I'm more interested in Yang's day job as the head of strategy for the marketing and PR firm Distilleri and the expertise he can lend to the sociological side of our increasingly futile feeling hunt for the missing Mavs Barbie. And in just a few minutes online, Yang has uncovered enough proof—a stock keeping unit number (20728) and several seemingly original photos—to conclude that the Mavs Barbie dolls do, in fact, still exist.

Yang then points out how the popular and new *Top Gun: Maverick* Barbies might be skewing search engines and hiding the NBA Mavericks Barbie in a kind of electronic Google desert.

He believes the burgeoning "clearance culture" of the late 1990s might have also been to blame. (Just a few months after they went on sale, the NBA Barbies were discounted to $6.99.) But his main theory as to why they've disappeared is so simple it's genius: We forget our beloved Barbie is a toy, first and foremost.

"We're only looking at the tip of the iceberg," Yang says. "Never forget that Barbie is a toy, primarily. Five percent of the people who consume Barbies are adults. The rest are a bunch of girls who have her in the swimming pool or buried in the sand with her head missing."

Another huge factor is that the NBA Barbies were from the "gymnast" line of dolls, meaning they had what was at the time the most bendable, articulated Barbie bodies in history which would have inspired even more "play" and less "save." To highlight this, in her original packaging, NBA Barbie's left leg is bent disturbingly beyond 90 degrees.

NBA Barbies were also made with flat feet, which means no high heels. In the movie trailer, modern-day Barbie has to deal with the horror of having her heels on the ground. She can blame the NBA Barbies for setting this in motion 25 years ago, back when having a functioning heel made Barbie a bit of a heel herself.

Knowing this it's easy to imagine a sweetly clueless dad in Dallas in 1999 excitedly giving his daughter a Barbie from his favorite NBA team, only to have their bonding moment ruined when she tears it open and responds, *Ugh, Daaad, you bought me the wrong Barbie!* and immediately puts the doll in a different outfit.

"So that Mavs doll still exists," Yang says. "There are probably a lot of them out there, actually, but no one has any idea she's the missing Mavs Barbie because she's wearing a dress."

Bronx, New York
Stupidly, I reach out to a fellow NBA Barbie collector on eBay and, being new to the collectibles game, I blab to the guy exactly

what I'm looking for and why. A retired mail carrier from the Bronx, Wade Lewis has been searching for the same missing Mavs Barbie since 1999. (Most days he does a minimum of four internet searches for the doll.) Among his 215 listings on eBay, Lewis is asking for a quarter million dollars for an Allen Iverson rookie card with a misprint. He's also got what looks like an actual portfolio from Vincent Van Gogh. What Lewis doesn't have is the Mavs Barbie.

As a result, when I first contact Lewis, his 1999 NBA Barbie collection has 27 dolls and is listed for $4,500. After our initial communication, though, Lewis doubles his efforts and, in early July, he locates a white Mavs Barbie in Memphis, Tennessee, and snags it, right out from under my stinkin' nose, for—get this—$47.31. And with this set, Lewis immediately (and, unapologetically) jacks the price up to...$75,000.

The smugness just oozes through the phone as Lewis giddily walks me through what it felt like to actually lasso a unicorn. "Twenty-five years, every day, I searched the world for her, so this was a gift from the universe for all the energy I put in," Lewis says. "I waited, watched. Waited, watched. Watched. Watched. Waited. Waited. She popped up out of one of these storage places with like five or six other NBA dolls and when I seen her, the Dallas Mavs doll, I yelled, 'Oh my gosh: Give me that!' It took me about a blink of an eye to buy it. Then I thought: I know what I have. I've got something nobody else in the world has, so let's throw some punches."

The next day, Lewis's 57-doll NBA Barbie collection (29 white Barbies and 28 Black Barbies) is listed for a cool $100,000.

"It's a big ocean," Lewis says of his Barbie search. "This is like looking for treasure. You just have to wait her out. But she'll show up. At some point, she will show up."

I'm beginning to seriously doubt it, though.

Orlando, Florida

A Boston Terrier relieves itself in the grove of palm trees outside the Hyatt Regency while its owner, dressed in jorts and a skin-tight Barbie tank top, juggles a coffee and a FaceTime call. A few feet away, the driveway to the valet stand is slowly piling up with cars as two grandmotherly women in heart-shaped sunglasses and huge pink poodle skirts pose for pictures in front of a pastel Barbie sprinter van with the license plate: BARBIER. I might never get my rental car parked, and I'm still reeling about getting outplayed by a Yankees fan, but I have officially arrived at the National Barbie Doll Collectors Convention, my last, and possibly best, chance at finding the missing Mavs Barbie.

After filling my phone with photos from a series of life-sized Barbie doll boxes and movie poster backdrops, I pay $10 for a sparkly gold wristband that gives me access to two massive ballrooms full of everything Barbie, from across the globe, as far as the eye can see. Once I catch my breath, I go straight to the biggest vendor, a woman from Chicago with a Moschino Barbie in a leather jacket on sale for $685, and explain my predicament. Before I even finish, though, she's already shaking her head. "Play line," she mutters, dismissively. Translation: never intended to be collected or protected.

For the next five hours, I wander around in a funk, hearing a slightly different version of this same explanation from, oh, 30 collectors or so. Everywhere around me are fencing Barbies, Olympic Barbies, skiing Barbies, tennis Barbies, NASCAR Barbies, cheerleader Barbies, but not a single NBA Barbie to be found. Suddenly, I long for the NFL season and to be back in the comparatively hospitable confines of a Bill Belichick locker room. And, I swear, if one more Barbie-quoting collector pats me on the back and tells me to "Hold onto your dreams" or that "Anything is possible" and "The magic really happens when you believe in yourself," I'm going to lose it.

I can't be sure because I lost track of time, but at one point I think I spent almost an hour with my nose buried in a stack of *Barbie Bazaar* magazines from the 1990s. Then, near the end of the day, when I catch myself humming "Barbie Girl" by Aqua while rummaging through a giant clearance pile of $5 unboxed bargain Barbies all wrapped in cheap plastic, the realization hits me like a runaway Barbie Dream Camper.

I've officially hit rock bottom.

Arlington, Texas

A day before this story is due, as I'm literally pacing back and forth in front of my desk staring at my phone working up the courage to call and update the Harveys, my cohort in this quest, Texas-based ESPN reporter Alonzo Olmedo (the Ken to my Barbie, if you will) emails to say he might have actually located a Dallas freakin' Mavs Barbie on Facebook Marketplace.

I message the seller and try to bluff my way through the conversation by throwing around terms like NRFB (never removed from box) and MIB (mint in box). But something feels off. At first she says she can take PayPal and will mail my Barbie to me. But after I offer her full asking price ($75) she then insists on cash and an in-person pickup...at a gas station.

Well, I've come this far, I mumble to myself, before typing my Hail Mary into Messenger. OK, where?

The address she gives is near Arlington, 15 minutes from Alonzo's house. Is this a Barbie Miracle?

I Venmo Alonzo the money and arrange for the cash payment and pickup at 7:45 p.m. the next night. Alonzo arrives 30 minutes early. After a scorching day in Texas, his car says the temperature is 109 as he watches the sun set behind a QuikTrip that is just a few minutes from AT&T Stadium.

At first, the seller is a no-show. But after a little bit of last-second cajoling and negotiating, she arrives at pump 9 at 8:25 p.m. on the back of a scooter driven by her boyfriend. Alonzo inspects the doll, a white Barbie with the Mavs uniform. The box is sealed. The hologram, barcode and stock keeping unit number all seem correct. The "Indiana Jones" moment is the hairbrush, hidden at the bottom of the box and unknown to most newbies. It's there. Alonzo hands over the cash and places the doll in the passenger seat of his car.

And then, like a dad leaving a hospital with a newborn, he makes the short drive home. "Very carefully," he says.

Several tortuous minutes after sending him a pleading "all good?" text, Alonzo arrives home and my phone lights up with a response.

Smiling back at me in the dark, it's her, it's actually her.

Brundidge, Alabama

The day after bravely securing it at the QT in Arlington, Alonzo bubble-wrapped our Barbie like she was the *Mona Lisa* and overnighted her to me in North Carolina as I scrambled to make travel plans to rural Alabama while alerting the Harveys of my visit without giving away too much. After a plane ride through a thunderstorm, a long drive through the night and a sleepless night in a hotel, I brace myself as I approach Marilyn's front door. The Harvey home is a red brick cottage set back off a crepe myrtle-lined side street in a tiny, tight-knit town once known for its peanut butter production just a few miles east of Troy University.

And then, the strangest thing yet happens: Candice, who is wearing a Barbie T-shirt, barely even acknowledges my giant Barbie pink gift bag. After a long night shift at the hospital, a subdued Marilyn doesn't inquire about it, either.

Some of the Harvey's prized 28 NBA Barbies are on display in Candice's childhood bedroom next to a sign: "Don't be afraid to dream…for out of such fragile things come miracles." The rest of the dolls are in Marilyn's room, organized by—of course—NBA divisions.

After nearly 25 years of aggravating and fruitless searching (Candice's phone still beeps with Google alerts for NBA Barbie), Marilyn had finally lost hope and become fully resigned to the fact that her dream doll just didn't exist. She sees my gift bag and figures I'm probably carrying a *Barbie* movie doll or some other consolation prize.

But as soon as I hand it to her and she sees my beaming face and the faint NBA logo underneath the bubble wrap, Marilyn—I don't really know how to describe this—she lights up and melts all at the same time.

"Oh, don't do this to me, David, don't tease me like this," she cries while pulling at the wrap.

A euphoric scream of "Oh God, oh my goodness" is followed by a long, high-pitched joyous, half laugh, half cry of "Ooooow." There's a moment of stunned silence. More gentle unwrapping. And then, tears. Lots and lots of tears.

"After all these years..." Candice sniffles.

Standing at the end of the kitchen table, practically cheek-to-cheek, with trembling hands and tear-soaked faces, together, mother and daughter finally unwrap their Dallas Mavericks Barbie.

"It's her! She's gorgeous!" Candice says.

Marilyn just says one word, over and over: "Faith."

And if you think this is all a little much, well, you just don't get Barbie, or what she means to people like the Harveys or the worldwide Barbie community that made this moment happen.

"I don't cry easily, but I'm emotional right now and it's about finally finding the doll but everything else around it, mostly my momma, mostly the kindness people, strangers, showed us," Candice says. "We will always have this connection and this moment together, forever. It's extremely special. I have been dreaming of this most of my life and it happened. We did it."

After a brief discussion about jumping in my rental car and driving to Texas so we can all give Alonzo a group hug, Marilyn goes right into collector mode, pulling Barbies out of rooms and shelves and drawers all over the house, finally, finally getting to line up her entire NBA Barbie Collection on the living room couch without that awkward, annoying chasm between the Bulls and Denver Nuggets. In all the hoopla, when the Miami Heat doll slips off the couch and falls to the floor, Marilyn coos at it: "It's OK, sweetie, you're OK, sweetie." Then she steps back, takes in the sight, tugs on her "Kindness Matters" T-shirt and giggles, "It's like I can finally exhale."

The plan now is for Candice to take the 29 dolls back to Georgia and display them in her new home, at least until next year's Harvey family reunion in Brundidge, where Marilyn plans to show them off and close the loop on her familial plea in 2004. Eventually Marilyn wants to donate the collection to charity or a museum. Maybe even the Smithsonian.

"I will never sell them," she says. "This is not about that. This is about finishing what you start and believing in what you're doing, and if it's meaningful to you, that's all that really matters. This is meaningful to me. This is a dream, realized, and a reunion, too! Barbie was missing, she was lost, for a long time. But now she's with the rest of her team. She's with her family.

"Barbie's home."

Additional reporting by Alonzo Olmedo.

DAVID FLEMING earned numerous national awards as well as a handwritten note from the White House during the last 30 years as a writer for *Sports Illustrated* and *ESPN The Magazine*. His fourth book, on the miraculous, disastrous 1952 Dallas Texans, the last NFL team to fail, will be published in 2025 by St. Martin's Press. His previous books include *Breaker Boys: The NFL's Greatest Team and the Stolen 1925 Championship* and *Who's Your Founding Father?* on America's first, true Declaration of Independence. Fleming is a Meadowlark correspondent. "Barbie" was his final story for ESPN.

Hazing, Naked Skates and a 'Mental-Health Hunger Games': The Dark Side of Harvard Women's Ice Hockey

HAILEY SALVIAN AND KATIE STRANG

FROM The Athletic • MARCH 10, 2023

On Jan. 21, hours after the Harvard women's ice hockey team fell 3–1 to Union College, Crimson coach Katey Stone walked into the Boynton Lounge, a hospitality suite within The Bright-Landry Hockey Center. It was the night of the HH Dinner, the marquee event of alumni weekend, and the room was filled with Stone's former and current players, athletic department officials and others.

Stone, 56, has coached Harvard for 27 seasons and has more wins than any other female coach in collegiate women's hockey history. Photos of the great players from her teams adorn a wall outside the lounge. Some of those players clustered with former teammates around the space, reconnecting, catching up about careers and families. Stone moved among them, buoyant. The drinks and stories flowed.

But amidst the socializing and revelry was an undercurrent of unease. Stone and many others at the dinner knew that the *Boston Globe* was about to publish an exposé about the program.

Days earlier, current players and some alumni received an email from Stone notifying them of a coming article that would accuse her of fostering "a culture that has emotionally damaged many of the girls I have recruited."

As they socialized, some attendees speculated about what the article might reveal and who spoke to the newspaper. Others denounced the story as a hit piece. When athletic director Erin McDermott praised Stone and her legacy in a speech, some saw it as a public vote of confidence. Holly Johnson, a member of Stone's first team (1994–95), forcefully reminded the players and alumni that their association with the program gave them credibility. She added that the reputation of the program is sacred.

To some of the approximately 50 attendees, the event felt like an effort to galvanize support for Stone and rally people to push back against any criticism to come.

Throughout the evening, Stone projected insouciance. She danced. She took a shot of alcohol off a goalie stick with others. She offered up her crystal-studded loafers to be auctioned off. And she enthusiastically thanked those in attendance for their support.

But later, Stone met with a smaller group of former players in the team's locker room. It is considered hallowed ground by many alumni, and printed on the door is one of Stone's edicts, a reminder that what is said and seen in the room doesn't leave the room. There, Stone shed the calm she displayed at the larger gathering.

"They're trying to light this program on fire," she said. "And we're not going to let that happen."

On Jan. 27, the *Globe* published the article, in which 16 players (three of them named), accused Stone of misconduct, including insensitivity to mental health issues, pressuring players to return from injuries, body shaming and more. The paper also reported there was hazing within the program.

The article's most detailed anecdote centered on a racially insensitive comment made by Stone at a meeting on March 5,

2022. Stone said the team had "too many chiefs and not enough Indians."

Stone self-reported that remark, made in front of two players of Indigenous descent, shortly after it occurred. It prompted a review of the program, but in an email to one player, McDermott wrote: "Please know that Coach Stone is not under investigation." In an April 8 email to the entire team, she called the review a "deeper dive" into players' experiences that would involve "conversations" with a faculty member and assistant dean. On July 19, McDermott let players know via email that "Coach Stone is our head coach and will remain our head coach."

Over the last month, The Athletic spoke to more than 30 individuals who played for Harvard or were associated with the program from this season and going back more than 20 years. The Athletic also reviewed audio recordings, videos and email correspondence from players, school officials and others. What emerged from that reporting was a portrait of a program that, for most of Stone's tenure, pushed and crossed the boundaries of acceptable treatment of athletes, players say, and in many years there were activities that some players considered hazing. Among the specific allegations:

- During the team's annual "Initiation Week," which concluded with "Freshmen Fun Night", upperclassmen urged freshmen to, among other acts over the years, put condoms on bananas, fake orgasms and act out skits that referenced their sexual orientation. Some years, underaged players felt pressured to consume alcohol, some until they passed out or vomited. In some years, alumni came back to campus and participated in "Freshmen Fun Night."

- There was a ritual called "Naked Skate" at The Bright-Landry Hockey Center that made some players uncomfortable. Players from 2005 to 2023 said they witnessed or participated in the event. In some of those years, freshmen were told to do a "superman" slide on the ice that left some with ice burns and bleeding nipples. The most recent "Naked Skate" occurred the day following the publication of the *Globe* story. After one player became upset about the event, Stone and her staff later met with the team and told them it was an unsanctioned activity.

- Players on teams dating as far back as 2002 recalled a fining system in which team members had to pay a monetary penalty for perceived offenses. Some women were fined for the clothes they wore or what they ate, for having a boyfriend or harboring a crush. Some players say they had to pay a "gay tax" or an "Asian tax."

The Athletic did not find direct evidence that Stone played any role in Initiation Week, the fining system or was present for Naked Skate. But, as one player from the last 10 years said, Stone would frequently remind the players: "There's not a single thing on this team that goes on that I don't know about." (That player and some others were granted anonymity because they fear reprisal from Harvard officials or the team's alumni.)

Stone was allegedly an active participant in other problematic behavior. Seven players described instances from three seasons when Stone would respond to a rule infraction by leading a chant against the offending player: "I hate (player's name)! I hate (player's name)!" Eleven players alleged that Stone showed indifference to injuries they or others suffered. One player who suffered a head injury during a practice early in her freshman year said Stone glanced at her while she was lying on the ice and crying and barked at a trainer: "Get this kid out of here!"

One year, Stone had players fill out a survey, which included a comment section where players had to write about their teammates' abilities. Stone then held a meeting with each player and showed those comments to them.

"It was like being a part of a cult," Tiana Harris, who played the 2011–12 season for Harvard, wrote in an email.

The remark by Stone on March 5, 2022, was not the first time she or a member of her coaching staff made a racially insensitive comment in front of the team. During the 2017–18 season, Stone made an insensitive comment to a player from Japan during a team meeting. The next season, an associate coach did the same, according to the Japanese player and another person present.

Concerns about the program's culture and Stone's treatment of players were raised to school officials at least four times over the past six years. Further, a 2019 survey of all Harvard athletes revealed that the women's hockey program ranked last among the school's teams in player satisfaction, according to players. And athletic department officials were aware of the program's high rate of attrition. In the last two years, nine players exited the program with eligibility remaining.

Abra Kinkopf, who played on the 2002–03 team, and many other players who spoke to The Athletic expressed frustration with Harvard's seeming inaction in the face of so many players leaving the program. "How many would you like? How many do you need? How many is enough for you?" asked Kinkopf.

On Wednesday, The Athletic spoke with Harvard spokesperson Rachael Dane and, in a nearly hour-long conversation, went over the allegations in this story and requested interviews with Stone, McDermott, associate coach Lee-J Mirasolo and Mike Smith, the school's faculty athletics representative. A reporter also spoke with Stone briefly over the phone and offered her the opportunity to respond to the allegations. Stone said she did not have time to go over them. Dane later said that Stone didn't wish to speak with The Athletic at this time. McDermott, Mirasolo and Smith also declined to comment, according to Dane. The Athletic had multiple phone conversations and email exchanges with Dane over a two-day period, answering her questions about this story. She provided a statement addressing one allegation in the story—included below—but otherwise declined to comment.

'A mental-health Hunger Games'

Stone grew up in Watertown, Conn., the youngest of four kids, nicknamed "The Big Banana" by her siblings because of her bright blonde hair. She played on her older brother's peewee team and wasn't shy about mixing it up with the boys. Her mother was a receptionist at the prestigious Taft boarding school; her dad was the athletic director. Stone recalled sitting in dugouts with her father, keeping stats during baseball games and skating on Taft's rink on Christmas mornings.

She played field hockey, ice hockey and lacrosse in high school—"She was just a fireball," her older sister told *Harvard Magazine* in 2014—before playing lacrosse and ice hockey at the University of New Hampshire.

Stone was hired to helm Harvard's hockey team in 1994 at age 28. In 1999, the Crimson won a national championship, thrusting the program on the level of powerhouses like UNH, Providence and Northeastern.

She smartly built the program, in part, by leveraging Harvard's academics and the network of well-connected alumni of the program. She preached the mantra 4 for 40—where an individual played for the next four years would dictate the following 40 years of that person's life. It helped her establish pipelines to hockey hotbeds such as Minnesota, elite prep schools such as Noble and Greenough, and feeder programs such as Assabet Valley.

When players arrive at Harvard, Stone demands total commitment, and they must abide by a stringent code of conduct. In the weeks prior to the season's start, new players wear their high school gear or their Harvard jerseys turned inside out and are not permitted to use the locker room. Those are rights they have to earn. When "Coach" enters the room, players are instructed to sit up straight, place their hands on their knees and make direct eye contact. Arriving on time means you're late. During the national anthem before puck drop, players know "not to move an inch." Skate blades are in the middle of the blue line, sticks in their right hands, and helmets in their left with numbers facing out.

When a player scores a goal, she has to point to the teammate who passed her the puck.

Some of the players interviewed by The Athletic said they had a positive experience playing for Stone. But she also favored a climate in which players were constantly on edge. One way she accomplished that, players say, was to create two factions, one comprised of Stone's favorites and the other the players she disliked or disregarded. The divide was not always by skill. Often it was players who were compliant versus those who dared to have "a streak of independence," as one player put it. The former were often deputized by Stone to monitor the latter, ferrying information to Stone about their teammates' eating habits, personal lives, extracurricular activities and more. Some team leaders were asked for input on playing time for their peers, discipline for teammates, even dispatched to enforce dress code violations.

One person likened the environment to the Stanford prison experiment, a controversial study in which college students became prisoners or guards in a simulated prison and adopted the behaviors of their respective roles.

Some players who felt out of favor tried to claw their way into Stone's good graces, which sometimes meant volunteering her information such as who was dating who, which players were drinking heavily on weekends and more.

"The whole team was centered around shame," said a player from the 2016–17 season.

Many players described a sense of constantly being scrutinized. One player was informed her pants were too short. Another that an exposed metal zipper was unacceptable. Some years, players were weighed regularly and what they ate was monitored. The player from the 2016–17 season said she and others had to send a trainer photos of their meals. The trainer chided her for having a muffin on her plate. ("Is that a breakfast cupcake I see?"). Another player who played a few years earlier was told she needed to gain weight and had to down protein shakes while team captains supervised. She gained 20 pounds in six months and felt slow and became more self-conscious about her appearance. "I was in a completely foreign body," said the player, one of three who told The Athletic they developed an eating disorder while at Harvard.

Two players on the 2016–17 team said that at the end of that season, Stone distributed something like a Likert scale survey for players to fill out that included questions about their teammates—example: *Does (player name) work hard?*—which they were to score from one to five. There was also a mandatory comment section and players were instructed to list their teammates' strengths and weaknesses. Once the surveys were completed, Stone and the other coaches called each player into a meeting and showed them what their teammates wrote about them. "It was like the burn book from *Mean Girls*," said one player. She said some teammates were shattered after reading harsh comments from their peers. And, the coaches didn't name who said what, creating more mistrust among teammates.

One parent of a player from a recent season, in describing how she perceived Stone ran the program, said it was "a mental-health Hunger Games."

In her 27 seasons coaching Harvard, Stone has 523 career wins. She has won 12 Beanpot trophies, and coached 24 All-American players, 15 Olympians and six winners of the Patty Kazmeier award (given annually to the top Division I player in the nation). She was the first woman to coach the U.S. Olympic women's team, at the 2014 Games in Sochi. However, Harvard has qualified for only one of the last seven NCAA Tournaments.

"The longer the season goes, the more the team just falls apart, because she pits us against each other and creates this dynamic where we're not rooting for each other to be at our best, we're waiting for someone to fall so we can be in their shoes," said Maryna Macdonald (2018–22).

After the five-win 2016–17 season, the worst in Stone's tenure, two parents of players met with Lars Madsen, the chief of staff to then-Harvard president Drew Faust. One of the parents in that meeting said they told Madsen about Stone's insensitivity to mental health issues, how she told players who were struggling that they were a burden to their teammates and that players don't speak up due to fear of retaliation. Those parents also collected comments from other parents via email and shared some of those comments with Madsen. In those parent emails, the program was termed a "secret society." Stone was called "a menace." And players were said to be "scared s---less" to report what they were enduring. (Madsen, now at Stanford, did not respond to multiple emails and a text message requesting an interview.)

The parent who spoke to The Athletic said they never heard from Madsen after that meeting. "All I could think was: 'Thank God my kid is finished here,'" said the parent.

'It reinforces the culture of silence'
The instructions would come via email or text sent to the freshmen class early in the school year. Those incoming players, most still teenagers, would be given costume assignments and a list of tasks to complete, with photo documentation required.

This, they were told, was the start of Initiation Week.

Most tasks were innocuous. Some were even a bit fun. Form a pyramid in the quad. Snap a photo in front of the "Pucks 9" license plate that adorned Stone's car. But there were other, more unseemly tasks. Lick the toe of the John Harvard statue on campus. Jump inside a dirty laundry hamper after an intense practice session.

Players also were ordered to wear or carry things around campus that made them look ridiculous but were mostly viewed as harmless fun. One player had to wear a cowboy hat and pigtails, another a leather jacket and biking gloves, another had to carry a stethoscope and medical briefcase. If a player was caught without the required costume or adornment, upperclassmen might demand they drop and do pushups on the spot.

The Athletic spoke to players spanning two decades of teams. Most did not take issue with what they were asked to do or wear or carry in the first part of Initiation Week. But some felt that what was asked of them in the early part of the week crossed the line. Harris remembers a group of upperclassmen coming to her dorm in her freshman year (2011–12) and filming her while she did pushups and goading her with insults about her long-distance boyfriend. "We know your boyfriend likes it fast, but we want them slow," Harris said they yelled.

Initiation Week culminated with Freshmen Fun Night. The newcomers met at a dorm room at a prearranged time in assigned costumes, some of which were chosen to poke fun at a freshman's insecurities. One woman struggling emotionally and who cried often had to dress up as Oscar the Grouch, with actual garbage attached to her. Another with a very muscular, athletic build had to go as Malibu Barbie.

At the dorm room, the freshmen were met by upperclassmen, and in some years alumni of the program—who came back to help with the initiation—all of them clad in black dresses and sunglasses. Freshmen were herded into a bathroom where the lights were turned off, the sink drains covered in tape and they were told to drink until the shots of alcohol or warmed-up beers were gone. Some years, freshmen were allowed to abstain. Other years, players felt that wasn't an option. One former player said she became so inebriated she never left the bathroom; she just laid down there.

Freshmen would eventually exit the bathroom and stand in the middle of the dorm room and be given commands. In some years, they had to recite Harvard hockey facts, like how many goals Nicole Corriero scored in her career. Sometimes, the freshmen were required to perform a song. Players also described skits simulating sex acts with each other or inanimate objects. Harris said she and others were required to do wall sits while alumni screamed at them.

When all the freshmen had gone through the gauntlet, the jeers and vitriol turned to smiles and hugs. The players were told they were now part of the team and were invited to go out partying with the upperclassmen. Some freshmen laughed off the experience, eager to be welcomed into the ranks, and found the night to be fun. But others were appalled.

"For me, it was hazing," Harris said. She added: "You had all these alum who were super intimidating."

One of the players from 2016–17 said she and others in her class tried to shield a classmate who was allergic to alcohol from having to partake during Freshmen Fun Night, but the classmate felt she couldn't abstain. When the initiation ended and they were invited out for a night of more drinking, the player said she and her classmate instead headed to Harvard Yard. The two sat on the steps and cried. The player who was allergic to alcohol vomited.

For some, the torment from upperclassmen didn't end with Initiation Week. Harris said older teammates would see her at parties and call her "titties," a reference, she felt, meant to shame her for dressing too provocatively. When she passed on team parties to hang out with friends from her dorm, she was given a teddy bear named "Shady Bear" because, team leaders explained, she was acting "shady."

Upperclassmen and team leaders also oversaw the fining system in which players were docked nominal amounts for perceived transgressions. Much like the initiation rituals, what a player was fined for depended on the arbiter. The offenses could be light-hearted, like for wearing the same outfit as a teammate. But players also recalled being fined for late-night hookups or associating with people not deemed "friends of the program." Players' bodies, eating habits and sexual orientation could all be fineable offenses. One team member was fined for having a crush on a teammate.

Players not in Stone's good graces often felt as if they were targeted with fines more frequently. "I was an easy target. Coach didn't like me, so they didn't have to like me either," said a player from the 2015–16 season.

"It reinforces the culture of silence," Kinkopf said. "It seems silly. It seems harmless. It's not."

Naked Skate, another tradition painted as a team-building exercise, occurred later in the season, typically after the longest road trip of the season.

As the team bus arrived back at campus, players were told by the upperclassmen to go to the locker room at The Bright-Landry Hockey Center. Once inside, the upperclassmen stripped down and instructed others to do the same until they were naked. They would then put on skates and gloves and take the ice. Some years, freshmen were ordered to take part. In other years, it was voluntary. Four players from 11 different seasons say they witnessed a Naked Skate when freshmen were told to superman slide on the ice.

Many players who spoke to The Athletic thought Naked Skate was fun or expressed indifference to it. But it made others uncomfortable. A player from the 2013–14 team said she worried about other people who had access to the rink, including the men's hockey team, and whether Naked Skate was being recorded by the arena's cameras. She said she took part for just a few minutes and then left, finding the whole experience "f---ed up."

Even amidst the fallout from the *Globe* article, the 2023 Naked Skate was held as usual. Confronted with that fact, Harvard emailed the following statement:

> Following the disclosure that a member of the Harvard women's hockey team was upset after a non-sanctioned team event on the evening of Saturday, January 28, the women's hockey coaches alerted Harvard Athletics to the comments and discussed next steps. Following that notification, the coaches were instructed to speak with the captains and members of the team to determine the events of Saturday, 28th. During those coach to student conversations, players involved acknowledged that they arranged a voluntary skating event at the hockey arena without the consent of Harvard Athletics. They further acknowledged that the event was not mandatory

and some students participated, while others chose not to. On February 1, the coaches held a full team meeting to reaffirm that this was a non-sanctioned event that did not reflect the expectations of the Harvard women's hockey team and clearly stated that all team activities that make any member of the team feel pressured or uncomfortable are not permitted.

In response to that statement, The Athletic emailed a Harvard spokesperson some questions, including: Did Harvard consider what occurred to be "hazing"? How did players gain access to the arena after hours? Was this the first time Stone has been made aware that team members were holding a Naked Skate? The spokesperson did not respond to that email.

All Harvard athletes must sign an anti-hazing pledge at the beginning of each season. One player from the mid-2000s felt a sense of relief when that form was distributed, only to find herself subjected to what she considered hazing a short time later during Initiation Week.

"It's something that you think you're protected against and it turns out there is no protection," said a player from the early-2000s.

'They wouldn't even call it an investigation'

When on March 5, 2022, Stone said to the team that it contained "too many chiefs and not enough Indians," Maryna Macdonald, a member of British Columbia's Ditidaht First Nation, said Stone looked at her as she spoke. Stone admitted almost immediately that she shouldn't have said it, but Macdonald was so obviously unsettled by the comment that, after Stone left the room, Macdonald's teammates consoled her.

Macdonald had considered leaving the program before. When she arrived as a freshman in 2018–19, some of Stone's policies and the team dynamic made her feel unwelcome. Macdonald was thousands of miles away from her home, and she felt isolated and grew depressed. She was frequently vomiting from the anxiety she felt each day.

After Macdonald sustained a head injury in a game on Dec. 8, 2018, Stone came to her hospital room to deliver a keepsake puck—Macdonald had scored her first goal before the hit. But when Macdonald described the on-ice collision to a nurse, Macdonald said Stone scoffed at her description and suggested that she was embellishing.

During winter break later in the season, Macdonald missed the first session of a two-a-day practice (which she could not participate in due to her concussion) because she was late flying back from British Columbia. She says Stone later scolded her in front of the coaching staff and two captains. Stone brought up that misstep continuously over the remainder of the school year and beyond, Macdonald said.

Stone, according to Macdonald, consistently harped on Macdonald's weight. Macdonald said she developed an eating disorder and lost 15 pounds the summer between her freshman and sophomore seasons.

Following her sophomore season, Macdonald told Stone she was struggling with the decision to return because of how Stone treated her. Macdonald said Stone apologized for making her feel that way. She also brought up Stone berating her for missing the practice she could not participate in because of her head injury. Macdonald said Stone said she wasn't aware Macdonald couldn't practice.

Macdonald returned to the team but says Stone continued to criticize her about her weight. Once, when Macdonald arrived late to practice because she was receiving medical treatment, Stone started a chant—"I hate Mac! I hate Mac!"—and goaded others to join in. (Macdonald does not know if Stone was aware she was getting treatment.)

When on April 8, McDermott, the athletic director, informed the players via email of the review of the program, Macdonald welcomed the scrutiny. Macdonald says she asked McDermott why it had taken about a month after learning of Stone's comment for the school to do something. She said McDermott told her that players needed time to "cool off," and that the university needed to find someone who "understands Harvard" to carry out the "conversations" with players. The school chose Mike Smith, Harvard's NCAA faculty athletics representative. He has worked at Harvard since 1992 and chaired the committee that hired McDermott.

"There was no separation on any level," Macdonald said. "They wouldn't even call it an investigation."

Macdonald still took part in the review, telling Smith and Katie Colleran, an assistant dean for student engagement and leadership, about the dysfunction and the manipulation and verbal and emotional abuse she experienced.

Another player told The Athletic she also met with Smith and Colleran and said she described her time in the program to them as "(verbally) abusive and unacceptable in every regard." The player from Japan said she told Smith and Colleran that, given how she was treated her senior year and how little she played, she felt Stone discriminated against her because of her race and background. (Colleran, who now works at Dartmouth, did not respond to an email and message on social media requesting an interview.)

On July 19, McDermott sent to the team an email with the subject "Onward and Upward." She thanked players for their candor during Smith's review and announced Stone would remain coach. "I believe in Coach Stone. I believe in you. And I'm excited for the future of Harvard Women's Ice Hockey...Go Crimson!"

The next day, Macdonald officially quit the team.

"I don't want to be dealing with this in my 40s," she said. "The fact that there's trauma that runs that deep in (former players) that have kids and careers and families, that's ridiculous to me. That shows how terrible this whole situation is."

'I haven't watched a hockey game or skated since'

Macdonald's exit was one of many.

Sydney Daniels, an assistant coach and former captain (2013–17) and a Mistawasis First Nations member, also did not return to the team. She has since filed a complaint against the school with the Massachusetts Commission Against Discrimination, which is being investigated. Taze Thompson, a member of Metis Nation of Alberta and Okanagan Indian Band, B.C., and the Ivy League Rookie of the Year in 2021–22, transferred to Northeastern in July.

Three other players left the program before the end of this past season.

They joined a lengthy list of players who left the program or finished their careers at Harvard disappointed and distraught:

- "I decided after two years I'd rather live my life not playing hockey so that I don't have to be on this team anymore," said an early-2000s player who quit because she felt constantly scrutinized and belittled by Stone. She recalled being scratched off one game-day roster after Stone looked at her plate of chicken and pasta and asked: "Is that all you're eating?"

- "There was this feeling of I'm completely worthless and nobody will tell me why," said another player from the early-2000s. She said Stone once criticized her for not smiling enough and told her that her teammates didn't want to be around her. She finished her career at Harvard and said she needed therapy to work through what she experienced.

- "If you are not producing for her, she doesn't give a s--- about you," said the player from the 2015–16 team. She was the player who laid on the ice, crying, after suffering a head injury, when Stone said: "Get this kid out of here!" Later, Stone repeatedly asked her why she wasn't practicing, the player said. Feeling pressure to return to the ice despite still suffering from symptoms, including light and noise sensitivity, the player said she performed multiple conditioning tests on a stationary bike and failed them. She later arrived at the arena, found her bags packed, and said Stone told her she was a "disgrace" and off the team.

- "It was like I wasn't even in the room," said the player from Japan. During her freshman season (2017–18), when she offered a dissenting opinion on a uniform decision, she says Stone said to her in front of the team: "In this country, we make decisions democratically." The next season, in November 2018, associate coach Lee-J Mirasolo used a team speech to lionize a WWII veteran who shot down five Japanese planes. The player had been a regular in the lineup her first three seasons at Harvard, but she barely played her senior season for reasons she says were never explained to her.

- "I haven't watched a hockey game or skated since," said a player who quit during the 2017–18 season. That year, she struggled with an eating disorder and felt depressed. When she met with an academic adviser to try to resolve a class scheduling conflict, she broke down in his office, sobbing, and confided in him that she wasn't eating or sleeping and felt miserable. The adviser offered a straightforward solution: *Why not quit the team?*

The player scoffed at the suggestion. It was absurd. She was an elite athlete. Like so many of the women whom Stone recruited to Harvard, hockey was who she was. But over the next few days, his words sunk in. She considered a life not filled with stress and anxiety. *I could just not do this*, the player realized.

She quit the team soon after and took a leave of absence from school to focus on her mental health.

The high number of players who recently exited the team—nine over the last two seasons—should have sounded alarms within the athletic department. So, too, should the results of a 2019 survey, commissioned by the faculty of Arts and Sciences, in which Harvard athletes were asked to respond to questions like "My coaches care about me as a person" and "I am treated fairly on my team." McDermott told the team that the women's hockey program ranked last in overall athlete culture and satisfaction. Yet no efforts to address those issues during the 2020–21 school year or the first half of 2021–22 were apparent to the people associated with those teams who spoke to The Athletic.

Said one player from the mid-2000s: "It makes me really angry and sad that it's continuing to happen to these girls because I know the harm and the pain it's caused me."

Added Kinkopf: "It's time to think, time to listen, time to make some changes."

'You graduated before I was born'

The alumni community that made Harvard women's hockey so appealing to recruits, that has contributed vast sums of money to the program year after year, is now a house divided. Some players desire a deep accounting of Stone's tenure, others shout down even the mere suggestion of wrongdoing. Multiple women said they no longer feel welcome at gatherings of former players, and fear being cut off from the powerful Harvard alumni network if they speak honestly about their experiences.

"We have this thing at Harvard about a Team First mentality. For me, Team First means if someone is hurting on the team and in our community, we have to do something for those players," said a third player from the early-2000s. "I feel like Team First for (Stone's supporters) is protecting the legacy and protecting Katey Stone."

After the Globe article published, a group of hockey alumni communicated in an email chain and discussed how to push back against the article. One player on that chain, Vanessa McCafferty (1999–2002), responded to the group that she felt the story was balanced. She wrote:

I'm glad so many of you cherish her and felt mentored/supported but team first for me means acknowledging that for many players, it was a very different experience to varying degrees. It may not be a vendetta but just speaking the truth. I'm torn because I witnessed behavior that was abusive and also observed her being wonderful to other teammates. Favorites had a completely different experience and coach.

My conclusion is that be true to your own experience but also sensitive to all of your teammates.

A subsequent email from Lauren McAuliffe (2001–04) informed the group that McCafferty had been removed from the email chain. (McCafferty declined to comment.) McAuliffe then encouraged alumni to sign a letter of support for Stone that would be sent to Harvard's current and incoming president.

It would be imprecise to say that the fissure within the alumni base is generational. There are some players from recent teams who have spoken in Stone's defense and players from her early teams who were critical of her in interviews with The Athletic. But the most vocal and public of her defenders are players from her first decade as coach, and the women who have put their names on allegations against her are predominantly from teams in the last decade.

Holly Johnson, the player from Stone's first team who spoke at the HH Dinner and is also on the advisory board for the Harvard Varsity Club, penned an op-ed in the *Globe* in which she defended Stone's coaching style as "characteristic of all coaches who demand excellence and don't champion mediocrity in players." McAuliffe shared an unpublished op-ed with The Athletic that stated that the criticism of Stone and the program was driven, in part, by "white players from privileged backgrounds that wanted Coach Stone fired because they weren't getting their way."

Meanwhile, younger alumni bristle at women from earlier generations dismissing what they endured. "You graduated before

I was born," said one of the players from the 2016–17 team. "How could you know what my experience was like?"

Editor's note: On Tuesday, June 6, 2023, Katey Stone announced her retirement.

HAILEY SALVIAN is a national women's hockey writer who writes primarily about the new Professional Women's Hockey League and international women's hockey. Previously, she covered the Calgary Flames and Ottawa Senators. **KATIE STRANG** is a senior enterprise and investigative writer for The Athletic, specializing in covering the intersection of sports and social issues, with a focus on sexual abuse and gendered violence. She previously worked at ESPN.

Livvy, Inc.

STEVE POLITI

FROM NJ.com • NOVEMBER 20, 2023

DULUTH, Ga.—There are hundreds of teenage girls screaming, and thousands of rabid fans waving pompoms, and club music playing at a volume that could make your eardrums bleed. There are sequin-covered gymnasts pounding their palms on floor pads, and blazer-clad judges looking sternly over their computer monitors, and numbers that look stolen from a math test—*9.825! 9.950! 9.875!*—met with approving roars as they pop up on placards in all corners of this madhouse.

It would seem impossible that a single human being could stand out during the two hours of sensory overload that is the SEC Gymnastics Championships, a four-ring circus with no clowns but dozens of the world's best acrobats. Then, early on the final night of competition at Gas South Arena this spring, that is exactly what happens.

Olivia Dunne, in a white-and-purple leotard with her blond hair pulled back into a messy ponytail, steps onto a mat and stares up at the uneven bars. She is not the most accomplished athlete on her Louisiana State team, but it feels like every neck in the building cranes in her direction as she tightens the strings on her wrist supports.

The gymnastics diehards want to see how the New Jersey native will perform with a much-coveted title on the line at the end of an injury-plagued season. But plenty of casual fans who have come to this suburban Atlanta venue don't know the difference between a salto and a split.

They are here just to see her—period.

Livvy, as she is known on social media, is the rare athlete who transcends her sport thanks to a rule change that allows NCAA athletes to cash in on their name, image and likeness. In a three-month span this year, she commanded a spot on the cover of *Sports Illustrated* and a multi-page spread inside fashion magazine *Elle.*

She is everywhere. That was her standing with boxing legend Mike Tyson on the red carpet at the ESPYs, riding a white horse at the Country Music Awards and posing on Puerto Rican beach during a *Sports Illustrated* swimsuit edition photoshoot. That was also her in a white suit discussing her business prowess with *Forbes* magazine, describing a social-media presence that has helped her earn a reported $3.5 million a year in endorsement deals.

"She is the equivalent of the five-tool player in baseball," said Darren Heitner, a Florida-based attorney who helps college athletes navigate this altered landscape in college athletics. "She has the following. She has the engagement. And she has the prowess—she is very good at what she does as an athlete."

The fame, though, has come with a cost. A threatening message on Instagram, she told NJ Advance Media, contributed to her decision to stop attending classes in person out of an abundance of caution. LSU had to increase its security presence at matches when an unruly crowd on a road trip last winter sparked safety concerns.

Then, some critics have taken aim at her success, wondering if she is doing more harm than good to the women's sports movement. She was a self-made millionaire before her 21st birthday for finding a way to monetize the harmless 30-second videos that appeal to teenagers, but somehow, there are people out there who think she's controversial.

None of this is on her mind as the public address announcer introduces her to the crowd here. This is the one place, with her teammates looking up from the edge of blue mats, where she can tune out the noise and put a lifetime of training to use. She rubs her chalk-covered hands together, takes a deep breath and stares up at the uneven bars.

Then she bounces off the springboard and soars into the air.

Dark side of celebrity

Most spectators at Gas South Arena are diehards who have traveled hundreds of miles to see their favorite teams compete. A sign outside the arena features the SEC's haughty logo—"IT JUST MEANS MORE"—and, from a gymnastics standpoint, that is undeniable. Nowhere else in the country does the sport garner this much attention on the college level.

But, when Dunne is competing, it is impossible to not look around the arena and wonder: Who *else* is watching?

The teenagers who hold up signs asking her to marry them are harmless enough, as are the fans who want her to stop for a quick photo. Dunne is every bit as friendly and approachable in real life as she is in her omnipresent TikTok videos, which is both part of her appeal and cause for concern.

"I love getting to know the people that follow me and what I do, so I always try to say hi to everybody I can that recognizes me when I'm out in public and I always try to take a picture," Dunne said in a phone interview last month. "But this past year, it's been a bit crazy."

Dunne told *Elle* this summer that she takes all her classes online for safety reasons. Speaking with NJ Advance Media last month, she said it wasn't her fellow students who concerned her when she made that decision, but a threat she received on the Baton Rouge campus. She said she no longer felt safe having a schedule that would allow potential bad actors to know where she was at a given time.

"I had a scare once with a message that I got about a class I was going to, and I was like, you know what, it's not worth it," Dunne told NJ Advance Media. "It was a threat. It seemed like they knew where I was at and what class, and I just decided better (to be) safe than sorry."

According to an LSU Police report obtained through an open records request, Dunne received death threats on Instagram on Dec. 2, 2021, from an apparent stalker who threatened to "shoot up" the university's campus. Dunne blocked the account on Instagram and LSU Police launched an investigation, but no arrest was made in the case. LSU officials did not respond to multiple requests for more information.

"(Dunne) added that due to her large social media following…she was used to getting strange messages from unknown accounts but has not received a message of this nature before," the report states.

Two months later, LSU head coach Jay Clark called the police when an unidentified man was seen inside the team's facility watching the gymnasts, according to a separate police report. Surveillance footage captured three men walking around the exterior of the building on Feb. 9, 2022, prior to the unknown male making entry, but no charges were filed.

LSU officials decided to provide more security for Dunne and her teammates after a road trip to Utah last January. A group of young men holding posters and a full-size cutout of Dunne disrupted the routines of other athletes as they chanted "We want Livvy!" throughout the meet. ESPN analyst Sam Peszek posted on X (formerly Twitter) that the scene outside at the team buses was "so scary and disturbing and cringey."

Gymnasts usually hang around at the end of competition, taking selfies with young fans or chatting with their friends and family, but the vibe is much more serious with LSU. After the SEC Championships, a man with the build of a professional wrestler made sure the fans didn't get too close before shepherding the Tigers to their locker room.

"The thing in Utah was weird," Clark said that night at Gas South Arena. "When I look back at it now, I wonder if it might have been orchestrated because the vitriol behind it was really intense. That's what alarmed us. It wasn't a positive thing, just signing autographs on the side.

"We've taken precautions since then to make sure (nothing bad happens). We don't want to deny people access to our kids, but we live in a world where we need to be aware of the environment that we're in and take care of all these things."

While Dunne takes her classes online at LSU, she said that she does not fear for her safety at campus events such as football games. Dunne posted photos from a recent game with her boyfriend Paul Skenes, a former LSU pitcher who was the No. 1 overall pick in this year's amateur draft, but said she never posts while still at an event for safety reasons.

"It's not about people swarming me—people at LSU are used to me at this point," Dunne said.

She doesn't see her fame as a burden, but her family works to make sure that she takes common sense precautions whenever possible and is grateful that LSU has stepped up its security measures. The success, of course, is a blessing.

The rest of it?

"I'm happy for her, that's for sure, because how many kids come out of college without debt?" her father David Dunne said. "But yeah, absolutely, I worry."

Homeschooled in Hillsdale

About a dozen rows up from the competition, Team Livvy watches her every move.

Her mother, Katherine Dunne, stops a conversation to study a practice routine. Her older sister, Julz, plots the next social media posts in her role as what Olivia calls the "brains behind the operation." David will offer moral support but doesn't pretend to have tips on TikToks or Tkatchevs.

"I'm the dad," he said with a laugh. "I don't get any of it."

He still marvels at his daughter's success. One day, she was an accomplished but mostly anonymous gymnast training out in Bergen County with her eye on Olympic glory. The next, she is such a big celebrity that security had to move the family's seats at a Yankees game in 2022 because the autograph and selfie seekers became too much.

Dunne, a 53-year-old lawyer, was a college athlete during a much different era. The Mount Vernon, New York, native punted for Rutgers from 1990–92, once holding the school record with a 75-yard boot. He met Katherine, a 48-year-old Pascack Valley High graduate from River Vale, when one of his teammates started dating her sister.

The couple married in 2000 and settled in Hillsdale, which is where their younger daughter's gymnastic career began. That origin story is now part of Livvy lore. She was an active 3-year-old girl who wanted the sparkly pink leotard that her cousin was wearing, and Katherine told her that she had to sign up for a preschool gymnastics class to get one of those.

She started taking classes at ENA Gymnastics in Paramus when she was 5 years old, and right away, co-owner Craig Zappa could see she had talent. "We gave her some advanced training above and beyond what other kids would do," he said, "and she just kept getting better and better."

She broke the New Jersey all-around record for her age group when she was 7, and when her training requirements reached 30 hours a week as an elite-level gymnast in the seventh grade, the family began homeschooling her. Those sacrifices are often glossed over in the telling of Livvy's rise, but she said she "100 percent" came close to quitting when the demands became too much.

"Doing elite gymnastics comes with costs," Dunne said. "I pretty much give up a lot of normal high school/middle school opportunities, like school dances, field trips and football games to go represent the USA. But it was definitely worth it."

In March 2017, she was named to the USA Gymnastics Junior National Team and started training at the controversial Karolyi Ranch in Texas with her eyes on the Olympics. It was a turbulent time for the sport, with high-profile scandals and coaching changes. Larry Nassar, the team doctor for the U.S. women's national team, was arrested for using his position of power to exploit and sexually assault hundreds of young athletes.

"All the bad, negative things that happened in USA Gymnastics, she was right in the thick of that," Zappa said. "It's hard. Every day you're wondering, 'What's next?'"

She managed to escape the abusive culture of youth gymnastics that made victims of so many of her high-profile peers. But she had to overcome a series of injuries and competitive setbacks, including what Zappa called "a very dark time" when she failed to qualify for the USA championships when she was 14.

The dream of sliding a gold medal over her neck in front of a worldwide audience had faded in her mid-to-late teens. Still, she earned a scholarship to her dream school, LSU, in a part of the country where college gymnastics attract massive crowds. She also found a new social-media platform that would change her life.

TikTok was, in her words, "kind of cringey" when she posted her first video in April 2019. She is almost unrecognizable with her natural brown hair in that short clip, dancing to "Old Town Road" by Lil Nas X in an oversized Rolling Stones T-shirt and a silly hat.

Her gymnastics videos would increase her following to over 100,000 within eight months, and that number would build exponentially during the pandemic.

"Making videos has always been something she's been very good at, and then during quarantine when (LSU) and the gyms were all closed, she was like, 'Okay, what am I going to do? I'm going to do this,'" Katherine Dunne said. "She zeroed in on it and she focused on it, and it grew. It grew really fast."

The Dunne Family rode out the first weeks of the COVID-19 reality in Jensen Beach, Florida, with Livvy's grandparents. With Julz working the camera and Livvy flipping effortlessly on the sand, they shot daily "beachnastics" videos that helped create an unrivaled social media presence for a college athlete.

This, in 2020, meant little. The NCAA prohibited athletes from accepting a cheeseburger while on scholarship, much less cold, hard cash. Finally, an antitrust lawsuit reached the Supreme Court, with justice Brett Kavanaugh writing on June 21, 2021, that the governing body of college sports could no longer rake in millions "on the backs of student athletes who are not fairly compensated."

The NCAA changed its rules just a week and a half later, and from the beginning, no athlete was better positioned to take advantage of this new world than Olivia Dunne.

Headline-creating pioneer

It isn't just the members of Team Livvy who are watching her as she grabs the bar with both hands and begins her routine. It isn't just the 9,554 fans at Gas South Arena, either, who are eager to see how she'll perform in just the third competition of her junior season.

Dunne's rabid following includes her clients, and while they might not be in the crowd, they have a vested interest in her success.

And Dunne chooses them as much as they choose her.

"Her brand is her image," Zappa said. "She is very careful not to align herself with something that will tarnish her image."

A month after the NCAA's about-face on NIL, Dunne hired the powerhouse WME agency to represent her and started signing business partners. Those companies—the list includes Vuori (sports apparel), L'Oreal (makeup), American Eagle (clothing) and Grubhub (food delivery)—know that Dunne can deliver an audience that has abandoned the TV remote for the smaller screen in their pockets.

These are not athlete endorsements from a different generation, when Steelers great "Mean Joe" Greene grabs a bottle of Coke
from a young fan. When Dunne slides down the polished floors of
her apartment in one eight-second video, her 7.8 million TikTok
followers might not even notice that she's mouthing the words to
Justin Bieber's "Maria" into a can of the energy drink Accelerator.

"She reaches 12 million people," Katherine Dunne said. "There
are people who want to reach that 18-24 demographic, and that
demographic doesn't want TV with commercials anymore. They
watch TikTok. They click through Instagram."

When the NIL started, most college sports observers believed
it would simply take the under-the-table payments to football and
basketball stars and bring them into the open market. Rutgers
football coach Greg Schiano joked that the three letters really
stand for "Now It's Legal." That has happened.

But NIL has also opened a path for female athletes to cash
in, too, although, unlike the star quarterbacks, they aren't getting
handed deals from collectives just for showing up. Heitner calls
it "real NIL," because while Dunne's videos might look effortless,
many of them are mapped out with her clients' wishes in mind. If
the lighting or the sound isn't just right, she will record it again,
and again, and again.

Everything she creates becomes viral content. Few will
notice that she effortlessly opens her bars performance at the
SEC Championships with a Tkatchev and a perfect pak salto.
Scan a random sample of stories about her on Google News on
a typical day, and you'll find precious few that have anything to
do with her chosen sport or, really, sports at all.

Olivia Dunne reveals stunning birthday looks as she turns 21

*Olivia Dunne cozies up to MLB prospect boyfriend in new
photo*

*Olivia Dunne gives intimate look at sun-soaked getaway in
new photos*

*Olivia Dunne fans 'can't get enough' of new BTS video of her
SI Swim shoot*

Dunne knows what's out there about her. She said she never googles herself, but as someone who makes a living online, the endless aggregations of her own social-media feeds are unavoidable.

"I'll only see stuff like that if it's sent to me," Dunne said. "I get random clickbait of myself on Snapchat. It's so funny, I'll see random Snapchat news articles. I try not to click on them because I know they're not true, but every now and then the headline is so outrageous that I get click-baited by my own self."

When told that some outlet probably will turn that quote into clickbait, Dunne lets out a loud laugh. "Exactly!"

It isn't Dunne's fault that, in this click-driven media landscape, everything she posts becomes a "story." But all that attention has led to backlash from some who believe that the focus on Dunne's appearance instead of her athleticism is harmful to the women's sports movement.

Dunne was the centerpiece of a *New York Times* column last November that wagged a disapproving finger at the female athletes who "post suggestive images of themselves that seem to cater to the male gaze." Tara VanDerveer, the longtime Stanford basketball coach, called it "a step back" for the women's sports movement.

The criticism surprised and angered Team Livvy. Dunne fired back, tagging *The New York Times* in an Instagram post of her in a leotard with the question, "Is this too much?"

"Honestly, it made me a stronger person," Dunne said. "I mean, they took a picture of me in my leotard by the beam and they used that photo as clickbait with the headline 'sex sells.' I was in my team-issued attire! Being able to brush it off is important—and to keep succeeding. The best revenge is success."

It isn't the only time Dunne has taken shrapnel from a national outlet. The conservative website The Free Press lumped her into a story about Haley and Hanna Cavinder, former college basketball players at Miami who also have raked in millions thanks to NIL. The headline: "The NCAA has a 'Hot Girl' Problem."

But what, exactly, is the problem?

Dunne and the Cavinders make more in endorsements than more accomplished athletes, but this is not exactly a new phenomenon. This is also true with many high-profile male athletes—former Jets quarterback Mark Sanchez wasn't on the cover of *GQ* years ago because he was good at football—with far less outrage or scrutiny.

The criticism ignores a simple reality: If it was easy to build an eight-digit social media following and rake in millions off of it, nearly everyone would do it. Dunne has never claimed to be the best gymnast in the world, but as a pioneer in the landscape of modern college athletics, she is unchallenged.

"Here's this young woman who's empowered," said Rutgers gymnastics coach Umme Salim-Beasley, who has followed Dunne's career from the beginning. "She is utilizing the fact she's a gymnast, the fact that she's a strong, beautiful person, to be able to capitalize on being a collegiate athlete. I think that's something that we should be celebrating."

Future in sports business
Twenty-one seconds.

That is how long it takes for her to complete her bars routine at the SEC Championships, and when she sticks the landing, she claps her chalk-covered hands before giving her coach, Clark, a two-handed high-five to celebrate. Her score is a season-best 9.850 as LSU finishes the event in third place.

Her teammates greet her at the edge of the padded platform like a conquering hero. The crowd roars its approval as this four-ring circus continues with the next performer.

It would be the final time she would be in LSU's lineup as a junior, bringing her total time competing during an injury-plagued season to just over a minute. Clark wonders if the "NIL thing," as he calls it, has only added to the challenges that high-level college athletes like Dunne have to overcome.

"This is uncharted territory," Clark said. "It's hard for her to manage. You're trying to be a student, you're trying to be an athlete, and you've got all these other obligations going on. And I know she's technically an adult, but she's still a kid to me."

Clark no doubt prefers the old days in which the college team was the center of an athlete's universe, and everything— even classes—fell in line. But in 2023, those so-called "other" obligations are what enable many star athletes to stay on campus.

For years, the NCAA has aired commercials celebrating the fact that most of its athletes will be "going pro in something other than sports." Those ads conveniently left out the part about college administrators and head coaches making a small fortune off the teenage competitors they buried under a pile of unnecessary restrictions.

Dunne is unlikely to make a dime after college as a gymnast. That she has parlayed her athleticism, her social media prowess and, yes, her good looks into a lucrative career before she hangs up her leotard for good is not a problem. It is, for many college or even high school athletes, an inspiration.

When Rutgers soccer player Riley Tiernan found herself dubbed "the next Olivia Dunne" in a headline this summer, she wasn't embarrassed or angry. She has signed small NIL deals with apparel giant Adidas and even her orthodontist, who traded Invisalign braces for her work as a spokeswoman.

"I hope I'm the next Livvy Dunne because she's extremely successful," said Tiernan, who has never met Dunne. "She's pretty smart with the type of posts that she makes, based on the audience she has."

What will Dunne do with that audience next? This was one of the big topics when she sat for an interview with *Forbes* recently as "Business Livvy," as she calls this side of her personality, and discussed her spot on the magazine's "Top Creators" list.

"I do feel like I have an entrepreneurial background so I want to put that to good use," Dunne said in that *Forbes* interview.

"Have my own product, my own thing…I'm not exactly sure what that is yet."

Dunne told NJ Advance Media that she wants to "do something in the sports world," and said that she is in talks to have a media role at the Olympics next summer. She wouldn't elaborate because the details are being finalized, but given that Paris is regarded as the world's fashion capital and gymnastics is among the most-watched Olympic sports, that seems like a no-brainer.

Jason Belzer, a Rutgers professor who helps universities run their NIL collectives, wonders if her success in college will translate to a career that will carry her through the next phase of her life. If she's not competing, does that change the dynamic with her corporate partners?

"The big question becomes, what happens when she's done being a student-athlete," Belzer said. "Is she going to leverage this? Can she become a singer? Can she become a movie star? I don't know if she's invested in that."

Zappa, though, isn't worried.

"She is so good at marketing herself and putting herself in the perfect spot at the perfect time, I don't even know what's next," Zappa said. "I don't think there's anything this kid can't do in this environment right now."

Dunne is trying to stay in the moment for her final season in college, and that means focusing on what brought her to Baton Rouge in the first place. She wants to help LSU win its first NCAA team title in gymnastics, and individually, stay healthy enough to remain a fixture in the lineup unlike last season.

She also wants to have fun. Those Instagram stories of her having a blast cheering on the LSU football team with Skenes, the mustachioed minor-league ballplayer, are not staged. She also has adopted a golden retriever named Roux—"a little light in my life," she calls the puppy—that requires a bit of attention (and, not surprisingly, has her own Instagram page).

"This past year has been a bit crazy," she said. "I deserve to enjoy this last year."

Dunne will leave behind a legacy. She created the Livvy Fund to provide future LSU female athletes with the NIL funding, industry tips and business connections that she didn't have when she started this journey. Will she stay in Louisiana when she's done? Will she move back to New Jersey? She doesn't know.

"You can just have it all in Jersey, and that's something I definitely miss sometimes when I'm down here," she said. "I do love Louisiana as well, but I love Jersey."

LSU will begin its season in early January, and once again, thousands of crazed SEC gymnastics fans—and more than a few spectators who know nothing about the sport—will fill arenas in hopes that they can catch a glimpse of her.

Dunne will step onto the mat in the one place where she can tune out all the noise. She'll eye those uneven bars and leap onto that springboard.

How high will she soar? The world will be watching.

Staff writer Keith Sargeant contributed to this report.

STEVE POLITI is the sports columnist for NJ Advance Media. The former *Star-Ledger* paperboy achieved a lifelong dream when he joined the newspaper's staff as an enterprise sports reporter in 1998, and his work has appeared in its pages and online at NJ.com ever since. He has won top honors from the Associated Press Sports Editors for columns (2019), long feature (2021), and investigations (2017), and his feature on a high school baseball coach who was sued after telling a player to slide was featured in *The Best American Sports Writing* in 2020. He and his wife, Nancy, live in Montclair, New Jersey, with their two children, Julian and Sara.

A Reckoning, Decades in the Making: Famed Olympic Runner Lynn Jennings Chases Down the Renowned Coach Who Abused Her as a Teen

BOB HOHLER

FROM THE *Boston Globe* • FEBRUARY 17, 2023

The call came into Cambridge police headquarters on Independence Day weekend in 2019. A three-time Olympian, the caller said, had filed a complaint with the US Olympic and Paralympic Committee, alleging sexual abuse by her coach, including assaults in Cambridge, when she was a girl.

The officer on duty, Sergeant Darlene Beckford Pearson, took the call from a committee official and asked for the Olympian's name.

Lynn Jennings, she was told.

Pearson trembled. She and Jennings, one of the greatest middle-distance runners in American history, had been fast friends in the 1970s as teen stars of Greater Boston's renowned Liberty Athletic Club. In all the years since, Pearson had guarded her own haunting secret: She too had been sexually molested as a youth by her coach.

Her hand quivering, Pearson logged the name of Jennings's alleged abuser: John M. Babington. A former US Olympic and Wellesley College coach. Pearson's former Harvard University coach. And, as her Liberty coach, her abuser.

In her 28 years on the Cambridge police force, Pearson, now a lieutenant, has witnessed chilling scenes that will trouble her forever, she said. But discovering that Jennings had also been robbed of her innocence by their coach—a running savant nearly twice their age—struck her like no other.

"I've seen some horrible stuff on the job, but I've never shaken like I did that day," said Pearson, herself a former collegiate record-setter and world-class runner.

After Jennings lodged her complaint with the Olympic committee, Babington acknowledged to the US Center for SafeSport and the *Globe* that he sexually abused Jennings, beginning when she was 15, and Pearson, when she was 17, while he was their Liberty coach.

"I wasn't right in the head," he told the *Globe* in a recent phone interview. "I have terrible remorse over it all."

As Babington rose through the coaching ranks, he concealed his misconduct long enough for the statute of limitations to expire on the offenses. But his scandalous acts had ignited a quiet rage in the girls he abused. That fire never died.

Jennings and Pearson kept their silence for decades, fearing that speaking out would only lead to further pain. Finally, in 2017, Jennings made it her mission to root out Babington's misdeeds, shine a light on those who enabled him, and exact a measure of justice.

"It got to the point that I couldn't live with myself if I didn't try to hold him accountable," she said. "I feared my silence put others in jeopardy."

What Jennings discovered, after digging through records and conducting more than 50 interviews over hundreds of hours, cast in razor-sharp relief the damage Babington had done.

By the time SafeSport permanently barred Babington in December from involvement in any Olympic-related sport because of his admitted sexual misconduct, Jennings had helped lead investigators to Pearson and two other women Babington had harmed: a promising runner in the late 1990s at Wellesley College, where Babington coached for 26 years, and an elite high school runner he tried to recruit to train with Jennings.

"My conduct was inexcusable," said Babington, now 77, of Ashland. "I deserve the punishment."

Jennings also found—and the *Globe* confirmed—that Wellesley, rather than fire Babington or report him to the police for molesting the student runner, placed him on unpaid leave for only a semester in 1998 and never formally notified his assistant coaches or the student-athletes he coached over the next 15 years about the abuse.

"We are deeply sorry for the pain suffered by our former student as a result of John Babington's sexual misconduct at Wellesley in the late 1990s," the school said in a statement. "Wellesley strives to create a safe environment for our students, faculty and staff and to prevent sexual harassment and misconduct with strict policies, and we do not tolerate these behaviors in our community."

For Babington, the school's handling of the case provided him a protected path to retirement in 2013, when he was lionized as one of the great running coaches of his era.

Nearly 10 years later, Jennings brought him down. But why did it take so long?

Assaults begin at age 15

Babington entered Jennings's life in 1975, when she was a girl from Harvard, a hilly town northwest of Boston abounding with apple orchards. She was 14. He was nearly 30.

Come run for Liberty, Babington coaxed her, after he spotted Jennings at a state high school track championship, flashing early signs of the global phenom she would become.

Babington himself had taken early to the sport. He competed at Williams College (Class of '67), and while he attended Harvard Law School (Class of '71), he began running the Boston Marathon, which he finished every year from 1968 to 1980.

A lifelong bachelor, Babington was new to training elite runners when he recruited Jennings. He had coached boys at the Mount Hermon School during a year off from law school, then helped train girls for the Greater Brockton Striders, before he joined Liberty, the region's top women's running club, in 1974.

There, he found his calling—and Jennings.

Babington became enthralled by Jennings's talent, he said, and while he trained her to become one of the world's premier young runners, he developed a self-described "crazy obsession" with her.

Jennings was just 15 when Babington took her to his Cambridge apartment in 1976 and sexually assaulted her. He sexually assaulted her there multiple times over a period of months, and again in a dorm room at the University of Oregon, where he had accompanied Jennings and fellow Liberty runner Joan Benoit to compete in the Olympic trials.

SafeSport found by a preponderance of the evidence that Babington, had the statutes of limitations not expired, could have been liable under Massachusetts law for rape of a child and under Oregon law for second-degree sexual abuse.

Jennings had never even kissed a boy before Babington abused her. The experience, she said, "produced an absolute kaleidoscope of terrible, terrible feelings."

While the molestation continued, Jennings began to gain stardom under Babington's tutelage. At 17, she was the undisputed best high school girls' middle-distance runner in America, having posted a 4:39 mile, captured national titles, and stunned a prestigious field of adults to win the inaugural Bonne Bell 10K for Women (now the Boston 10K for Women). Her likeness appeared on Wheaties boxes, and the *Globe* declared her "New England's Teen Angel of distance running."

Jennings kept Babington's misconduct secret to keep her dreams alive. She wanted to be a world champion, and to get there, she would need a world-class coach.

"I knew that if I said anything, it would have been taken away from me, the thing that I loved," she said. "I became a whiz at compartmentalizing."

Second Liberty teen

Pearson, born Darlene Beckford, joined Jennings at Liberty in 1977 at the urging of a club member. She was a city girl, a sophomore at Cambridge Rindge and Latin High School, the youngest daughter of a single mother struggling to make ends meet in working-class Cambridgeport.

Pearson and Jennings bonded quickly and trained together despite their different strengths—Pearson at shorter track distances, Jennings on longer road and cross-country courses. Jennings, dutiful and often icily determined, marveled at Pearson's lighthearted irreverence.

"She was lightning fast, but she hated the longer runs and would let Babington know it," Jennings said. "She used to make me laugh, giving it right back to him. I would never do that."

Babington fell hard for Pearson, too. She was 17, he was 33 when she found herself alone with him and he sexually abused her. By then, he had stopped assaulting Jennings.

Prosecuting Babington could have been proven difficult in Pearson's case because the age of consent in Massachusetts is 16. But there was nothing ambiguous about what Pearson endured.

She said simply, "It changes a person."

For his part, Babington choked up while reflecting on the harm he had done.

"To this day, I love Darlene," he said. "She is the finest person I've met in my life."

As a teenager, Pearson, like Jennings, suppressed her feelings about Babington's abuse in order to focus on her running career. In high school, she won the national Junior Olympic mile championship and captured the 800-meter and 1,500-meter titles in the national AAU Junior Championships.

Her fame as a high school runner catapulted Pearson to Harvard, where Babington joined her, walking away from his legal career to become an assistant coach of the Crimson cross-country and track teams. Babington said he did not tell Harvard about his abusive relationship with Pearson. They both said he did not molest her after high school.

As a Harvard freshman, Pearson set a national collegiate and world junior record of 4:32.30 in the indoor mile. She later became the first Ivy League woman to win a national collegiate championship in track and field, at 800 meters, en route to Harvard's Hall of Fame.

As for Jennings, she departed for Princeton University, but not before breaking away from Babington. As their relationship frayed, her chance to end it came when he forbade her from running the 1978 Boston Marathon because it could disrupt her regular training.

"He told me, 'If you run Boston, this coach/athlete relationship is over,'" she said. "I remember thinking, 'Screw you, pal.'"

Jennings was 17, too young to register for the Marathon. But she ran defiantly and was the third female to finish, unofficially less than two minutes behind 30-year-old Gayle Barron's winning time of 2:44.52. Along the way, thousands cheered the girl running without an official number.

She would not speak to Babington again for more than a decade.

'A deal with the devil'

Jennings's teen glory dimmed at Princeton, where she was a three-time All-American and set an Ivy League record at 3,000 meters but fell far short of her potential.

She was miserable and so detached from her identity as a national champion that she left school and was out of competitive running for a year. Over time, she fully grasped the cause of her psychological tailspin.

"The weight and darkness of the secret I carried was a burden I could not overcome," Jennings said.

The pain was exacerbated by seeing Babington coaching Harvard during meets with Princeton. She said she had been accepted by Harvard but chose Princeton to distance herself from him.

"Seeing him, while I was emotionally fractured, was a slap in the face, a fresh reminder of what he had done to me," she said.

Babington, in hindsight, understood.

"She was troubled, and it was because of my conduct," he said.

Jennings turned pro two years out of Princeton, running for Nike, then its affiliate, Athletics West. Mostly coaching herself, she earned her first Olympic berth and finished sixth at 10,000 meters in the 1988 Seoul Games. But she wanted a medal and believed she needed a coach to secure it, spurring an unsettling decision.

She asked Babington to be her trainer again.

"I literally remember thinking, if you do this, you are making a deal with the devil," she said. "But I also remember thinking, I'm 29 now, fully in command of myself. I will have total control."

So, Babington, already coaching for Wellesley and Liberty, went to work for Jennings. She paid him roughly $1,000 a month plus travel expenses. They never spoke about the sexual abuse, although she thought about it often.

"I disliked being around him, but the disdain drove me even harder," she said.

Babington said his memories of abusing Jennings were buried "somewhere in the dark recesses of my mind." He was "singularly focused" on training her, he said.

With Babington back, so was the magic for Jennings. In 1989, she won the first of five consecutive Boston 10Ks for Women, a feat that remains unmatched. More remarkably, she won three straight World Cross-Country Championships from 1990–92.

She set the world indoor record at 5,000 meters, the world road record at 8,000 meters, and the US road record at 10,000 meters.

And in perhaps her greatest achievement, Jennings won bronze at the 1992 Barcelona Olympics, setting a US record at 10,000 meters on the track and becoming the first American, male or female, to medal at the distance since 1964.

At age 32, she had forged her legacy. There would be richer sponsorship deals, endorsement contracts, speaking and appearance fees—so many financial rewards that she would be set for life.

And yet she continued to employ Babington. But while she was training for one of her final races, the 1999 Boston Marathon, Babington confided to her that he had been temporarily barred from the Wellesley campus for taking a student to his apartment.

"I knew exactly what that meant," she said, "and it sickened me."

She would walk away again from Babington, this time forever.

Emboldened, she strikes back

In retirement, at age 40, Jennings moved to Portland, Ore., far from New England and Babington. But even there his shadow loomed.

In 2006, she was inducted into the USA Track and Field Hall of Fame and was invited by Nike mogul Phil Knight to fly to the ceremony on his private jet. But she declined to attend, too discomfited by the prospect of publicly citing Babington's role in her career.

She also discovered in 2006 that Wellesley College was prominently featuring her in its website profile of Babington, and she called the school to demand her name be removed.

But she felt powerless to hold him publicly accountable. That changed one autumn morning in 2017, after she had moved deep into the Maine woods, when she read a first-person account in *The New York Times* by famed long-distance swimmer Diana

Nyad about the "perpetual trauma" she had endured since her coach sexually molested her as a girl, decades earlier.

"I could feel my heart rate go wild as I read it," Jennings recalled.

Long burdened by misplaced shame—"It was humiliating to say somebody had done that to me and I hadn't run away screaming," Jennings said—she became emboldened by Nyad's story.

Her first step was to contact the *Globe*. She was not yet ready to be publicly identified, however, and her account lacked corroborating evidence.

Then came the "SafeSport Authorization Act of 2017," signed into law the following year amid outrage over USA Gymnastics doctor Larry Nassar sexually abusing scores of young athletes.

Jennings reported Babington in 2019 to the Olympic committee, which notified SafeSport, and when an investigator asked her for leads on other possible victims, she went to work with an Olympian's tenacity.

Her case was placed on hold for a year while the FBI offices in Boston and Oregon, and the police in Cambridge and Eugene, Ore., all alerted by SafeSport or the Olympic committee, investigated her allegations; no charges were brought. All the while, Jennings scoured old Liberty and Wellesley rosters and questioned former athletes and officials. She ultimately provided SafeSport leads to Pearson and the women Babington mistreated in his Wellesley career.

In 2021, nearly two years after the Olympic committee's call to the Cambridge police, SafeSport contacted Pearson to ask if Babington had abused her. She replied, "I've been waiting for you to call."

Pearson had phoned Babington after taking the Olympic committee's call about Jennings. She had confronted him for the first time about him sexually abusing her, but he offered little in the way of contrition.

"I told her that I couldn't imagine what was going on in my mind at the time," Babington recalled. "It was like it wasn't me."

Pearson ended the call by saying, "You are never to contact me again."

More violations and concealment

Babington, as it turned out, had been violating ethical boundaries for nearly a quarter-century. In 1991, he was in Belgium, recruiting Melody Fairchild, a high school sensation from Colorado who won a bronze medal for the US at the World Junior Cross-Country Championships. Babington wanted Fairchild to move to Boston so he could train both Jennings and her.

He was 45 and Fairchild was 17 when they crossed paths at a postrace party in Antwerp. Fairchild told SafeSport and the *Globe* that Babington chastised her for dancing with a fellow athlete, as if it showed a lack of commitment to competing, then he removed her bandanna and caressed her hair. He denied doing so to SafeSport and the *Globe*.

A year later, Babington took Fairchild to dinner in Colorado. There, she said, he bought her alcohol while she was underage. Over her objections, she said, he then began walking her home, tightly hugged her, and, while she resisted, said something like, "Do you know how you make me feel?" She then broke free and ran away.

Babington said he may have provided Fairchild alcohol and hugged her but not in a sexual manner. SafeSport, however, found that Fairchild's version of the events was credible.

Fairchild, who went on to become a national champion and Hall of Famer at the University of Oregon, told the *Globe*, "I was put into situations with him that felt threatening to my young nervous system, but which I came out of physically unscathed."

She also said, "The knowledge of my hero, Lynn Jennings, and other women who I admire enduring horrific abuse at his hands is heartbreaking, enraging, and confusing."

One of those other women was a gifted runner who enrolled at Wellesley in 1996, just after Babington returned from helping coach the US track and field team at the Atlanta Olympics. The woman, who asked not to be identified because she remains traumatized, said in interviews with SafeSport and e-mails to the *Globe* that Babington took her to his Cambridge apartment, where he provided her alcohol and made sexual advances. She was 19. He was 51.

The woman and her parents reported Babington to Wellesley College. Babington acknowledged to the school that he kissed her, fondled her, provided her alcohol while she was underage, and used marijuana in her presence, he said.

But Wellesley, rather than fire Babington, placed him on unpaid leave for the 1998 fall cross-country season, on the condition that he receive counseling and produce a psychologist's written opinion that he would not pose a risk to other young women.

Soon, Babington was back. He did not inform Wellesley or the psychologist about his previous sexual misconduct, he said, and the school reinstated him, based in part on the therapist's opinion that his improper behavior was an isolated episode.

Babington and Wellesley concealed the reason for his absence from his interim replacements, assistant coaches, and student-athletes, many of them said in interviews. They recalled him saying he had taken a sabbatical.

"It's shocking for me to learn the truth," said Laura Woeller Hill, who served as an interim coach during Babington's leave. "It almost makes me feel like I was complicit in something that I wasn't."

Alison Wade, who accepted Babington's offer to serve as his last assistant coach at Wellesley, said, "It certainly would have changed things for me if I had known what he had done. In retrospect, Wellesley should have gotten rid of him in the first place."

The Wellesley runner who was abused by Babington felt so betrayed by him and the school's handling of her complaint that she transferred to another college. She said the experience irreparably damaged her.

Babington "robbed me of my innocence, made a college coming of age story that should have been beautiful and memorable into something I have tried to forget in order to survive," she wrote to the *Globe*.

Babington described his misconduct with her to the *Globe* as "a midlife crisis."

Unburdened at last

While Babington avoided criminal prosecution, he became haunted by the anguish he caused. Speaking of Jennings and Pearson, he said, "I understand the anger and betrayal they must feel. They were part of some sort of strange total obsession that I had with them, which obviously got into a very dark and bad area. I understand how permanently I have harmed them."

In a gesture of remorse, Babington told SafeSport and the *Globe* he would offer to financially compensate the two women, with no strings attached. He said he would return to Jennings the $120,000 she paid him over a decade and give Pearson $100,000.

"I can't undo the harm, but I can hope that by telling their story, Lynn and Darlene gain some measure of closure and satisfaction," Babington said. "Although we never spoke about it, I have deeply regretted my misconduct ever since it happened, and I will regret it for the rest of my life."

The women declined to comment on the financial offer, saying they have received nothing and haven't had the promise confirmed by anyone associated with Babington (SafeSport banned him from contacting them).

Meanwhile, their lives go on. Babington, living alone in retirement, has lost his place in the running world. Pearson, 61, continues to serve the city where she grew up, and Jennings, 62, remains an exceptional athlete, training regularly as if for another race.

But she no longer chases Babington.

"I am unburdened now in ways I have never been since I was 15 years old," Jennings said. "Telling what happened has freed me."

BOB HOHLER is a sports investigative and enterprise reporter for the *Boston Globe*. He joined the *Globe* in 1987, served in its Washington bureau from 1993 to 2000, and was the beat writer for the Red Sox from 2000 through the 2004 championship season. He has received many national awards for his investigative, breaking news, and feature writing. His work also appeared in the 2007 and 2010 editions of the Best American Sports Writing. He is the author of *"I Touch the Future...": The Story of Christa McAuliffe*.

Feared and Loved, Iowa's Caitlin Clark Is Taking Women's Basketball by Storm

BEN GOLLIVER

FROM *The Washington Post* • MARCH 14, 2023

IOWA CITY—Ten years later, her brother's hair still hasn't fully grown back.

Before Caitlin Clark was making her case as college basketball's most thrilling talent, she was a middle child in West Des Moines, Iowa, who insisted on tagging along with her two brothers and countless cousins. The 21-year-old junior guard, who has risen to national prominence thanks to her Stephen Curry-esque shooting range and video game-like statistics, spent summers bicycling and winters yearning for a snowboard she could use to cruise down hills. She played softball and soccer before briefly experimenting with piano, only to conclude that her breakneck approach to life clashed with the instrument's varied pacing.

Basketball was the constant as she climbed from all-boys youth leagues to become Iowa's top prep recruit at Dowling Catholic High. Now the Naismith player of the year semifinalist is preparing to lead the Iowa Hawkeyes on her third March Madness trip. Clark's intensity and demonstrative nature on the court have won her plenty of fans but also some critics, who think she shoots too often and talks too much trash. Hecklers targeted her in high school, and Iowa Coach Lisa Bluder said opposing coaches have told Clark during games that she's not as good as she thinks.

If the shade from rivals gets to her, she doesn't let on. Clark is on a mission to lead Iowa (26–6) to its first Final Four since 1993, to be a No. 1 WNBA draft pick and to defy gender-based preconceptions much like Serena Williams, her favorite athlete.

Indeed, Clark will stop at nothing, as she proved during a game of basement basketball with her younger brother, Colin, when both were preteens. One minute, the siblings were trading buckets on a Nerf hoop. The next, Clark shoved Colin headfirst into a wall, leaving him with a nasty gash that required a trip to urgent care and four staples.

"When it gets really quiet, that's a sign of danger," Anne Clark, Caitlin's mother, said over dinner at an Altoona, Ia., steakhouse. "We were trying to stop the bleeding. We had just put in light carpet. I might have said, 'Not the carpet!' Colin still has the little cut in his head. It's his war wound now."

Clark doesn't cringe at the memory or offer a belated apology, instead noting that she was merely giving as good as she received. Perhaps that helps explain why she was ready to take the reins at Iowa as a freshman and why her coaches invoke Kobe Bryant to describe how she craves pressure and conflict.

"If I wanted to hang out with the boys, I had to hold my own," Clark said during an interview at Carver-Hawkeye Arena. "They didn't take it easy on me. Every family function, it seemed like I would go inside crying. They wouldn't pass me the ball. In the Easter egg hunt, I wouldn't get enough eggs. It was just one thing after the next. I got picked on, but I loved it. That's what made me who I am."

A homegrown prodigy

In the heart of basketball season, Interstate 88 out of Chicago is flanked by frozen lakes, silent farms and foggy cornfields, a trucker-friendly route with hardly any elevation change. The parking lots at Herbert Hoover's presidential library in West Branch, Iowa, were nearly empty on a weekday in early January, as were downtown Iowa City's bars and restaurants during the university's winter break. Even the souvenir magnets at Eastern Iowa Airport in Cedar Rapids acknowledge the solitude: "What happens in Iowa, stays in Iowa…but nothing happens in Iowa."

Clark has changed that, as the home crowds have swelled to more than 15,000 and young girls crowd the court to take photos with her postgame. The state of Iowa has a rich women's basketball history dating from the 1920s, when teams fielded six players instead of five. An Iowa City boutique sells T-shirts that proclaim the state as the "center of the women's college basketball universe," with coastal powerhouses such as Connecticut and Stanford well over 1,000 miles away.

No one here, or anywhere, has seen a player quite like Clark. The 6-foot floor general has driven record television ratings for the Big Ten Network and received social media shout-outs from NBA stars LeBron James and Kevin Durant, who appreciate her refined game, showmanship and competitiveness in the face of double teams, traps, full-court presses and junk defenses.

"When you couple her edge with her skills and her IQ, that's what takes her over the top and makes her rare," Durant said in a telephone interview. "She can pretty much do everything on the floor, score from any angle, shoot deep threes and create for her teammates. But she has that feisty side to her. She has that dog in her, as people call it. She's trying to do everything for her team because she can't lose."

Clark's athletic gifts and drive were obvious to her sports-obsessed extended family from an early age. Her father, Brent, played baseball and basketball at Division III Simpson College; her older brother, Blake, played football at Iowa State; and several of her cousins have played collegiate sports.

Brent, a sales executive at Concentric International, and Anne, a former marketing executive, wasted no time enrolling their young daughter in a local boys' basketball league. Before long, an angry parent from an opposing team, who was upset after a blowout loss, went to the league's director to demand that Clark's team forfeit because she is a girl. The request was denied, and Clark was named the league MVP at the end of the season.

"They were really [upset] about how a girl could beat all these boys," Clark said. "I definitely deserved MVP. It wasn't a pity award."

Around that same time, Clark's first-grade teacher phoned the family to discuss the results of a timed math challenge. Clark had finished second in her class, and she was devastated. The teacher offered advice that never stuck: "Caitlin needs to relax."

When Clark was a third-grader, her father drove her to watch the WNBA's Minnesota Lynx in Minneapolis, and she briefly met Maya Moore. Too excited to ask for an autograph or a selfie, Clark settled for a bear hug—an embrace she now credits as the moment she fell in love with basketball. The Clarks stoked their daughter's burgeoning hoop dreams by gathering her siblings and cousins together in the laundry room, turning off all the lights and holding mock player introductions, complete with flashlights to mimic an arena's spotlight.

Recruiting letters began hitting the mailbox when Clark was a seventh-grader, though her parents shielded her from the attention until she was a high school sophomore in hopes of preserving a normal childhood. The handwritten notes and promotional posters eventually filled two oversized Tupperware tubs.

By the time Clark was 13, she had switched to girls-only leagues and was playing up several grade levels in search of better competition. With no interest in video games, she hit tennis balls against the garage, threw tight spirals with her father and lobbied her parents for a full-size basketball court in the backyard. They compromised by placing a hoop above the garage and by extending the driveway so she could spray paint a three-point line at the appropriate distance.

Battling wind gusts that buffeted her shots, Clark honed her three-point range. Her father rebounded and encouraged proper shooting form from all distances. To compensate for her skinny frame, Clark studied Moore, James and Durant to see how they used their bodies to finish in traffic. Playing soccer helped her see passing angles, as did grainy YouTube video of Pete Maravich.

The Dowling Maroons played a fast-paced style, and they turned Clark loose as a freshman starter. She dropped soccer after her sophomore year so she could focus on basketball year-round, given that she was juggling her school team, her All-Iowa Attack AAU commitments and invites from USA Basketball. In time, she racked up all-state and McDonald's all-American honors, and she was named Iowa's Miss Basketball in 2020.

"The student sections loved to chant 'Overrated!' at me," Clark said. "It brings out your best. I laughed."

Clark led the state in scoring as a junior and senior but graduated without winning a state title. Her high school career ended with a stunning upset loss to Sioux City East in the regional finals.

"I can still see her," Brent Clark said. "She crumbled and fell to the floor. She came to me not long after the game and was kind of tearful. I said to her that she had a fabulous career. She was the first one in the line to congratulate the other team. The next morning, she was up and at a 7 a.m. faith-based discussion group. No matter who you are, that's hard to do."

Her own stage

Shared values brought Clark to the Hawkeyes.

Clark never changed high schools or AAU programs, and Bluder has been an institution at Iowa for 23 seasons. Clark was a homebody, according to her mother, who had little interest in far-flung blue bloods. Jan Jensen, the Hawkeyes' associate head coach, had played college basketball in Iowa, and she sold Clark on the program's family culture during a six-year recruiting marathon.

Most importantly, Iowa was prepared to give Clark the keys to its up-tempo, read-and-react offense from day one. While dining at Orchard Green near campus, Bluder found out that the Hawkeyes had prevailed over Notre Dame, Iowa State and others for Clark's commitment. The ecstatic coach ordered champagne to celebrate.

Clark made an instant impact, leading the country in scoring as a freshman and becoming the first woman to rank first in both scoring and assists during her sophomore campaign. This season, she has emerged as a leading candidate for Naismith Player of the Year honors after averaging 27 points, 7.5 rebounds and 8.3 assists while leading Iowa to the Big Ten tournament title and the Seattle 4 Region's No. 2 seed in the NCAA tournament. The Hawkeyes' offense ranks first in scoring and third in pace, so her exploits often blur together.

"I don't think I could play basketball any other way, honestly," she said. "I do everything fast. I drive fast. I do my homework fast."

Clark is best known for her deep shooting range: She feels comfortable pulling up from 32 feet—roughly 10 feet behind the women's three-point line. When she can step into her shot off the dribble or while running up the court, she can launch from even deeper than that. Clark blushed at the Curry comparisons, noting that the Golden State Warriors star only counts his three-pointers as makes during practice if he swishes them. Clark dreams of getting to that level and holds herself to the swishing standard when she works on her free throws.

When she has made a few threes in a row, Clark can't resist a heat check. During one practice scrimmage, she scored 22 points in a two-minute stretch, capping the flurry with a one-legged floater while falling out of bounds. Yet Clark, who ranks second nationally in points per game and stands first in assists, prides herself on being a "general," not a gunner, because of her wide-reaching authority.

"There's always backlash that I take too many shots or that I'm a ball hog," she said. "My assist numbers speak for themselves, too. I'm scoring. I'm facilitating. I'm leading."

Clark has showcased her wide-reaching game throughout her junior season, registering four triple-doubles and sealing the Big Ten tournament title with 30 points, 10 rebounds and a season-high 17 assists in a blowout of Ohio State. Her most electric moment came in a Feb. 26 victory over Indiana, which was ranked second in the country at the time. With her team trailing by two with 1.5 seconds left, Clark raced around the top of the key, corralled an inbounds pass and stepped into a deep game-winning three-pointer that rattled through at the buzzer, causing the Iowa City crowd to erupt at the 86–85 victory.

"She's the best all-around player that I've ever coached," Bluder said. "She's the player of the year because of her impact on our team compared to other players who have surrounding people who can take some of the pressure off mentally or defensively. Having that name 'Connecticut' or 'South Carolina' helps you get votes automatically. She gets a lot of shots, but she also gets the best defensive player all the time. When the [stakes] get higher, that's when she gets better."

Team staffers insist that Clark has an off-court alter ego, that she is a goofball who might stroll into lunch wearing a bathrobe. Her parents encourage her to find time in the offseason to relax on the beach in Florida or at Lake Viking in Missouri, and the entire family attended a Kansas City Chiefs game over Christmas break.

These attempts at balance are mostly in vain; Jensen said molding Clark has been "the challenge of a lifetime."

Iowa's coaches describe an ongoing tug-of-war between Clark's innate self-assuredness and her growing willingness to trust her teammates. Clark has been instructed to save her longest attempts for the end of quarters or late in the shot clock, and she has learned that feeding center Monika Czinano can crack the opposing defense from the inside out.

The Hawkeyes thrive off Clark's confidence and marvel at her audacious Michael Jordan shrug celebrations when she hits a big three-pointer, but they also must cope with the nagging issue identified by her first-grade teacher: She can be too hard on herself. That perfectionism can manifest in knee-jerk reactions, which occasionally cause her to lose focus. Iowa's coaches have stressed the importance of moving on from mistakes, and Clark's teammates have learned to assemble like security guards around her to de-escalate brewing confrontations with referees or opponents.

"I get mad," Clark admitted. "You have reactions that you don't always love in the heat of battle. I'm full of passion no matter what I'm doing. I'm going to give you every single part of me. I'm going to give my heart to this. I want young girls to know that you can play with joy and passion."

In a January win over Northwestern, a frustrated Clark received a technical foul for shouting a profanity to herself after missing a shot. Though Bluder put Clark through a leadership course aimed at refining her communication skills and tone, the 61-year-old coach was quick to push back against criticism concerning on-court demeanor.

"What makes me upset is that a men's basketball player can act like that, and he's just being a player," Bluder said. "But if a women's basketball player does the same things, oh, it should stop. I don't know why we should be judged differently based on our sexes. I hope she changes some of these conversations."

Ready to dance

Clark's craftsmanship and flair will undoubtedly make her a top pick in the WNBA draft, and she said she "obviously want[s] to be the number one pick." Durant can already envision how she will transform her first professional team.

"Whoever gets her is going to fill the seats up, win some basketball games and have some fun while she's there," he said. "She's one of those players who attracts other players and who attracts casual fans and turns them into real fans."

When, exactly, Clark enters the draft remains to be seen; she could stay at Iowa for a fifth season because of the NCAA's coronavirus eligibility guidelines. While she won't need to make a decision for at least a year, the NCAA's new name, image and likeness rules, which allow athletes to earn endorsement income, could play in Iowa's favor. Clark, a marketing major with a 3.88 grade-point average and dreams of working as a front-office executive in pro sports, already has struck lucrative deals with Nike and the Hy-Vee supermarket chain.

"It will be very difficult," said Clark, who is "50-50" on whether to stay for a fifth season. "I love this place. You're playing in front of a lot of people, doing it in your home state, doing it with your friends. Turning pro, you're traveling all the time, you're only playing three months a year, you're moving to a whole new city where you probably don't know anybody. NIL definitely makes it more of an incentive to come back, in a way. It adds another pro on the pros and cons list."

For now, Clark is focused on making the Final Four after a second-round loss to Creighton last year. That upset represented a step back from her freshman season, when the Hawkeyes advanced to the Sweet 16.

Clark spent last summer adding eight pounds of muscle and chewing on the fact that the pinnacle of her sport has, so far, remained just beyond her reach. Iowa's NCAA tournament losses stung just like her final game at Dowling. And second place will never be good enough, whether it's a first-grade math quiz or the Naismith Player of the Year voting.

"It does drive you," Clark said. "Growing up, I've always been right there, chasing the number one spot. I feel like I am the best player in the country. I've put in a lot of time in the gym to believe that. The confidence I have when I shoot the ball is because of the work I put in during the summer. Why wouldn't I want to be at the top?"

BEN GOLLIVER is the National NBA Writer for *The Washington Post*. The Beaverton, Oregon, native and Johns Hopkins University graduate has written about all levels of basketball since 2007, including as a senior writer for *Sports Illustrated*. His first book, *Bubbleball*, chronicled his 93-day stay inside the NBA's COVID-19 bubble. He lives in Rolling Hills Estates, California.

Tragedy That Put Andy Reid's Son in Prison Can't Be Ignored at Super Bowl 57

JARRETT BELL

FROM *USA TODAY* • FEBRUARY 10, 2023

SCOTTSDALE, Ariz.—If you just so happen to wonder what Andy Reid's favorite Mexican dish is, you would have been enlightened during a mid-week media session with the Kansas City Chiefs coach at the team's Super Bowl hotel.

What a show, an entertaining hype-fest, some of these pre-Super Bowl news conferences can be. And the jovial Reid can play along with the best of them.

No, that wasn't Bill Belichick at the podium when someone asked the coach to name his three favorite rappers.

"Do The Fat Boys count as one rapper?" Reid replied, prompting an outburst of laughs from the assembled audience.

Reid was also asked how he takes his coffee. He doesn't.

"I've got endless energy for a chubby guy," he said.

His favorite cheeseburger? You get the picture. A lot of fluff stuff.

During the two Reid sessions that I attended this week, which included the presence of dozens of national and international journalists, no one bothered to ask about the tragic incident that occurred three days before the Chiefs were last in the Super Bowl in February 2021. Or the aftermath of an accident caused by a then-Chiefs assistant coach, Reid's drunken son, Britt, that left a then-5-year-old girl, Ariel Young, fighting for her life.

The matchup pitting Reid and the Chiefs against the franchise he coached for 14 years, the Philadelphia Eagles, is a big reason why he is one of the most compelling storylines of Super Bowl 57. Reid is 3–0 against the Eagles since continuing his Hall of Fame–credentialed career in Kansas City, and he readily acknowledges the sentimental twist added to the game on Sunday at State Farm Stadium that features the teams who shared the NFL's best record this season.

"Once the game gets going, it's football," Reid said. "Who's got the better team? Better players? Better coaches? Who gets a break, here or there? All the things that normally happen in a football game."

Still, the tragedy that marred the ramp-up to Kansas City's last Super Bowl appearance should not be ignored—as much as the Chiefs and the NFL seemingly would want it to just go away.

Britt Reid is in prison now, serving a plea-bargained three-year sentence after pleading guilty to felony driving while intoxicated resulting in serious physical injury. Then a Chiefs linebackers coach, he left the team's headquarters the night of Feb. 4, where court documents suggest he had consumed alcohol, and rammed his truck into two vehicles that were idled on the shoulder of I-435 near Arrowhead Stadium. He had a serum blood alcohol concentration of 0.113 approximately two hours later, well above the Missouri limit of 0.08. According to police, his truck was speeding at 84 mph in a 65 mph zone, and he admitted to an officer that he had mixed alcohol with the prescription drug Adderall.

Young was sitting in the back of one of the vehicles that Reid struck and suffered a traumatic brain injury after being pinned behind the driver's seat. She was in a coma for 11 days and hospitalized for two months. Thank God that she survived. Yet at the sentencing hearing for Reid in November, Young's mother,

Felicia Miller, told the court that while her daughter's condition has improved, she will have to deal with the impact of the crash for the rest of her life.

"The positive thing is that the little girl is doing better. A lot better," Andy Reid told *USA TODAY* Sports. "That's the positive of this whole thing."

Reid, always one of the most engaging and approachable coaches in the NFL, responded to a handful of questions following one of his media sessions this week. As he prepares to coach in his third Super Bowl in four seasons, surely it wasn't the ideal topic for him. But it's fair game, given his high-profile role in the public eye—and the connection to his job with the Chiefs.

And it's also apparent that the manner in which Reid has handled crisis is part of the example that he has set as a coach and leader, earning him tremendous respect and empathy.

When asked for a lasting impression of Reid from the crisis before the last Super Bowl appearance, defensive end Frank Clark told *USA TODAY* Sports, "The main thing I learned about Coach Reid was just his grit. His will to keep on going, no matter what the situation."

The NFL, which previously said it would review the case under the umbrella of its personal conduct policy—which it vigorously pursues regarding issues involving players—has not publicly released any findings from the review and did not respond to an inquiry from *USA TODAY* Sports this week.

The Chiefs engaged in an undisclosed settlement with Young's family that covers medical and, conceivably, other expenses.

Reid, who lost his son, Garrett, to an accidental heroin overdose in 2012 while working on his father's staff with the Eagles, hired Britt to his Chiefs staff despite scant experience that basically consisted of one year of coaching at the high school level. Like the conditions of the plea-bargained sentence that reportedly outraged Young's family, the hire that led to Britt joining the Chiefs raises serious questions about privilege. Britt came to the Chiefs with a record that included previous jail time stemming from drug abuse, a road rage incident and had undergone drug rehab treatment.

The compassionate efforts by Reid to help his son—much like he provided a second chance to Michael Vick after the star quarterback served his prison sentence for dogfighting—were noble enough. But the opportunity afforded Britt that many qualified candidates don't get a chance at, backfired.

"Britt will do his time and he'll be back and get back on his feet," Reid told *USA TODAY* Sports.

It must be tough to separate the non-football issues related to the tragedy from his job.

"You've got to do the best you can," Reid said. "Absolutely. It's all part of life."

When Reid lost his son, Garrett, while he coached the Eagles, he came back to work days after the death. The auto accident involving Britt was obviously a different circumstance, but it forced Reid to compartmentalize on the eve of coaching in one of the biggest games of his life.

How did he try to reconcile what happened?

"Tried to stay focused on the job the best I could," Reid told *USA TODAY* Sports. "There was a little girl involved, too. My son was hurt. She was hurt. For that time being, you've got to put that distraction aside the best you can."

Distraction. For the most affected victims, it was so much deeper than that. Yet that form of "coach speak" might also reflect why players and staff members describe Reid as a rock of consistency while employing a certain type of tunnel vision. In Reid's case, though, his personal challenges have made him more human with the men he is charged to lead. The humanism that makes Reid such a hit on the podium works behind closed doors, too, in relating to players.

"We can look at the (head) coach title and think that this person is so out of touch with reality, so out of reach, but he's a normal person," Clark said. "He goes through normal things. You look at the course of his career, he's had real-life situations, dealing with players, dealing with his own kids, his own family and the situation (before Super Bowl 55). Eventually, does it affect the man? I'm sure it does.

"It just shows his grit to continue to come in here, smiling in our faces, he's giving us everything that we want. He's not short-changing us with the coaching, either. He's giving it all to his players."

Like Clark, Chiefs tight end Travis Kelce saw another dimension of Reid's persona revealed through the crisis in early 2021. The accident occurred the night before the Chiefs flew to Tampa for Super Bowl 55, their departure later in the week than usual for a Super Bowl team due to COVID-19 restrictions.

"I learned how strong of a guy he is," Kelce told *USA TODAY* Sports. "Mentally, how strong his family is, how tight-knit this entire locker room is and how much we love that guy, man. It wasn't an easy time for him and we're definitely trying to make this year that much better. I've got to get another one for Big Red, man. I love that guy too much."

The Chiefs lost Super Bowl 55 against the Tampa Bay Buccaneers, and it wasn't even close. Kelce insists that the sudden crisis dealt to Reid and the team had no impact on the 31–9 result.

"All you saw in that game was how we played on that field," Kelce said. "I don't think anything like that got in the way."

Yet the tragedy was still part of the storyline.

NFL Columnist **JARRETT BELL** has covered the NFL for *USA TODAY* since 1993, and has served on the Pro Football Hall of Fame Selection Committee for 27 years. He was the 2022 recipient of the Bill Nunn, Jr. Memorial Award, the highest honor for the Pro Football Writers of America, for lifetime achievement. He received a Salute to Excellence Award (2020) and an Outstanding Book Award (2021) from the National Association of Black Journalists. Previously he worked as a San Francisco 49ers beat writer for the *Marin Independent Journal* and as editor of *The Dallas Cowboys Weekly*. Detroit native. Michigan State grad. Father of two. He resides in Smyrna, Georgia.

Greg Oden's Long Walk Home

MIRIN FADER

FROM The Ringer • MARCH 8, 2023

Greg Oden is early. Earlier than most of the players he's about to coach. He steps out of his Denali on this bright, windy February morning in Indianapolis and lumbers into Hinkle Fieldhouse.

Shootaround at Butler University's historic basketball arena doesn't start for another 45 minutes, but Oden isn't wasting a second. He takes a seat at the edge of the scorer's table and studies the practice plan, jotting down notes. Soon, players file in, and Oden breaks out into a giant, jubilant smile, almost humming with excitement, as if the game in five hours is nearing tipoff.

He slips a tiny red mesh jersey over his gray hoodie, which looks like a baby's bib on his 7-foot frame, barely covering the top of his chest. But he isn't the least bit bothered; he's in his element. He joins the scout team on the court, whispering bits of advice to players between sets. He throws down a dunk, soft and clean, offering up a glorious glimmer of the player everyone in this gym, in this city, remembers him to be.

Back then, when he starred at Lawrence North High School, just 20 minutes from Butler's campus, he was seen as the NBA's next great big man. He led Lawrence North to a 103–7 record over four years and three consecutive Class 4A state titles. He was the Gatorade National Player of the Year in 2005 *and* 2006. And in a state like Indiana, where basketball transforms mortals into gods, Oden became a massive celebrity. *The New York Times* called him a "once-in-a-basketball-generation center," mentioning his name next to Bill Russell's. He went on to lead Ohio State to the national championship game as a freshman, 16 years ago this month.

But Oden is mostly known for what came next: After being selected no. 1 overall in the 2007 NBA draft over Kevin Durant, he suffered debilitating knee injuries that prevented him from living up to the Herculean expectations set for him. For years, he carried a burden so heavy it nearly crushed him. Cruel, dehumanizing comments have followed him since: namely that he's *the biggest bust in NBA history.*

That narrative, that four-letter word, haunted him for a long time. It hurt to hear. It hurt to explain. But that word doesn't capture the spirit of his struggle, his journey, his resilience, his joy, and, most importantly, where his path has taken him today: He's finding new purpose as a coach. He's wrapping up his first season as Butler's director of basketball operations. And he's doing it alongside his former Ohio State coach, Thad Matta, who is now at the helm of Butler's program: a man who never gave up on Oden, even when many did.

Oden could have given up basketball. He could have gotten a regular job that had nothing to do with the game. But that peach-dotted leather ball kept tugging at him, kept reminding him of the deepest love he's ever known, even as it tried to break his heart again and again. Because as long as he can remember, basketball wasn't just something he did. It was *him.*

Hired last April, Oden now dreams of becoming a head coach someday. "It's fun. It's hard. But I really do enjoy it," he says. He beams when thinking about the future: how excited he is for this summer, when he'll get to spend more individual time working out with players. He thinks about what it would be like to run his own program one day, what his own coaching philosophy will ultimately be. "I really think I can do this."

In a way, he's a rookie all over again, paying his dues. Admittedly, with slightly less pressure and in more anonymity. Without the cameras, without the hype, he is left with the untarnished love he has had for basketball since he was a kid, scoring his first bucket by grabbing the opponent's rebound out of the air and putting it right back up in their basket.

He spends hours breaking down game film and pulling clips of opponents for Butler's other coaches. He embraces the grind. "I know I've got a lot to learn, and I'm going to keep working at it," Oden says.

He is constantly soaking up as much wisdom as possible. He often asks the other coaches about strategies and schemes or how they handle certain situations. And, most often, Oden says: "Is there anything anyone needs help with? How can I do more?"

Oden picks things up quickly and often points things out in film that the other coaches without his athletic pedigree might miss. "When I coached him, he had a great mind for the game of basketball," Matta says. "It wasn't only his physical characteristics. His understanding [of the game] is what made him special.

"Now, he's in that position where he is studying and he has to teach more because the guys that we're dealing with aren't as talented as he was, and they don't have the characteristics that he had," Matta says. "I think that in the end's going to make him a lot better basketball coach."

Some of Oden's most dominant high school games were actually played at Hinkle. He never expected to return. Anyone who has gone through the injuries and setbacks and disappointments Oden has might never want to *look* at a basketball again. But Oden kept gravitating toward it. He never lost his love for the game.

He still needs it.

And maybe part of him needed to come back *here*. To Indianapolis. To the very house he had lived in back when he bought the place in 2012. He had just been released from Portland after playing just 82 games over five seasons, missing three campaigns entirely, and then sitting out another season before joining the Heat. He left the house to pursue an NBA comeback with the Heat in 2013, but various family members occupied it in the years since.

The home, painted blue and gray, is every bit the sight Oden remembered. It's surrounded by trees, near the woods, a bit nestled away from the surrounding old-time neighborhood. That was one of the reasons he bought it after his tenure with Portland ended. He needed his space. He was devastated.

"I just secluded myself from everybody," he says.

Sometimes, he stayed in the house for two weeks straight. He felt too ashamed to go outside. He feared running into anyone from high school. "I felt like a loser," he says.

On the rare times he did venture out, he'd put his hood up far over his head, hoping to shield his face, his eyes, and, quite impossibly, his 7-foot frame. "I just felt like a failure. I felt like I let a lot of people down," he says. "Letting Portland down, letting the whole entire staff and organization down. I felt like I let my family down and everybody who coached me and believed in me."

Oden often thinks about how much life has changed since then, how much *he* has changed since then. He has a family now. He and his wife, Sabrina, have a young daughter, Londyn. Rooms in the house that were once empty are now filled with love.

But there are rooms he can't bring himself to go in, like the theater room. That was where he used to sit and drink until he passed out, until he temporarily numbed the pain and the shame of his basketball dreams slipping away.

He became addicted to painkillers during his time with the Blazers. And as the years wore on, he grew more frustrated at his inability to will his body to perform the way he needed to. In the way he expected it to.

Oden has spent years unpacking off-the-court issues that led to his darkest moments. He has been working to heal, to move forward with his life. Coaching has given him a new joy. He feels buoyed by possibility.

He has finally found...peace.

But he is human. He still struggles. It still hurts sometimes when someone calls him a "bust." He sometimes watches his old highlights on YouTube, especially the '07 national championship game against Florida, where he notched 25 points, 12 rebounds, and four blocks. Some part of him still needs to see those clips. To remember what he could do then. Who he was then.

But Oden doesn't necessarily see himself as another person these days. He doesn't view coaching as a second act either. He's come to accept all parts of his journey: the things he wished would have happened and the things he wished never would have happened. It's all one long, continuous road. "I've been on this ride for 35 years now," he says.

Oden's journey has now brought him back home, back to the place where it all started. It's been a long road back: a long road that began just a short drive away.

Dozens of spindly, leafless trees line the streets leading to Lawrence North. It's only 8 miles from Butler, and on this February morning, the roads are nearly empty. A cluster of suburban brick houses sits across from the high school. Every other driveway has a hoop. After all, it's Indiana.

Inside the school's gym is a prominent Hall of Fame wall. There's a photo of a baby-faced, much slimmer Oden in the right corner, flashing both rows of teeth and spinning a ball on his finger. His National Player of the Year trophies sit in a glass case nearby.

Back then, no one could contain him on the court. The lane was *his*. It seemed like he could block a shot from anywhere, anytime. But Oden seemed almost oblivious to his own talent. "It was almost like he didn't understand why they thought he was the next big thing," says Jimmy Smith, whom Oden considers a kind of adopted father. He and his wife, Tami, consider Oden family, a son. Their biological son, Travis, was Oden's best friend since age 9, and Jimmy coached the boys team.

Alongside Oden's mother, Zoe, Jimmy and Tami helped Oden navigate his budding fame, as his teenage face would grace the cover of seemingly every hoops magazine. He would become anointed as the next great American prospect, as LeBron James had been just four years earlier. Tami remembers how much pressure followed Oden. "It was absolutely huge," Tami says. "But he was also just so humble.... He would always be like, 'I've got to work.'"

The spotlight only intensified at Ohio State as he dominated the competition, despite playing with a surgically repaired wrist all season. Cameras followed him everywhere. He'd kindly sign every autograph, every picture, but the attention was overwhelming. "You could just see in his eyes sometimes, you'd just want him to hide," Matta says.

But the hype, the promise of what Oden might bring to the NBA, hung in the balance when he arrived in Portland. Before the season, Oden knew something was wrong with his right knee. He tried to stay optimistic even as doctors told him: *There's a possible chance you may have season-ending surgery. We need to go in there and look.*

Shortly thereafter, Oden woke up to the devastating news: *You're out for the year.* He soon had microfracture surgery, a now infamous procedure. Sitting out the entire season as the top pick and watching sports pundits talk about his absence on TV was painful. He was supposed to be the savior to rescue Portland from its Jail Blazers era, coined for its players' legal troubles. Meanwhile, Durant was proving to be an immediate superstar in Seattle.

Oden burned to get back on the court but was stuck inside his home, eight hours a day, with his leg wrapped inside a machine that would continuously stretch his leg. He continued working hard in rehab but felt lonely off the court. He felt like he was letting so many people down.

He didn't feel like a part of the Blazers organization either, spending so much time away from the team. He was 19 and living in a new city. Everyone seemed to know him, but he hardly knew anyone, making him feel even more isolated. "I was kind of depressed," he says.

He began drinking more and more, especially when the team would go on weeklong road trips. Time would pass, but the relief never lasted. "It got pretty bad when I got to Portland," he says. "I was always injured, and I was always at home, and it was just an everyday thing."

Few knew he was also grieving. Travis, the only true friend he felt he ever had, the one who never wanted anything from him but friendship and love, died in a car accident about five months before Oden was drafted.

Oden would usually give Travis a ticket to his Ohio State games. But this time, ahead of a late January contest against Michigan State, Oden told Travis that his mom and grandmother were in town, and he was going to give them his two tickets. Hours before the game, Oden's mom and grandmother told him they were no longer able to come. Oden talked with Travis about 30 minutes before tipoff, but didn't tell him about the now-available ticket because he feared Travis would speed to Columbus to try to make it in time.

But something did happen that night, albeit unrelated to Greg's game. Travis died in a car accident. For months, Oden blamed himself for his friend's death. If he had just told Travis his grandmother and mother were no longer coming, Oden reasoned, if he had just given him that spare ticket, maybe this wouldn't have happened.

Matta broke the news to Oden after the game. Oden walked out of the locker room, got in his car, and drove around Columbus all night, sobbing until he couldn't anymore.

Oden tried to cope as best as he could, but injuries kept haunting him as he returned to the court for his first true season in 2008–09.

He left his NBA debut with a foot injury after just 13 minutes of play. He played off and on the rest of the year, recording several double-doubles, but later missed extended time with an injured kneecap. In the following 2009–10 season, he had stellar stretches of play, showing flashes of his massive potential. But 21 games in, he suffered a fractured patella in his left knee, prematurely ending his season.

It was agonizing: continuously getting injured, working so hard in rehab, trying to get himself back, only to get hurt again and again. He wouldn't give up on the player he knew he was, but he wished his body could just *do* what his mind instructed.

Then, Oden suffered yet another loss. Trail Blazers assistant coach Maurice Lucas, who had empathized with him and always had him over to his family's home for Thanksgiving so he wouldn't feel alone, passed away of cancer. And Oden's cousin, who had come to live with him his second season, was suddenly diagnosed with cancer and soon passed away.

So many people he cared about were disappearing. And the surgeries kept mounting: He had *another* microfracture surgery, this time on his left knee, in November 2010, causing him to sit out for another full season.

Some wouldn't want anything to do with basketball after going through what Oden experienced, but Greg was drawn closer to it. His passion for it wouldn't allow him to even consider the possibility of letting it go. He'd watch his highlights on YouTube, see himself dunk over people, and think about how he could get back to *that*.

This is what I used to be able to do, he'd think.

And, perhaps, a more fragile thought lay underneath:

This is who I used to be.

THE IDENTITY HE had clung to since he was a teenage basketball prodigy was becoming blurry. He didn't even feel like a basketball player anymore. His sense of self-worth had long been conflated with his achievements. Who was he if not a basketball player?

To make matters worse, it hurt when people would walk up to him and say: "That's Greg Oden! You were a bust!" before snapping a photo of him, as if he weren't a real person deserving of dignity and respect.

All his life, Oden truly just wanted to be *liked*. He was a sweet, goofy kid who just happened to be much taller and bigger than his peers. When he was younger, he initially worried about not fitting in, not just because of his size, but because he was one of the few Black players in the area. As beloved as he would become on all of his teams throughout high school—he was able to make anyone laugh with a funny face or joke and was incredibly talented and a good teammate—he still worried about being accepted.

Heading into his freshman year at Ohio State, after he had won every national award imaginable, he called Matta one day: "Coach, I'm worried that the guys may not like me when I get there."

There was an innocence to him: a bit of naivete. Ahead of the 2007 NBA draft, he walked the streets of New York for the first time. He was astounded by how aggressive people were, pushing him every which way. He felt so overwhelmed that he had to duck inside a pizza shop just to catch his breath.

He liked cartoons and movies, referencing *Shrek* in a predraft interview. "He's a kid at heart," Tami says. A kid who was praised from such a young age, placed on such a high pedestal, only to be thrown back down as an adult once his body couldn't function the way it had in the past. It left him with a jarring dissonance that was difficult to reconcile.

Years later, as he tried to cope with the disappointment of his injuries and the isolation of working through them by himself, he would turn to other methods. Jimmy says the Blazers' front office would call him, concerned about the company Oden was keeping in Portland and his partying. He had partied in college, too, but this seemed different. And the truth was, as he entered the pros, when the parties ended, when everyone left, when he was finally alone, he felt profoundly sad.

He had been taking painkillers since his first surgery his rookie year. He couldn't sleep without them. He says he needed Percocet, Vicodin, Tylenol P.M., Benadryl, and a drink just to get five hours of sleep. And for a period of time, he kept scratching his body, not understanding why. "I felt like a crackhead," he says. Later, he learned he was allergic to Percocet but kept taking whatever he could.

"I was kind of numb to it," he says. "It's just at a point where you get used to them and to get some type of relief. And then at one point, I was taking them just to take them."

There wasn't much relief. He wasn't thinking deeply about it either, trapped in his habit. *This is what I do*, he'd think to himself.

One day, he ran out of pills. "I ransacked my house looking for any more," he says. In the bathroom. In old bags. In every room. He frantically tried to remember where he last put them, what each pill individually looked like. *Maybe it could be here?! Maybe I dropped one there?!* "That was pretty eye-opening," he says.

That's when he realized he might need help. He had tried to confide in therapists over the years in Portland but didn't feel the mostly white therapists could relate to his experience as a 7-foot-tall Black man. He wasn't sure he could trust them either, because they were hired by the team.

He started drinking more. Drinking in the club turned into drinking at the house, which turned into drinking beer, wine, and hard liquor in the same day: "Whatever will get you there until it's just time to pass out." As much as he tried to shut the door to the theater room and drink, hoping to hide his habits, he soon learned that he didn't have to tell anyone for them to know. "They can smell it on you," he says.

That only added to his shame.

A month after having two additional surgeries in February 2012—a third microfracture surgery on his left knee and arthroscopic surgery on his right knee—he was released by Portland

Only 24, he felt so far from *Greg Oden, the no. 1 pick.* "Now, I'm *the party guy*," he says. "I'm *the drinking guy*."

He returned to Indiana. And as much as he tried to stay in his house, he would inevitably run into old classmates. It surprised him how genuinely nice they were. "Greg! Man, it's good to see you. I'm sorry for everything that's happened to you."

It tore him up. The shame inside him, the part of him that felt like a failure, struggled to process kindness. The part of him who feared he wouldn't be liked, who always feared disappointing others, wasn't sure how to move forward.

Still, he wouldn't quit. Basketball was something he loved with every fiber of his being, so he kept pushing to return to the court, eventually signing with the two-time defending champion Heat in August 2013, more than three years after his last NBA action. He played 23 games with Miami, helping the Heat make it all the way to the 2014 NBA Finals, where they lost in five games to the Spurs. But none of it would matter after that summer.

On August 7, 2014, around 3:30 a.m., police were called to Oden's home. Court documents state that Oden had punched his ex-girlfriend, whom an officer described as having "blood [and] swelling to the nose." His mother, who'd been awoken by the commotion, had to pull Oden off the woman, according to the documents. Oden was arrested and charged with two felony counts of battery and two misdemeanor counts of battery. According to the police's incident report, Oden told responding officers: "I was wrong, and I know what has to happen." Oden eventually pleaded guilty to one felony count, while the other three charges were dismissed. He received 909 days of probation and was ordered to complete 26 weeks of domestic violence counseling and alcohol counseling. A no-contact order was also put in place.

Oden has since expressed remorse for his actions but has said he cannot legally comment on the situation, per the no-contact order. Tami, who spoke to Oden in the immediate aftermath of the arrest, recalls him telling her: "I know what I did was wrong. It could never happen again. Women can't be treated like that." She also recalls him saying that he had been drinking but reiterated that his actions were inexcusable. Indefensible.

"Talk is cheap," she told him. "Until you practice what you preach, nobody is going to believe anything you say." He knew she was right. And he knew he needed help getting sober. "We told him he had no option but to go to rehab," Jimmy says.

Oden headed to rehab in Minnesota for the next month. He also attended therapy. He stayed completely sober for about half a year. "I went through a process of trying to clean my body out of where I was at," he says.

He was able to wean himself off of the strongest painkillers. He was beginning to piece his life back together. "He took immediate accountability for his actions," says Tami, who was often his contact in Alcoholics Anonymous and would receive regular reports from his counselors about his progress.

She could sense in his voice that he was improving, starting to sound like himself again, but he knew the work was ongoing. "Therapy didn't stop in Minnesota," she says. "Minnesota was just the very tip of it. This is just an eight-plus year ongoing recovery.... And it still has to continue every day."

Meanwhile, he was still drawn to basketball, still unwilling to accept that he was past his prime and that he could not do the thing he enjoyed most. He worked to make a comeback, and he was ultimately willing to go all the way to China to prove that he could still do it.

He played for the Jiangsu Dragons in 2015–16, but as fate would have it, he broke his right thumb in the preseason. He had to rehab for a month over there before even getting onto the court. His back was hurting too. He started enjoying himself more though, finally playing, finally in his element. But the team missed the playoffs, and he was soon cut from the team.

Throughout his comeback, he feared reinjury: the cycle repeating again.

Before leaving for China, Oden called Matta late one night. "I'm scared. I'm afraid it's going to happen again," Matta remembers Oden saying. "I just don't know if I can keep doing this."

"G," Matta said, "just come to practice."

MATTA INVITED ODEN to return to Ohio State as a student manager for the 2016–17 season, which would allow him to simultaneously complete his undergraduate degree. It wasn't a paid position, but Matta understood that Oden needed something more than money, more than a job: He needed support, someone to affirm to him:

You still belong.

Oden returned to his alma mater and began coaching, seeing another therapist, and attending Alcoholics Anonymous meetings. He also juggled a full-time course load as a student.

"It takes a lot of humility to do that, to go back to school, to walk to class every day, for, again, a guy who was the no. 1 pick," says Jon Diebler, Butler's director of recruiting and a fellow former Ohio State star.

Being around college students made Oden feel younger. He was able to slip back into *Greg Oden who led Ohio State to the national championship game.* He needed people to see him in that way: "I really did," he says. "That [I] wasn't *no. 1 draft pick that didn't turn out to nothing Greg.*"

Oden didn't realize how much he truly loved basketball until he returned to his alma mater. As a kid, basketball was just something he fell into. He enjoyed playing with his friends. He had been a fan of the NBA. But when he could no longer play as an adult, he found himself watching more basketball than ever, falling in love with the game on his own terms.

He felt valued again. Ohio State's players were asking *him* questions. Counting on *him* to explain concepts.

For so long, he was labeled as past his prime, as having unfulfilled potential because of his injuries. But when he was on the court with OSU's players, he had access to a different view of himself.

People still like me, he thought.

But he was realizing that *he* needed to like himself. *He* had to face his shame, his feelings of inadequacy, his guilt. The parts he wanted to see and the parts he may not have wanted to see. Those surgeries in Portland. That night in Indiana at 3:30 a.m. The pills. The bottles. The people he hurt. His fears. His remorse. His resilience.

"It's all still me, struggling to be the best person I can be," Oden says.

"There was a lot of ups and downs in my life. I did a lot of things I'm not proud of," he says. He realized he had to own it. "This is my path.... I made these decisions. I've got to live with it, and I've got to move forward with it. I just got to be able to look at myself in the mirror."

In really *seeing* himself, he had to try to let go of how others perceived him. He wasn't a bust. He wasn't a failure. He was simply a flawed human being trying to find his way.

"He had to learn to forgive himself," Jimmy says. "Everyone deserves a second chance, but it is ultimately your own decision what you choose to do with that."

GREG AND SABRINA, who had been friends for some time, reconnected while he was in China. She had long been one of his closest confidants, the only person besides Travis who could get him on the phone for longer than 10, 20 minutes. She understood his struggle and was there for him as he tried to rebuild his life, and they became serious. She helped him step outside of his comfort zone. "He was in a bubble, a shell," Sabrina says. She'd say, "Let's go see a movie. Let's just hang out." She isn't a person to sit in sorrow, and she wouldn't let Oden wallow. "Life will *life*," she'd say. "No matter what yesterday was, just *go*. Chin up.

"You have to just put your best foot forward," Sabrina says, "and do the work on yourself to improve.... You're not going to be able to do that if you're stuck staggering in just one spot."

The two had Londyn in 2016 and married in 2017. Oden graduated in 2019, almost 13 years since he first stepped foot on campus, with a degree in sport industry.

Right before Oden joined Butler's staff in 2022, he took his family to Miami on vacation. The Heat were playing the Nets, and Oden wanted to watch Kevin Durant, the player he'll forever be tied to for surpassing as the no. 1 pick in '07.

Oden never forgot how Durant, the no. 2 pick, responded in 2016 when asked on ESPN if he thought Oden was a bust. "Nonsense," Durant said. "He didn't get a chance. He was injured.... When he did play, he was a force. Protecting the paint." It meant a lot to Oden to hear Durant dignify him in that way.

And, during halftime of the Heat-Nets game, Durant came over to chat with Oden. Oden pointed out Sabrina and Londyn, and Durant waved to them. Then, the two top picks embraced. The small gesture meant more to Oden than he had words for. "That was big time," Oden says. "I'm a KD fan for life."

He realized, being in the arena, how much he was enjoying being *present*. It didn't matter that he was in the stands, that his life turned out so differently than Durant's.

"I can look in the mirror and just realize that in this moment, I'm happy," he says.

Happiness, Oden was learning, was about having gratitude for his *own* path. "It's accepting what you've been through," he says. "Being able to keep your head high."

He's been sharing some of those insights with Butler's players since taking the role last April. "What we're trying to go through, he's already been through," says guard Jayden Taylor. "So I feel like anybody could come and learn from him."

He often tells Butler's 6-foot-10 senior center Jalen Thomas, "Take your time in the post."

"Just being able to pick his brain, asking him how it was going against other guys, bigger guys, being able to ask him those questions is great," says Thomas, who transferred to Butler this season after spending the past three years at Georgia State. Finding out Oden was coming to coach helped seal the deal. "Definitely a big part of why I came," Thomas says.

One practice, Oden noticed center Manny Bates kept missing easy shots because he was off balance. He pulled Bates aside. "He showed me film when I was on balance," Bates says. Bates has become more efficient than ever this season, shooting 62 percent from the field.

Sometimes, when Oden is asked to fill in during practice, the former Ohio State star will resurface, and he'll become ultracompetitive, dunking on anyone in his way: even student managers. One of them, Tommy Niederpruem, remembers Oden giving everyone a *look* after stuffing a spectacular one down. "It's just really fun to see that come out," Niederpruem says.

Another time, the post players were doing a pick-and-roll drill. Players scored on Oden five times in a row. "All right, bet," Oden said. The next four trips, nobody scored. He blocked everything in sight.

"That energy, that enthusiasm, that passion is infectious," says Mike Pegues, Butler's assistant coach. "It circulates throughout this building." Oden often asks Pegues how to develop solid relationships with players and how to hold them accountable. Pegues can tell how badly Oden wants to succeed as a coach: "[He's] really, really intrigued by longevity and how you go about extending your career in this business."

He doesn't act entitled because of his name. He was surprised to learn that the assistant coaches share rooms on the road—very different from the perks he used to have as an NBA player. "I haven't shared a room since college," he says. But, he nodded his head and accepted it.

There's a door inside Pegues's office, right behind his desk, that leads into the tunnel to the gym. Every member of the staff parades right through.

Not Oden though. He'll ask: "Mike, can I come through?"

Every home game, Oden sits in the same spot on the bench: last coach, with nearly all the players to the right of him. He is quiet but impactful whenever he speaks up, busy tracking fouls, timeouts, and the possession arrow. And no matter how the game is going, he always turns around, finding Sabrina and Londyn in the same spot in Hinkle.

MAYBE ODEN'S CALLING will prove to be at the end of the bench, not the paint. Maybe his potential can be reincarnated. He's realized that it's okay to change course, change careers. Sometimes, he thinks about former child actors and how it disheartens him when he sees that people shame them for doing something different as adults. "What did you expect them to do? Sit in the house and live off the one thing that you know them from?" Oden says.

Things aren't perfect. He still feels pain in his left knee. He still watches his old highlights. And he still has to be mindful of alcohol, though he knows his limits now. "I'm not going to say I'm a recovered alcoholic and I don't have a drink," he says, "because I do have a drink every now and then."

For managing pain, he tries not to go near anything strong, as he used to. "That's something I really try to stay away from, knowing how bad it got."

He's still recognized wherever he goes. These days, though, he actually enjoys running into old classmates, no longer hiding in his hoodie. Well, only a little, for other reasons. "My hair is bald a little bit," he says, laughing.

Somehow, his mind circles back to his house, as it often does. He says the place is aging too, creaking in certain spots. "There's a lot of work to be done in the house," he says. The carpet has to be changed. The driveway needs to be redone. The outside could use a fresh paint job. The pool needs attention. He makes a mental note to follow up with the repairman. Then there's the theater room, a demon he has yet to conquer.

But after a long day of practice and compiling video clips for Butler's coaches, he returns home to rest. The night is dark, but he can see the beauty of the house: how perfectly imperfect it is. There's still time to tend to it.

What a gift, he realizes. A chance to wake up tomorrow and take a closer look. A chance to rebuild.

MIRIN FADER is a senior staff writer for The Ringer, writing long-form human interest sports features. She's the *New York Times* bestselling author of *Giannis: The Improbable Rise of an NBA Champion*. Her work has been honored by the Pro Basketball Writers Association, the Associated Press Sports Editors, the U.S. Basketball Writers Association, and the Los Angeles Press Club.

This Gifted Clubmaker's Handcrafted Driver Made Him a Star. Then It All but Derailed Him

BRENDAN PRUNTY

FROM *Golf* • MARCH 31, 2023

She was in an aquarium. They all were. Her brothers and sisters, all submerged in 10-gallon mixtures of boiled linseed oil and turpentine. God, the smell was terrible. Sitting and soaking. Waiting to float. That's how you knew. This one, this perfect 208-gram block of persimmon wood, was in there for days. Weeks. *Months.* Every time she was removed to get weight-checked, she wasn't quite there yet, so back into the bath she went. Finally, after a few months, it was time.

You could tell, right from the get-go, this one was different. She was more fickle than most. A little more temperamental. She took longer during the drying process, too. Sheesh, that was a pain—there were deadlines to meet, you know?—but finally the time had come. By this point, she had acquired a name: *Christine.* Named her after that Stephen King novel where a '58 Plymouth Fury has a mind of its own and a little murderous streak to boot. He carried Christine out to the side of the workshop, opened the trunk of his Datsun B210 hatchback and placed her down to cure under the hot Texas sun.

Clubs of character is how Dave Wood always believed golf clubs should be made, but hot damn, the good Lord never created a block of persimmon like Christine.

"It was perfect in every way," Wood recalled. "But it had a little bit of Elvira to it. All the markings were different. This was a block of wood that had a hard heart to it."

By the time Wood had polished her up, screwed on the identifying sole plate at the bottom—the one with the big, shiny silver silhouette of Texas, with "TEXAS GOLF CO." across the middle of it—affixed her to a 43½-inch Dynamic Gold X100 steel shaft, adjusted her to a 10-degree loft, a D-3 swing weight, and gripped her up, she looked like the dozens of prototypes that he would roll up to PGA Tour events with on a weekly basis. She was ready in time for his trip to the 1986 Los Angeles Open at Riviera Country Club, where he was scheduled to meet with several of the world's best players. Among them, was a potential new client: a 28-year-old mild-mannered German, who was the reigning Masters champion.

Bernhard Langer needed a new driver and wanted Dave Wood to make him one. As he tested a few different models on the range, Langer liked some of them, but the connection wasn't quite there.

Then he saw Christine.

"It had a nice pear shape," Langer recalled the other day. "It seemed solid, it would go a good distance when I hit it. I was always interested in performance, but these didn't just perform well, they looked good, too."

Langer took her, teed it up and began swinging away. His caddie, Peter Coleman, stood at the other end of the range at Riviera, signaling with his arms which way the ball would move. (Think prehistoric Trackman.) Wood stood a few feet back and smiled, as Langer drilled ball after ball perfectly. He had made clubs for some of the up-and-coming players on Tour for a few years, but bagging a current major champion would be a coup for his growing outfit. He knew what was coming next.

"Bernhard took it right there," Wood said. "He wanted to keep it. And that was kind of the beginning of that. That's how that relationship began with Wood Brothers."

Bernhard Langer and Wood Brothers Golf. Hard to find a more dynamic pairing in golf through the late 1980s and early 1990s. Langer would take *Christine* and then her descendants all over the world, winning more than a dozen times, playing in three Ryder Cups and, in 1986, becoming the first player to be ranked No. 1 in the new Official World Golf Rankings. Dave Wood and his small club-making business soon exploded alongside Langer's success. By the end of the 1980s, the best players in the world were playing his handcrafted persimmon woods: Seve Ballesteros, Greg Norman, Ben Crenshaw, Steve Elkington, Bob Tway, Hal Sutton, Jeff Maggert and Jeff Sluman. They would win PGA Tour events and major championships, and achieve career highs.

And each time, more orders would pour in for Wood.

The business grew. He added employees, staff, executives. Soon, Japanese partners entered the mix. He was global now. Had to fly around the world, including numerous trips to Nagoya.

It was there, in 1993, that he watched the final round of the Masters. Langer would pull away from the field to win, using his Wood Brothers Texan persimmon driver—making him the last player to win a major championship using a wooden driver. Halfway around the world, Wood beamed with pride in the early morning as he watched Langer slip on his second green jacket.

He was at the height of his sport.

The peak of his profession.

What nobody knew, was that Dave Wood would soon walk away from it all.

CAMELLIA.

This is Bernhard Langer. Standing on the tee box of the 10th hole on Sunday afternoon at the 1993 Masters, with a one-shot lead over Dan Forsman and two shots over Chip Beck. Langer is

*wearing a yellow golf shirt, olive pants, white visor, staring down
the hole where the "tournament really begins."*

*He pulls out his Wood Brothers driver, the one that has lifted
him to this point, on this resplendent Easter afternoon, and swings
away. The ball flight is textbook: arrow straight, with a little fade
at the end.*

It finds the perfect spot on the left side of the fairway.

"I was driving the ball pretty good," Langer recalled. "Augusta
for me, in those days, had the big fairways. So, I never thought it
was a hard driving course, except for a couple of holes like 10."

THRU 9
Langer -9
Forsman -8
Beck -7

Soup. Why did he order soup?

It was 1982. Dave Wood had been summoned to Champions
Golf Club in Houston at the behest of Jackie Burke and Jimmy
Demaret. Golf royalty. Texas royalty. Four green jackets between
them. Wood had done some small club work for Burke, but to
get an audience with him and Jimmy? *What was this about?* They
were seated in the dining room of the clubhouse overlooking the
course, the crisp white linens, shiny silverware, napkin rings.
Probably the most formal meal Wood had ever been to. He was
so nervous that he couldn't really think, so he panicked and
ordered...soup?

Burke cut right to the chase.

"All of the good clubmakers are dead," Burke said from across
the table. "Nobody makes 'em any good anymore. You don't manufacture a golf club, you build it. With your hands."

OK...

"A golf club is an instrument, not a piece of equipment,"
Burke continued. "I've seen some of the work that you do. You
have a skill for this. I know you're also trying to make it out

there professionally, but I'm telling you right now, Dave—this is your destiny."

Wood couldn't swallow. He had come for lunch, he presumed, as a thank you or something for the work he'd done, and now he was supposed to throw away his dreams of making it to the PGA Tour in order to...*build golf clubs?*

As he listened to Burke talk about the need for serious golfers—ones with professional aspirations, legendary aspirations—to have drivers that were handmade and the absence of that skillset as golf became more modernized, it began to strike a chord with him. Wood's small club repair gig that he did on the side to supplement his professional dreams allowed him to see what equipment players were using. Many of the top players in the area, whether it was professional, amateur or collegiate, used old equipment that was made and designed before they were born. Only the top 1 percent of professional golfers—the Palmers, the Nicklauses, the Players—had equipment that was designed for them.

Wood had been toying with getting onto another career path, so...maybe this could work? He took a shot and began asking Burke what he wanted and looked for in a driver. Wood figured if Burke thought he could make a career of this, who better than a Masters champion to be his first customer?

Over the soup he never finished, Wood talked with Burke about weight, shape, shot type. Demaret then walked him through the painstakingly long oil-hardening process, and how getting a solid block of wood that was the perfect weight—between a 205- to 215-gram starting weight—was so important to the final finished product. Wood started to think that this seemed doable enough.

"I was already living in a world of specifications," Wood said. "My own, players I worked with whose clubs I worked on. Balance, weights, where you wanted the flex point on the shaft—all those things. So, I started to think this wasn't much different than the work I had already been doing."

Burke's final piece of advice was a necessary one.

In all his years working on clubs, Wood had never carved a driver head from a block of wood. He asked the great man, *How, exactly, do you go about shaping it into its final form?*

Burke smiled.

"There was this old member at Champions, who carved ducks as a hobby," Wood remembered. "One day Burke had asked him, 'These things are so life-like, how do you do it?' And the man told him, 'It's simple, you carve away anything that's not a duck.'"

Wood laughs thinking of Burke's counsel.

"He never gave me any specifications for his driver," Wood said. "So, I went and got a block of wood and carved away anything that wasn't a golf club."

Wood Brothers Golf was born.

WHITE DOGWOOD.

This is Bernhard Langer. Standing on the tee box of the 11th hole on Sunday afternoon at the Masters, still with a one-shot lead over Dan Forsman and two shots over Chip Beck. Langer is about to begin the stretch of holes that define how the tournament is won or lost: Amen Corner.

He pulls out his Wood Brothers driver, the one that has lifted him to this point, stares down the hole on this resplendent Easter afternoon, and swings away. The swing is loose, the ball flight wayward: a push to the right.

It lands softly with a perfect line into the green.

"I knew that I wouldn't win the tournament unless I played aggressively," Langer *would tell* Sports Illustrated *afterward. "Nobody was going to give it to me."*

THRU 10

Langer -9

Forsman -8

Beck -7

WHEN YOU WALKED into the front door at 101 East Main Street, you knew exactly what awaited you inside. The reception desk was smack in the middle of the room—Dave's sister, Sue, would be behind it answering phones, taking orders that sort of stuff— and around the walls were a menagerie of golf club items: Old MacGregor woods, Ben Hogan irons, showcases with golf collectibles to peruse. A couple of chairs were scattered about.

This was the Texas Golf Company—part custom club outfit, part Elks Lodge.

Pink Floyd often blared from the backroom as Dave worked on clubs by hand. He was the artisan, founding the company on his own. Later, as more work came in, his younger brother Charlie, and then Don, would float in and out of the business, occasionally helping out. But when you walked in the door, you shouted to the back for Dave, and out he would come with your club in tow. *He* was the company.

"When people ask me about it, I tell them 'Everything came together at once there,'" recalled Dr. John Kendall, one of the first Wood Brothers customers in the late 1970s. "It was kind of like a magical time."

Kendall was a low-handicap member at Sugar Creek Golf Club in Sugar Land, just southwest of Houston. A director of R&D for Riviana Foods in the city, he would routinely make the 20-mile drive up I-69 at lunchtime to Humble to spend time in the shop. Not just because he would begin enlisting Dave for custom orders, but because you just never knew who you would run into inside. Everyone from John Mahaffey and Andy Bean to T. Boone Pickens and Darrel Royal to Willie Nelson (yes, seriously) and George Strait.

(That's really where the "Wood Brothers" name would *actually* come from: Not from Dave's family members—some of whom would work for him in limited capacities over the years—but from the close-knit relationships of the individuals who frequented the place. "Wood Brothers" wasn't formally established as an official brand until 1988, operating under Texas Golf Company, until the company disbanded.)

Despite its sprawling scale, Houston is a relatively tight-knit golf community. As Wood began to put the advice of Burke and Demaret into action, word began spreading about his craftsmanship. The University of Houston golf team were the first true converts, creating a pipeline of sorts for business. Keith Fergus and Ed Fiori were the first in the late 1970s, going to Dave for repair and small custom work. By 1982, another future star—Steve Elkington—began hanging around the shop so much, Dave would put him to work one summer.

"You'd have collectors, afficionados, great amateur players, Tour players, mini-tour players, club pros that would hang out," Dave Wood said. "Everyone was very knowledgeable about golf equipment and history. But the top collegiate players really helped us get some traction, because these guys would use our early products as amateurs, come up, make it big, and then everyone would want to know what they were playing."

Within a year after his lunch at Champions with Burke and Demaret, Wood began to see the vision they saw. He began to push harder to accelerate the timeline to develop a persimmon model that a PGA Tour player could utilize week-in and week-out. The prototypes they developed were good, strong models for amateur players and top collegiate ones, but to capture the upper echelon of golf, Dave needed a driver that was perfect.

Late into the night, the lights would be on in the back room in the shop on Main Street, right next to the old Union Pacific railroad tracks. A Texas golf nut tinkering and toying, all in the hopes of finally cracking the code that would let him unlock the next step in the journey. It would be a calling card for Dave throughout his career—his nickname would become "The Count"—the late hours he spent obsessing over the details that would make his clubs great.

He circled the 1984 U.S. Open at Winged Foot as the debut site to bring it to the masses. He knew they were close. But nailing the finishing weight of 200 grams, took time.

"I had it in my mind," Wood recalls. "I had it in my mind before I even made it. Other ingredients had to come together—and that took time—finding that perfect, solid block with the exact gram weight. Jimmy Demaret gave me the recipe, but the ingredients took time. It's a natural resource, wood is. It comes in different weights, different densities. So, it was a very careful process. My world was all about balance."

By the end of 1983, it was finished: He named it "The Texan."

AZALEA.

This is Bernhard Langer. Standing on the tee box of the 13th hole on Sunday afternoon at the Masters, with a one-shot lead over Chip Beck. Dan Forsman is gone now. Put two in the drink at the 12th for a quad. Langer is now stepping up to the risk-reward par-5 that can seal the deal or open the door.

He pulls out his Wood Brothers driver, the one that has lifted him to this point, stares down straight into the dogleg on this resplendent Easter late-afternoon, and swings away. The ball flight returns to textbook: a perfect fade to match the shape of the hole.

It lands softly on the low, left side of the fairway.

"Going in Amen Corner, I missed a little putt on 12 that just went right," Beck would recall. "I thought, 'Oh man, that was a missed opportunity to get one', because he made par."

THRU 12

Langer -9

Beck -7

WHEN DAVE WOOD arrived at Winged Foot for the U.S. Open in 1984, change was happening right in front of him. For the last handful of years, golf club manufacturers had begun introducing a new product to the game: metal drivers. They promised more power, more control, more distance. A fad, many thought.

The first one showed up on the PGA Tour in 1979, and
then two years later—right in Dave's backyard—it would have
its breakthrough moment at the Michelob-Houston Open,
when Ron Streck became the first golfer to win a sanctioned
event with a metal driver. (Purists still scoff because the event
was shortened to 54 holes.) While the upper crust of players
looked down their noses at the clubs, they began to gain traction. Soon, players spoke about the distance advantages and
how that helped them get over the awful tinny sound the clubs
made at impact.

"I remember going to the driving range in Fayetteville, N.C.
and L.B. Floyd, Ray's dad, had these metal woods," said Chip
Beck, a four-time winner on the PGA Tour, who transitioned to
metal woods in the late 1980s. "And they went farther than any
club at the driving range. I knew they were hot, but they were
never really available early on."

The sight on the range at Winged Foot was jarring: Some
of the most strident persimmon stalwarts were showing up
with metal woods in their bags. Dave Wood, though, remained
undaunted. He had worked too long, too hard, to abandon the
quest now.

There was an element of perfecting a dinosaur.

But it was a dinosaur that was still in high demand.

Players of skill were still clamoring for a driver that placed
a premium on accuracy, and the ability to shape a shot. Because
of the precision nature that went into creating every driver—and
the growing list of top players from the Houston area espousing
their excellence—the business was booming, even as metal woods
crept into the market.

As Dave Wood took on more and more business, the simple
grounded nature of his company's origins began to become more
complicated.

Things had become so big that Dave expanded beyond the
shop in Humble, and would add more than 100 employees by
the start of the next decade. His weeks were spent travelling to

meet with ad executives, to meet with marketing executives, back to Texas, then off to a tour event, then back home for more club work, then back out on the road.

Life would become even more frenetic when in 1987, he was wooed and eventually entered into a partnership with Japanese textile company, Nihon Hymo. The company's chairman, Keitaro Takagi, flew to Humble to meet with Wood for days to get a sense of how his operation ran. Then he flew Dave and his wife Laura to Nagoya to seal the deal: Nihon Hymo would be the official Japanese distributor for Wood Brothers Golf. A year later, they created a joint venture, and Nihon Hymo gave Wood Brothers an infusion of capital.

By the end of the 1980s, Wood Brothers was at the top of the golf world.

The price was the Japanese corporation getting 48 percent share of the company.

"I think by that time, for me, it just started to consume my life," Dave admits now.

FIRETHORN.

This is Bernhard Langer. Standing on the tee box of the 15th hole on Sunday afternoon at the Masters. He has a three-shot lead over Chip Beck. Somehow rolled it in for eagle at No. 13. Langer is now facing the hole where Gene Sarazen made double-eagle and where eight years earlier Curtis Strange found the water to give Langer his first green jacket.

He pulls out his Wood Brothers driver, the one that has lifted him to this point, stares into the 500-yard par-5 and the setting sun on this resplendent Easter afternoon, and swings away. The swing is a little across his body, but the result works just fine.

It lands softly on right side of the fairway.

"I was trying to figure out how to make three birdies and get into a playoff," Beck remembered 30 years later. "I knew how well I was playing, and I knew what the opportunities were."

THRU 14

Langer -11
Beck -8

"I WAS A Disneyland dad."

Even 30 years later, there is a pain in Dave Wood's voice as he admits the truth out loud to himself. He had built Wood Brothers from a club-repair hobby to the most sought-after custom clubmaker in the game in just more than a decade. He made friends all over the world, the sport. Built clubs for Vice Presidents, Secretaries of State, Prime Ministers, CEOs, some of the most powerful people in the world. He had it all.

Except at home.

His children, Sally and Nick, were entering middle school when dad went from a guy with a golf club-making shop to an international sporting goods maven. Went from being home and taking them to games, practices, school events to calling from far-flung outposts around the world. Home for a day, gone for four. Back for two, gone for six.

The business was becoming a monster that needed to be fed at all times: more ads, more slogans, new products, new pros playing the products. With the Japanese involved, they pushed to expand Wood Brothers into other areas of the golf business—they wanted bags, gloves, hats. Anything to stick a "WB" on to sell to the global markets.

Dave was in deep.

He felt the ownership of what he built slipping away. He felt his family slipping away. He felt *himself* slipping away.

Then, it did.

"Almost overnight, I became a single parent," he says solemnly. "My world changed."

Dave prefers to keep the details private, but around the time of the 1993 Masters, he phoned home from the road. The housekeeper answered. He asked where his wife was. Housekeeper said she was gone. Took her belongings and left. Dave was stunned. There had been problems of late, but he chalked it up to the job.

But when he arrived home, he immediately knew what he had to do next.

He had to become Dad once again.

He also began to wonder whether staying at Wood Brothers—in its current form, with its current demands—was a tenable situation. Yes, he was living a nice, comfortable life, but what would that end up costing him? What would be the next domino to fall? His marriage? His family? His friends? Wood didn't want to wait around and find out.

When he would leave, he didn't yet know—or even figure out for more than a year—but that moment, when he walked in the door and hugged his children and let them know that Daddy wasn't going anywhere, was the planting of the seed.

"My kids needed me," Wood said. "I didn't walk away right then and there—I hung in there—but everything changed. I knew that I couldn't keep things the way they were."

He would stay on until early 1996, but mostly phased himself out of the company he created and built from scratch. His brother, Charlie took over a good amount of the club-making work—most of which was being manufactured now—but once Dave stopped being the engine, the Wood Brothers aura quickly faded. Pros stopped calling. Orders slowed. The shop on Main Street saw fewer and fewer friends stop by.

Then, at age 40, Dave Wood walked away from Wood Brothers for good.

NANDINA.

This is Bernhard Langer. Standing on the tee box of the 17th hole at the Masters. He's the owner of a five-shot lead over Chip Beck. Tournament is basically his now, after Beck bafflingly laid up on No. 15 and made par, then followed it up with a bogey on 16. The sun is beginning to set alongside any hopes of a collapse from the German.

He pulls out his Wood Brothers driver, the one that has lifted him to this point, stares down the tricky short par-4 with the

Eisenhower Tree on the left. As a resplendent Easter afternoon gives way to the eve, he swings away. The swing is once again as he has practiced it countless times before: consistent, effortless.

It lands and rolls out on right side of the fairway.

"He wasn't doing anything extraordinary," Beck said. "It wasn't like he was out-driving me or hit it any different than I'd ever seen him. I'd beaten him in tournaments before. But not that day."

THRU 16

Langer -12

Beck -7

FRED CLARK CAN still remember the exact date: Nov. 10, 2009.

His wife was a few months pregnant, and he once again found himself on eBay late at night perusing through classic golf clubs for sale, when he stumbled on a listing, that he was sure was a con. It was a pristine Wood Brothers Texan. Mint condition. Clark couldn't believe his luck. He had foolishly given away his first and only Wood Brothers driver a few years back and had been searching for another for a while. But a Texan? In *this* good of a condition?

He clicked on the page and found a description that almost read as the club's biography.

"I'm reading this whole thing, and it's so detailed, I couldn't believe it," Clark recalls with a laugh. "And I get to the bottom of it, and it says, 'From the collection of Dave Wood.'"

Nah. Couldn't be.

Could it?

It was. Nearly 15 years after leaving Wood Brothers, Dave Wood was preparing for his life's next chapter. He had just wrapped up a nearly eight-year run working for MacGregor Golf and decided it was time to pursue his true passion: art. He had opened a studio in downtown Houston, split time between Texas and Oregon, but had decided it was time to part with the dozens and dozens of Wood Brothers clubs in his possession.

Clark—a software sales executive who lives in Salem, Mass.—is one of hundreds of devoted Wood Brothers fanatics who have kept the company's name alive even after the company shuttered. Because the clubs were designed custom for low-handicap players, they remain rare and hard-to-find on the collector's market. Often they come from the hands of a Tour pro or accomplished amateur, and when they do pop up for sale on eBay, easily fetch north of $500.

"They were very hard to get back then," said David Bass, a persimmon club restoration expert. "You just didn't have an average golfer walking around with one. And you hardly ever see one that's been restored. That's because they've held up over the years. I very rarely see one because the things just don't beat up."

There are Facebook groups devoted to Wood Brothers, Instagram pages and dozens of threads on GolfWRX.com with collectors and enthusiasts sharing knowledge, history and more about their persimmons. It's given Dave Wood a second burst of celebrity within the golf world. Wood Brothers has regained traction even as modern drivers promise speed and distance combinations once unimaginable.

But the persimmon drivers—particularly from Wood Brothers—carry equal parts nostalgia and practicality. You can pick one up out of an attic or garage or from another collector and put it into play immediately. The oil-hardening process passed down to Dave from Jimmy Demaret is a big reason why, but also there was minimal invasion of the club's heads during the building process. Screws were smaller, thinner. There were no artificial materials.

So, imagine Clark's surprise when, a few weeks after buying the driver from Wood, another email popped into his inbox:

Fred – you seem very anxious to build your collection. Would you like buy the Bernhard Langer driver from me? It was his tour demo.

No.

Yes.

It was Christine.

Wood had retrieved her from Langer around 1989, at the PGA Merchandise Show in Orlando, after making him another set of drivers. She sat in Wood's storage for more than 20 years until he began cleaning out. Clark didn't hesitate and has even taken her for a test spin once or twice. He was immediately the envy of every Wood Brothers collector, even receiving offers from around the globe to buy it.

"I would never get rid of it," Clark beams.

It's a prized possession. Which is why, two years after he bought it from Wood, Clark made an unusual request: He wondered if the man who made it would refinish the club and bring it back to its original luster. Wood happily obliged.

Clark shipped the driver out to him and when they initially talked about stain color and restoring it, Dave mentioned an idea for a "special stain." Clark was intrigued but left it up to Wood to come up with the idea. A few days later, Clark received a surprising message: It was a picture of a scalpel and blood all over the clubhead.

"I'll never forget it as long as I live," Clark recalled. "I get an email back from Dave, that says that as he was refinishing the club, it was so special to him that he decided to add something to the stain so that he would be bonded with it."

Clark pauses, and then laughs because it still sounds wild to say out loud.

"His blood."

HOLLY.

This is Bernhard Langer. Standing in the back of the tee box of the 18th hole at the Masters. He has a five-shot lead over Chip Beck. They're getting Langer's green jacket—the one from 1985—out of the Champions Locker Room, and bringing it down to Butler Cabin for the TV cameras. A couple of shots left until the end. It's been a perfect Easter Sunday for Langer, his favorite holy day.

He pulls out his Wood Brothers driver, the one that has lifted him to this point, for the final time on this day, as he tries to navigate his way home. With the setting sun at his back, and 465 yards in front of him, he takes what will be the final-ever swing with a persimmon wood by a winner at a major championship.

He lashes at the ball, squinting as he watches it come down out of the baby blue sky.

It takes three bounces and lands--

THRU 18

Langer -11

Beck -7

DOES IT MATTER where that ball landed? Does it matter that if it took three bounces and landed in the front bunker near the elbow of the fairway on the 72nd hole? Does it matter if Langer would make a bogey there? Does it matter that once his ball landed, he turned to his right, handed his well-worn Wood Brothers Texan to his caddie, who put it back in the bag, only to never take it out again?

Does that matter?

Should it matter?

Dave Wood doesn't think it does. He prefers to think of Langer and his ultimate creation—hand-in-hand, methodically bruising their way across the manicured grounds of Augusta National in the pounding sun on a beautiful Easter Sunday—showing the golfing world just how years of dedication, practice and endurance can triumph over modern technology. That's the vision he has of Wood Brothers these days. He'll think about it from time to time, when he goes out early on Tuesday or Thursday mornings with a couple of irons and wedges—Wood Brothers brand, of course—to hit balls in the warm air at Country Club de Chapala, a short drive from his home in Ajijic, in Central Mexico, just south of Guadalajara.

He moved there full-time during the pandemic. Loves it. Nestled up against Lake Chapala, he lives a life that seems like a fantasy. Walks along the cobblestone streets, or along the water. It's the perfect place to have fully embraced his true artistic side. Now, he spends his days painting, drawing inspiration from the beauty around him.

Every now and then, he'll think back to the long nights grinding away with a newly cured persimmon head or putting the finishing touches on The Australian or traveling the world preaching the gospel of the game. He'll think about the players he met, how he helped change and shape their careers—their legacies—and how they changed his life from a wannabe tour pro to the craftsman on call for the world's best players.

"Apples don't fall too far from their trees," he said with a laugh. "As much as I love being a part of the art world and that community, I still love to go out and hit balls. Love to be out in the sunlight and the grass. Life here is so easy, so low stress. It's the world of mañana."

Tomorrow.

Once he knew the end was approaching with Wood Brothers, he invariably found himself thinking about the tomorrows to come.

That's why shortly after Langer slipped on that green jacket for the second time, Wood began one final journey. After he returned home from Japan, he flipped on the lights in the back of the shop on Main Street in Humble—where the city slogan is "Where people make a difference"—and placed a perfectly weighted solid block of old-growth persimmon into the aquarium bath. He would check back on it every couple of weeks, in between he would begin sketching out the other aspect of his masterpiece.

Langer was a devout Christian, his success deeply rooted in his faith.

Wood always admired that about Langer, and immediately following the win at the Masters 30 years ago, Wood set on what would be *his* masterpiece: He meticulously copied Leonardo di Vinci's *The Last Supper* by hand, stenciling it first while the block of wood readied itself. Once the clubhead was prepared and ready to be turned into a golf club, he began engraving the depiction of Jesus and the Twelve Apostles across the skirting of the driver head.

"I wanted to thank him in a very personal way," Wood said. "To me, as an artist, it was a great ambitious project."

The driver would be built with a 54-degree lie, slightly flat. Little bit open at address. Nominal face progression, with a 9-degree loft. It was designed to hit that piercing, launched trajectory that Langer was known for.

Wood began with Bartholomew, then on to James Minor, Andrew, Judas, Peter and John. Then came Jesus Christ—that was the one Dave felt the most pressure on, "It was pins and needles"—before finally moving to the other side of the table: Thomas, James Major, Philip, Matthew and Thaddeus. Finally, came Simon. There is a wicked irony in that. The most obscure Apostle, the one who was only identified as a zealot. Who traveled far and wide, making sure that the truth was known.

The Apostle who was a missionary, spreading the gospel.

A man who seemed so much like Wood himself.

Once he was done with the club, Wood admired it in all its beauty. A light, sandy color with a green fiber inserted in it, as a tribute to Langer's victory at Augusta. The club took him more than a year to construct, and by the time Wood was finished, Langer had already switched to metal woods for the 1994 season. Wood knew the end was coming. He packaged up the work of art, put it in a neat white Wood Brothers box with the black and red lettering, and sent it to Langer's home. He never knew if it would reach its destination.

Never knew if the man who it was intended as a tribute for would even see it.

It would be the last persimmon driver Wood ever made.

"It's a beautiful piece of art," an excited Langer recalled recently. "It truly means a lot to me."

Not until a few years ago did Wood even know that Langer had it in his possession. He didn't find out until a friend sent him a video tour Langer did of his home during which he pulled it out and showed it to the camera crew. Almost immediately the thoughts of the lunch with Jackie Burke and Jimmy Demaret came flooding back to Wood; the early days in the shop curing the persimmon heads in the broiling Texas heat; the first success on the PGA Tour; Bob Tway and Jeff Sluman both winning PGA Championships with a Wood Brothers driver; the camaraderie among the shop stalwarts; the highs, the lows.

The clubs.

At the end of it though, it was always about the clubs.

Down to the very last one.

"I didn't know that was going to be my last golf club I built a driver from scratch," Wood said. "It was all very poetic when you think about it. That club was my—*our*—Last Supper."

BRENDAN PRUNTY has been a nationally recognized sportswriter for more than 15 years, writing for *The New York Times*, *Esquire*, *Rolling Stone*, and *Sports Illustrated*. He began his career at the *The Star-Ledger* in New Jersey, covering college sports and golf. His work has been honored by the Associated Press Sports Editors, U.S. Basketball Writers Association, and twice was named honorable mention by the Best American Sports Writing series. A graduate of Saint Joseph's University in Philadelphia, he lives in his hometown of Cranford, New Jersey, with his wife, Amanda, and daughters, Quinn and Parker.

The Prodigy and the Protégé: The Pain of 'Baby Jordan' and the Power of Kami Miner

AISHWARYA KUMAR

FROM ESPN • NOVEMBER 29, 2023

*K*ami *Miner stands in a makeshift gym in the garage of her family's Las Vegas home. Storage boxes line the back wall, and exercise gear—a leg press machine, a treadmill, a cycle, ropes and dumbbells—takes up the rest of the space. Her father points a camera at her.*

"I'm about to do 30-inch box jumps," says Kami, a USA sticker on her right cheek.

"You're 10. And you're about to do 30-inch box jumps? Are you serious?" her father asks, his voice deep.

Wearing a white tank top and her curly hair in a messy bun atop her head, Kami turns and looks at her father.

"Neck's in a neutral position," her father says. "Explode."

Kami squats and pumps her arms. She jumps, tucks her knees to her chest. She lands like a ninja, her toes making contact with the box first. "Whoa!" her father says. He peppers her with instructions, tells her to hop, step and jump, like in volleyball. She hops, steps and jumps. She repeats the move three more times.

"Unbelievable talent," her father says. "She is going to be a volleyball star, folks. Mark my words."

Kami smiles at the camera.
"I get it all from my daddy."

HAROLD MINER NEARLY fills the frame of the front door at his
condo in Redondo Beach, California. Wearing a black hoodie,
joggers and a black hat, backward, he stands, all 6-foot-5 of him,
next to his wife, Pam. At 52, Miner has filled out since his NBA
playing days, but his shy grin remains the same.

Miner doesn't care for attention. In fact, for nearly 15 years
after Miner's basketball career ended, reporters tried and failed
to get him to even answer his phone.

But now, he's inviting me to spend time with him and his
family in his home.

The two-bedroom condo is modest, painted in an off-white
color. A few abstract art pieces hang on the walls. The brown
sectional sofa in the living room is covered with memorabilia.
Harold points to a red jersey. His eyes light up, and his grin gets
wider. "She wore this when she played for Team USA for the first
time," he says. He points to a printed speech on the dining table.
"This was in sixth grade. She talked about her dreams to play
volleyball in the Olympics. She loved public speaking." A laptop
on a table contains folders titled "Pics for ESPN volleyball," "Pics
for ESPN childhood," and "Kami's Home Videos Training."

He asks Pam, who is sitting in front of the computer, to
click on one of the videos. Pam smiles. "They just loved training
together," she says.

The room contains no evidence of Harold's accomplishments.
He rolls his eyes when he's asked why.

"It's Kami's time now," he says. "It's Kami's story."

What Harold Miner doesn't say is this: Kami's story might
never have happened if not for his own story. Sports robbed him
of his dream, spat him out, and left him with little more than
regret and painful lessons he learned too late. Love profusely,
he told his daughter, but not exclusively. Train with fervor, he
instructed, but preserve your body. Distinguish yourself, he

demanded, but fight off comparison. Today, Kami Miner is one of the best volleyball players in the country. She credits a man who could have been one of the best basketball players in the world.

"That was 30 years ago," Harold Miner says. "Who cares?"

The Prodigy

They called him "Baby Jordan." Not at first, when Harold Miner was 6 and followed his father and brother to Normandie Park in Los Angeles to watch them and other older men jump and twirl on the basketball court, elbow each other and belly laugh.

And not when he devoured books about basketball, taking meticulous notes in the margins. *Heaven Is a Playground* by Rick Telander is one of his favorites. He loved watching "Pistol Pete" Maravich, Julius Erving and Magic Johnson on TV, and after processing what he saw, he would go back to the park and imitate their moves. For hours, for years.

The nickname might have originated in the summer of 1986, when Harold was going into his sophomore year of high school. Rod Higgins, who would play 13 seasons in the NBA, held a camp in Fresno, California, and Harold was invited. He won MVP of the entire thing. As he stood next to his campmates, cheesing, Michael Jordan, whom he had watched score 63 points against the Celtics in an NBA playoff game earlier that year, walked up to Harold and asked to play one-on-one. A five-point game, one point per basket. Harold took a 4–0 lead. No joke. *I'm gonna win this*, he thought.

"The next shot, I went to shoot the ball, he looked at me and went up, just flew in the air and just grabbed the ball out of the air, blocked my shot, and went and scored," Harold says.

Jordan won 5–4.

Afterward, Jordan told him to keep grinding. Harold nodded, and his confidence soared.

By the time he was a junior at Inglewood High, everybody was calling him Baby Jordan. It wasn't just that one-on-one game. Harold shaved his head. He soared above the rim. He dunked with style. At first, Harold loved the tag.

"When somebody compares you to the best player of all time, you're going to take notice of it and it makes you feel like you're on the right path," he says.

He averaged 27 points in his junior season and 28 in his senior season.

Coach George Raveling recruited him to USC and told him he would build the struggling team around him. During his freshman season, wearing his No. 23 jersey, Harold could hear fans' conversations during timeouts. "It was that empty," he says. But Baby Jordan and his high-flying game became a draw, and he led the Trojans to the NCAA tournament as a sophomore.

By his junior year, in 1992, Harold walked into an arena that was regularly packed with fans holding Baby Jordan posters and screaming the nickname.

"I'd like to think that I played a pretty big role in that just because of my style of play and the way I played," Harold says. "People were excited to come watch me play."

He averaged 26.3 points per game and led the Trojans to a 24–6 record, but they fell in the second round of the tournament. Still, Harold was named *Sports Illustrated* Player of the Year ahead of future NBA stars such as Shaquille O'Neal, Christian Laettner and Alonzo Mourning. He skipped his senior season and left as the program's career scoring leader.

When he was picked 12th in the 1992 NBA draft and walked up to collect his Miami Heat cap after hugging his crying mother, Baby Jordan was everywhere. People on the streets, strangers in restaurants and, almost every day, on TV.

"Now you start feeling the pressure of it because you realize that you're a talented player," Harold says. "But you're not Michael Jordan."

BABY JORDAN'S LEARNING curve in the NBA was steep, but by the time 1993 rolled around, he was getting more minutes and more points, including a stretch in January when he had three straight games of 20 or more points.

As a rookie, he was invited to compete in the 1993 slam dunk contest, and he clinched the title before his final dunk. He dribbled in from the left baseline, jumped with the ball clasped in his left hand, twirled 360 degrees and slammed it down. As he raised his hands in the air, the arena in Salt Lake City erupted in applause. He grinned as the commentator announced, "Our new Slam Dunk king."

"Has 'Baby Jordan' grown up now?" the interviewer, Craig Sager, asked. Harold smiled. He couldn't remember the last time he went through an interview without the nickname making its way into the conversation. "I think so. I came out here and represented myself well," he said. "Hopefully this is the first of bigger and better things."

Self-doubt already was creeping in. Midway through his rookie season, he began experiencing pain in his right knee. First it was a twinge. He felt it after a heavy practice session. It became persistent.

Some days, he would wake up pain-free and put up big numbers for the Heat. Other days, he couldn't bend his knee at all.

"I started to lose that burst, that quickness and explosiveness that I had," Harold says.

He finished the season—he even scored in double digits 10 times during the final month—and returned home to Los Angeles. Doctors diagnosed him with a torn meniscus and told him he needed surgery. All the years playing on asphalt growing up resulted in overuse. After his surgery, he spent months at home rehabbing before returning to Miami.

"My knee was never the same," he says.

THERE WERE GAMES that provided glimpses of what could have been, like when he scored a team-high 28 points in a 111–80 home win over the Celtics on Dec. 11, 1993. But consistency never came. His knee wouldn't allow it.

He appeared in just 45 games in the 1994–95 season. He also won his second slam dunk contest, something only Dominique

Wilkins and Michael Jordan had done before him. He sat out the final six games of Miami's season. Months later, the Heat traded him to the Cavaliers.

In Cleveland, he spent every day in pain. Doctors said he needed another surgery, this one more complicated. He had developed cysts in his right knee in addition to another torn meniscus. He played in just 19 games and went scoreless in seven of them.

Pam, whom he had been dating for a year, flew to Cleveland to support him through the surgery. She cooked him a catfish dish and brought it to the hospital. She slept in a chair next to his bed.

Cleveland released him at the end of the season. He flew to Toronto to try out with the Raptors. Basketball was all he wanted. He clung to hope.

During a training session, he slipped on a wet spot and landed on his right knee. Pain radiated through his leg. Doctors taped him up, ran some tests. The pit in his stomach never left. God, he felt, was telling him it was over. He was 25 years old. He had played in exactly 200 games. Fatefully, his last one was on Feb. 20, 1996, when he went scoreless in five minutes in a Cleveland loss to Michael Jordan's Bulls. Later, Raveling said the Baby Jordan nickname was the "worst thing to happen to Harold."

"I grew up studying the game, watching the game, being in love with the game and being a fan of the game," Harold says. "And it felt like basketball was turning on me."

Pacing his hotel room in Toronto late that night, Harold dialed Pam's number.

"This is it," he told her. "It's over."

HAROLD MINER STOPPED reading about basketball. He stopped watching it. He stopped responding to reporters requesting interviews. He gathered his awards and jerseys in boxes and put them in storage.

"I just didn't want to deal with that, because I would just have to keep reliving it over and over and over and over again,"

Harold says. "And why put yourself through that? Why torture yourself with that?"

There was one torture he chose to endure: the All-Star Game. The year after his retirement, in 1997, his stomach churned as he pressed the button on his remote from his home in Los Angeles. There was Jordan, strutting on Harold's former home court in Cleveland. Tears streamed out of Harold's eyes. He wiped them away and continued to watch. Jordan had a triple-double.

"I would cry because I always wanted to be an All-Star," Harold says. "And I never made the All-Star team."

His mom tried to provide solace. She moved into his home. Just the two of them. Some days Harold sat quietly in her presence. Other days, he let his hurt and regrets tumble out. *I gave basketball my everything. This is so unfair. Why me?* She patiently listened, and told him he was enough, that basketball was just one part of his journey. He nodded, but the words felt empty. He felt empty.

He stopped exercising. He gained weight. He stopped answering when former teammates called. He felt ashamed. He hadn't lived up to his potential. He hadn't lived up to his nickname. The calls stopped coming. In silence, Harold prayed for healing.

He felt better when Pam was around. She had never cared if he could dunk a ball or shoot a 3. His fame neither fazed her nor enticed her. He felt certain that when she looked at him, she didn't see a failed prodigy. It was a certainty he felt with nearly nobody else.

Living in Los Angeles made him restless. It reminded him too much of his past. He and Pam got married in 1999, and they bought a house in Las Vegas, near a condo Harold had bought years earlier. He and Pam settled into the house. His mom moved into the condo. He worked hard at being a good husband and son and tried to shun his basketball memories. But Pam would watch him spend hours at home doing nothing. *He needs to get out and do new things.* Sometimes, she noticed a faraway look on his face, and she knew he was grieving his life as a basketball player.

Basketball gave him community. Basketball gave him purpose. Basketball was gone.

"That was his whole life," Pam says. "From childhood, that's all he did."

In 2003, Pam gave birth to their first child, a daughter named Kami. Months later, Harold got a call from his mother's doctor, who told him that his mom had advanced liver cancer, that she had just weeks to live. Harold spent 18 days in his mother's presence. Then she was gone. He was 33 years old.

"I'm still processing my career, and then my mother passes and I've got to process that too," Harold says. "It was so painful."

KAMI MINER LINES up her feet in front of an agility ladder on the floor of her family's garage in Las Vegas. She's wearing a white tank top and black shorts.

"What kind of quick-foot drill would you like me to do?" she asks.

"You know the drill. You know what we do," Harold responds, pointing a camera at her. She begins, stepping in and out of the square boxes in quick bursts. She reaches the end of the ladder and stops, looking up at her dad.

"This is for quick, explosive movements with your feet," Harold says.

"Exactly," she responds. "I'm training for volleyball."

The Protégé

Before anything else, Kami Miner loved playing the piano. It soothed her. It challenged her. And Kami loved a challenge.

One of her earliest memories: participating in a piano recital and beaming at the end as the audience cheered loudly.

Maybe, in another world, Kami would have chosen to become a pianist. But Kami Miner had Harold Miner as her father. He knew squat about the music industry, but he knew exactly what Kami needed to do—and not do—to become a star athlete.

"Having that kind of visual aid to be an inspiration, it's invaluable knowledge from someone who's been to the top of sports," Kami says.

When she was 8, some of her soccer friends persuaded her to try volleyball. She loved that she could see every point play out much like a grandmaster would a chess game. She loved hugging her teammates after every point. Tennis was too lonely, soccer too slow. Volleyball was the perfect concoction of speed and team spirit.

"I felt like I was doing the right thing and I was in the right place," she says. "I knew I wanted to be able to play it for as long as possible."

USC retired Harold's jersey in 2012 and asked him to give a speech at halftime of the UCLA game. His hands felt sweaty as Kami and her little brother, Brayden, walked next to him on court, her fluffy pink dress bobbing along with each stride.

She stood by her father as he thanked Raveling and the USC community for believing in his abilities. Kami's eyes darted between her dad and the adoring fans. It was the first time Kami consciously thought of her father as something other than her father—a basketball prodigy, a revered athlete.

"It's really cool because my brother and I, sometimes we [used to be] like, 'What does this guy know? He played 20-something years ago. He's an old dude now,'" Kami says. "It was very powerful in getting to hear him firsthand talk about his experiences while he was playing."

When Kami was 10, Pam told her she needed to choose between piano and volleyball. Simple. Piano was something she imagined doing in her free time. But she couldn't imagine a world without volleyball.

"I'm going to be a volleyball player," she said.

She had power in her right arm. She could soar like her father. Thanks to those 30-inch box jumps, she could spike hard over the net.

But Kami's club coach, April Chapple, noticed something else about 11-year-old Kami that nobody else had.

She had massive hands.

Chapple approached Harold with an idea: Kami should become a setter. *Mark my words, she is going to be an elite setter,* Chapple said to Harold.

Harold, who had spent the past three years poring over books like *Inside College Volleyball, Misty: My Journey Through Volleyball and Life, The Sand Man: An Autobiography*, and watching college and international volleyball games to prepare his daughter, loved the idea.

Volleyball had several highly successful Black players—Hall of Famers Flo Hyman, Tara Cross-Battle and Danielle Scott-Arruda—but with few exceptions, they were attackers.

"I liked that idea of her doing something that people don't expect African Americans to do in terms of position," Harold says. "It became exciting to be one of the forerunners at that position."

Kami loved a new challenge. She was all-in.

HAROLD HIT THE store and came home with a hooplike contraption for setting practice. Almost every evening, Harold and Pam drove Kami and Brayden to a public gym in Las Vegas and lugged the equipment from their car so Kami could get in two extra hours of practice. Harold paid for the gym, set up the equipment and threw balls at Kami. Sometimes Pam took over to give him a break. Kami, who already was playing above her age group, elevated and pushed the ball into the net.

"If you're going to play it, if you've chosen to play it, you want to be the best that you can be, and so I took it upon myself to help her get there," Harold says. "And I knew what it was going to take, it was going to take a lot of hard work."

A part of Harold began to come alive. Even relatives noticed.

"[Harold] lights up when he's training Kami," says Denise Malveaux, Pam's first cousin. "It's like watching him fall in love with a [new] sport all over again."

Kami welcomed the grind. She also remembers laughing a lot. Harold was the "biggest jokester," Kami says. He would say something ridiculous and burst into giggles. A song would play on the speakerphone, and Kami would start swaying her hips—and Harold would follow suit. Soon, they'd all be dancing and laughing.

There were times when Kami pushed back. "I want to hang out with my friends," she snapped at Harold. "I'm tired," she complained. "There's no free time, and I'm doing it almost every single day," she fumed. But, at the end of every practice, she made the "active decision" to go back. She wanted to get better, and she wanted her father to help her.

To Harold, that meant emphasizing recovery as well as training. After intense workouts, Harold drew an ice bath in their tub, and Kami would get in. "His body didn't cooperate," Pam says. "So he is always making sure her body is right."

Pam focused on nutrition, making sure Kami got enough complex carbs and protein.

Harold showed up to every one of Kami's club matches and stood on the sideline, sweating. Sometimes Chapple sent him to the second floor. She didn't want Kami reacting to Harold's energy or looking at him for validation. He paced, peering down to get glimpses of the action.

To coaches, Kami seemed wise beyond her age. Players four years older than her called her a "role model," Chapple said.

As Kami's college recruitment process began, Harold began opening up to her and Brayden. During dinnertime, he coyly talked about his USC recruitment process, his experience playing in front of sold-out crowds, and what it felt like to hear his name called at the NBA draft. Some days, he kept it light. Other days, he waded into stories he hadn't allowed himself to think about in years.

He told them about his knee injuries and how he had failed to take care of his body. He told Kami how important it was that she put her body first.

Harold sometimes found Kami icing her knees or adding an extra scoop of protein to her meal and knew his stories had resonated.

"I poured all that stuff into [Kami] for years and years, and it helped bring me out of dealing with the disappointments I dealt with from my basketball career," Harold says. "It was therapeutic for me to be able to use all that stuff and just pour that stuff into my daughter."

IN 2017, THE Miners moved 290 miles from Las Vegas to Redondo Beach in California so Kami could play for Redondo Union High. Coach Tommy Chaffins remembered watching her tape with his mouth open. At 13, she was making plays only very few seniors in high school could.

It had been nearly 20 years since Harold left California to flee his basketball memories. Now he returned—some 20 miles from where he grew up—hoping to make volleyball memories with his daughter.

Kami quickly settled in. She made eye contact when Chaffins coached, nodded her head, and immediately executed a set he expected of her. Sometimes after practice, Harold would ask Chaffins' permission and hit balls really hard at Kami. "Kami is not afraid of a hard hit," Chaffins says.

When Kami was a sophomore, she and Harold began having regular mental health check-ins. "Are you feeling unnecessary pressure from me? If so, what can I do to change that?" Harold asked. Some days, Kami told him to back off, that she didn't have time for an extra practice. Other days, she said, "Dad, just chill out and be a parent in the stands."

Says Pam: "Kami can say, 'You need to back off,' and Harold accepts it."

Sometimes Harold didn't even need Kami to voice her feelings. He could see it in her face. "I could read her and how she's feeling, and I would let her know that, 'OK, so we gotta shut it down today,'" Harold says.

USC was among the first major colleges to show interest in Kami, but the idea of playing at a school where her father's shadow would follow her to every nook did not appeal to her. If anything, Harold felt more strongly than Kami. Their visit cemented that. People walked up to the Miners and shook Harold's hand, telling him how much they loved his game.

In spring 2018, Stanford reached out. Kami had not given Stanford any serious thought. It was an academically rigorous school, and she didn't know if she would fit in. But she fell in love with the volleyball team and the campus. The feeling was mutual.

"I was blown away at the whole family, to be honest," Stanford coach Kevin Hambly says. "Her dad's perspective and how she's developed...I'm like, man, this is certainly a good fit."

When the Miners rode to the airport after their visit, Kami burst into tears. "This is where I want to go to school," she told Harold and Pam.

For the next two years, to meet Stanford's academic requirements, Kami took on eight AP courses at Redondo Union, in addition to playing on her high school and club teams. Sometimes Brayden, with whom she shared a room, woke up late at night and found the desk lamp on, Kami's head bent over a notebook. Brayden could hear her scribbling away in the otherwise quiet night. Still, getting seven hours of sleep was nonnegotiable. *Your body needs to recover*, Harold told her.

Whenever she found gaps in her schedule, Kami cooked. Pam's mom instilled a love of cooking in Kami when she was a kid. Every time Kami would go to Louisiana to visit Pam's mother—and Whitey, the horse she inherited from her grandfather—she came back with a notebook full of recipes and dragged her parents to the grocery store to buy ingredients. Her specialties: monkey bread and pot pie.

When Kami was in high school, Pam had to travel to Louisiana for a stretch to take care of her ailing mother. After practices, Kami cooked for her dad and brother. She looked forward to the hours she spent in the kitchen. It was her time to unwind, and to put together a delicious meal.

"It's for sure wanting to have an identity outside of volleyball and have things that I do that I'm passionate about, that have nothing to do with athletics at all," Kami says.

Usually, thanks to Harold's warnings, she packed her meals with protein and whole grains. *It didn't matter if you got into the best school if your body wasn't ready for it.*

In August 2020, she committed to Stanford. She led Redondo Union to a 108–14 record in the three seasons—the COVID-19 pandemic wiped out her senior season. Her favorite memory? Winning the California Interscholastic Federation Division 1 championship against Mater Dei in her junior year.

After the last point, Kami joined her team in a dogpile. "It's something I'll watch back," Kami says. "My parents still have it recorded on the television."

Looking back, Kami had a realization: Harold had an urgency to teach her everything he knew—the good, but particularly the bad—when she first began playing volleyball. By the time she finished high school, her father had changed.

"He backed off and was along for the ride with me," Kami says. "That shows the growth, the healing he did go through in being a part of my journey."

KAMI MINER STANDS inches from a red brick wall in her brother's bedroom. She's wearing a gray T-shirt and camo pants, her hair in a ponytail. Her arms are lifted above her head, and she's slapping a volleyball against the wall. Quick rhythmic wall sets.

"Keep it up," Harold says. She lets her left hand go for a second, continuing to set with her right. After a second of break, she resumes setting with both hands.

"Two hundred," Harold calls. Kami keeps setting. She groans.

"Keep it up," Harold says again, this time his voice louder. "It's dropping." Kami picks up the pace. She's breathing harder.
"Three hundred," he calls.

The Pioneer

Kami's eyes fill with tears as the national anthem plays over the speaker at Villanova's Jake Nevin Field House. Standing next to her Stanford teammates, wearing her Cardinal jersey for her first match, a wave of emotions overtakes her.

Harold is not in the stands, but memories of her father play in her mind like scenes from a movie. The hours they spent in the gym, the ice baths he drew for her, the dinnertime conversations when he opened up about his past.

"It was the culmination of so much time…my dad has put in," Kami says.

Before leaving for Stanford, Kami approached Harold in their Redondo Beach living room and asked him if they could talk. Ever since she told him she wanted to play volleyball, he had been her guide. A big change was coming. She needed him to know she was going to be OK. She needed to know whether he was going to be OK.

"I have this great community around me, these great coaches, staff," she said. "I want you to enjoy just watching me play and watching all that work that we both put in over all these years pay off."

Kami remembers Harold nodding, but then struggling with the change. As months passed, Kami saw him beginning to embrace his new role as her cheerleader. Even as she and the Cardinal were struggling.

Despite having players like sophomore star Kendall Kipp, Stanford lost to Minnesota in the second round of the 2021 NCAA tournament and ended the season with a 19–11 record. Kami was named Pac-12 Freshman of the Year.

The turning point came in Kami's sophomore season.

Five thousand fans—most of them wearing Gophers' maroon and yellow—sit in the bleachers as Kami walks onto Maturi Pavilion in Minnesota in her red Stanford jersey. Stanford has lost back-to-back games, and the season seems to be teetering.

Kami's hair is pulled in a tight bun and her eyes are locked in, but her face reveals nothing. She doesn't say a word to anyone. Hambly feels her energy, and so do her teammates. This is the day Kami Miner becomes Kami Miner.

"She absolutely took charge of the game, blocking, defense, was flying all over the place," Hambly says. "That was the first time I really saw her [say] 'This is how I compete, I'm going to take over, it's mine, I'm taking this match, I'm going to show you that I'm the best.'"

Kami had 43 assists and 10 digs, and Stanford beat No. 3 Minnesota 3–1. That match put her on a path to become a first-team All-American and Pac-12 Setter of the Year. "We have a real setter now," Hambly remembers thinking.

Kami felt as if her father had prepared her all her life for that very moment. His advice echoed in her ears.

When in the biggest, most critical moments of any match, attack the situation all-out. Never hide from the moment! Embrace that moment!

GRINNING FROM EAR to ear, Kami jogs out of the locker room at Maples Pavilion in her white-and-red Stanford jersey and black shorts. Her hair, up in a bun, glistens with sweat. It's September 2023, and Stanford has swept Arizona State. Kami finished with 44 assists and seven digs.

One end of the arena has been cordoned off, and young girls holding posters of Miner and other Stanford players wait. A group of young Asian American girls huddles nearby. "Is that the setter? Is that Kami?" they whisper as a smiling Kami approaches. "Oh my god, she's here!" another one responds. Kami stops to take pictures.

A young Black girl in a blue hoodie smiles sheepishly at Kami.

"I loved your sets today," she says, handing Kami a Stanford volleyball poster. "I'm a setter too."

"Thank you," Kami says, smiling widely. "And you are? That's amazing!" She grabs her Sharpie and signs the poster.

"Keep practicing your setting. Love - Kami Miner," she writes.

Over the past year, Kami has heard the word "pioneer" attached to her name. She has sat with it, considered it and journaled her thoughts. Of course, she has discussed it with her parents.

"Being called a pioneer, and have little girls that were my age trying to look up, find someone that can visually represent them and that they resonate with, I think that's just so incredible and really, really powerful," Kami says. "It's important to talk about the fact that being a Black setter is not the norm and it has not been the norm."

The weight of the epithet is not lost on Kami.

"It's a lot different being a role model of a group versus my dad being linked to another person and trying to replicate it with their game in everyone else's eyes," she says.

Harold no longer feels the need to be present for every practice session or match. But he still checks in—constantly—sending Kami text messages in all caps. "BE AUTHENTIC." "GET YOUR BODY RIGHT." "ARE YOU STILL ENJOYING VOLLEYBALL?"

The messages make Kami laugh. "Like, Dad, why are you yelling at me?"

Deep down she knows. Sports left Harold with little more than regret and painful lessons. He wants to make sure Kami is ready. It's her turn now.

"He spent so much time and effort into my career," Kami says as a tear falls down her cheek. "And I didn't even realize that it was therapeutic for him."

Pam thinks it was his therapy, sure, but it was more than that.

"Being taken out of the game was the biggest blessing that could have happened to him," she says. "Kami and Brayden wouldn't be here."

Harold—who is, to this day, USC's leading career scorer—says his daughter has become better at volleyball than he ever was at basketball.

"I wouldn't change a thing," Harold says.

Says Kami: "It honestly shows the power of sports and the power [it] has to heal us and how massive of a role that that can play."

One morning before the season even started, Hambly woke up to a text from Harold. "How is she developing?"

"I'm like, Harold, come on, man," Hambly says. "She's literally the best setter in the country right now. I don't think there's any argument about that."

Kami has led Stanford (26–3) to the No. 2 overall seed in the NCAA tournament. The Cardinal open against Fresno State (19–13) on Friday at home hoping to win the program's 10th national title. Harold will be there.

Kami and the Cardinal got a wakeup call early in the season, losing to Florida and Nebraska at home. They went 20–1 the rest of the way, including a gritty five-set win over Louisville five days after the loss to Nebraska, the top seed in the tournament.

Does Kami think she can lead the team all the way to the trophy?

"We're absolutely prepared and ready for it," Kami says. "This group deserves it."

The Promise

Harold Miner is nowhere in sight.

Pam Miner, sitting next to an empty seat, cranes her neck. She can't, for the love of God, figure out where the man went.

She opens her purse and fumbles for her phone.

"Get your ass here right now," she texts him.

It's the regional final of the 2022 NCAA tournament, and Stanford has just lost to San Diego in a brutal five-setter at home. Kami finished with 52 assists and nine digs. It wasn't enough.

Minutes earlier, Pam watched an emotional Kami disappear into the Cardinal locker room. She knew Kami would run over any minute now and ask: "Where's Daddy?" Just as she did after every loss growing up.

Pam needs Harold to be present when Kami comes looking for him after the biggest loss of her career.

Just then, Pam spots Harold in the crowd. Sweat pouring out of his forehead, he comes running. He had been pacing the top section for the past two hours. He began making his way to the bleachers as soon as the game ended, but the crowd slowed his progress. The only thought running in his head: *My girl, she needs me.*

Moments later, her eyes puffy, Kami exits the locker room. She has been crying, holding her teammates. *I need to find my dad.*

Kami spots Harold. She runs into his open arms, tears streaming from her eyes. Harold kisses her forehead.

"I know it hurts so badly right now, but I am proud of you because you played your heart out against a great opponent," he whispers in her ear.

And then, Harold holds her face, looks into her eyes.

"You're a champion. You will get another chance."

———————

AISHWARYA KUMAR is a feature writer for ESPN's Investigative and Enterprise Unit. Born and raised in South India, she moved to the U.S. 10 years ago to pursue a master's degree at Northwestern's Medill School of Journalism. On graduating, she joined ESPN, where she covers the intersection of sports, immigration, culture, race, and identity. Her ESPN feature "The Grandmaster Diet" appeared in *The Best American Sports Writing 2020*. She's been a working journalist in three continents—Asia, Africa, and North America—and her work has also been published in *National Geographic*, VICE, Independent Media, *The Hindu*, and *The New Indian Express*. She lives in Hartford, Connecticut, with her husband, Jack Sullivan, and their 60-pound cream goldendoodle, Laddu. On Sunday mornings, she teaches yoga at a local studio in Hartford.

Preston Mattingly Felt Helpless as His Mother Battled Alcoholism. Here's How They Discovered Her 'Second Life' Together.

ALEX COFFEY

FROM *The Philadelphia Inquirer* • MAY 10, 2023

Preston Mattingly still has the sweatshirt. It is old and gray and dirty, with red wine stains set into the fabric. They might come out in the wash, but that would defeat the purpose. He wants to hold those painful memories close. Sometimes, he needs a reminder of how far he and his mother have come.

It was his favorite sweatshirt. He wore it all the time, including one night in 2010, when he was standing on the back porch of his childhood home in Evansville, Ind. Mattingly was having a heated argument with his mother, Kim, over her drinking problem. He began to yell, and she splashed wine in his face.

He sat there for a while. He decided, in that moment, that he was done helping her. His life would certainly be easier. But he could never follow through.

Mattingly prided himself on fixing problems, and his mother's alcoholism was the ultimate problem. Kim had been in and out of rehab since he was in high school. She'd been arrested for public intoxication, driving under the influence, and disorderly conduct. Her ex-husband, former Yankees star Don Mattingly, filed a protective order against her in 2008.

She was depressed. When she was in rehab, she became bulimic. At one point, Kim weighed only 85 pounds. Mattingly had a solution to every problem but this one—which was maddening, because to him, it seemed like a simple fix. When she was anxious, she could just feel better. When she was drinking, she could just stop. To Mattingly, these were all choices his mother was making, to both her and her family's detriment.

He has since realized that they are not choices. Mattingly, the Phillies' farm director, now knows alcoholism is a disease. He knows bulimia is a disease, too. It took him a while to get to this point. But sitting in his office one morning in mid-March, with his mother by his side, you wouldn't realize it.

Kim is 61 years old and five years sober. She no longer struggles with bulimia. She talks with her son almost every day, and like most mothers, she likes to give him grief. She says Preston, 35, has some of Donnie's characteristics. They are both hard workers, they both treat people well, but the trait she focuses on most is their perfectionism.

"When she walked in here for the first time, she was like, 'Oh my God, the water bottles in your fridge aren't lined up perfectly?'" Preston said. "What a shock."

"Yeah, I was like, 'I better straighten up those things at the bottom,'" Kim said.

They don't dwell much on the past. Kim and Preston made mistakes. Preston could have had more patience. He says his fiancée, Ellie, has helped him with that. Kim spent most of her adult life feeling like she let her three sons down. That guilt keeps her sober.

"For so long, I couldn't forgive myself," she said. "Because I felt like my sons were ashamed of me, for what I did. For what they had seen. I think any mother would have felt that way."

Preston has told her that's not remotely the case. Kim doesn't have an American League MVP award, or 2,153 hits, or a retired number at Yankee Stadium, but in a way, he's every bit as proud of his mother as he is of his famous father. There was a time when he wasn't sure she'd live to see his wedding. Now, she is as healthy as she's ever been.

"I have a lot of admiration for who she has become," Preston said. "It's almost like her second life. She's so happy every day. That's probably what I'm most proud of—how great a life she has. She's had to overcome more than most people I've seen.

"I love my dad. He's helped me a ton. But this is the story I think people should know."

The cost of a Yankees lifestyle

Don and Kim met when they were teenagers. Kim's father, Dennis, was an assistant coach of a local American Legion team near Evansville. Don, who respectfully preferred to not be interviewed for this story, was one of his players. Kim would go down to the dugout to ask her father for sunscreen. This was less about protecting her skin and more about getting close to the team's first baseman.

"The rest is history," she said.

Don was 18 when they got married; Kim was 17. They didn't have much of a grace period before he was shipped to the Yankees' low-A affiliate in Oneonta, N.Y. Three years later, in September, he was called up to the big leagues, and the next season, in 1983, he stuck on the big league roster. He'd stay there for the next 12 years.

The transition from Evansville to the Bronx wasn't easy. There were aspects of the Yankees lifestyle that Kim liked. She had a good relationship with owner George Steinbrenner, and enjoyed meeting former players, like Mickey Mantle. Her kids loved spending time at the ballpark—especially Preston. But it all came at a cost.

Don was a fan favorite. He was the humble son of a mailman, which appealed to hardworking New Yorkers. He had a sweet swing and a deft glove, but didn't act like a superstar. At a time when the Yankees weren't winning, he set a standard of professionalism and grace that would carry them to their glory years.

They were private people whose lives became very public. Don and Kim couldn't go to a grocery store without being mobbed by crowds. Sometimes, fans would show up to their house in the middle of the night. It got so bad that the police needed to barricade their property.

When Don was going through a slump, fans would yell at Kim. When he returned to his normal, MVP-caliber self, she became an afterthought.

It wasn't just that she was married to a celebrity. It was that she was married to a man who could do no wrong. She put pressure on herself to be perfect but was crushed by the weight. So, she started to drink.

"It was always chaotic," she said. "'Donnie Baseball' this, 'Donnie Baseball' that. Hollering and screaming and pushing. I chose to use alcohol to try to quiet out some of the noise.

"Everywhere we went, it was a cocktail party. When he'd go on road trips, I'd get into a bottle of wine or something. I knew it was becoming a problem because I was doing it when he was gone. I was doing it when I was alone.

"My dad was an alcoholic. So was my mom. It was definitely prevalent within me. I swore within myself, growing up, that I would never be like that. But that's what I did."

The tabloids quickly caught on to her drinking habit, and the narrative changed. They weren't high school sweethearts anymore. The story became about Don, the golden man, and his troublesome wife, who held him back in his career.

Don did the best he could, but their relationship got more fraught as the years went on. Kim developed bulimia while she was at a rehab center in 2005, and suddenly found herself battling not one but two diseases. In 2007, after 28 years of marriage, they filed for divorce.

'Tell me what to do'

Kim became severely depressed. In the months after the divorce, she would show up at Don's home in Evansville late at night. One time, she tried to kick down his door. She grew closer with two of her children, Taylor and Jordan, but distanced herself from Preston. He thinks it's because he reminded her of Don. She'd look at her son, who had her ex-husband's eyes and smile and temperament, and she would feel shame.

When they did talk, it was adversarial. There wasn't much of an existing relationship to lean on. Preston always aligned himself more with his father. They both liked playing basketball and baseball. His mother liked riding horses and spending time outdoors. They didn't seem to have mutual interests.

He would beg her to stop drinking, and sometimes, she would. But that would last for only a few weeks or so. It stayed this way until 2015. She'd vomited so much that she needed surgery to reconstruct her esophagus. The doctors told her that if she kept drinking, she would die.

One day, Preston was driving her home from an appointment. While they were stopped at a red light, he started to cry.

"I don't know what to do anymore," he told his mother. "Tell me what to do."

Kim started to cry, too. It was a humbling moment. The boy she'd raised was breaking down because of her own addiction. From that moment on, she decided to find a solution. She moved in with some family friends who were involved in Alcoholics Anonymous. She began going to meetings two or three times a week, and still does to this day.

But above all, Kim forgave herself.

"I decided to just start a new life," she said. "Not worry about anything from the past. That's gone. That's done. Wipe it clean."

Preston has helped her do that. Because of Kim's health problems, she developed some memory loss. Preston would make her a daily checklist, reminding her to brush her teeth, eat breakfast, and get some exercise. Now, she doesn't need reminders. Kim spends most of her days going on walks, or running errands, or doing her crossword puzzles by the pool. She is happy in her new life.

"Preston keeps me honest," she said. "And to stay sober and to stay healthy, you have to stay honest. You have to stay in the day. I can't go back. And we don't know what the future holds."

For years, Kim hated baseball. It brought up painful memories. But in 2022, she began watching the Phillies' playoff run. It reignited her love for the game. Kim sent Preston pictures of herself in a Phillies cap. Her favorite player was center fielder Brandon Marsh, whom she calls her "mountain man."

"I felt like a little kid, watching games again," she said. "I was like, 'There goes my mountain man!' He just seems so normal. I don't like the prima donnas, you know? My ex-husband wasn't like that."

Her trip to Clearwater, Fla., this spring was the first time she'd seen Preston at work. She believes that player development is the perfect job for him. He sticks up for the underdog. He's observant and kind. He gives second chances. She says he is like Don in that way.

In his seven seasons in baseball front offices, starting with the San Diego Padres, Preston has come to better appreciate mental health. He is proud of the work the Phillies have done to make it a priority, particularly in the minor leagues. Players have access to counseling, psychotherapy, and psychiatric support. The Phillies now have a mental health department, headed by a board certified psychiatrist.

It's all about giving resources to those who want help. Preston knows there is no such thing as a perfect person or a perfect family. He has the wine-stained sweatshirt to prove it. But he also knows that if you replace judgment with empathy, frustration with patience, anger with kindness, you might just change a life.

"Everybody deserves a second chance, and some are afraid to take it," Kim said. "They don't think they will have the support. I'm very blessed that I did."

ALEX COFFEY has covered the Phillies for *The Philadelphia Inquirer* since 2022. She began her journalism career in 2019, covering the WNBA's Seattle Storm and then the Oakland A's for The Athletic. She is a proud second-generation sportswriter.

The Table-Slamming, Ketchup-Spraying, Life-Saving Bills Mafia

STEVE RUSHIN

FROM *Sports Illustrated* • JANUARY 12, 2023

Behind wrought-iron gates, beneath a polished granite slab, James Ambrose Johnson Jr. whiles away eternity in Buffalo. His earthly life ended in 2004, in Los Angeles, after 56 years, but Johnson returned for posterity to his hometown, to the city of his angry youth. That anger, Johnson long ago said, was fed by tributaries global ("I was angry about the poor people in Ethiopia"), national ("I was angry about the politics of the country") and, most notably here, local: "I was angry that the Buffalo Bills were losing."

Johnson rose to fame as an R&B artist whose stage name, Rick James, gets top billing on his headstone at Buffalo's Forest Lawn Cemetery, etched in larger font above his real name, so that Johnson appears to be opening for his alter ego in the afterlife. In 2020, Bills receiver Stefon Diggs paid homage to the "Super Freak" singer by wearing on his cleats a portrait of the same Rick James, as Dave Chappelle played him on *Chappelle's Show*. Diggs had learned that the real-life Rick James was a Buffalonian and a Bills fan from a local dentist who was capping one of Diggs's teeth following a root canal. This was the Buffalo way, finding higher purpose in pain, the Bills and their fans raising one another up in the self-styled "City of Good Neighbors."

That nickname never got much traction outside of Buffalo, whose Good Neighbors are now better known to the world by another handle, one that embraces the same virtues of small-town civic connectivity through cold-weather football. That new name, Bills Mafia, is barely 12 years old, but it feels ancient, timeless and eternal, with an origin story that is downright Biblical.

IN THE BEGINNING, there was Adam and Steve. On Nov. 28, 2010, Bills receiver Stevie Johnson dropped what would have been a game-winning touchdown pass in overtime against the Steelers, triggering a public crisis of faith. "I PRAISE YOU 24/7!!!!!!" Johnson later tweeted to God. "AND THIS IS HOW YOU DO ME!!!!!" Nearly a day later, a Buffalo web developer named Del Reid noticed that ESPN's Adam Schefter had retweeted Johnson's already-viral outburst. In Reid's opinion, Schefter was late to the news, his RT needlessly extending Johnson's misery. And so, like other Bills fans, he tweeted a benign bit of mockery at the NFL insider...who promptly blocked him. "It seemed like a gross over-reaction," says Reid. But Reid didn't dwell on it. Life and Twitter moved on.

Months later, Reid was at his parents' house, in Tonawanda. He had grown up in that Buffalo suburb as a Bills fan, an impressionable teen when the team lost four consecutive Super Bowls, from 1991 through '94. "A lot of Catholic families have a picture of the pope on their wall," he says. "We had a picture of O.J. Simpson." After an awkward silence, Reid adds: "It came down in '94. We're not monsters."

Reid left his childhood home that night for Fratelli's, a local pizza joint, to pick up a takeout pie. Arriving 20 minutes early, he did what he does too often: pulled out his phone. He idly tweeted out the Twitter handles of some friends and fellow Bills fans—all of them Schefter block-ees—in a custom known in those early days of the bird app as Follow Friday. At the pizza counter, without much in the way of thought, the then 35-year-old father of two young girls added a hashtag to his football family. He called them, without really thinking about it, #BillsMafia.

This was April the twenty-second, in the year of our Lord two thousand and eleven. Reid's coinage, Bills Mafia, received, he says, "a few laughs" from his small group of friends. He picked up his pizza and left.

WHEN NICK BARNETT signed with Buffalo as a free-agent line-backer in 2011, after eight years with the Packers, he noticed the Bills Mafia hashtag, which Reid and his buddies—he calls them the "cofounders" of Bills Mafia—had continued to use. Bills fans, hungry for football after that summer's NFL lockout, were congregating on Twitter in great numbers. So Barnett embraced the hashtag, and not just online. He had the phrase printed on his mouthguard, literally spreading the idea by word of mouth. Stevie Johnson, whose Old Testament crisis of faith had started the whole mishegoss, began embracing the Mafia name, too. And Bills running back Fred Jackson. As a phrase, "Bills Mafia" gained traction the way that companies go bankrupt: gradually, and then suddenly.

As a concept, however—as an *ethos*—Bills Mafia had not yet coalesced. Reid was working at the Roswell Park Comprehensive Cancer Center in Buffalo, in web development, upstream from the medical professionals giving hands-on care to patients. He also attended a men's Bible study group that focused on male accountability. He likes to quote the overlapping wisdom of the gospel writer Luke ("To whom much is given much is required") and Spider-Man's Uncle Ben ("With great power comes great responsibility"). Now that Bills Mafia was gaining traction as a happy epithet, one of Reid's original "cofounders" asked: "Should we *do* something with this?"

"We were absolutely *not* looking to monetize it," says Reid, who created some Bills Mafia T-shirts that mashed up the Twitter and Bills logos and approached the development office at his hospital, asking whether they'd like to become the beneficiary of a Bills Mafia shirt sale. "It was a very confusing conversation," he recalls, "because they didn't understand this combination of the Bills, Twitter and the word *Mafia*." Finally, Reid says, he asked more directly: "Can I just give you money?"

From that seed he started a one-year community service project, with a goal of producing a different T-shirt every fortnight. An ORCHARD PARK shirt would echo the *Jurassic Park* logo, with a buffalo in place of the T-Rex. A Seussian shirt reading BLUE CHEESE AND WINGS would offer a sly homage to the cover of *Green Eggs and Ham*. Each would be created by a different Buffalo-adjacent artist, with proceeds going to a different family in need, beginning with a Bills fan whose daughter had eye cancer. Eventually, in 2015, Reid was laid off and urged to apply for another role within the hospital—but, as he explained over the phone to his wife, Chrissy, he had something more ambitious and less secure in mind: to turn the Bills Mafia into a full-time, philanthropic calling through a nonprofit he would name 26 Shirts. Chrissy, at the time, was in Manhattan, visiting the 9/11 Memorial, and thus open to the idea of making the world a more hospitable place.

"So from the jump we have tried to associate Bills Mafia with giving back and charity," Del Reid says.

"*Later*, Bills Mafia became associated with people jumping through tables. And look: People can celebrate their fandom in their own way; I'm not here to pooh-pooh anybody. Just please be safe.... But for a while, it was *just* the tailgate antics that were the focus."

THOSE TAILGATING ANTICS are certainly part of the Mafia's global brand. Table-slamming involves throwing oneself—or perhaps a close friend—onto a Lifetime brand fold-in-half church-banquet table, usually on video, to be instantly posted for likes and lolz. Sure, the occasional knucklehead has been slammed onto a burning table and engulfed in flames. And yes,

Simpson, the disgraced former Bills running back, *did* attend a home game last winter and found fans eager to pose for photos with him, including one guy in a Rumple Minze hoodie, and another gentleman wearing a novelty trucker hat with plastic bird poop on the bill, its crown emblazoned DAMN SEAGULLS. But these are not the bulk of the Bills Mafia, whose tailgates are a welcoming combination of cosplay and communal drinking. Comic Con meets Omicron.

Infiltrating the Bills Mafia at the 50-year-old venue now called Highmark Stadium, the neutral observer feels like a real-life mob informant. The man *not* wearing Zubaz, a Steve Tasker jersey, face paint and a horned helmet from the Loyal Order of Water Buffaloes risks looking conspicuous, especially if he's not two-fisting tallboys of Labatt Blue Light at 9 on a Sunday morning. When a man emerges from a port-a-potty in Lot 7 wearing a full Bills uniform, replete with visored helmet, it's the guy he holds the door for—in khakis and a quarter-zip—who appears to be attending a costume party.

In a private parking lot across the street from Highmark, 65-year-old Ken Johnson is soberly dressed and soberly comported. "My costume is a hat," says the gray-bearded Johnson, better known to the Bills Mafia as Pinto Ron because he grills on the hood of his 1980 Ford Pinto wagon and 25 years ago was misidentified as "Ron" in an *Athlon Sports* NFL preview magazine.

Pinto Ron, a Rochester software engineer, says he has attended every Bills home game since 1984, and every Bills game *period*—463 straight, home and away—dating back to '94, excluding the COVID-19 contests that were closed to the public. In Orchard Park, he cohosts the joyous pregame tailgate at the private parking area known as Hammer's Lot, whose tough-but-fair owner, Eric "Hammer" Matwijow, firmly prohibits, as his sign says, "funnels, dizzy bats [and] table slamming." (A dizzy bat, for the uninebriated, is a Wiffle ball bat filled with beer and weaponized in a vertiginous drinking game.)

Instead, drinks in Hammer's Lot are largely dispensed from the thumbhole of a bowling ball that Pinto Ron long ago liberated from a stranger's curb. The son of a Buffalo truck driver whose family of six lived in a 10-by-55-foot trailer, Pinto Ron grew up in poverty, and so Trash Day treasure hunting is rooted in his childhood. "The big trip of the year was going to McDonald's," says Pinto Ron, whose craving for grilled meats has occasioned a slight overcorrection in adulthood.

Today, on the hood of his street-legal Pinto, he has "six main grills" going. He's cooking chicken wings inside of an Army helmet, cocktail wieners in a hubcap, hamburgers and hot dogs on a rake, bacon on a handsaw, a breakfast menu—pancakes, eggs and omelets—in a shovel, and ribs and shish kebabs in the wheel rim of the auto racer Colton Herta's Indy car. (Long story.)

Parked next to Pinto Ron, operating out of an off-white 2002 Dodge Ram van, his pal Pizza Pete is making pies inside of a filing cabinet, jerk chicken inside of a rusted mailbox, Italian wedding soup inside of a watering can inside of a wheelbarrow, and pulled pork in the oil pan of a Buick Regal.

In the 1980s, Pinto Ron—back then still d/b/a Ken Johnson—and his buddies would end their meaty Bills tailgates by setting up their empty beer bottles like tenpins and knocking them down with the aforementioned bowling ball. In '89, at a Rochester bar called Marge's, he drank a shot of the house specialty, Wiśniówka, on a dare. The Polish cherry liqueur tastes "like 100-proof NyQuil," Pinto Ron says. "Naturally, I went running around to every liquor store in Polish neighborhoods and got some for the next tailgate." When his shot glass shattered at a game sometime in the '90s, the bowling ball became the obvious new dispenser of Wiśniówka.

And so: Two and a half hours before the Bills and Vikings kick off in November, with a needle-like snow slanting down, a 40-year-old woman takes the bowling ball in both hands, does a shot from the thumbhole, drops the ball, pulls an antiseptic baby wipe from a pouch and cleans her lips, perhaps unnecessarily.

The liqueur, at 71% alcohol by volume, is practically its own disinfectant, Pinto Ron insists. "One hundred proof will sterilize almost anything."

By now a crowd has gathered around Pinto Ron, hundreds of Bills and Vikings fans jockeying for position around the Pinto where—90 minutes before kickoff, by longstanding custom—he will be doused in ketchup and mustard, dozens of squeeze bottles aimed at him as if he were facing a fast-food firing squad.

It's a ritual that dates back to the time his brother Frank, out of sheer laziness, shot a perfect dollop of ketchup onto Pinto Ron's waiting hamburger roll from five feet away, rather than walk all the way over there. Now, revelers massed five-deep on the berm behind the Pinto have cameras poised in their trembling hands. "They won't be able to see anything," says Pinto Ron, who's slightly burdened by his attendance streak and his litany of ridiculous rituals. In three days he will be in Toronto, shooting a commercial for Mailchimp in which he'll be doused with ketchup and mustard for five consecutive hours, breaking only for lunch and the occasional hosing down. "You do something stupid long enough," he sighs, "you become known for it."

It can be burdensome. Heavy lies the head crowned in ketchup. Pinto Ron had open-heart surgery in February 2021 to repair a heart valve. "Last year I pushed myself too hard during the season, and it definitely affected my recovery," he says. Over the last three games of this regular season—for the first time in 30 years, outside of the height of COVID-19, when large gatherings were discouraged—he suspended the condiment ritual. "The ketchup ceremony in the cold, and the 20 minutes or so of selfies after, takes a large toll on me," he says.

And besides, Bills Mafia has so much more to offer than spectacles on social media. "We had been taking on this image of table-crashing, this negative image of stupid Buffalo things," says Pinto Ron. "Then the charity stuff took over. Now it overshadows the table-crashing."

When the Bengals beat the Ravens in the final week of the 2017 regular season, sending Buffalo to the playoffs for the first time in 17 years, the Bills Mafia returned the favor. In a happy, spontaneous wildfire on social media, Buffalo fans began donating to the Andy & JJ Dalton Foundation, which fundraises for "seriously ill and physically challenged children." Andy (then the Bengals' quarterback) and the foundation he started with his wife were flooded with donations. "I sent 17 dollars; I can tell you that," says Pinto Ron. And he was hardly alone: The Bills Mafia donated more than $442,000.

Three seasons later, when 80-year-old Patricia Allen died just before her grandson Josh led the Bills to a Week 9 win over the Seahawks, the Bills Mafia raised a million dollars for Oishei Children's Hospital in Buffalo. Again, many of the donations came in $17 increments, for the Bills quarterback's uniform number.

After Baltimore quarterback Lamar Jackson was concussed against Buffalo last season, the Bills Mafia donated another half a million dollars to Jackson's favorite charity, Blessings in a Backpack, which provides food for children when they're not in school. "Bills Mafia showed amazing generosity by helping so many kids in need," the QB said. But the truth is: Almost any worthy cause might benefit. Mafia munificence is now an ever-sweeping searchlight; no one really knows where its beam may fall next. Example: Feeling robbed by the referees in a six-point loss to the Buccaneers last year, the Bills Mafia raised $65,000 for a charity called Visually Impaired Advancement.

By the time Bills superfan Ezra Castro—known as Pancho Billa, for his signature sombrero and leather luchador mask—died of cancer in 2019, fellow fans had raised more than $60,000 for his family. (The PANCHO POWER T-shirt produced by 26shirts proved so popular that it remains available in perpetuity.) When Buffalo briefly disappeared beneath seven feet of snow this past November, Good Neighbors took shovels in hand and dug out the driveways and sidewalks of Bills players and coaches, allowing them to get to the airport for their game, which had been relocated to Detroit. The Bills Mafia had done the same thing in '14, when ski-masked strangers on snowmobiles picked up players in front of their homes and conveyed them, like sacks of Christmas toys in Santa's sleigh, to the practice facility in Orchard Park. And in December, when another blizzard killed at least 42 people in Erie County, Buffalonians continued to draw from their bottomless well of empathy.

When Dolphins quarterback Tua Tagovailoa was concussed against the Bills in September, and showed alarming difficulty walking to the huddle, more than 1,000 Buffalo fans donated to the Tua Foundation for youth initiatives. After the teams met again, in Buffalo in December, Tagovailoa gave a postgame "shout-out to the Bills Mafia." He hadn't forgotten their generosity and concern. "I really appreciate that," he said.

And then came the horror in Cincinnati. Bills safety Damar Hamlin went into cardiac arrest Jan. 2, on *Monday Night Football*. As players wept and the game against the Bengals was abandoned, fans—strangers to Hamlin and one another—found the GoFundMe page that the 24-year-old had set up in 2020 with the meager goal of $2,500 for a Christmas toy drive in his native Pennsylvania. Within days, the Chasing M's Community Toy Drive had received $8 million in donations, a patchwork quilt of 10s and 20s, and larger sums ending in 3 (Hamlin's uniform number), like Colts owner Jim Irsay's contribution of $25,003.

"If you get a chance to show some love today, do it!" Hamlin had tweeted, apropos of nothing, in 2021. "It won't cost you nothing." Now Del Reid and 26 Shirts did what they do: They made a new T-shirt. SHOW LOVE—IT COSTS NOTHING, it read, and proceeds went to Hamlin's toy drive. "Typically we try to bring families into the spotlight, as opposed to walking towards an existing spotlight," Reid tweeted. "But Damar's situation is the intersection of who we are and what we do."

A second T-shirt—a bengal tiger and buffalo embracing—benefited the University of Cincinnati Trauma Center where Hamlin was treated. (Hamlin, too, is selling a T-shirt to benefit the trauma center. He also announced this week that he'd direct some of the $8.6 million from the toy drive to help support young people through education and sports.)

All this largesse is "just an expression of who we are as a community," says Reid, "both in Western New York and around the world through the Buffalo diaspora."

THE BILLS MAFIA is a global family, but that family is rooted Up Here, in the 30th row of the third deck of Highmark, where the game arrives as a rumor, carried on the shifting winds off Lake Erie. In 2026 the Bills will move into a new billion-dollar stadium, with roughly 60% of its seats covered, but for now we sit on metal bleachers, wet from snow, using a La Nova pizza box as a seat cushion.

"My wife's afraid of heights," says the red-bearded guy to my left, summiting the snow-capped peak of Section 333 to take in that November game against Minnesota. "I can't believe I got her Up Here—except that tickets Down There are $800." To my right is a grandfather wearing a hooded snowmobile suit that exposes only his eyes. "You know what a small town this is?" he asks through a slot in his camouflage suit of armor. "I saw Jim Kelly and John Murphy this morning, just walking through the parking lot." Kelly, of course, is the Bills' Hall of Fame former quarterback, Murphy the voice of the Bills on Buffalo's WGR-AM. (Murphy suffered a stroke earlier this month. Within days someone on Bills Reddit had posted "Let's do what we do, Mafia," and linked to a donation site.)

Overnight, the weather had turned from unseasonably warm to unreasonably cold. As if cued by the Bills' game-ops crew, snow first began to fall when the parking lots opened at 9 a.m. The weather made a prophet of the meteorologist who promised on Saturday night that the Vikings would be welcomed by "stinging ice pellets," "blustery winds" and "that battleship gray sky we're used to this time of year." And while the stinging, blustery, battle-ready weather is actively hostile, even confrontational, the Bills Mafia is neither of those things.

Beneath that darkening sky, an aging Vikings fan in a horned helmet turns to the rest of Section 333 and screams, "In Minneapolis, we call this a sunny day!" But the Vikings play indoors, at U.S. Bank Stadium. Before that, they played beneath a Teflon dome. "You know what we used to call the Metrodome?" asks Snowmobile Suit Guy. "We called it The Pussydome." But he says it softly, confidentially, so as not to be overheard by the women, children and Vikings fans in our midst.

Concerned friends, knowing that you're at the Bills game, will text to ask whether you've been thrown through a table yet, or been hit by an airborne sex toy (as one was lobbed into the end zone during a 2018 game), or done a shot of Polish cherry liqueur from the thumbhole of a bowling ball. Buffalo has been fighting disparaging national stereotypes for at least 150 years. Mark Twain had been a Buffalonian for just 20 months when he wrote to a friend, in 1871: "I have come at last to loathe Buffalo so bitterly (always hated it) that yesterday I advertised our dwelling house for sale."

Ninety-eight years later, the greatest sports columnist of the 20th century deemed the city unworthy of Simpson, the Heisman-winning USC running back. "What do you endorse in Buffalo?" Jim Murray of the *Los Angeles Times* asked his sun-tanned readers. "A snow shovel? A ball bearing? An overshoe?"

When Pat Phillips was the head golf pro at Tan Tara Golf Club in North Tonawanda, the club's Texas-based management company wanted to know what Phillips could do in September and October to get more people out on the course. "What happens after Labor Day," Phillips, now 57, patiently explained, "is bowling season starts. People *bowl* here." Phillips hates bowling, but he joined a Monday-night league, anyway, out of civic duty.

The other thing Buffalonians do in the fall is watch the Bills. "Mondays after victories are great; Mondays after defeats, people are down in the dumps," says Phillips, who helped tear down a goalpost after a home win in the 1990s. "When the weather starts getting like this, it can get depressing. The Bills—and the Sabres, too—are a shot in the arm. They get people through the winter."

This is also true of our metaphorical winters. When Phillips was diagnosed with Stage IV kidney cancer, in 2014, he and his wife, Michelle, were raising three teenage boys. Pat's doctor said that he'd typically seen patients live 11 months to two years under similar circumstances. "Good thing he was wrong," Pat says today, eight long football seasons after his left kidney and a massive tumor were removed.

Among the first Buffalonians to rally to the aid of the Phillips family were Del Reid and 26 Shirts, who made a tee for Pat that read BUFFALO WILLIAMS, a play on the Bills and their many players at the time with that surname. "It was a great thing," says Phillips. "Not just the money [raised], but to know someone is looking out for you. That's the biggest thing about the Bills Mafia, what the Buffalo community is all about: If you're in need, people rush to help you. We don't know any different."

PERHAPS BECAUSE THEY'VE been collectively reduced to snow-bound, Super Bowl–losing gobblers of beef on weck, Buffalonians have historically been alive to one another's pain. They're "so empathetic," says Sherry Brinser-Day, from the city's north side. "They get the working man, down on his luck, and connect with that. People here *know*. Our reputation is more than the economic downfall that we had; it's more than the blizzard of '77. But those things also made us who we are."

Buffalo is more than wings, Wide Right and table-slamming. Buffalo is more than the Bills and bowling and roller derby, the sport that Brinser-Day took up at age 46 when she joined the Nickel City Renegade Roller Derby, competing first as Sherry Bomb and later as All-Fight Knocks, a play on Buffalo's venerable art museum, Albright-Knox.

She joined the league at Kiddy Skateland, on the north side of Buffalo, during the two years when her husband, Tim, was waiting for a heart transplant. Tim was a cop in Tonawanda—Officer Day worked nights—when, at age 45, he had what he thought was a heart attack but turned out to be, after agonizing months in the hospital, hypereosinophilic syndrome (HES), in which white blood cells attack internal organs. The Day children were 4, 5 and 7 years old at the time, kissing their father goodbye for weeks on end.

Ultimately, a left ventricular assist device kept Tim alive; and so, in a way, did the Bills Mafia. At the time, Day knew, as all Buffalonians did, that a nonprofit called Wings Flights of Hope was flying Jim Kelly to and from his jaw-cancer treatments at Memorial Sloan-Kettering hospital in New York City. Tim contacted the organization, and soon Wings was flying him to Boston for his own life-saving treatments in the Mass General transplant program. He also saw, on the Buffalo news, that a local boy with brain cancer had benefited from one of Del Reid's T-shirts. When Sherry met Chrissy Reid, Del's wife, at the elementary school that their daughters both attended, Chrissy told Sherry: "We're gonna do a shirt for you." And so the Bills Mafia searchlight fell on the Days.

"Twenty-six shirts became a vehicle to share our story," Sherry says. The Days began to see people wearing "their" shirts—a bison in a Bills uniform, based on a 1960s soda pop ad—around their Kenmore neighborhood. A niece in Boston spotted one of the shirts in a bar, and the guy wearing it said, "Oh, yeah, we bought it specifically to support your uncle." Strangers approached Tim Day at his local Wegmans—the beloved Rochester-based grocery chain, purveyors of Bills Mafia Wing Sauce—and told him they were praying for him.

More than seven years after he finally got his heart transplant, 55-year-old Tim Day now coaches his teenage son in hockey. He's able to walk the dog. He and Sherry have bought plenty of T-shirts to support other Buffalonians in need. "Being good to your fellow man, caring about each other, helping each other... we need to do that," says Sherry. More important than money (which can be anywhere from a few hundred bucks to $13,000 for any given 26 Shirts beneficiary), Del Reid has delivered love, compassion and concern to his fellow Bills fans. He embodies, Sherry says, "the kindness and empathy that all Buffalonians understand so deeply. Del is representing our humanity."

DEL REID DOESN'T want credit for that. He'll scarcely take credit for his own coinage, Bills Mafia, which is now in the world's water supply. It's everywhere in Buffalo and beyond: on sweatshirts, in commercials, affixed to car bumpers—the all-encompassing epithet for Bills fans and Buffalonians everywhere. On a building in downtown Buffalo, there's a four-story mural painted in Bills blue that says KEEP BUFFALO A SECRET. But it's getting to be too late for that. On the Sunday morning in November before the Bills visited the Jets, Reid woke up to text messages informing him that the Bills Mafia had been name-dropped in a *Saturday Night Live* sketch. "The dragon's awake now," Reid says of his creation. "Like Smaug."

If you go looking for the birthplace of that dragon—the old Fratelli's pizzeria, at the corner of Sheridan and Loretta in Tonawanda—bear in mind that it's now an Italian restaurant called Romeo and Juliet's. But the building deserves landmark status, a place in local lore alongside the Anchor Bar, birthplace of Buffalo wings, another creation that started here and was bequeathed to the wider world.

Rick James, another one of those global exports, is gone, but Buffalonians are still making music. Jeremie Pennick, the local rapper who performs as Benny the Butcher, has a song that plays during games at Highmark Stadium. "Bills Mafia Anthem" goes: "[When] we say Mafia, that means family to me."

The eccentric uncle of that family, Pinto Ron, reserves parking spots for visiting fans at every tailgate in Hammer's Lot. He says the conviviality of Bills supporters has ever been thus. "Bills Mafia has always been here," he says of Western New York and its émigrés worldwide. "It just never had a name. Now, it's got a name. Del Reid did that."

Like William Shakespeare, Reid has made a permanent contribution to the English language. He and Chrissy have two daughters, Delaney and Chloe, in addition to Bills Mafia, another offspring conceived of love. "Bills Mafia is a celebration of our team, our love, and it's pure," Del says. "Any time you're thinking of margins—money and profit—that ruins things. It takes the purity out of it. Looking back: My 'cofounders' and I, none of us were looking to do anything but enjoy our Bills fandom. That's one of the reasons ['Bills Mafia'] stuck around so long before [the team itself] adopted it. They saw that it *wasn't* being exploited. I've been protective of it."

Look at them now. Del Reid and 26 Shirts have raised more than $1.6 million for Bills fans in need. Meanwhile, his other brainchild, the Bills Mafia, "grew up and left the house and belongs to all Bills fans," he says, watching in wonder as his intangible invention travels the world. "It's really cool to be a footnote on my favorite football team's Wikipedia page. That's enough for me."

STEVE RUSHIN is the author, most recently, of *Sting-Ray Afternoons* and *Nights in White Castle*. He has written for *Sports Illustrated* since 1988.

Pelé Finally Comes Home, after a Lifetime of Belonging to the World

SAM BORDEN

FROM ESPN • JANUARY 4, 2023

SANTOS, Brazil—At 3:57 Monday morning, the Vila Belmiro neighborhood of Santos began to glow.

A swooping helicopter shined its spotlight from a black sky. Firecrackers exploded in neon reds and blistering whites. Lamps in bedrooms flipped on, almost in unison, and more than a few heads poked out the windows of the line of squat, flat-roofed houses.

On the corner, seven helmeted policemen stood stout in front of the old soccer stadium. They were starkly still amid the racket of the fireworks' *pop-pop-pop*, save for one officer who shouted a single word into the walkie-talkie pinned to his shoulder: "*Chegando! Chegando!*"

Arriving.

It was Pelé. A line of vehicles turned onto Rua Princesa Isabel. There was a white police cruiser and a motorcycle. An SUV and another bike. A white passenger van followed by a black Chevy Tahoe. Then, slowly, came the black Mercedes hearse.

An old man watched by the curb. His name is Alemão, and he owns the bar just 25 paces from the stadium gates. He has a tattoo of the club's crest in the middle of his forehead.

Pelé was Alemão's friend. Pelé would come to his bar, as a player and in retirement, to talk football. To drink guarana. To get his haircut from Didi, the barber next door whose shop sign says, "Pelé's hairdresser—and yours, too."

Alemão needed to be there on Monday, even if it was before dawn. He needed to see. He watched Pelé's hearse go past and make a left down the side of the stadium. He watched Pelé's hearse turn right into the stadium's belly. He nodded and rubbed his hands together as Pelé went. He whispered, *"Seu casa,"* under his breath. His house.

Pelé played in Vila Belmiro, won in Vila Belmiro, became one of the best-known athletes in history in Vila Belmiro. Then, somehow, he grew even larger, going all over the globe to spread the message of the sport he loved. He died from complications related to colon cancer on Dec. 29 at 82, and the only thing bigger than his fame was the smile he flashed, over and over, in all those pictures and speeches and films and commercials.

It was his life. It was his way. It was what he wanted. For more than a half-century, Pelé belonged to the world. On Monday, he came home.

A DAY EARLIER, while his customers drank from beer cans wrapped in yellow sleeves in the sticky afternoon heat, Alemão sat at a table. "There have been a lot of tears these last days," he said. "But there should also be a party."

Pelé played 18 years for Santos and scored a staggering 1,283 goals in 1,367 matches for both his club and his country, according to Brazilian records. He led Santos to 10 state titles, six national titles and two continental trophies. He remains the only soccer player to win the World Cup three times and is regarded by many as the best player the game has ever seen. At his peak, the only athlete who might have even approached his renown was Muhammad Ali.

There was something magical, something sublime about watching Pelé on the field, and talking about it sent Alemão—a thick, doughy man who walks with a slight limp—into a contemplative space. His eyes twinkled. "*Lindo, lindo,*" he said, describing what it was like to see Pelé dribble. Beautiful.

To take just two examples, Pelé's pair of goals in the 1958 World Cup final stand as museum-quality pieces of sporting art: In one, he traps the ball on his chest, drops it to his foot, flips it over his head (as well as his opponent) before ripping a shot into the net. On the other, he jumps so high he seems to be stepping on the defender's skull as he heads a laser past the goalkeeper.

There were countless moments just like these, whether with Santos, a club Pelé elevated out of a small, provincial city on Brazil's south coast, or later when Pelé came out of retirement to play (and get paid handsomely) in the United States, essentially introducing the sport to Americans as part of the juggernaut New York Cosmos. Wherever he was, Pelé's strength was relentless.

But the allure of Pelé, the quality that made him an iconic Brazilian, runs deeper.

"It is how he made us feel," Alemão said, rubbing his thumb over the Santos tattoo on his head (he got it after losing a bet). Brazilians can often be self-critical and, especially in today's political environment, fiercely divided, Alemão said. With Pelé, though—especially in Santos—there is a sense of gratitude and pride.

"Everything he did with soccer out in the world, he first did here in Santos," Alemão said. "He built soccer out there, but first he built Santos. He made it into something."

Just down the block from Alemão's bar is a tiny house that sits only a few steps from the main gate fans use to enter the stadium. Jose Nunes, who is 84, has lived in the house with his family for 50 years. He specialized in electronics and came to Santos to work at a company for which Pelé was a spokesman. Nunes struck up a relationship with Pelé after helping him set up a television ("He called me a genius, can you imagine?"), and Nunes's teenage son, Sidnei, befriended one of Pelé's sons. "When we were 18, I'd go over there and we'd sneak whiskey together," Sidnei recalled.

Years ago, Sidnei was living in Florida and Nunes came to stay with him for a few months. The two were at a house where some construction colleagues of Sidnei's were working on installing a new floor, and Nunes accidentally cracked several pieces of tile.

"They were so angry at first, and I didn't know what to do because I didn't speak their language, I didn't know if they'd want money—I was worried," Nunes said with a laugh. "But once I could make them understand that I was from Santos, that I knew Pelé, they started smiling.

"They were soccer fans from Puerto Rico and they loved Pelé, so they shook my hand. They weren't mad anymore. They just said, 'The floor is OK now—you're from Santos.'"

NUNES DIDN'T GO to Pelé's wake in the stadium Monday—he worries about COVID exposure, and his granddaughter wouldn't give him back the autographed Pelé jersey he wanted to wear anyway. So he watched the crowds from his porch, sitting in his chair behind the glass window he slides open when he wants to hear the sounds of Vila Belmiro.

Lines stretched for nearly a mile as hundreds of thousands of people waited hours for their turn to walk past Pelé, whose body lay beneath a white veil in an open casket at midfield.

The mourners came in all ages and life stages. There were shopkeepers and trash collectors, bakers, chefs, architects, students, engineers, retirees and toddlers. Memories hung heavy. Ellie Manhas brought her 14-year-old daughter and 12-year-old son because she wanted them to see what Pelé meant to her grandparents. Paulo Roberto Grosso brought his grandson and told the story of the night he saw Pelé score twice in a 5–1 Santos win. Romildo Peroni Santos, who works on the docks as a third-generation stevedore in this port city, came because as a child he'd heard on a loop how Pelé was like nothing anyone had ever seen.

There were plenty of well-known figures, too: former Brazilian stars, like Ze Roberto; local and national politicians; Neymar's father; a Brazilian supreme court justice (who said his chambers has a de facto shrine to Pelé in it); as well as FIFA president Gianni Infantino, who suggested that every country in the world should name at least one stadium after Pelé.

But Pelé's legacy clearly lay in the everyday people who loved his sport. They ate in line, sang in line and sweated quite a bit in line as temperatures reached well into the 80s and they criss-crossed the avenues to get their turn with *O Rei*. The King.

Each had their reason. Haroldo Stampaccheo is now 62, and he has had the image of Pelé on the field—lanky build, long-sleeve jersey, No. 10 on the back—burned into his brain for as long as he can remember. He first saw Pelé as an 11-year-old, and while he always enjoyed watching Pelé play, those game moments aren't what brought him to Vila Belmiro.

"My father worked at a bank—every day from 7 to 5, he just worked and worked and worked," Stampaccheo explained after he emerged from the stadium. "I didn't see him so much. It just wasn't like that in that time—we weren't...close. But on Wednesdays, he would take me in the car because it was a match-day. And the roads were terrible but we would bump and bump and bump our way to the stadium. And we would sit and watch the game and talk about Pelé. My father really, really loved to talk to me about Pelé."

Stampaccheo paused. Then he looked back at the field and said, "My dad died in 1993. I think I came today because I thought I might see him here, too."

AWAY FROM THE stadium, a few miles back toward the ocean, Dida Dias finished her usual morning coffee and cut a path among the sandy vacationers and tourists. As she dodged families lugging baskets and beach chairs, she passed one of the many stores with a sign for Pelé out front, but Dias barely looked up.

"It is very, very difficult—especially here—to take a position that isn't exactly like everyone else's when it is about Pelé," she said. "But there are things that matter."

Dias, a 66-year-old retired professor, has worked as an activist with feminist and anti-racism groups for most of her adult life. She understands the lionization of Pelé—"what he did as a footballer is undeniable"—but believes that shouldn't erase the feelings of some Brazilians, especially some Black Brazilians who feel there are areas where he fell short.

Throughout Pelé's career, Dias said, he consistently denied that racism was an issue in Brazil even as he personally experienced it. When he first came to Santos as a teenager, Pelé was sometimes called "Gasolina," a reference to the color of oil, and even once he became a star player in the mid-1960s, Dias said, he wasn't allowed to join the exclusive (and all-white) Santos Tennis Club.

Some other Brazilian stars used their platforms. Dias recalled Reinaldo, who played on Brazil's national team at the 1978 World Cup and famously celebrated goals by raising a fist—which angered the Brazilian military dictatorship.

"Reinaldo was pushed away, left out of the 1982 World Cup team because they didn't like what he was saying," Dias said. "Pelé never said anything. He never used his fame in service of the anti-racism movement. He just spent most of his life saying he'd suffered because he was poor, not because he was Black."

Even in 2014, when the Santos goalkeeper Aranha claimed to have been the target of racist chants from opposing fans, Pelé was critical of Aranha for making an issue of it. "If I were to stop the game or scream…every time they called me a creole or a monkey, then every game would have to stop," he said then. "The more attention is paid to this, the more this thing will happen."

Pelé's charity work, his work with children, his global diplomacy were meaningful, she stressed, and he modeled the importance of higher education, going to college even as many of his contemporaries never did. "That was important, especially for young people here, Black or white, to see," she said.

"It isn't about saying he's not special—of course he was," she said. "But he was not a god. He was a man. And we should remember that no man is perfect."

AS THE LINES stretched farther and the wait to get into Vila Belmiro grew to three hours on Monday, Doraci Ribeiro cut flowers.

Ribeiro works at Flor de Lotus, a flower shop across the street from the Cemitério Memorial Necrópole Ecumênica—the peculiar vertical cemetery where Pelé was to be buried.

Ribeiro, who has been a florist for 30 years, acknowledged that the vertical cemetery is "unusual." Instead of plots in the ground, the vertical cemetery looks like a high-rise apartment building, with floors of graves, ossuaries, mausoleums (and a car museum and aviary in the rear). Pelé's body will stay on the second floor in a large mausoleum decorated to look like a soccer field so as to be more accessible to visitors.

"It is different," Ribeiro said, "but people will still want flowers."

Ribeiro saw Pelé several times, usually at the restaurant next to the cemetery. He always sensed a calmness from Pelé, he said, an ease or comfort with his life, with his place.

So as Ribeiro sat in his white plastic chair at his orange plastic table on the sidewalk tossing stems into a bucket, he began to make small bouquets for the mourners he knew would come to the cemetery across the street. For the blooms, he chose mostly tigerlily and chrysanthemum, he said, because they felt appropriate.

"These are white flowers," he said. "They bring peace."

ON TUESDAY MORNING, Luiz Inacio "Lula" Da Silva, Brazil's newly elected president, came to Vila Belmiro to pay his respects.

He was one of the final mourners—some 230,000 came during the 24 hours that Pelé lay in state—and at 10 a.m., the wake was over. Pelé's coffin was carried outside by eight uniformed cadets and was set atop a fire engine to begin a final trip around the city. A Brazilian flag and a Santos club flag were draped over the casket and a soccer ball hung off the back of the truck.

Alemão was there again. He stared. The last time he'd seen Pelé—when Pelé was clearly struggling physically—he'd said, "King, you looked f---ed up," and Pelé laughed and replied, "What do you mean? I'm going to play soccer right now."

The procession began. The journey through the city was languid. Music blared, Samba drums thumped. Horns rang out. Santos songs and chants erupted from storefronts. Children sat atop their parents' shoulders and waved.

The procession inched along the beachfront, the sand where Pelé played *pelada*, pick-up soccer, as a teenager. Sergio Fernandes de Aguiar, who played in those games on Saturday afternoons, remembered how Santos officials were so worried that Pelé, their prize prospect, might get hurt that they demanded he only play as a goalkeeper in *pelada*.

"He had good hands—he was actually an excellent goalkeeper," Aguiar said, giggling at the fact that he was saying such a thing about a man who was maybe the greatest scorer in history. "We were so young. I just remember so much laughing."

The crowds along the route began to swell as the procession approached Canal 6, one of the city's drainage channels that divides Avenida Coronel Joaquim Montenegro. Thousands, including one of Pelé's old teammates, the goalkeeper Lalá who lives around the corner, squeezed into the narrow road between the canal and a modest, white, rectangular house where members of Pelé's family, including his sister, Lucia, waited at the second-floor balcony. "I came because we were friends," Lalá said.

As the procession came near, the fans began to sing a favorite, "*Mil Gols*," about how Pelé is the only player to score a thousand goals (no Brazilian has ever cared that FIFA disputes that statistic) and Celeste Arantes, Pelé's 100-year-old mother, who is in poor health herself, looked out of a window just for a moment.

The fire truck turned down Avenida Montenegro. Police officers cleared a path. The engine stopped directly in front of Pelé's family's house, and suddenly thousands dropped their heads in prayer with Pelé's loved ones.

"*Pai Nosso, que estas no ceu,*" they all said together, the words ringing out across the canal. Our Father, Hallowed be thy name. "*Venha o teu reino; seja feita a tua vontade; assim na terra como no ceu.*"

On Earth, as it is in Heaven.

THE FIRE ENGINE approached the cemetery. It came around the bend in the road, rolled past Doraci Ribeiro and the flower shop and then reversed, backing toward the front steps. The eight pallbearers removed the Brazil flag and the Santos flag, folding them carefully. They picked up the coffin. A man named Cassio Mandu stepped forward.

Mandu clutched a trumpet. He is 45 and, despite being an accomplished musician who often plays at ceremonies, he confessed that he was terrified. A light mist was falling and his country's greatest athlete was coming toward him and his emotions were roiling so much he worried his lips might fail him. "I was scared that I wouldn't be able to play," he said.

Mandu put the trumpet to his mouth and the first notes of "Il Silenzio," a haunting melody about a soldier, flew up between the raindrops as the coffin was lowered down off the truck. In the sky, a helicopter circled. Across the street, two women clutched chrysanthemums. On the second floor of the vertical cemetery, Pelé's relatives wiped away tears.

Mandu finished "Il Silenzio." A cheer went up from those behind the fences set on the street, a final shout for their star. *Eterno Rei!* a man yelled out. Eternal King.

It was time. He had welcomed all who wanted to see him. He had moved through the streets of his city. Now, finally, he would rest.

Mandu lifted his trumpet again. The cadets raised Pelé's casket high. The first notes of "Amazing Grace" sounded out, soft and steady, as the pallbearers climbed the steps.

Mandu lowered his instrument and wiped his face. It was over. His next job is playing at a wedding.

"Without pain," he said, looking back toward the cemetery, "we might not know what happiness feels like."

Flavio Ferreira contributed to this report.

SAM BORDEN has been the global sports correspondent for ESPN since 2017. Before that, he spent six years at *The New York Times*, where he first served as a beat reporter covering the New York Giants and then as an international correspondent based in France. A graduate of Emory University, Borden lives in Connecticut with his wife, Jessica, and their daughters, Riley and Hannah.

Kobe Bryant's Little Mambas Are Still Playing, for Him and Each Other

MICHAEL LEE

FROM *The Washington Post* • APRIL 7, 2023

NEWPORT BEACH, Calif.—Every year they gather at the jetty here, teenage girls in matching black hoodies, their toes clinging to the edge of the rocks as the Pacific crashes into the shore below. They cling to each other, too, crying quiet tears onto each other's shoulders as they toss eight flowers apiece into the ocean.

"Everything we do is for the eight," Amalia Holguin says of their mantra, which, naturally, is also now a hashtag: *#4The8*.

Since Jan. 26, 2020, it's a bond these eight girls have shouldered as much as they have shared. On that date each year, when the sun begins to set, they remember what was lost when a helicopter plunged to the ground and one of the most famous basketball players in the world died alongside their best friends, their friends' parents and another coach. The flowers leave their hands, and they again become teammates—and family—in time.

A red poppy for Gianna Bryant because red was her favorite color. The bright pink Gerber daisy for Payton Chester. A light pink dahlia for her mother, Sarah. The yellow Gerber daisy for Alyssa Altobelli because she was an Oregon fan. Orange for her father, John, who coached baseball at Orange Coast College. The white hydrangea for his wife and Alyssa's mother, Keri Altobelli. And a lilac Hawaiian hibiscus for Christina Mauser, the coach whom they called "MOD," as in mother of defense.

For Kobe Bryant, the Los Angeles Lakers great known as "The Black Mamba"—and the co-founder and CEO of Mamba Sports Academy, where the girls learned to work on their games and dream their dreams—a light purple and black poppy.

"It's just really therapeutic," says Emily Eadie, 16, who curated the floral arrangement.

The photo apps on their phones remain loaded with images of those practices and tournament victories, holiday gatherings and beach parties. They have filled scrapbooks and photo albums that never get dusty because they're flipped through so often. "Mamba 8," their black-and-white wristbands all read, as the flowers are strewn in the sea.

In the first two ceremonies, the tide came in and the flowers were swept back to shore. Every time they want to move forward, it seems, the mourning and pain return. They return to the shore anyway, waiting for the current to carry those flowers toward the horizon.

A master plan

Eleven girls can say they were coached by Kobe Bryant. Three were on that helicopter. The remaining eight feel fortunate they were once part of his plan to build them a basketball nirvana.

"A great opportunity that no one else has besides us girls [had]," says Kat Righeimer, 16. "So we soaked up every moment, every lesson that he taught us."

Bryant retired in 2016, his ferocious will and relentless pursuit of Michael Jordan's greatest player baton having led to five NBA championship banners and two Lakers jerseys hanging in the rafters. He soon found an outlet in coaching, pouring his passion into being a #girldad to his second daughter, Gianna. She shared his competitive fire and love for the game. By investing in her and her basketball buddies, Bryant got the chance to teach in the gym lessons he found more challenging to instill at home.

Kobe being Kobe, this wasn't just about putting together a great AAU team; he had a master plan. He sought players whose personalities and playing styles complemented one another. His plan, according to the girls' parents and his associates, was to drill them on fundamentals and methodically cultivate their skills and intangibles. By the time they were high school seniors, the plan went, they would be state champions and AAU national champions, able to pick the colleges of their choice. A select few, he was sure, would play in the WNBA.

Vicki Lamkin, Zoie's mother, says, "Kobe knew what he was doing when he brought us all together."

As a player, Bryant had a reputation for being a single-minded loner. But for Gianna, he created a warm, tightknit atmosphere. Siblings were included. Emily's mother still has a text message from Bryant after their last Christmas party together.

"He said that he was so incredibly blessed to have such an extended family," Allison Eadie says. "But, you know, he created that family. And because he created that family, the girls were able to continue on."

Five of the eight players were able to follow through on Bryant's plan to play at Sage Hill School, a nearly $45,000-per-year private school founded in 2000 with a strong academic reputation and little athletic prominence. Bryant had considered Mater Dei High School, the private sports powerhouse in Orange County. But something about creating a new standard at Sage Hill appealed to him.

Jim Righeimer, Kat's father and the former mayor of Costa Mesa, wanted his youngest daughter to attend Mater Dei, where his older daughter, Morgan, went. Kat's mom set her husband straight with a simple question: "How can you deny your daughter six years with Kobe?" That morning, Jim let Bryant know he changed his mind. "We're in 1,000 percent."

'Hogwarts'

Located on a rangy hill in Newport Coast, with sandy brown brick buildings and scenic views, Sage Hill has a charming, 28-acre campus. Bryant, a Harry Potter fan, affectionately referred to the place as "Hogwarts."

Inside the gym on a February evening, inspirational signs such as "Embrace Our Journey" are taped on black padded walls, and the bleachers are halfway filled, mostly with parents and friends, waiting for Sage Hill's last regular season game to tip off.

As the Lightning's 12 girls take the court, the five Team Mamba alums lead the way—a team within the team, a little like Michigan's Fab Five from a generation ago.

"Em," as Emily is known, is a team captain, a steadying, reliable presence on and off the court whose play and academic performance have drawn interest from Ivy League schools. Kat, who has also drawn interest from Division I schools, stretches the floor with her range and sets the tone with her optimism. Annabelle Spotts does her work in the low block and generally maintains a stoic approach on the court. When the team needs a timely stop or shot, Zoie steps up. They understand their roles, complement each other and get the expected contributions.

Those four enrolled at Sage Hill seven months after the crash and, as sophomore starters last season, led the school to its first state title. There were comebacks and buzzer-beaters and an instant-classic championship game. Coming back from down 13, the Lightning took its first lead on Em's reverse layup with a minute left. Kat helped seal the dramatic 51–47 victory with clutch free throws. The players mobbed one another at midcourt to celebrate.

"It was just a great milestone, especially to do it with these girls," Annabelle says. "Basketball has allowed me to meet my family. So it's just more than a game."

This year, Sage Hill moved up a classification, testing its reign as state champion against some of the larger powers in California. With a win over Portola, the girls can add the school's first girls' basketball league title to the green-and-white state title banner that already hangs.

To help them get there, they were able to finally welcome Amalia, a promising freshman who was a mere fourth-grader when Bryant found her. He had told his then-12-year-old girls that he was going in search of some size. But he showed up to practice one day with a little blond 10-year-old with a nice jumper and plenty of moxie and told anyone who was perplexed by the addition, "We'll grow a big."

(Team Mamba, the AAU team, did later add a big: Mackenly Randolph, daughter of former NBA player Zach Randolph. But she attends Sierra Canyon, a basketball power in Los Angeles that is closer to her home.)

Amalia remains the little sister, shy but playful. "Our fourth-grader at heart," Annabelle calls her. She keeps the team loose with a celebratory dance after a big play while staying ready to attack the opposition with the same zeal—all as she chomps on bubble gum. On Instagram, Amalia goes by "Junior Mamba," and she is the only member of the team who wears one of the jersey numbers Bryant once wore, donning his international No. 10.

"She was the missing piece," Zoie says of Amalia.

Despite a height advantage, Sage Hill gets off to a slow start against Portola. But there's calm on the floor, as if the girls know a push will come. And it does. The Lightning eventually celebrates a 36-point victory by trusting in one another.

"The biggest thing that Coach Bryant wanted us to do is don't be robots on the court," Kat says. "Like, just figure it out yourself."

The next day, the Mamba girls meet for lunch at the Mustard Cafe. They munch on salads and avocado toast and gab about teachers and class assignments before an afternoon skills training session with former NBA player Darren Collison. Given their previous coach, the girls' commitment didn't surprise Collison, an 11-year NBA veteran.

"I know how hard he works. And I felt like if you can be around Kobe, with his mental disposition, then you can do a lot," says Collison, who has trained players such as Zach LaVine, Chet Holmgren, Jalen Green and Evan Mobley.

Em, Zoie, Kat and Annabelle show up wearing their lime-green Kobe Grinches, the signature Nikes Bryant preferred for Christmas Day games. Amalia packs for a slumber party later that night at Em's house but doesn't get the memo for the footwear: She's in the black-and-white Kobe 6 Mambacita shoe, with Gianna's No. 2 near the heel.

They spend an hour at a caged half-court gym in Lake Forest doing drills on ballhandling, shooting and finishing contested layups with both hands. Collison and his crew offer professional pointers on how to get separation from defenders, including little tricks referees won't catch given their hand position.

Afterward, Collison congratulates the girls on winning the league title but adds, "You haven't done nothing yet." Amalia looks at him, eyebrows pressed with confusion. But before Collison can explain what he means, her teammates help by shouting an old Kobeism:

"Job's not done!"

A night in

Friday night frees up when Sage Hill Coach Kerwin Walters cancels practice, a reward for their win over Portola. They load into Em's black Volkswagen Tiguan to watch the Sage Hill boys' team play. During a postgame ice cream run, Amalia tries to befriend kids circling on an electrical bicycle, in hopes she will get a chance to ride herself. She strikes out.

They get back to Em's house a little after 10 p.m. Annabelle, Amalia, Em, Kat and Zoie climb into a huge mattress on the floor of the living room and watch the most recent remake of *The Great Gatsby*, starring Leonardo DiCaprio. Em and Kat read the book in English class this year. The movie was good, Em says, but "the book was better."

They wake early the next morning for a 7 a.m. weight training session. Em loads them up again, cruising along the coastline as the sun crests above the Pacific. They stop for doughnuts before arriving at their destination: the Laguna Beach studio of Brenan Ghassemieh, Kobe Bryant's former personal trainer.

Ghassemieh began working with Team Mamba shortly after Bryant took over as coach. After six years, Ghassemieh knows them well enough to push them hard while keeping the mood light, with dance music from the Weeknd blaring in the background.

On this chilly (for Southern California) morning, they're still wearing hoodies and coats for the opening stretching exercises. The giggles that precede the workout disappear once it begins.

Sage Hill recently named Ghassemieh an assistant coach, a nod to his bond with the girls, which intensified after the crash. Ghassemieh was supposed to be on the helicopter that day, his seat taken at the last minute.

"I'm just hoping to do right by him," Ghassemieh says of Bryant, adding that the girls have "helped me just as much as I've helped them."

"The types of processing that you're going to need to do with events like this, in the end, you can't do it alone," he says. "And we're grateful to not have to."

Just don't 'die twice'

Something was off that cloudy Sunday morning in 2020. They had been waiting too long for Bryant, Mauser, their three teammates and the others to arrive at Mamba Sports Academy, the 100,000-square-foot training facility in Thousand Oaks where they had a tournament that day.

Jon Spotts, Annabelle's father and one of Bryant's business partners at the academy, summoned the families to a conference room above the courts, where he announced that Bryant's helicopter had crashed. The full details weren't known, he said, but there were probably some fatalities.

"A lot of these girls didn't even know what the word fatalities meant," Allison Eadie says, adding that these were "people that they had just been playing with on the court the day before."

Panic fell over the room, and soon a parent was reading the news on TMZ. Screams could be heard through the door.

Coach Bryant used to joke about all the weddings this extended family was going to attend. Now he was gone. He had preached to always show up, to never be late; now every friend's tardiness would bring a surge of anxiety. You're not supposed to die on your way to a basketball game.

The academy happened to have a therapist on hand, and a representative from a nearby church came to pray with them. They spent hours weeping and praying. Finally, Spotts ordered transportation for every family to make it home, sparing them from driving nearly two hours in a fog of bewilderment and sadness.

Lene Righeimer wasn't at the gym that morning, but embedded in her brain is the image of her daughter returning home, her eyes red and watery. "I remember seeing Kat come out of that bus like a wet cat," she says, "I told her that no matter what, you're going to be okay."

The Righeimers had experienced grief some 16 years earlier, when their 4-year-old daughter, Rebecca, died of a heart ailment. Kat never got to meet Rebecca, but her picture still hangs in a hallway of the home, and her parents always shared stories about what she was like.

"There is something that they say in our grief group that a person can die twice," Lene Righeimer said. "Once, when they die a physical death, and the second time they can die is when you stop talking about them."

'Mamba mentality'

Team Mamba, the AAU program, shuttered after Bryant's death. The girls scattered, finding homes among some of Southern

California's top programs, including three at Team Why Not, a program backed by Clippers star Russell Westbrook.

Their coach, Marlon Wells, happens to have a runaway favorite NBA player: Kobe Bryant. Kobe's signature shoes. Kobe's jersey. Shirts. Jackets. Wells is often decked out in Bryant gear, leading him to wonder last year, during a bus ride to an AAU tournament, whether he was risking causing the girls pain with his constant reminders of their mentor.

So he asked them. "And they were like, 'Oh, no—we love it!'" Wells says.

That enduring affinity for Bryant is reflected in their own footwear. Amalia, Annabelle, Em, Kat and Zoie wear his signature Nike sneaker at almost every game. They have several pairs of Kobes, but their preference, given Sage Hill's green-and-white school colors, is those Grinches. By the end of this regular season, the girls had to switch sneakers because the tread was so worn.

Bryant's words still ring in their ears, pushing them at times when they least expect. If a player missed an easy layup, Bryant would always tell them, "Finish your breakfast." Em says she will repeat that phrase to herself while on the court but also when she has a challenging assignment in school.

Every time Kat leaves her bedroom, the last image she sees are two black wooden plaques on the wall. One is Bryant's 10 rules for success. The other is how Bryant defined the "Mamba mentality."

"Haters are a good problem to have," it reads. "Nobody hates the good ones. They hate the great ones."

To them, he wasn't Kobe or the Black Mamba. He was Coach Bryant: the one who threatened to make them run sideline to sideline 17 times if they smiled on the cover of *SLAM* magazine. The one who tried a zen-like approach on the bench, calmly letting them figure it out—until he unleashed with the occasional scream. The one who demanded they give their all to the game while focusing on what they were doing to get better, not what *he* had done or how *he* had done it.

"He was such a real person that you would just kind of forget that he has fans all over the world," Annabelle says.

Bryant's level of fame became apparent only when they traveled to AAU tournaments and had to take the back entrance to avoid a mob. Or when large crowds gathered around their courts to catch (and record) a glimpse of a legend in his element. Team Mamba was also guaranteed to get the best effort from its opponents.

Yet despite the attention it brought, Bryant was dedicated. Most days, an associate said, Bryant would finish practice and show up to his Kobe Inc. offices in Costa Mesa around 8 p.m. or later, a bag of basketballs draped around his shoulder. He would then spend three or four hours working on a film or a book project. Bryant rarely missed practice. The times he did, he checked in through FaceTime.

"He never made it seem like he wasn't going to be there," Em says.

His pupils reciprocated, arriving early and staying late. Amalia's mother, Flora, says Bryant once explained how that extra work accumulated, leading to marked improvement. It was the same work Bryant did, he reminded her, when others were resting or enjoying the fruits of their labor.

Plus, he told her, he always had to work on Christmas. "I know you used to watch," he told her. She smiled and replied, "I did."

The girls received basketball lessons but were also able to get a peek at Bryant's playful side. Em recalls Bryant taking the team to a WNBA game between the Los Angeles Sparks and Las Vegas Aces and asking the players to choose sides. Those who picked the losing team would have to eat chicken feet, pig intestines and scorpions later that evening. Em chose the Sparks, who lost.

"I'm not going to lie. Like, it wasn't the worst thing," she says of the food. But she could do without the scorpion.

The team once went go-cart riding for a birthday party. Afterward, Bryant started talking about his own experience driving. He called on Alyssa and asked, "What do people do when they see a yellow light?"

"Slow down," Alyssa replied.

"No," Gigi said, "you punch it!"

The players laughed. Coach Bryant nodded approvingly.

The girls and their families have kept most of their memories private, declining to post pictures from team dinners or of Bryant belting out "Happy Birthday" after practice as one of the girls blew out a candle on a cupcake. Bryant once told the parents, "You can either be a friend or a fan," his way of telling them not to exploit their relationship with a Hall of Famer for likes on Facebook or Instagram. Understanding their fortune in having one of the all-time greats teaching the game to their daughters, the choice was simple.

"We always pinched ourselves," Jim Righeimer said.

'Our everything'

They were just middle-schoolers when their coaches and team-mates died. Roughly six weeks later, the pandemic hit. At the exact moment they needed repeated hugs from one another, the girls had to socially distance.

Ghassemieh did individual workouts through Zoom until Amalia asked whether he could have all the girls together on the video calls. But understanding the importance of keeping them together, some of the parents later found whatever facilities or tournaments that they could. The game was more than a sanc-tuary; it became their lifeline.

"I think they can all agree basketball is like our everything," Em says.

Their friendship has become everything else. After the win over Portola, Annabelle tries to reminisce about Payton, her best friend since kindergarten, who died in the crash. But she gets too emotional for the words to come. Em wraps her arms around Annabelle and brings her in, allowing Annabelle to collect herself. Nothing needs to be said. Even if no one else ever gets them, they get each other.

"I don't know what I'd do without them," Kat says. Zoie, one of the few Black students at Sage Hill, puts it this way: "These girls are definitely like extra sisters."

They play for those who are no longer with them, trying to navigate and perform through the pressures of social media and the spotlight that comes from their association with one of the greatest players to pick up a basketball.

Bryant spent the final few years of his life mentoring his basketball admirers, promoting the women's game and making sure the wisdom he acquired while aspiring for greatness wasn't wasted in his mind. What he instilled in these girls extends his legacy. The weight of those responsibilities could at times be a burden, but it also has provided a purpose to the ones left to honor him and their friends.

"Not only were they given the chance to be taught by the very best, they're able to continue on with the goal," Allison Eadie says, "They didn't just throw their basketball shoes aside. They just kept going out there."

Walters credits their resilience for making his job easier: "They inspire me."

But for Flora Holguin, there are also the what-ifs whenever she takes a step back to appreciate what her daughter has accomplished. "I think if Kobe were still around, where would they be? What would they be doing? Like, where would their basketball level be?"

The tide turns

It's dusk when they gather at the ocean's edge again this time, on Jan. 20, 2023. Their season, in the end, wouldn't go as planned, ending with a loss to Mater Dei in the state playoffs. And for all the reminders of what Coach Bryant always said—that their journey was about progress, not perfection—sometimes even progress feels hard.

"We go through the year just trying to live our normal life," Zoie's mom says. But Zoie "just crumbled and was like, 'Oh, Mom, I don't know how I can keep doing this.'

"It's hard because everybody expects so much from them."

But their ritual carries on, and they suspect it always will. Deep down, they all know they can't let those who still mean so much to them die a second death.

Zoie, Emily, Amalia, Kat, Annabelle. Ellie Robinson and Annika Jiwani, two other Coach Bryant protegees who don't go to Sage Hill, surprise the five who do, showing up at the cliffs and wrapping their former teammates in hugs. There in spirit this year because it conflicts with a game: Mackenly Randolph.

The eight survivors of Team Mamba. #4the8.

One by one, they toss their flowers into the ocean, just as they have in years past. But this time, the girls notice, instead of sweeping the flowers back to shore, the tide carries them out to sea, out toward the descending sun.

MICHAEL LEE is a sports enterprise reporter at *The Washington Post* focusing on the intersection of gender, diversity, and how sports shape our society. He returned to the *Post* in 2020 after working previously for the newspaper from 2004 to 2015, serving as the national NBA writer and beat writer for the Washington Wizards. A longtime NBA beat reporter, Lee provided expertise and wrote colorful profiles about the league's most intriguing players and teams for more than two decades. He has also worked at the *Atlanta Journal-Constitution*, Yahoo! Sports, and The Athletic. He has covered three Olympics (2004 Athens, 2008 Beijing, and 2016 Rio de Janeiro), 15 NBA Finals, the World Series, and the NCAA men's basketball tournament. Lee helped lead the *Post's* "Black Out" project, which examined the NFL's hiring practices regarding Black head coaches. The project received in 2023 numerous honors, including an Edward R. Murrow Award for excellence in sports reporting, and was a finalist for a Scripps-Howard Award. The National Association of Black Journalists awarded Lee in 2009 with sports story of the year. His work has also been recognized multiple times by the Associated Press Sports Editors. A native of Kansas City, Missouri, Lee is a graduate of Florida A&M University and resides in the Philadelphia area with his wife, Ingrid, and sons, Jacob and Isaac.

Advisory Board

The Year's Best Sports Writing 2024

J.A. Adande is the director of sports journalism at Northwestern University's Medill School of Journalism, Media, Integrated Marketing Communications. He is also the graduate journalism Sports Media Specialization leader. Adande has worked in sports media for more than three decades, including multiple roles at ESPN and 10 years as a sports columnist at *The Los Angeles Times*, in addition to jobs at *The Washington Post* and *Chicago Sun-Times*. He has covered a broad array of sports and events, including the NBA Finals, Super Bowls, the World Series, the Stanley Cup finals, the Olympics, the World Cup, Wimbledon, the U.S. Open, and the Masters. He also served as the guest editor of *The Year's Best Sports Writing 2022*. He continues to appear on ESPN's *Around the Horn*, where he has been a panelist since the show's beginning in 2002. In 2024, he was the recipient of the Curt Gowdy Print Media Award from the Naismith Basketball Hall of Fame.

Kavitha A. Davidson is an award-winning sportswriter based out of New York. She was most recently a correspondent on HBO's *Real Sports with Bryant Gumbel*, for which she won an Emmy Award. She also serves on the Board of Directors of the Yogi Berra Museum and Learning Center. She was previously a sports and culture writer for The Athletic and the host and editorial director of *The Lead*, The Athletic's flagship daily podcast, for which she won an Edward R. Murrow Award, a Gracie Award, and a Webby Award. She was also a weekly columnist and feature writer for espnW and *ESPN The Magazine*. Before that, she wrote a daily sports column for Bloomberg with a heavy focus on the intersection of sports and business, policy, race, gender, and culture.

Richard Deitsch is a media reporter for The Athletic. He previously wrote for 20 years for *Sports Illustrated*, where he covered seven Olympic Games, multiple NCAA championships, and U.S. Open tennis. He served as the guest editor of *The Year's Best Sports Writing 2023*. He also hosts *The Sports Media Podcast with Richard Deitsch*.

Sandy Padwe has been a sports journalist, columnist, and editor, and through decades teaching at Columbia Graduate School of Journalism he has had a direct impact on generations of writers. He started off as a wire reporter for the Associated Press, United Press International, and Newspaper Enterprise Association before becoming a columnist for *The Philadelphia Inquirer*. Later, he was the Deputy Sports Editor for *Newsday*, *The New York Times*, and a Senior Editor for *Sports Illustrated*. At Columbia's J School, he taught sports journalism and investigations for more than two decades.

Notable Sports Writing of 2023

Selected by the Editor and Advisory Board of *The Year's Best Sports Writing 2024*

The Year's Best
Sports Writing

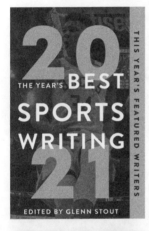
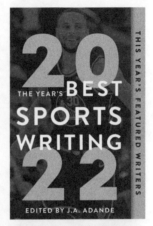
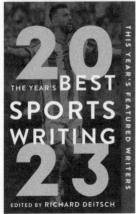
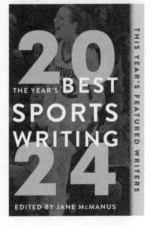